Effectual Entrepreneurship

What are you waiting for?

Whether you're dreaming about starting a business, learning about entrepreneurship, or on the brink of creating a new opportunity right now, don't wait. Open this updated bestseller. Inside you'll find everything you need, including:

- A newly established and popular way to learn about and to practice entrepreneurship.
- New practical exercises, questions, and activities for each step in your process.
- Specific principles derived from the methods of expert entrepreneurs.
- 70+ updated and renewed case briefs of entrepreneurs across industries, locations, and time.
- Applications to social entrepreneurship, technology (new!), and to the creation of opportunities in large enterprises.
- 60+ "Research Roots" connections to current and foundational research in the field.
- Brand new chapter on "the ask"—strategies for initiating the process of co-creating with partners.
- Data that will challenge conventional entrepreneurship wisdom.
- A broader perspective on the science of entrepreneurship and the ways in which individuals can shape their own situations.

In this vibrant updated edition, you will find these ideas presented in the concise, modular, graphical form made popular in the first edition, perfect for those learning to be entrepreneurs or those already in the thick of things.

If you want to learn about entrepreneurship in a way that emphasizes action, this new edition is vital reading. If you have already launched your entrepreneurial career and are looking for new perspectives, take the effectual entrepreneurship challenge! This book is for you. If you feel that you are no longer creating anything novel or valuable in your day job, and you're wondering how to change things, this book is for you. Anyone using entrepreneurship to create the change they want to see in the world will find a wealth of thought-provoking material, expert advice, and practical techniques in these pages and on the accompanying website: www.effectuation.org.

So, what are you waiting for?

Stuart Read is a Professor of Strategic Management at the Atkinson School of Management, Willamette University.

Saras Sarasvathy is the Isidore Horween Research Associate Professor at The Darden School of Business, University of Virginia.

Nick Dew is an Associate Professor of Strategic Management at the Graduate School of Business and Public Policy, Naval Postgraduate School.

Robert Wiltbank is the CEO of Galois, a software firm based in Portland, Oregon.

Praise for the first edition:

'Entrepreneurship is the most powerful tool we have for economic and social value creation and this book is destined to be recognized as the secret weapon all entrepreneurship educators have been waiting for! An accessible and comprehensive guide for all who aspire to both make and find opportunities. Bravo!' – *Len Schlesinger, President, Babson College, USA*

'Both in form and content, this expansive volume captures the excitement of the entrepreneurial enterprise and the opportunities and challenges presented at each development cycle. Written by European and US academics, this volume is a great starting point to explore notions of innovation and entrepreneurial activity. Summing Up: Highly recommended. All levels of undergraduate students; practitioners; general readers.' – *S. A. Schulman, CUNY Kingsborough Community College, CHOICE*

'A pragmatic, comprehensive book on entrepreneurship that talks about the key aspects and principles for establishing and sustaining a successful business.' – *Businessworld*

'This work has been absolutely instrumental in the development and continued growth of our company. We apply the 5 principles of effectuation everyday at Forgetful Gentleman. If you've ever thought of being an entrepreneur, this book will literally change your life.' – *Nathan Tan, Co-Founder, Forgetful Gentleman, Darden MBA '09*

'An entrepreneurial blueprint for those who don't like blueprints. The authors have distilled the essence of entrepreneurship in a new and vital way. Anyone who wants to know what matters to the global and local economies of tomorrow should read this book.' – *Jim Zuffoletti, Co-Founder of OpenQ*

'I knew that effectuation was a game changer as I witnessed my sixty MBA classmates fight and squirm to digest the material; this topic isn't for those wanting some gentle stretching – it's a majestic contrast to the typical MBA way of thinking. As someone who already exhibited entrepreneurial tendency, effectuation provided an indispensable framework that organized and explained my previously chaotic yet intrinsic style of thinking.' – *Ian Ayers, Co-Founder of Nova Global, Founder of Happy Rickshaw and CTO of LightWind Energy*

Effectual Entrepreneurship

Second Edition

Stuart Read,
Saras Sarasvathy,
Nick Dew, and
Robert Wiltbank

Routledge
Taylor & Francis Group

LONDON AND NEW YORK

First published 2011

Second edition 2017
by Routledge
2 Park Square, Milton Park, Abingdon, Oxon OX14 4RN

and by Routledge
711 Third Avenue, New York, NY 10017

Routledge is an imprint of the Taylor & Francis Group, an informa business

British Library Cataloguing in Publication Data
A catalogue record for this book is available from the British Library

Library of Congress Cataloging in Publication Data
Names: Read, Stuart, author.
   Title: Effectual entrepreneurship / Stuart Read, Saras Sarasvathy, Nick Dew and Robert Wiltbank.
   Description: Second edition. | Abingdon, Oxon ; New York, NY : Routledge, 2017. | Includes
   bibliographical references and index.
   Identifiers: LCCN 2016003538 | ISBN 9781138923775 (hardback) | ISBN 9781138923782 (pbk.) |
   ISBN 9781315684826 (ebook)
   Subjects: LCSH: Entrepreneurship. | New business enterprises. | Success in business.
   Classification: LCC HB615 .E453 2017 | DDC 658.1/1 – dc23
   LC record available at http://lccn.loc.gov/2016003538

ISBN: 978-1-138-92377-5 (hbk)
ISBN: 978-1-138-92378-2 (pbk)
ISBN: 978-1-315-68482-6 (ebk)

Typeset in Minion and Frutiger
by Florence Production Ltd, Stoodleigh, Devon, UK

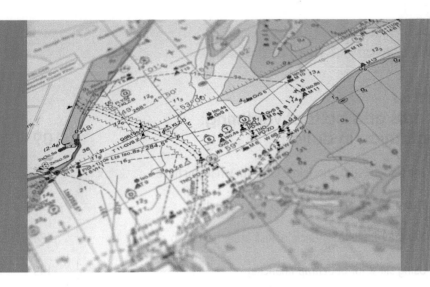

Contents

Acknowledgments

Writing any textbook is an effort that extends well beyond a team of authors. And writing one about effectuation involves an enormous network of self-selected stakeholders, many of whom we would like to recognize here. First, we would like to thank our families for their enduring patience as we talk endlessly about this topic and then disappear endlessly to write about it. Second, we recognize the entrepreneurs. As you read this book and enjoy the uniqueness and color of the stories, please appreciate that they were enabled by individuals willing to share their time with us. Here we would particularly like to thank Jack Roseman whose conversations from the very beginning and through the years inspired and gave life to several passages in this book. Third, we have had many useful inputs from individuals active in new venture financing, and we would like to call special attention to Artie Buerk and Andy Dale of Montlake Capital for their access and patience in exploring ideas around new ventures. Fourth, we would like to express gratitude to our institutions. Willamette University, Darden and IMD have offered us the freedom, funding, and encouragement to pursue big projects, and we are deeply grateful. And finally, though not least, our writing collaborators: Anne-Valérie Ohlsson brought enormous creativity to the presentation of this work in the first edition. Beverley Lennox spent tireless hours trying to turn our Word documents into English. Among the new additions in this edition is the chapter on the "Ask," written by Amy Halliday who did an amazing job capturing a new idea and putting it into the tone of this book. The story of Bacania Veche was written by Andreea Rosca, and we appreciate her self-selection both in creating it and sharing it. Catherine Egli, Kevin Baumer, Emma Brown, and Sinead Waldron patiently gathered permissions for the interesting art in the book. Leigh Wilkerson Ayers and Abby Skolits of Half Studios turned our sketches into intelligible graphics. Terry Clague, Elisabet Sinkie (in the first edition), and the team at Taylor & Francis co-created something novel and valuable with us, and we appreciate their pioneering spirit. Furthermore, we appreciate the inputs we received from users of the previous edition. We have done our best to incorporate your valuable suggestions and hope you can see your own mark on this edition. Beyond that, a large cast of editors and reviewers within the academic system have provided us over many years with challenging questions and great suggestions for our academic papers that have significantly refined the ideas in this book. That said, all errors and omissions are completely our responsibility, and as entrepreneurs, we will use these unexpected surprises to inform and improve the next revision. Effectually yours, the author team.

Introduction:

The science of entrepreneurship

D EAR READER,

Whether you come to this book as an entrepreneurship student, a corporate manager, or a seasoned creator of new ventures, you already know that entrepreneurship is the primary engine of growth, innovation, and that most delicious of personal freedoms—financial self-reliance.

What you will discover in this book is that there is a science to entrepreneurship—a common logic we observe in expert entrepreneurs across industries, geographic locations, and time. We call this logic "effectuation," a word you probably don't run into every day. The concept, though, isn't new. In fact, the underlying principles are the same ones that enabled Josiah Wedgwood in the eighteenth century to transform a pottery business into an enduring brand, helped Earl Bakken, the founder of Medtronic, to turn his college job into a company that has become a global leader in medical technology, and allowed Muhammed Yunus, the Nobel Laureate founder of the Grameen Bank and microfinance pioneer, to transform the lives of millions of women in Bangladesh. In a nutshell, effectual entrepreneurs work with things already within their control to co-create valuable new futures with people who want to work with them.

As you begin the book, you will come face-to-face with some common misconceptions about entrepreneurship, as well as some of the fears every entrepreneur faces. In the heart of the book, you will find the four core principles of effectuation expert entrepreneurs have learned in the process of creating new ventures, products, and markets. Each will be explained through cases, stories, thought exercises, and a variety of practical applications. Though simple and easy to put into action, these principles challenge and even invert the traditional logic mature organizations follow:

1   **Start with your means**. Don't wait for the perfect opportunity. Start taking action based on what you have readily available: Who you are, what you know, and who you know.

2   **Set affordable loss**. Evaluate opportunities based on whether the downside is acceptable, rather than on the attractiveness of the predicted upside.

3   **Leverage contingencies**. Embrace surprises that arise from uncertain situations, remaining flexible rather than tethered to existing goals.

4   **Form partnerships**. Form partnerships with people and organizations willing to make a real commitment to jointly creating the future—product, firm, market—with you. Don't worry so much about competitive analyses and strategic planning.

Together, these principles enable entrepreneurs to co-create opportunities with other people who choose to work with them. When you can make the future happen by working with people who want to work with you and working with things you control, you don't need to worry about predicting the future, determining the perfect timing, or finding the optimal opportunity.

Throughout the book you will find examples of consumer and business-to-business ventures, technical and non-technical, in as many industries and locations as we could find. As you reach the conclusion of the book, you will find applications of these principles in contexts ranging from social entrepreneurship to large firms. And you will understand the challenges entrepreneurs face, as their lovingly created ventures become mature businesses.

When you start a new venture—for-profit or not, individually or within an existing organization—you are not only trying to make a good living but also expanding the horizon of valuable new economic opportunities. This book is designed to help you do that from start to finish. And, in form and content, the book embodies the expert entrepreneur's logic—bold, systematic, pragmatic, and, at all times, full of energy, mischief, and fun.

How to use this book

We designed this to be much more than a textbook. Certainly, it can accompany you through a course in entrepreneurship, and we hope it will.

But it is also prepared to venture outside the academic environment into the uncertain world of startup creation.

As much as the chapters, in sequence, tell a story, each chapter is designed to stand on its own. So whether you start at the beginning and read through, or jump to Chapter 14 on partnerships in the moments before a meeting with a prospective stakeholder, we intend this book to be your partner in creating new opportunities.

As you read through, you will also find different special topics, outlined below, that provide more detail on the material in the chapter. Each is designed to help with a specific aspect of thinking about or starting a new venture:

What Now?

Let's face it, entrepreneurs like to do things. So at the end of each chapter we have prepared a series of things you can do to put the ideas in the chapter into practice. Like everything else in the book, these are designed to accompany the sequential story or to stand alone. So create your roadmap as you read, or review the entire "What Now?" inventory to get a feel for what a complete new-venture journey might look like.

Practically Speaking

In every chapter, you will find brief stories of new ventures. Every one of the more than 70 stories about entrepreneurs illustrates at least one of the principles described in this book. You will find stories matched with topics in each chapter. But if you choose to focus on just the "Practically Speaking" stories, you can skip from one to the next and quite literally tour the entrepreneurial world. Alternatively, you can select specific stories using the directory we created to connect stories with effectual principles, industry, or geography.

Research Roots

There is an enormous body of academic research on entrepreneurship—far too much for us to include in a book you could actually carry in your laptop case. So we searched for foundational research that has shaped thinking over the years and contemporary research that reflects current knowledge to date. In the context of a chapter, we summarize the key points of a research stream in "Research Roots" to give you an idea of what other scholars are working on and to offer directions for further reading.

So What?

Impatient? Eager? Want the bottom line? We have tried to summarize the one idea we hope you will take away from each chapter in "So What?" The goal is not to encourage you to skip the chapter. Quite the contrary. If you are wondering whether a chapter is worth your time, skip to "So What?" If the idea seems relevant to the challenge you face, know that you will find a whole lot more detail in the chapter.

Think It Through

Collectively, the authors of this book have more than 10 new ventures under their belts. So we understand the need for practical, immediate, and relevant material. At the same time, we have provided space to consider some of the larger topics entrepreneurship opens up: the more intellectual questions that you may not find appealing when you have to close a financing round, but you might appreciate on a long contemplative hike with your partner during the weekend. We keep these for the very end of each chapter so as not to distract from the business of getting a venture going. But we hope you will enjoy taking the time to step back every once in a while and consider the broader implications of what you are accomplishing.

PART I

What we know about entrepreneurs and entrepreneurship

The five chapters that constitute the first part of the book present the four most common myths about entrepreneurship and the associated and pragmatic questions that hold individuals back from starting a new venture—namely, "I don't have an idea, the money, I'm afraid to fail and I don't know where to start." These fears arise from misconceptions similar to those ascribed to the pioneering explorers who set sail on the open seas several hundred years ago. History has stylized these early adventurers as visionary heroes, possessing superhuman abilities and extraordinary luck. In fact, the process of drawing the map of the world is similar to the process an entrepreneur employs in starting a new venture. Both explorers and entrepreneurs do what they can with the things they have available. Both embrace surprise as an asset. And both create new maps that define our world for generations to come. We encourage you to look past the glamorous retelling of entrepreneurial lore and instead focus on the systematic principles that experts follow—principles detailed in this book that you can apply yourself as you create your own map.

Hold up a mirror and ask yourself what you are capable of doing, and what you really care about. Then take the initiative—don't wait for someone else to ask you to act.

Sylvia Earle

Popular mythology around entrepreneurship has created a number of barriers that hold people back from becoming entrepreneurs.

Most of them are not true.

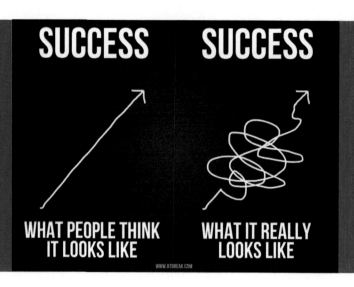

Roadmaps, myths, and the Bahamas

■ ■ ■

If you are reading this, you are most likely looking for a roadmap to success. You are, of course, not alone. Most human beings whose basic needs are satisfied share this quest with you. Each may define success differently. For some it may be to make a meaningful difference in the world, for others it may be power and fame and for yet others it might simply be independence, dignity, and the opportunity to achieve the creative potential within themselves. And perhaps, make oodles of money in the process.

There are probably as many ways to define and achieve success as there are human beings. However you define success, the principles of entrepreneurship you'll learn in this book can help you achieve it, for entrepreneurship is about the very creation of new roadmaps, not only for you but also for a subset of humanity around you.

As you read this book, we encourage you to actively consider your own roadmap. Yours may be based on existing paths that work well or new ones that reshape the terrain and perhaps even make new worlds altogether.

Regardless, we hope you are prepared for an adventure of mind-bending possibilities rooted in street-smart realities, all culled from rigorous academic research.

THE MYTHICAL ENTREPRENEUR

Entrepreneurs are heroes of our times. Jeff Bezos, Sachin Bansal, and Richard Branson are seen as the daring visionaries of our business culture—conquering new markets, thriving on risk, and pursuing opportunities others simply could not see.

THE FAIRY TALE JOURNEY

How do they do it? Let's begin by sketching out the roadmap generally ascribed to the mythical entrepreneur:

1. Searches for a "new, high-potential" opportunity.
2. In a lightbulb moment, discovers something nobody has thought of before.
3. Writes a business plan.
4. Raises lots of investment money—especially from venture capitalists (VCs).
5. Hires a great team.
6. Builds a product.
7. Orchestrates a big launch.
8. Achieves steady, or better yet, hockey-stick growth.
9. Sells the venture or has an initial public offering.
10. . . . and, finally, retires to the Bahamas.

This all sounds great, but there's a problem: when we look at the startup histories of companies and the biographies of the entrepreneurs who founded them, this roadmap has no bearing on their actual course.

Consider just a few data points along this journey. One academic study found that only 28% of a sample of Inc. 500 firms had completed a formal business plan (Bhidé, 2000). More than 73% of Initial Public Offerings (IPOs) are not funded by VCs (Gompers and Lerner, 2001: 145), and the average amount of money it takes to create a business in the US is less than $30,000 (Kaufmann Foundation, 2009).

These and other data suggest that the mythical entrepreneur's roadmap is a fantasy. But if many great entrepreneurial stories don't involve business plans and huge venture capital investments, how do entrepreneurs actually create enduring companies? For the past 15 years or so, we, along with many collaborators around the world, have been engaged in research to answer that question and identify specific techniques people actually use to create new firms. The results of our investigations point to the principles detailed in this book. The results challenge us to rethink several key issues about how great entrepreneurship happens. The core insight is that anyone who wants to be an entrepreneur can (learn to) be an entrepreneur.

THE COMMON ENTREPRENEUR

Let's put Richard Branson and the popular media aside for a moment and reconsider the waypoints on our fantasy path to success. As we examine each, see if you can begin to diagram the real entrepreneurial journey.

Search or divine inspiration

Our path started with an entrepreneur searching for an opportunity and having a lightbulb moment. Which means that the opportunity could be found by anyone smart enough or alert enough. It means our mythical entrepreneur's clients would recognize the solution when she presented it to them. It also means that our entrepreneur could assess the value of and risks in the opportunity when she discovered it. But imagine trying to predict the returns of creating a new "airline we hope you love" in an industry which has been notoriously unprofitable? Of putting a bookstore online in 1990? Or, of then trying to challenge that unexpectedly successful bookstore in India in 2007?

Only with the benefit of hindsight, Virgin Air, Amazon, Flipkart, and countless others appear brilliant and inevitable. Only with the benefit of hindsight is it also possible to distinguish those successful businesses from some equally spectacular failures, such as Pets.com or the Internet currency, Flooz.

Furthermore, as you will discover in Chapter 2, there is little magic in the initial idea anyway. Ideas are cheap and plentiful. And because most ventures start with an idea that has little relation to the company which subsequently emerges, success is in the active perspiration, not the divine inspiration. In reality, many companies you know are based on ideas that were co-created by the

Research Roots

WHAT IS ENTREPRENEURSHIP, REALLY?

One issue that has caused a lot of debate among entrepreneurship researchers over the years is the question of what entrepreneurship is, really. If you do it, what are you doing? And if you study it, what are you studying? What is the central phenomenon? Though this issue may seem silly, it isn't atypical; it turns out that biologists have a surprisingly hard time defining "life" and physicists have a hard time agreeing on what "matter" really is. Perhaps understandably then scholars have had some difficulty defining precisely what entrepreneurship is, and isn't.

One way to tackle the question of what entrepreneurship is (really) is to focus on the activities entrepreneurs engage in, i.e. what entrepreneurs do. We take this approach in this textbook. The emphasis is on the actions and behaviors of entrepreneurs. One key entrepreneurial activity is creating new ventures. Other key activities include developing new markets, discovering and creating opportunities and entrepreneurship inside corporations.

An important implication of defining entrepreneurship in terms of activities is that it shifts the focus away from seeing entrepreneurs as special people with particular personality characteristics. Instead, we focus on the central activities that are involved in entrepreneurship and look at how these activities can be learned and done well (Gartner, 1988).

---

entrepreneur and her partners—ideas not anticipated when the entrepreneur started the venture and might have looked dubious in the form of an initial business plan.

Money

As your journey through mythology continues, we investigate the actual data on new venture financing in Chapter 3. In addition to those data, consider that the number of businesses funded by VCs in the year 2014 in the US (a good year for raising venture capital investments) was 4,356 (PricewaterhouseCoopers, 2014). And the number of new businesses started in 2014 in the US was about 1.8 million (SBA, 2015). A little quick math indicates that only 0.2% of new firms

received venture funding in 2014 (these numbers are very similar year after year). The rest of us, 99.8% of US entrepreneurs, somehow manage to get a new firm going without big investment money from a VCs.

Failure

Nobody sets out to fail, yet despite every effort, some ventures don't make it. Coming back to the legendary Richard Branson, even he is not as invincible as you might imagine. Having failed 16 businesses along the way to creating his current entrepreneurial empire, Branson says,

"Business opportunities are like buses, there's always another one coming."

So as obvious as it may feel to hire a team, scale up operations and take big chances on a big idea, even Richard Branson manages things conservatively enough so that he is always ready for the next bus.

Barriers

We share the roadmap and its flaws with you not to pick on VCs or even Sir Richard Branson, but to shed light on the barriers that can keep prospective entrepreneurs from starting a new venture. As you compare the mythical roadmap with the data summarized here and detailed in the chapters in this section, it is easy to see where those barriers come from. And, it is also easy to see why they are false. More specifically, if you are

Practically Speaking

MURKY BREW

Perhaps over a grandé mocha nonfat latte, it is useful to consider the insight that created today's fabulously successful Starbucks. Unfortunately, the alternatives suggested by the mythical journey do not help much:

1) Market analysis cannot be credited with helping Howard Schultz discover the opportunity in Starbucks. Daily per capita coffee consumption in the US had declined from 3.1 cups in the 1960s to 2 cups when Schultz was assembling the ingredients for Starbucks.

2) Nor did a functional prototype point to the opportunity. The original Starbucks, founded in 1971, was a shop that sold beans, tea and supplies, but not coffee by the cup.

3) Furthermore, Shultz' vision of bringing the Italian espresso bar format to the US has little relationship to a Starbucks store today. In fact, when Schultz joined Starbucks in 1982 as head of marketing he was unable to talk the founders into offering drinks, so built his own coffee bar and called it Il Giornale (merged with Starbucks in 1987).

The daily grind

In its original form, Il Giornale struggled. Customers did not like nonstop opera music. They wanted chairs. Some asked for flavored coffee. A menu printed mainly in Italian was inaccessible. The baristas' bow ties were untidy. Schultz adjusted in response to those customers who chose to buy from him and those employees who chose to work for him, providing chairs and playing more varied music. The baristas stopped wearing ties. "We fixed a lot of mistakes," Schultz said, although for many years he chose not to grant the request for flavored coffee.

Making your own cup

So the story of Starbucks, like the story of many enterprises, is full of stakeholder (e.g. investors, customers, employees and strategic partners) input and entrepreneurial action. This is the insight from the story of Starbucks, and it highlights two elements of the real entrepreneurial journey. First, it explains why you didn't think of Starbucks. Based on market information at the time, Starbucks was not an opportunity waiting to be found. Had Schultz not taken the series of actions he did to  create and shape the firm, there might not be a mainstream market for premium coffee cafés today. Second, it informs you about what you should do. If opportunities are created, as opposed to found, then taking action is more important than doing research. So stop looking and start doing.

Practically Speaking

FROM BAGS TO RICHES

Exotic destination

Debbie Watkins was looking for a little respite from the hustle and bustle of corporate life in London, so she booked a trip to Cambodia. Images of Buddhist temples, lush jungles and warm smiles intermix with a history of conflict and a unique Southeast Asian cuisine. But that was 11 years ago, and as is so often the case with entrepreneurs, the destination became the starting point.

New direction

By some combination of wanting to engage deeply with the culture of Cambodia, create economic opportunity and social progress in the region and meet the man of her dreams, Watkins turned her respite to resolution. Over beer one evening with her future husband, Marc Lansu, the pair imagined a venture that could animate Watkins' aspirations, and thus Carpe Diem, a non-profit tour operator providing small group excursions in Cambodia, was born. Instead of checking off a list of top local photogenic spots, Carpe Diem would facilitate tourism deeper into the country, exchange with local people and cultural interaction.

Terrific trip

Carpe Diem Travel has delivered on Watkins' aspirations, and more. The organization employs more than 20 people today, including Willemijn Wellens who bears the title of "Wheelchair Travel Specialist," and is a wheelchair traveller herself. The firm has expanded into Laos, and educates and engages visitors on issues including conservation and social welfare. But this story is not about Carpe Diem Travel. Carpe Diem is only a waypoint on the journey of an entrepreneur who, during her travels, could not help but continue to see problems and opportunities everywhere around her.

Littered landscape

Many who have travelled to interesting destinations in emerging parts of the world have seen what caught Watkins' eye. The pervasive plastic bag. Handling waste in the developing world is hardly a systemic activity; most often, individual entrepreneurs extract whatever value they can from the refuse of others. Glass and metal can be resold. Organic waste goes to feed livestock or fertilize fields. But plastic bags, because they have no value once used, cover more and more of the countryside. Cheap and non-biodegradable, they are more than an eyesore; they harm animals that eat them and clog waterways and drains.

Practically Speaking *(continued)*

Trash transformation

And so Watkins' next venture was born. She formed Funky Junk (www.funkyjunkrecycled.com) in 2009 to weave those plastic bags into something of value. And not just something of value for her clients, though they appreciate

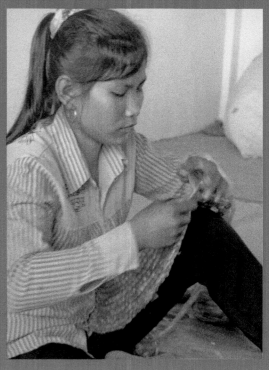

Practically Speaking *(continued)*

the colourful, eco-friendly floor cushions, laundry baskets, sun hats and shoulder bags. But the value provided by cleaning up the environment. Value for her local Cambodian employees, who she trains, manages according to fair-trade best practice and compensates. And value to entrepreneurs in other parts of the world with whom she "franchises" her model.

The job of creating

Watkins also provides value to us. She illustrates for us the job of the entrepreneur. Indeed, that job is not to wait in the shower for the moment of divine intervention but rather to get out in the world and create something. The process of creating does not happen in isolation; instead, it is a function of interacting with others, using mundane resources already at hand. Resources that may be as unattractive, common and valueless as the plastic bag by the side of the road … until those resources get into the hands of the entrepreneur and are transformed from foul to funky. Glamorous? You decide. Valuable? Absolutely.

not starting your dream venture because you think:

"I don't have a good idea"

. . . you now know that expectation came from the mythical entrepreneur, but real entrepreneurs probably iterated and co-created until they generated an opportunity worth pursuing, as we discuss in Chapter 2.

If you think:

"I don't have the money"

. . . it is only because stories about firms securing $10 million in venture funding are the ones that make the news, perhaps because they are so rare. Most entrepreneurs start firms with little or no capital, and more information on the truth about investments in new ventures is in Chapter 3.

If your worry is:

"I'm afraid to fail"

. . . you will find both good company in failure and good learning from failure. Described in more detail in Chapter 4, you will understand that failure is part of the entrepreneurial process. It is not a question of whether ventures fail (as some do) but how you set yourself up to survive failure. Also, it is how you use what you learn from failure to inform your venture moving ahead.

And finally, if you feel like:

"I don't know where to start"

. . . that's really why we wrote this book. Because once we break through the barriers that hold people back from starting a new venture, the idea of taking the plunge into entrepreneurship (Chapter 5) is not so scary. So the next natural question is how to get going, and effectuation offers tools for doing just that. A simple, pragmatic approach to starting up.

Research Roots

THE ENTREPRENEURIAL PERSONALITY?

Every era, and every country, seems to have its arch entrepreneurial stereotypes that perfectly illustrate our perceptions about the nature of wildly successful entrepreneurs. Whether it is Mark Cuban or Mark Zuckerberg, human beings are such incredible pattern recognizers that we quickly put together an identifiable pattern for an entrepreneurial "type" of person.

So, do entrepreneurs have different personalities than non-entrepreneurs? Research on this issue dates back at least to work by Harvard psychologist David McClelland in the 1950s. McClelland was interested in why some countries grew economically, and posited that individuals with a high personal need for achievement would be driven to become entrepreneurs of high-growth ventures. In the 50 years since McClelland's work, many studies of the entrepreneurial personality have been published and several meta-analyses confirm that there are personality differences between entrepreneurs and non-entrepreneurs. For example, measures of self-efficacy and autonomy needs are both strongly related to business creation, while a person's need for achievement is strongly related to business success (McClelland, 1965).

While these past patterns are interesting to know about, tomorrow's entrepreneurs are not determined by them. Indeed, entrepreneurs founding firms today are continually creating the patterns that psychologists will investigate in the future (Rauch and Frese, 2007).

The Bahamas

We have addressed or will address the first nine steps in the mythical roadmap with data and examples to show why that map leads people to imagine artificial barriers to starting a company. But what about the 10th step?

. . . and, finally, retires to the Bahamas.

Retirement isn't really the topic of this book. Everyone's journey takes them to a different place. For some that place may be a warm sandy beach in the Bahamas. But not for many entrepreneurs. There is such a deep sense of personal satisfaction that comes from creating your own venture that it also creates the serial entrepreneur—that person who creates multiple, perhaps even dozens of ventures over the course of a career.

Of all the myths around entrepreneurship, the story of the individual organizing her next business while she is selling—or even running—her current one seems the most accurate.

TAKEAWAY: ENTREPRENEURSHIP IS ACCESSIBLE

We will not advocate that everyone should become an entrepreneur. Our purpose is far more specific. Which is to cast light on the realities of starting a new venture so those people who want to become

entrepreneurs understand the facts. And while more complete information may make people more or less likely to start a new venture, those who do understand the facts should have a better sense of the real barriers, heuristics and practicalities associated with entrepreneuring.

■ ■ ■

So What?

Many of the issues that hold people back from starting a new venture are not based in reality. As a result, potential entrepreneurs may be distracted from the real issues, and might even be delaying for no good reason at all.

What Now?

Identify what you believe are the three biggest things holding you back from launching your new venture.

- [ ] Identify one thing that if true, would immediately make you start. Is it about money? Try harder.

- [ ] See for yourself. Go talk to an entrepreneur or three; ask them about their path and how they started.

- [ ] On your path through this book, will it be helpful to read Chapters 2–5 about barriers to getting started?

- [ ] Or are you ready to skip to Part II to get into the details of entrepreneurial thinking?

Think It Through

Beyond the immediate topic of this chapter, think about the following questions:

- [ ] If real entrepreneurs aren't working through the 10 steps in the roadmap at the start of this chapter, what are the real steps associated with creating a new venture?

- [ ] What do entrepreneurs actually do each day?

- [ ] If you had to start a venture right now, what are the first three things you'd do? Write them down and keep reading.

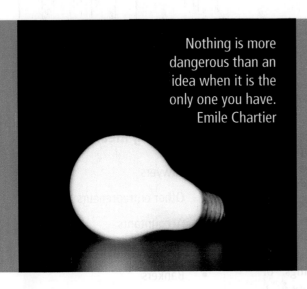

CHAPTER 2

Nothing is more dangerous than an idea when it is the only one you have.
Emile Chartier

Many people who want to start a venture say they haven't yet because they don't have a good idea.

The fact is that good ideas are cheap and plentiful.

It's what you do with them that matters.

Good ideas are everywhere

■ ■ ■

One clear fact emerges from research into entrepreneurial expertise and early stage histories of new ventures—it is not possible to know with any certainty whether an idea will turn out to be a good business opportunity. In fact, successful entrepreneurs and experienced investors state that there is only one way to determine whether a given idea is a good business opportunity—go ahead and give it a try. Implement it creatively with very low levels of investment and either find real customers who are willing to buy the product or service at a reasonable price, or locate partners willing to commit resources to the venture early on—or, ideally, both.

Understandably, most first-time entrepreneurs, especially those who have good job-market prospects, worry a lot about finding the "right"

opportunity. Hence, the angst about waiting for an idea that is "good."

What is a good idea? Where do ideas come from? Who decides whether an idea is good? When and how do you recognize if an idea is feasible?

As you think about these questions, consider Medtronic. In 1949, inspired by the impact of electricity on life, as depicted in the 1931 movie Frankenstein, Earl Bakken founded the medical devices firm. But it was a long time until he conceived the cardiac pacemaker, the company's first breakthrough product. Bakken spent his first eight years working as a medical equipment repair technician. In 1957, after years of interactions with doctors and the medical industry, he began developing the pacemaker. Even then, the device was much more a collection of

knowledge from his repair work than a flash of visionary genius.

Once the device was introduced, a medical industry analyst organization predicted a world market for pacemakers of, at most, 10,000 units—not per year—but 10,000 units in total. Although the analysts considered that a small market, Bakken and his team rejoiced—they were selling fewer than 100 units a year at the time! Today, Medtronic is a US$20 billion business (FY2015 revenue) and a leader in the medical devices field.

Where do ideas come from?

In theory:

- Patent Office Gazette
- Government (NASA, CERN)
- Technology transfer
- Trade shows
- Doctoral dissertations
- Invention expositions
- Brainstorming

In practice:

- A personal satisfaction or dissatisfaction
- Market knowledge from prior job
- Hobbies
- Other people
- Acquisition of a company or product already launched
- The news
- Rejects from employer or other company
- Customers

So, set aside your worries about having a good idea.

IDEAS ARE A DIME A DOZEN

One simple way to come up with an idea is to think of things we like and things we don't like, things we wish we had, things we would like to get rid of, things we care about, and so on. In fact, like the queen in *Alice in Wonderland*, most of us can come up with six "impossible things," or six new venture ideas, before breakfast. But we don't necessarily know what to do with them. Or even whether we want to do anything with them.

It is important to reiterate here that there is no such thing as a "good" idea up front—there are only ideas we implement and ones we don't. A good idea can be wasted, just like a bad idea can be turned into an opportunity.

Useful contacts for generating ideas

- Lawyers
- Other entrepreneurs
- Accountants
- Venture capitalists
- Bankers
- R&D professionals
- Patent attorneys
- Purchasing agents
- Businesspeople
- Salespeople or distributors
- Trade associations
- Executives
- Potential customers

Research Roots

THE STARTUP GENOME PROJECT

A research project out of Berkeley sought to "decode the startup genome" by trying to figure out as many predictors of success as they could from their sample of new ventures.

One interesting finding shows that entrepreneurs not only change the idea they started with, but also that change is positively associated with financial success. The study reported that startups that pivot once or twice raise 2.5 times more money, have 3.6 times better user growth and are 52% less likely to scale prematurely than startups that pivot more than two times or not at all (Marmer et al., 2011).

The complete report is available for free download and contains a variety of additional interesting data on startups.

Practically Speaking

TURNING A HOBBY INTO A BUSINESS

When John Vence sent his son Michael off to college, he equipped the young man with a loft bed to maximize tight space in the campus dormitory. Word of mouth soon spread, and Vence was delivering loft beds hundreds of miles from his home in Horseheads, New York. Demand got so great that Vence investigated what was necessary to ship his beds nationally and turned the hobby into a full-time business. Today, College Bed Lofts employs 18 people, making and selling about 5,000 unfinished wood lofts a year to customers coast to coast.

Think of successful ventures you know and where their ideas came from. Throughout this book, there are examples of ventures that grew out of mundane, even silly, ideas. Ventures like Agilyx and unsicht-Bar, formed on top of things we might label as negatives—trash and blindness. Or enduring financial successes, like Colgate and Tiffany's, started with ideas that have little bearing on their current businesses. What we see in the stories of all these firms is the relative importance of the entrepreneur and the action over the idea.

EXAMPLES OF RADICAL BUSINESS MODEL CHANGE

Company	Where they started	What they do now
Tiffany & Co.	Started as a provider of stationery in 1837.	Not until 1853 did the firm shift over to jewellery.
Colgate	Soap, candles and starch were the first products.	Founded in 1806, Colgate did not make toothpaste for nearly 70 years.
Nokia	Since its founding in 1865, Nokia has been in industries from rubber to paper.	More than 100 years after founding, in the 1980s, Nokia started to make phones.
Hasbro	Textile remnants were the first offering from the Hassenfeld Brothers.	Toys were not offered until 1952, some 30 years after founding.
John Deere	Started as a blacksmith, making plows.	A full range of farm products, but best known for making its iconic green tractors.

Practically Speaking

TURNING A DISABILITY INTO A BUSINESS

Ever been on a blind date? Most people say it's simultaneously scary and exciting, and it's always memorable. Which is also what people say about Axel Rudolph's unsicht-Bar. unsicht-Bar is a small Cologne eatery run by the blind where patrons enjoy wine, cuisine, and conversation in the pitch dark. Even the glow of a mobile phone is not permitted in this establishment. Diners are attended by blind waiters/guides who describe the food in terms of both its preparation and its location on the plate.

Practically Speaking *(continued)*

Success without looking

Since its opening in 2002, unsicht-Bar has won acclaim from critics and restaurateurs alike. In addition to the novel yet empathic experience of spending the evening with someone who can't see, eliminating the sense of sight intensifies the rest of the senses so that unsicht-Bar's simple fare (the chef seasons with only salt, pepper, garlic, onions and herbs) comes alive in a way you might never have tasted before. According to Rudolph:

> **You smell better, you are more receptive to differences in texture, consistency and temperature . . . it's a holistic experience.**

unsicht-Bar's popularity has led Rudolph to open additional locations in Hamburg and Berlin, and has brought an intriguing innovation to the rather old and boring restaurant industry.

Vision inversion

Rudolph's venture embodies a powerful insight into the source of many successful innovations. Blindness is generally considered a liability—a handicap. Rudolph inverts it. unsicht-Bar makes blindness a point of differentiation and a basis for advantage. It takes a negative and makes it a positive.

Seeing upside down

Inversions like this are everywhere. Take Post-it Notes. Who would have thought you could develop a blockbuster product from a glue that wasn't very sticky? Or consider violent video games. Criticized for their disruptive psychological effects on minors, games like Full Spectrum Warrior are now the basis for an emerging software market in treating war veterans with post-traumatic stress disorder. Retro styles are an inversion of the idea that clothing goes out of fashion. And celebrities driving inexpensive, compact Toyota Priuses invert the notion that wealth and prestige are embodied in an enormous luxury car.

An eye to opportunity

The next time you feel you are on a blind date with destiny, look around you. Look for things that evoke a negative response. And think about transforming them into a positive basis for a new venture. For, as experienced entrepreneurs will tell you, opportunities are usually blind dates—simultaneously scary and exciting, yet memorable and, more often than you might think, worth embracing.

Practically Speaking

TRASH TO CASH

Good ideas for new companies can come from anywhere—from a frustrated customer, a breakthrough invention, or, as Kevin DeWhitt would tell you, from the trash. In 2004, he and his wife founded Agilyx Corporation (originally Plas2Fuel) with the idea of taking plastic waste and turning it into something better than money—crude oil. From a chemical engineering perspective, it makes perfect sense. Plastic is a petroleum product. Why not reverse the process when you're done with the plastic? Simple enough, in theory. In practice, the science turned out to be difficult, and the business even more difficult.

Converting the idea into action

You need customers to generate revenues. You need a product to attract customers. And you need cash to build a product. DeWhitt had none of these at the start. The team's solution was to partner with a customer willing to make an angel investment and at the same time assist in the development of an operational prototype. By creating with its customer, Agilyx built a working system that could be demonstrated to potential new customers, provide real-time environmental data to regulators, and give the team ideas for optimizing the system for full commercial deployment.

Using action for more action

Today, Agilyx can convert several thousand pounds of mixed waste plastic into hundreds of gallons of sweet synthetic crude oil each day. While this is exciting, it is utterly dwarfed by the fact that 26 million tons of plastic are sent to landfills annually in the US, and more than three times that amount are disposed of in Europe and China. Having proven the concept, Agilyx now has to figure out how to scale the business up to be able to handle this enormous quantity of fuel.

Ideas from nothing

Starting with trash might not be the most intuitive basis for a new venture, but with the potential to process mixed waste plastic into nearly 250 million barrels of crude oil annually in the US alone, the Agilyx opportunity ends up being pretty big. If you think Agilyx is unique, consider that eBay's 2014 sales volume was US$255 billion—much derived from sales of someone's unwanted items (i.e. their trash). Like Agilyx, eBay did not exist 20 years ago but turned waste into a business. So, if you are looking for a good idea, one of your assets might just be another person's trash.

Practically Speaking

EVERYONE IS DOING IT

There has been much research directed at discovering the unique characteristics of entrepreneurs. In particular, we might want to know whether entrepreneurs are psychologically different from the general population. But perhaps we are asking the wrong question. Instead of asking how psychology makes entrepreneurs, we may want to ask how entrepreneurs make psychology work for them.

Peer power

Generating more energy and using energy more efficiently have become central issues of our time. One interesting approach to the problem seeks to turn psychology into energy savings. Dan Yates and Alex Laskey founded Opower in 2007 to help their public utility customers reduce consumer peak-power usage, build fewer power plants and better utilize existing facilities. Opower is effective. About 85% of its clients' residential customers cut home power consumption by about 3.5%. But where did such a good idea come from?

Fuelled by competition

The results of a 2007 experiment make the psychology behind Opower transparent. Researchers hung announcements on the doors of 1,207 homes in San Marcos, California. All urged residents to use fans instead of air conditioning, but offered one of four alternative reasons. Some informed residents they could save $54 a month on their energy bill. Others indicated that using fans would eliminate 262 pounds of greenhouse gases per month. A third notice described fans as the socially responsible option. And the last group was told that 77% of their neighbors already used fans instead of air conditioning, closing with a caption of "San Marcos' popular choice!" Subsequent meter readings found that recipients of the "everyone's doing it" notice reduced their energy consumption by 10%, while no other group reduced their energy use by more than 3%.

THE IDEA-TO-VENTURE FORMULA

So now that you know divine intervention is not the source of opportunities, where do viable ventures come from? In this section, we outline the kinds of transformations an idea goes through on its way to becoming something valuable. You may well find more steps in your own process. But this is the point where you are beginning to create your own roadmap. So perhaps the steps here offer initial waypoints—the beginnings of how you will make sense of how this book can help you fill in the details of your roadmap.

We start the idea-to-venture formula by acknowledging that ideas are a good and important first step. Viable ventures often start with an idea. And ideas generally start with a transformation of the means you already have:

IDEA = ANYTHING + YOU

But we also know that ideas are plentiful and commonplace. It is action that turns an idea into a valuable opportunity:

OPPORTUNITY = IDEA + ACTION

At this point, we need to be clear. Gathering information does not count as action. Action is proposing a deal with a client. Action is getting a supplier to assemble a prototype. Action is asking a co-founder to join the business. Action goes beyond observation and calculation to invoke transformation, manipulation, fabrication—it's a function of interaction with the world:

ACTION = FUNCTION (INTERACTION) ON MONEY, PRODUCT, PARTNERS . . .

Finally, opportunity is transformed into a viable business through commitment. Commitments result in revenue, hiring and production lines starting up at suppliers:

VIABLE VENTURE = OPPORTUNITY + COMMITMENT

When putting together all the pieces of this formula, starting with you, it is important to see that at every point, there exists the possibility that your actions combined with the means and commitments of others may slightly or significantly redirect the course of your venture.

Research Roots

INNOVATION ADOPTION

Everett Rogers (2003) identified five attributes of an innovation that are highly predictive of whether it will be adopted. They include:

- **Relative advantage.** Is the innovation perceived as better than what it replaces?

- **Compatibility.** Is the innovation consistent with the values, experiences, and needs of potential adopters?

- **Complexity.** Is the innovation perceived as difficult to use?

- **Trialability.** Is the user able to experiment with the innovation?

- **Observability.** Are the results of an innovation visible to users?

Whether or not you like the words, these research-based tests provide a good common-sense basis for deciding whether an idea is likely to gain adoption.

Most enduring firms start very differently from where they end up. Their founders repeatedly act to create more valuable opportunities than would have been expected from their original ideas.

On the importance of commitment

We will look at partnerships, asking, and commitments in greater detail in Chapters 14 and 15, but there is at least one thing you need to consider at the outset: if you can't find anyone besides yourself who thinks it's a good enough idea that they are willing to make some kind of commitment (time, money, etc.), maybe it's not a good idea. And don't be too easy on yourself or your idea. There is no such thing as tentative commitment.

But how long do you look for someone to commit before simply dropping the idea? That question depends on how much you can afford to lose (more on this in Chapter 12). Maybe you can afford to wait for years for your idea to come of age. Early investors in video-conferencing technology did so. Sometimes ideas, especially technology-based ideas, such as certain kinds of renewable energy today, stew on the back burner for a long time. Affordable loss puts a limit on how much time you commit.

TAKEAWAY: EVERYBODY HAS A GOOD IDEA

Eric von Hippel (1994) at Massachusetts Institute of Technology (MIT) examined the sources of successful invention in large corporations. He found that the overwhelming majority of new ideas that turned out to be profitable product lines came not out of research and development departments, but out of customer inputs such as complaints and suggestions piped in through support and service departments.

The ability to act, learn, and change is critical as well. FedEx began with the idea of delivering spare parts, and RealNetworks began as an interactive television channel. Most successful entrepreneurs find that they have to abandon the ideas they first perceived and be willing to change their "vision" in response to feedback and stakeholder negotiations, both in the early stages of their venture and as they grow.

Sticking close to who you are, what you know, and who you know tells you not only what to do, but also what not to do. The problem with most novice entrepreneurs is not that they do not have great new ideas for ventures—it's that they have too many ideas and are too excited by them.

Novice entrepreneurs tend to see opportunities everywhere and, if they have the resources, feel tempted to expand production too soon, or jump into too many new market segments all at once. Especially if they have some initial success, it is easy to feel prescient (i.e. believe they can predict the future) as well as omnipotent (i.e. believe they are invincible). But good ideas are often a lot less glamorous than that.

Robert Reiss, founder of R&R, a company that brought games like Trivial Pursuit to the US, once said:

> People think they shouldn't go into business unless they have a blockbuster idea that's going to change the world. It doesn't really work that way. There are few new blockbuster ideas. There are just mundane kinds of ideas. You do something better than someone else. You take an existing thing and you add a new twist. It is just like Scrabble. You take an existing word, you put one letter on it and you get credit for the whole word—your letter plus the whole word.

Implicit in Reiss' statement is that you have to be in the game in the first place. You have to be playing Scrabble in order to be in a position to add that extra letter which makes a great venture.

■ ■ ■

So What?

You can begin with a simple problem for which you see an implementable solution—or even something that you believe would be fun to attempt—and start. Waiting for that blockbuster idea or "billion-dollar" opportunity is more likely to hold you back than to carry you to new heights.

What Now?

As you work toward taking the plunge into a venture:

- [ ] List five ideas that you think are really good and five that you think are terrible. What is the difference between them?

- [ ] Think of an idea you love, identify the critical hurdle to making it happen. How would you overcome that one hurdle? This may change the scope and nature of your idea. Why is that hurdle there?

- [ ] Consider the extreme case: How about becoming an entrepreneur without having any ideas at all? What would be the first step?

Think It Through

Beyond the immediate topic of this chapter, think about the following questions:

- [ ] If it's unrealistic to identify the best idea ever, what would it take to recognize one that's just good enough?

- [ ] Do we live in societies that encourage innovation? How would one know?

- [ ] Now that we realize that the magic of entrepreneurship is not in the idea, where is it?

CHAPTER 3

Starting without money is more challenging than starting with money, which is exactly why starting with little money generates strong new ventures.

Most ventures require little startup capital

■ ■ ■

IN THIS CHAPTER:

Of all the reasons wannabe entrepreneurs give for why they haven't already started their ventures, one that often tops the list is the lack of adequate startup capital. So, how much money is enough to get started?

WHEN US$90 MILLION IS NOT ENOUGH . . .

One of the most promising startups of all time in Silicon Valley was a company called Zaplet. In early 1999, Brian Axe and David Roberts created the concept of Zaplets—dynamic, updateable, web-like messages and applications delivered through email. Zaplet's history followed the textbook path for high-tech ventures—from two techies in a garage to pitching to VCs in the Valley, using systematic market research leading to the perfect plan focused on delivering a financial home run that every new entrepreneur naively dreams of and every investor hopes for.

Zaplet did everything right. VCs fell in love with the product. Silicon Valley buzzed with the market possibilities for Zaplet. Wall Street could not get enough of the story. By July 2000, Zaplet had hired 27 product managers, and 30 developers were writing code for six independent, potentially revenue-generating product areas.

Before it began its descent into oblivion in 2001, Zaplet had raised, and consumed, a total of US$90 million in venture funding.

How much does it take to start a business?

- Dell computers launched in 1984 with US$1,000.

- According to Inc. Magazine's October 2002 survey of the 500 fastest-growing companies, 14% were started with less than US$1,000 (Bartlett, 2002).

- The Wells Fargo/National Federation of Independent Businesses report shows that 70% of small business owners started with less than US$20,000 (Dennis, 1998).

- A 2009 survey found that US entrepreneurs average about $30,000 in total to start a business from scratch (Scott, 2009).

. . . YET US$5,000 IS PLENTY

Around the same time, in Bozeman, Montana (population 28,083), Greg Gianforte built RightNow Technologies to commercialize a software product that helped companies respond to their customers' emails quickly and effectively. Starting with a goal of creating 2,000 jobs in his beloved Bozeman, Gianforte invested US$5,000 of his own money and booked about US$20,000 in revenue in the first year.

Working alone, coding a bare-bones product with specs derived from a series of cold calls to customers, Gianforte often took price out of the equation by offering bargain-basement deals such as a few thousand dollars for a two-year lease of his software to early customers. Because his costs were so low, he could even afford to give the product away for free in return for actual early adoption and detailed real time feedback-in-use.

Once he had about 40 users, Gianforte hired five employees. With his relentless focus on revenue, all of his first hires were salespeople. Gianforte does not believe cold calling is disreputable work, nor does he believe fundraising or even product building has to precede sales. Instead, he waxes poetic about selling. For example, he told Professor William Sahlman and Research Associate Dan Heath of the Harvard Business School:

> Some entrepreneurs don't like sales very much. They do it only because they have to, and as soon as they can, they hire someone else to do the selling. They may even feel that there's something a little bit sleazy about calling up strangers for money. Yes, sales can be hard work. No one likes making cold calls. But sleazy? On the contrary, I think sales is actually the noblest part of business. It's the part that brings the solution together with the customer's need.

The little venture grew from an investment of US$5,000 and sales of US$20,000 in its first year to revenues of over US$35 million and a post-money valuation of US$100 million in its third year. In 2011, the firm was acquired by Oracle Corporation for US$1.5 billion.

> Nothing happens until somebody sells something.
> Greg Gianforte
> Founder
> RightNow Technologies

MONEY MATCHING

To stay in business, every venture (profit and non-profit alike) must take in at least as much cash as it spends, and in the case of for-profit ventures, ideally a bit more. It's true that "it takes money to make money," but taking investment money at the outset starts a new venture off in a deficit position. As far as the venture is concerned, any money it does not generate through sales is money it owes someone. This is what we call the "money matching principle." Simply put, any cash out needs to be matched with cash in.

Practically Speaking

DRAGON LADY

What would you guess happens to this book after you read it? If you are a social person, you might share it with a friend. If you are a resourceful person, you might resell it. And if you recycle it, chances are good it will end up with Yan Cheung of Nine Dragons Paper Holdings Limited in China. It won't take long, either. "The newspaper that you put in your newspaper bin— three weeks later, it's in the hands of someone in China," explains Bill Moore of Moore & Associates in Atlanta, a consultant on recovered paper. Amazing—but how does this happen?

Resourceful recycler

Rewind to 1990. In that year, Cheung created America Chung Nam (ACN) with just US$3,800. Her plan was to buy recycled paper in the United States and export it to China. She observed that Americans love to consume paper, using more than 700 pounds per person each year. And the Chinese desperately need to produce paper-based cardboard boxes in which to export domestically manufactured goods to the world. Driving around the US from dump to recycling facility in a Dodge minivan, Cheung and her husband filled containers (likely ones that had just arrived from China) with waste paper, and sent them to China. It wasn't long before they were filling a lot of containers.

Printing money

Five years later, armed with the new means of a strong cash flow from ACN, a reliable source of high-quality recycled paper through ACN and a clear understanding of the appetite for packaging materials in China, Cheung returned to Hong Kong. There she launched Nine Dragons to take that stream of waste paper and process it into kraftlinerboard, testlinerboard or corrugating medium—the basic papers used to make a cardboard box. Over the next 15 years, Cheung's operation may as well have been printing cash directly. Nine Dragons built capacity to produce more than 8.8 million tons of paperboard a year and today it is the largest producer in China and among the largest globally. Cheung is the self-crowned "Queen of Waste Paper," and rivals Oprah Winfrey and J.K. Rowling as one of the richest women in the world.

Paper trail

There are two useful insights from Nine Dragons that can be boxed up and shipped to entrepreneurs everywhere. The first is that new ventures can be created with things that already exist. It is easy to believe that in order to start a company, you need a technological innovation or a huge investment. But Cheung started with nothing more than trash. Second, ideas don't become opportunities until somebody acts. The fact that Americans were generating paper waste

Practically Speaking *(continued)*

and that China needed massive amounts of cardboard was no secret to anyone, even in 1990. Yet someone, an entrepreneur, had to get into her Dodge minivan and make the opportunity happen.

Packaged solution

Also contained in this story is a bigger idea. It's about where solutions to big problems come from. The problem of paper waste is huge. Every 120 pounds of recycled paper saves a tree. Paper made from recycled paper requires 64% less energy than paper made from raw materials. While governments try to convince people to recycle, Cheung gets the job done, using an average of 85% to 90% recovered paper in the manufacturing process. That's a lot of trees and a lot of watts. She and entrepreneurs like her build businesses and sustainability.

While our mythical entrepreneur may seek to raise US$10 million in venture capital as part of her roadmap to success, we take a different tack. We encourage you to try to think about not having money as an asset in itself—an asset that challenges you to build a more robust business, forces you to be more creative in how you deal with customers and partners, and allows you to maintain more control over your venture.

Research Roots

WEALTH IS UNRELATED TO STARTING A FIRM

It is easy to read the stories of new ventures that secure millions in venture funding and assume that lots of cash is a necessary prerequisite for starting a company. But in a study published in 2004, Erik Hurst and Annamaria Lusardi showed that wealth is not important for starting a business. The median amount of capital used by households founding their own businesses was US$22,700, and nearly a quarter were started with less than US$5,000. These results are consistent with the work of Amar Bhidé (2000), who found that most of the firms in Inc. Magazine's 500 fastest-growing list started with little capital, and 26% started with less than US$5,000.

MONEY MATCHING: ACCOUNTANTS VERSUS ENTREPRENEURS

Accounting works to extend the money matching principle over time. For example, if it costs US$500,000 to buy a new machine, accountants don't put that entire amount in the expense column of the balance sheet that year. Instead, they spread it out over the number of years the machine will be producing product revenue— say, 10 years. Through this process, accountants match the expenses and the revenues using the idea of depreciation.

How can this possibly matter to an entrepreneur? The answer is that depreciation happens only on paper. Where accountants rationalize actually paying out the US$500,000 in full for the machine, and writing it off on paper over 10 years, entrepreneurs seek to find ways to pay out only a fraction of the cash up front for the same machine—and work hard to match funding to actual use in each time period.

This difference in matching mirrors the difference in Zaplet and RightNow. It is the difference between matching funding to a vision and matching it to an implementation. It is the difference between selecting courses of action based on five-year return projections fuelled by imagined uses for a technology or focusing on the immediate next step that is underwritten by current commitments from actual stakeholders.

To match expenses and revenue, ask yourself questions like these:

- How much output do I need right now?
- Are there ways to get cash for that output before actually producing it?
- What are the ways I can delay cash outflows and accelerate cash inflows?
- Can a customer pay half up front?
- Will suppliers let me pay in 60 days instead of 30? Would they be willing to go to 90?
- Can I focus on non-cash-intensive parts of the business first so I don't need funding now and can raise money later on better terms?
- How can I use technology, including social media for marketing, Internet telephony for communications, and online payments for invoicing to make the most of my limited capital?

CREATIVE CAPITAL

One of the most common ways to match expenses and revenue—and thus reduce the need for cash—is to convert fixed costs into variable costs. Instead of buying the US$500,000 machine, you might find someone who owns a similar machine and is willing to sell you units from it. You may have to pay a premium for this option but now you don't have to raise US$500,000 to buy the machine yourself. Creative thinking along these lines often leads to the discovery of slack resources (i.e. resources lying around) such as periods when an existing factory is underutilized.

You may be able to access this capacity at a discount or even for free on a trial basis.

Move from asking, "Can I raise US$500,000 to pay for the new machine?" to asking, "How can I make the US$500,000 without incurring the fixed costs of buying and owning the machine?"

CREATIVE CAPITAL VERSUS INVESTED CAPITAL

Entrepreneurs don't always see all the costs associated with capital and make two common mistakes:

High cost of invested capital

They walk away from an opportunity to convert a fixed cost into a variable cost even though it has a premium price, only to turn around and sell a large percentage of their firm to an investor, i.e. obtain expensive capital, instead.

Not considering creative capital

They weigh the cost of one type of invested capital against the cost of another, overlooking the cost of invested capital versus the cost of creative capital.

Costs of creative capital

At the same time, there are caveats with the creative capital approach.

Creative financing gives entrepreneurs more time—but at a cost. Contrary to what you might have learned in a finance course, the cost of capital is not just the interest rate or the return your investors require. The cost of creative capital also includes:

- Paying a premium variable price (for example, paying top rental rates for a factory) in order to avoid a major fixed cost investment (for example, building your own factory).
- Exposure to renegotiated terms from suppliers if you turn out to be successful.
- Exposure to opportunistic partners if you don't control the parts of your business that are most competitively valuable. (At the start it's not always clear what will end up being your competitive advantage.)

If you make all your fixed costs variable, the total cost might be too high to make a profit. If the asset you decide not to buy—say, the US$500,000 machine—turns out to be critically necessary to the business, will the owner of that asset have you over a barrel, perhaps forcing you to buy output at a premium price? The answer is that these things can happen and each entrepreneur needs to make these trade-offs idiosyncratically, according to his or her own level of affordable loss, staying focused on keeping the venture going. Early in the life of a venture, the greatest threat is survival. When time and money run out, the venture stops.

We have yet to see the cost of creative capital kill a new venture. Many ventures, however, have ended in the pursuit of invested capital. The simple fact is that the market for lending and investing surrounding new ventures is far from easily accessible. Even if you effectively evaluate the true costs of your sources of invested capital, and venture capital comes out as the most cost effective source, the reality of striking a deal for venture capital is another thing entirely. Furthermore, chasing venture funding may be expensive in terms of the cost of your time, since you miss all the venture building you could have been doing (customers you do not talk to, suppliers you do not negotiate with, employees you do not build long-term relationships with) while you are out chasing VCs. You may spend six months

Research Roots

THE LEAN STARTUP

Few popular books on entrepreneurship have proven to be as well liked as Eric Ries' Lean Startup. Published in the wake of the global financial crisis of 2009, Lean Startup was very much the right book, with the right message at the right time.

Central to the book's message is the notion of "lean" which borrows from the lean manufacturing philosophy pioneered by Japanese auto manufacturers such as Toyota. To make a production process "lean" means to eliminate all the waste in it. Leaning a startup means eliminating the need for elaborate business plans, fancy product development, and large amounts of outside funding. Instead, Ries urges founders to focus on just the necessary things to get a new venture going. Therefore, in place of developing the perfect instantiation of a product or service, just develop the "minimal viable product" (MVP) version. In place of doing elaborate market research, validate the MVP by getting direct customer feedback on it. In place of investing heavily in a particular direction, stay flexible and "pivot" when necessary.

Lean Startup may not be based on a careful program of published research in the way that effectuation is, but the popularity of the terms "lean," "pivot," and "MVP" suggests that Eric Ries has written a book that many entrepreneurs find exceedingly useful (Ries, 2011).

Research Roots

FUNDING VIA THE MASSES

Crowdfunding is a unique category of fundraising that draws on practices in micro-finance and crowdsourcing. It refers to efforts by for-profit, social, and cultural ventures to fund projects by amalgamating small contributions from a large number of individuals, usually via Internet crowdfunding sites.

A recent research paper by Ethan Mollick of Wharton investigated data on 48,526 US projects crowdfunded on Kickstarter, an internet crowdfunding site, encompassing $237 million in funding (averaging around $5,000 per project).

Mollick's analyses showed several interesting patterns exist in crowdfunding. First, success in crowdfunding a project appears to be linked to the perceived quality of the project, with higher quality projects more likely to achieve funding. Second, a bigger presence on social networking sites such as Facebook was linked to more success in achieving funding. Third, there is a strong association between projects and the culture of the places they come from. For example, crowdfunded projects in Los Angeles were likely to be in the film industry, whereas projects in Nashville were mainly music-based. Lastly, Mollick found very little fraud among the projects, but around 75% of crowdfunded projects were delayed, with the bigger, more complicated projects being more likely to be delayed (Mollick, 2014).

chasing that cost-effective capital source unsuccessfully, leaving you without time and capital, which results in the end of the venture. The cost of obtaining capital, even well managed, can be higher than the cost of NOT getting it.

In the event of venture growth and success, the cost of creative financing tends to go down even more. At the same time, the cost of invested capital becomes higher, because the investors claim a fraction of the total value created in the venture. As a result, setting up milestones for addressing success as well as failure, "alternative" contracts, and even pre-negotiated changes that are different for "good" versus "bad" situations, can be an important part of your effort to use those creative sources of capital. Beware, of course, that you don't let your predictions of the future take over in these moments. For example, your predictions of the assets you think are most strategic (and those that you don't) can lead you to seek narrow control rights over those assets rather than continue to work creatively with potential partners.

BOOTSTRAPPING BENEFITS

In their book *Bootstrapping Your Business*, Gianforte and Gibson (2007) make the case that starting with nothing is a good idea. We agree, and summarize the highlights:

- *You can start now.* Instead of waiting for a prospective funder to come along, be inspired by your business and write you a

Practically Speaking

BRINGING A CAREER BACK FROM THE DEAD

At first glance, Vidal Herrera seems just like any person trying to make his way in the world. He lives in Los Angeles, drives a white SUV and his firm sponsors local baseball and polo teams. Average enough, except that the baseball team he sponsors is named "The Stiffs" after Herrera's business, 1-800-AUTOPSY. Of course, with the advent of the Internet, he has added ".com" to the name, but Herrera still offers the same thanatology services to private clients he did when he started the firm 21 years ago.

Job in a casket

Autopsy on demand is not the first idea that comes to most people when they start on their entrepreneurial careers. And it did not occur to Herrera until he became disabled and unemployed as a result of lifting a 5'2" 284-pound female corpse in 1984. After he lost his job as a field deputy coroner investigator (CSI) in Los Angeles County, try as he might, no one wanted to employ him. Necessity being the mother of invention, he started doing contract work to make ends meet, retrieving tissue for Veterans Administration researchers.

Alive, well, and growing

As part of the job, Herrera visited local funeral homes and met grieving families anxious to understand the fates of their loved ones. People wanted answers to questions ranging from the cause of their relative's death to paternity mysteries, and they had no viable ways of obtaining this knowledge. Based on his interactions with next of kin, Herrera began to form the basis of a service offering. He launched 1-800-AUTOPSY in 1988 using nothing more than his meagre retirement income, because banks refused to lend him money.

Conception of a new market

Unwilling to invest more cash in advance in new businesses, Herrera has since granted franchisees the right to operate in Orlando, Florida, Northern California, and Las Vegas, Nevada. So instead of investing his money in expansion, he gets paid when someone else takes the risk to expand. The business grew through the financial crisis and seems likely to expand further as the baby boomer generation ages. As Herrera puts it, "Death is a recession-proof business."

Practically Speaking (continued)

Post mortem

It is the sheer unlikeliness of this story that offers an interesting insight: who would have thought there is in fact a market for private autopsy services? If Herrera had not started 1-800-AUTOPSY, would the independent thanatology market exist at all? In fact, 1-800-AUTOPSY gives us a rare glimpse at how markets and firms are conceived. We tend to assume that the entrepreneur's job is to track down economically inevitable opportunities hidden in the sand through careful sifting and prophet-like prescience. Reality often points the other way. Herrera's story shows us that firms and markets are created when entrepreneurs, driven by all kinds of motivations (needing income is a primary motivation, but not the only one) and the peculiarity of their individual circumstances, begin interacting with potential customers and other stakeholders, and end up creating something novel and valuable. The ventures they begin almost always spring from things they already have or already know.

check, you can start your business today. There is nothing holding you back.

- *You can start learning now.* Most ventures we know and love were created through entrepreneurs' interactions with suppliers, customers, partners, and employees. Cash can encourage you not to engage in those interactions and, thus, not learn as quickly.
- *Cut your waste.* When you have money, it is easy to waste it on speculative ideas. But if you have none, it's hard to throw it out the window.
- *Limit your downside.* If you do not have a huge amount of cash invested in the venture, the mistakes you will inevitably make will likely be proportionately smaller.
- *Increase your upside.* Taking investment generally means selling equity. And the more you sell, the less you have when it comes time to realize the value created in your venture.
- *Increase your creativity.* Studies show that constraints increase creativity. When you have money, you'll spend it. When you don't have money, you add a constraint that makes you more creative.

TAKEAWAY: HAVING NOTHING IS A GOOD THING

The reality is that most firms in the world operate without any outside funding; instead, they make decisions with an eye to what they can afford to lose. Their priority is to stay in business, and so they make sure the downside risks are acceptable.

Starting without invested capital means that you get the feedback and cash you need from customers, so you refine your idea and develop new and productive partnerships with people whose slack resources you put to valuable new use. Starting without invested capital also forces you to try to make a sale, which is when you learn whether you really have a business or not. If you fail, you fail cheaply and early, and you don't have to give away a lot of equity or control in the process. Starting a venture with little or nothing may be a good thing after all.

So What?

The most important inputs come from you: who you are, what you know, and who you know. You plus a customer and a shared solution gives substance to the venture, not external investment.

What Now?

- ☐ Take stock of your monthly expenses and ask yourself how much you could do without.

- ☐ What slack resources (not money, but capabilities) could you tap into that belong to other people?

- ☐ Imagine that it is illegal to raise money for you to develop your new venture. How would you then take on the challenge of starting your new venture?

- ☐ What are "gross margin dollars" and how do you get them?

- ☐ Find resources on the web that will get you started in creating your own budget: (http://www.inc.com/encyclopedia/businessbudget.html).

Think It Through

- ☐ What would happen if a rich uncle died and left you several million dollars? Would you still want to start a venture?

- ☐ What is it about money that makes it valuable? If it's about what it can buy, think about how you can get those things without having to use money to buy them.

Fewer than 2% of new ventures reach an IPO.

92% of ventures exit without outstanding debt.

Soooo ...

If success is defined as an initial public offering, 98% of ventures fail.

But if failure is defined as bankruptcy, only 8% of ventures fail.

Fail cheap and learn quickly

■ ■ ■

No entrepreneur sets out to fail. But what, exactly, constitutes failure? And what counts as success? The answers to those questions are not as straightforward as you might think.

Most people would agree that a failed venture is one that closes down owing money to creditors. But most would also say that there are other kinds of failure, too. Success is just as hard to pin down. We all have different personal definitions of success and failure.

For some, quitting is the only form of failure. For others, earning less than they could working for someone else is equivalent to failing.

Similarly, for some, only an initial public offering (IPO) can be considered a true success, while for others, simply being able to make a decent living without answering to a boss is a sign of having truly made it.

The matter is further complicated by cultural differences. In Europe, business failure is perceived to be a death knell, financially and socially. In some parts of the world, an entrepreneur, whose venture doesn't work out, may find it difficult to get married and move forward with a productive life. But in Silicon Valley, if you are an entrepreneur who hasn't failed, you're a suspicious creature, an oddity.

In Europe, those who go bankrupt tend to be considered "losers." They face great difficulty getting financing for a new venture.
Communication by the European Commission, 1998

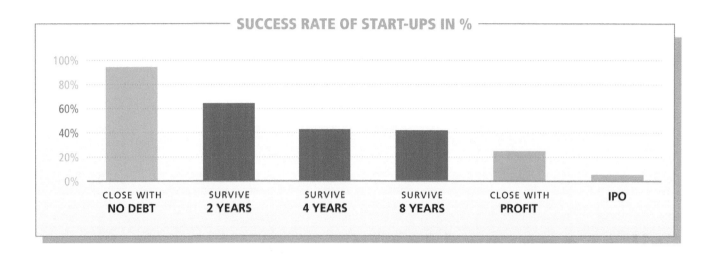

SUCCESS RATE OF START-UPS IN %

| CLOSE WITH NO DEBT | SURVIVE 2 YEARS | SURVIVE 4 YEARS | SURVIVE 8 YEARS | CLOSE WITH PROFIT | IPO |

The fear of failure, whatever it means, certainly looms large for many of us considering starting a business. But it shouldn't. If you are among those hesitating to dip your toe in the water for fear of being burned, consider these equations:

- Success ≠ success
- Success ≠ money
- Failure of the firm ≠ failure of the individual
- Failure = learning

In this chapter, we'll discuss each of those equations, and look at how entrepreneurs learn to make failure non-terminal, and instead, make it a learning experience.

SUCCESS ≠ SUCCESS

We know—this first equation looks nonsensical. We're not trying to be difficult, but are suggesting that success (and failure, too) is a slippery concept. If we need to overcome our fear of failure by reconsidering what failure actually

means, then we should do the same for success. Take a look at the statistics in this chart (Headd, 2004: 51–61; US SBA, 2009; Kirchhoff, 1997; Knaup, 2005). If success is nothing short of an IPO, your chance of succeeding is less than 2%. But maybe success is running a

business that closes with no debt. In that case, you have a 92% chance of success. On average, new ventures have around a 40% chance of success if that means creating a venture that lasts for eight years— long enough to have the experience of being your own boss, learn a few

Research Roots

VENTURE FAILURE— URBAN LEGEND AND MISCOMMUNICATION

The popular press and our political figures are informal about their use of research in narrating venture failure rates. Glenn Kessler (2014) recently penned an article in the Washington Post entitled "Do nine out of 10 new businesses fail, as Rand Paul (2016 US presidential hopeful) claims?" The answer in the article is "no," and the article goes on to summarize research on venture survival figures similar to ours in this chapter. Furthermore, a recent Forbes article (Wagner, 2013) entitled "Five Reasons 8 out of 10 Businesses Fail" cites the failure rate from a Bloomberg study that simply doesn't exist (Jarvis, 2013). But in a separate article, Forbes also reports a new venture failure rate of about 55% after five years (Pozin, 2012), again similar to ours. It appears that the high failure rate in entrepreneurship is another urban legend that though popular, simply isn't true.

Research Roots

ON THE ORIGINS OF FAILURE

In his book *Born Losers*, Scott Sandage (2006) explores the historical origins of failure. Failure, he argues, is a social construct that was invented during the nineteenth century. Of course, people have always stigmatized others for one reason or another. The Greeks and Romans, for instance, stigmatized slaves, criminals and traitors. But the idea of failed individuals didn't really exist before the late 1800s, and so we are still figuring out how to define and how to deal with this relatively new social concept.

things, and maybe even stash away a bit of money.

The chart also tells us that one in every four companies that closes down does so with a profit. Because most statistics track only firm closures, these firms are counted as failures—though they were making money right up to the point where operations ceased. Interestingly, this suggests that financial "failure" is not the only reason people close down a business. Maybe the owner retired, moved, accepted a job offer or simply got bored.

Now that we're thoroughly confused about what success is and isn't, read the following short stories. Think about whether each demonstrates a success or a failure, and tick the appropriate box.

Story 1

Lucy launched four ventures that failed before she moved onto her fifth one. This one and the one that followed were enormously successful, financially. Unfortunately, the sixth venture was wiped out by a natural disaster in which Lucy lost everything.

❑ Success   ❑ Failure

Story 2

Mark meets a San Francisco VC to pitch his next idea. He is feeling confident. His previous venture sold after only 18 months, making over four times its original investment for its founders and stakeholders. The VC looks at the previous venture as

a failure. Her argument: They sold too soon and could have made more money.

❑ Success   ❑ Failure

Story 3

Jack, a serial entrepreneur, looks at the company he founded 15 years ago. It makes an 8% return for its shareholders, pays the bills, and is highly respected in its industry. Jack quit the company seven years ago,

Practically Speaking

FAIL TO SUCCEED

Isaac Larian is a busy man. Since his immigration from Iran to the United States 38 years ago, he has washed dishes, studied engineering, imported brass goods from Korea, and sold refrigerators and microwave ovens. Building on his Asian connections, he was the first to bring Nintendo handheld LCD games to the US, and from there he expanded into the toy business, licensing popular brands like Mighty Morphin Power Rangers, Hello Kitty and The Hulk.

Taking control of the toys

That got Larian started, but the reason you likely already know him is Bratz. In 2001, tired of making profits for his licensors, Larian decided to create his own toy brand and launched a line of fashion dolls. In just three years, Bratz dolls successfully challenged Barbie's supremacy on toy store shelves and created more than US$2 billion a year in revenue for Larian's firm, MGA Entertainment.

> [Bratz] are everything Barbie is not. Who in Britain can identify with a six-foot-two blonde? The Bratz exist in a changing world—children today are exposed to change at a very fast pace, so the Bratz change too . . . In ten years, they will be something completely different.
>
> Isaac Larian

In 2007, Larian was named Ernst & Young's Entrepreneur Of The Year. But with the award came disappointment. The year proved bittersweet for Bratz. Panned by the critics, the Bratz Fashion Pixiez movie Larian released with Lions Gate Entertainment generated less than US$3 million in revenue. And adding insult to injury, 4Kids.TV canceled the Bratz animated television series. A closer look at these disappointments offers the real insight into Larian's entrepreneurial expertise. His investment into both of these experiments was sufficiently low that failure did not translate into catastrophe for the firm. Instead, he shared risk and the potential rewards with partners. As Larian says, "You should not be afraid of failure. In order to succeed, you need to fail."

Understanding failures to understand success

Looking back at Larian's career offers another insight. Entrepreneurship is less about vision and more about the journey of creation. From his start, it would have been impossible to predict that he would become the head of the third largest toy company in the world, yet in retrospect the pieces came together and make sense. And by failing gracefully when failure came, Larian was always ready to learn from the experience and do something better in the next round.

The Girls with a Passion for Fashion!

selling his shares to his managers because he knew he could never take it public.

❏ Success   ❏ Failure

That may have felt like a quiz, but it wasn't. There are no right or wrong answers. Clearly, how you view success (and failure) depends on your environment and on the expectations of others who are involved. It also depends on your role in the process. If you are a VC, you want at least 10 times the money you invested. If you are a supplier, you only worry about whether the startup will pay its bills. The fact that success and failure mean different things to different people makes the statistics we discussed earlier a lot less alarming because whether you succeed or fail really depends on what your objectives are and what your committed stakeholders want. This takes us to our next equation— success and the reasons why entrepreneurs start businesses have to do with more than just the financial return.

SUCCESS ≠ MONEY

Before you launch your venture, hoping to become the next Bill Gates, consider the following:

- On average, the self-employed earn about the same as those employed and working for a wage.
- Having said that, the distribution of earnings is skewed by a few superstar entrepreneurs who make

> ### Persistence pays, or who decides it's a bad idea?
>
> Within a month of submitting the first manuscript to publishing houses, the creative team behind the multimillion-dollar book series *Chicken Soup for the Soul* (Canfield and Hansen, 1993) got turned down 33 consecutive times. Publishers claimed that "anthologies don't sell" and the book was "too positive." Total number of rejections— 140. Then, in 1993, the president of Health Communications took a chance on the collection of poems, stories and tidbits of encouragement. Today, the 65-title series has sold more than 80 million copies in 37 languages.

incredible amounts of money (e.g. Bill Gates). Most entrepreneurs earn below the average.

- Those who earn below average officially earn about one-third less than a comparable employed person does.
- Recent research suggests that this pattern is reversed when income under-reporting is taken into account. It is an established fact that entrepreneurs under-report their income to tax authorities.

Of course, there are things other than money that matter to entrepreneurs (such as being your own boss, doing something that's important to you, or even just trying to solve a problem that irks you).

FAILED VENTURE ≠ FAILED INDIVIDUAL

Entrepreneurial performance is almost always confused with firm performance—the success or failure of the company is the success or

Twain on learning

We should be careful to get out of an experience only the wisdom that is in it—and stop there; lest we be like the cat that sits down on a hot stove lid. She will never sit down on a hot stove lid again—and that is well; but also she will never sit down on a cold one.

Mark Twain (1897)

Success is a lousy teacher. It seduces smart people into thinking they can't lose.

Bill Gates

Practically Speaking

MILTON HERSHEY

Born September 13, 1857, on a farm near Derry Church, a small Pennsylvania community, Milton Hershey was the only surviving child of Fannie and Henry Hershey. His mother raised him in the strict discipline of the Mennonite faith. Frequent family moves interrupted his schooling and left him with a limited education. He only completed the fourth grade.

A bitter start

Following a four-year apprenticeship with a Lancaster candy maker, he established his first candy-making business in Philadelphia. That initial effort failed, and his next two attempts, in Chicago and New York went bankrupt as well. Returning to Lancaster, Pennsylvania, in 1883, Hershey established the Lancaster Caramel Company, which quickly became an outstanding success. It was this business that established him as a candy maker and set the stage for future accomplishments.

New ingredients

Hershey became fascinated with German chocolate-making machinery exhibited at the 1893 World's Columbian Exposition. He bought the equipment for his Lancaster plant and soon began producing a variety of chocolate creations. Hershey sold the Lancaster Caramel Co. for US$1 million in 1900 in order to concentrate exclusively on his chocolate business. Three years later, he returned to Derry Church to build a new factory. There he could obtain the large supplies of fresh milk needed to perfect and produce fine milk chocolate.

Sweet success

Excited by the potential of milk chocolate, which at that time was a Swiss luxury product, Milton Hershey was determined to develop a formula for milk chocolate and sell it to the American public. Through trial and error, he created his own formula for milk chocolate. In 1903, he found success and began construction on what was to become the world's largest chocolate manufacturing plant.

failure of the individual. This is a mistake for several reasons.

First, as we have seen, although entry is common, survival is less so. Second, many companies enter a market in its infancy. As this market matures, only the fittest survive. A lot of work has been done on the corporation, looking, for example, for a correlation between the age of the firm and survival rates. (Do firms die young or degenerate with age?) But little is known of the success or failure rates of entrepreneurs.

The primary reason is that evidence on failed firms is hard to obtain (the data usually disappear along with the firm), while evidence on individual entrepreneurs who have failed a firm is well-nigh impossible to come by. People simply do not walk around with business cards that say, "Failed entrepreneur." Most founders of failed firms dust themselves off and go on to start other firms. In any case, entrepreneurs tend not to mention their failed firms, except long after the fact and as part of uplifting anecdotes in public speeches.

Separating entrepreneur from firm

The corporation was invented to separate the success or failure of the firm from that of the individual. If an individual closes the business to pursue a new opportunity, does that constitute individual failure? Too often, we think that if the business fails the individual has failed. This is not the case, as the Hershey story illustrates (see the nearby box). Milton Hershey's early business missteps did not destroy him; some of his ventures may have failed, but he, as anyone who eats chocolate knows, did not.

Words of wisdom

A CULTURE OF LEARNING

. . . part of creating an entrepreneurial culture is to celebrate failure. It's very hard to be an entrepreneur inside a company if you feel you're going to get crucified for failing because there's risk in being an entrepreneur. If you've tried ten things, five will fail. Besides, if you wait too long so that you can do enough research to be sure an idea will work, you're probably going to be too late. So you've got to create an environment where people know it's okay to fail and, that way, they'll try a lot more. They'll think outside the box. They're willing to think differently because they know that if it doesn't work, they won't be scorched and they'll still have a career.

At times, like when we've closed out a business, we've had something like a celebration of what we've learned. We celebrate what we now know that we did not know before because it will help us make much better decisions in the future. We celebrate those people who fail and everyone around them knows that they produced value. It wasn't the value we intended, but it's okay as long as we learn from it.

In one of the businesses we launched last December, the marketing person was someone who had failed on her prior assignment. She had worked on a project where we were trying to set up a business for lending to small businesses on a very low-tech basis. We developed, launched, and got ten financial institutions to back it, but we couldn't get the volume to make the business fly. But then last December, working out of our Boston office, which is one of our most entrepreneurial operations, the same person and her team succeeded at launching a whole new business called QuickBase. It's a revolutionary product and is off to a huge start.

Scott Cook

Practically Speaking

PERSIST EASY; SWERVE HARD

The city of Bangalore, India, has over 200,000 three-wheel auto rickshaws—short distance, open taxis that provide critical transportation in a metropolis of more than six million inhabitants with no metro or underground rail system. Efficiently ferrying both people and goods, these simple machines challenge the urban environment. Their entrepreneurial drivers cruise the edges of the streets eagerly soliciting passengers, choking traffic and adding smog to an already congested city. Meanwhile, frustrated businesspeople, merchants, and families await rides in other locations without a free auto rickshaw in sight.

Smooth solution

When the commissioner of traffic police approached Padmasree Harish, an entrepreneur and self-taught web designer, to build a software system that would connect available auto rickshaws with waiting passengers, Harish saw both a natural answer to her city's problem as well as a good business opportunity. The system would receive SMS messages from drivers indicating location and availability, and calls from passengers with location and interest. The system would match passengers with the closest auto rickshaw and dispatch the vehicle to the passenger. Harish could charge a setup fee for each driver and a small fee for each fare her system was able to connect. All she had to do was let the software do the work while the rupees rolled in. And so, in 2007, Easy Auto kicked into gear. In theory, that is.

Hard stop

In practice, after the announcement of the initiative, the system never got beyond the rave press write-ups of its potential. This left Harish with a software system she and her team had spent six months developing, a call center filled with people hired to take calls from passengers, a tech team ready to roll out the system, extra uniforms for the drivers of the spruced-up rickshaws, and even 50,000 rupees worth of coolers and inventory from Pepsi for in-transit sales and additional revenue. The bumps in the road seemed never-ending. Drivers were reluctant to pay a setup fee and were unwilling to send SMS messages with their current location. But the unseen pothole that derailed Harish was the regulatory environment. It turned out that the traffic commissioner who initiated the project did not have permission from the branch of the bureaucracy that oversaw auto rickshaws. So the entire project was brought to a screeching halt.

Practically Speaking *(continued)*

U-turn?

Harish's inclination was to return to her profitable web hosting and design business, leaving physical traffic to someone else. But her personal cell phone was one of the three numbers provided in the Easy Auto announcement for passengers to call an auto rickshaw on demand. And whenever it rained, as it often does in Bangalore, Harish would get 200 to 250 calls. The market had her number, and it simply would not hang up. But when does tenacity become foolishness? And how does an entrepreneur know when to quit?

A new route

Harish started looking for work-arounds. She took courses in entrepreneurship so she could get others chewing on her problems. She actively observed every auto rickshaw she rode in and then some. In one, she saw an advertisement. She saw taxis with GPS units. Nearly every website she saw offered free services to end users but made money from someone else. So when the head of transportation came back to her in 2009 and asked her about getting Easy Auto going again, she was ready to negotiate:

- The approvals had to be complete before she would spend a rupee.

- The auto rickshaws would have to be equipped with units containing LCD screens showing promotional videos and GPS units for precise location information.

- The video would be funded by a company that builds the auto rickshaws.

- The drivers would receive compensation for signing up with Easy Auto.

- The GPS and LCD hardware would be provided by the manufacturers in advance with payment once the system started generating income.

- The call center would be out-sourced to a firm willing to set it up at no charge.

Harish was prepared to do everything differently than she had on her first try. She left behind the choice between the straight road of persistence and the sad U-turn. She had learned to swerve hard.

Enduring logic

Conventional wisdom describes the doggedly determined entrepreneur enduring in the face of adversity. But a closer look reveals an unexpected combination of persistence and flexibility. Persisting hard for a particular solution can be counterproductive and even end in despair. But hardheaded flexibility may transform the problem into an opportunity that attracts unexpected shareholders. Especially when problems persist, entrepreneurs need to be able to swerve hard to co-create new answers that can form the basis of new firms, new products, new markets, or even that unlikeliest of novelties—smoother traffic flow in Bangalore.

FAILURE = LEARNING

There are smart ways to fail and not so smart ways. Without failure, there would be no learning, no progress. In fact, the essence of the scientific method—the most rigorous learning process we humans have—is the design of well-thought-out failures—experiments that seek to falsify hypotheses. As some hypotheses are shown to be false and others continue unscathed, we begin to get closer to workable truths that lead to valuable technologies and cures for diseases.

The same is true of good engineering. In a book entitled *Success through Failure: The Paradox of Design*, Henry Petroski (2006) shows how success often masks potential modes of failure and how throughout history failures have led to technological progress and better design.

The key to learning from failures is to keep them small and kill them young. The affordable loss principle, which we'll learn more about in Chapter 12, is useful here. The idea is to limit your investment in a new opportunity to what you have consciously chosen as an acceptable level of loss. This has the benefit of reducing the magnitude of failure as well as limiting the psychological hit likely to come with unanticipated failures.

Resilience at work

When greeted by a heckler's boos—generally acknowledged to belong to Reginald Golding Bright—during the curtain call on the opening night of his play *Arms and the Man*, George Bernard Shaw responded with his now famous remark, "I assure the gentleman in the gallery that he and I are of exactly the same opinion, but what can we do against a whole house who are of the contrary opinion?"

William Butler Yeats, who witnessed the event, wrote of the sensation that ensued, "From that moment Bernard Shaw became the most formidable man in modern letters, and even the most drunken medical student knew it."

Practically Speaking

PRODUCT LAUNCHES AT APPLE COMPUTER

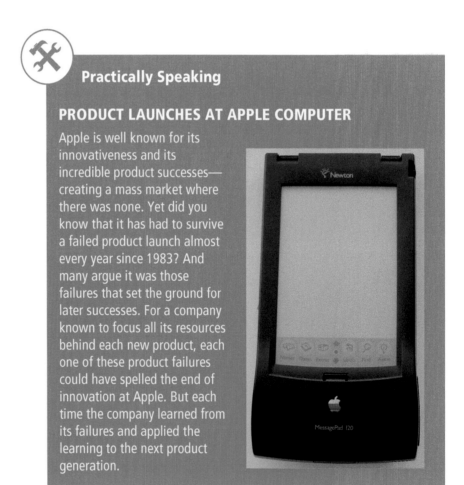

Apple is well known for its innovativeness and its incredible product successes—creating a mass market where there was none. Yet did you know that it has had to survive a failed product launch almost every year since 1983? And many argue it was those failures that set the ground for later successes. For a company known to focus all its resources behind each new product, each one of these product failures could have spelled the end of innovation at Apple. But each time the company learned from its failures and applied the learning to the next product generation.

		FAMOUS FAILURES FROM APPLE COMPUTER
Product	**Launch**	**Apple's product failures: Lessons learned**
Lisa	1983	The Lisa was the first computer to boast a graphical interface and a mouse. Aimed at the business community, it was priced at today's equivalent of US$20,800. Unsurprisingly, the business community voted for the cheaper IBMs. Lesson learned: Price does matter.
Apple IIc	1984	The Apple IIc was hailed as the first portable computer. It did have a carrying case, external power supply, built in floppy drive, and peripheral expansion ports. But it lacked upgradeability, and it had an extremely short-lived LCD display. The lessons learned from the Apple IIc's shortcomings would drive the design of the Macintosh.
Mac TV	1993	A combination of a Sony Trinitron and an Apple Performa 520, the product lasted barely 12 months before it was discontinued. Its major problem? It was incapable of showing TV feeds in a desktop window. Although only 10,000 units were produced, it was the precursor to today's successful AppleTV.
Newton	1993	The best known of Apple flops is probably the Newton. Released in 1993 as a revolutionary personal digital assistant (PDA) (but not as revolutionary as its first prototypes), it was available for four years with nearly no sales. When Steve Jobs returned to Apple in 1997, he axed the product he had tried so hard to launch. The Newton was bulky and relied on handwriting recognition software, which wasn't yet very good. Once Apple got those deficiencies fixed in the form of an iPad, the Newton became a good example of a product ahead of its time.
Pippin	1996	With the Pippin, Apple tried (once again) to enter the video game market with a product that was co-marketed with toymaker Bandai. The Pippin was sold as a cheap machine on which one could play games, but it also served as a network computer—one of the first multimedia platforms. It failed for several reasons, including a lack of software and competition in a market dominated by players such as Sega, Sony PlayStation, and Nintendo. Rumor has it Apple has just filed a patent for a new 3D gaming device, so we may soon be able to tell whether the company learned from the Pippin flop.
Hockey Puck Mouse	1998	The mouse that was shipped with the first iMacs was small, un-ergonomic and awkward to control. It was almost immediately phased out and replaced by the Mighty Mouse. Lesson learned: Sometimes a classical shape is good.
G4 Cube	2000	While the Cube was meant to fill the gap between the iMac G3 and the PowerMac G4, it was killed by the critics before it got anywhere. Its major problems: it lacked a monitor and it had a high price tag. However, its designer, Jonathan Ive, won several international awards for its design, and he remains as head designer for Apple. Apart from its design, it also set the stage for fanless cooling in PCs. The G4 was also an improvement on the NeXT computer, which Jobs had designed based on another major learning: don't build in proprietary software.

Practically Speaking

INVEST IN THE PERSON, NOT THE VENTURE

Imagine your dream is to create change on a national or, better still, global scale. And the bureaucracy at your employer, the US Federal Government, severely constrains what you can accomplish. What would you do?

Not many people would think of taking their own money and paying "salaries" to individuals in developing countries, even if those individuals showed promise in reforming their national environments. But that is exactly what Bill Drayton did when he launched Ashoka in India in 1980.

People and ideas

From the start, Drayton knew that he alone could not solve the world's problems. But he had travelled extensively in India and Indonesia, and knew people were already generating practical solutions to society's problems at a local level. These people and their ideas would provide him with resources—they would give him a place to start, and he would give them a chance to disseminate what they had designed and learned.

Investing in people

When Drayton created Ashoka, he created the concept of an Ashoka fellow—someone with an idea with potential for significant social impact, an idea he or she has proved locally and wants to roll out on a larger scale. But Ashoka carefully selects the person, not the idea. Once selected, an Ashoka fellow is rewarded with training, a monthly living stipend (for three years), and networking opportunities that encourage them to share their idea and create new ideas.

> Our job is not to give people fish, it's not to teach them how to fish, it's to build new and better fishing industries.
>
> Bill Drayton

Model citizen

Consider one of the first fellows, Fábio Luiz de Oliveira Rosa. Saddened by the exodus of farmers to cities in his native Brazil, Rosa developed a cheap way to bring electricity to poor, remote areas, allowing, for example, the irrigation of farmlands. For an investment of about US$400, rural farmers could install a

PASSION

Passion serves an important role in managing failure, helping to breed the resilience that's necessary to learn from mistakes. Remarks on passion from the comedian Seinfeld can be summed up as saying, "It is not that bad things do not happen when you love what you do. It is just that passion makes it easier to live with and deal with and overcome those difficulties."

All the same, failure is never easy. Dean Shepherd (2003) suggests that the emotions associated with having to close down a business are somewhat similar to those we feel when we lose someone dear to us. Business owners see the closure of their business as a personal loss and experience feelings of grief.

The ability to learn from the loss of a business depends on recovering from that grief. Shepherd suggests that confronting the reality of the loss and acknowledging the emotions as normal while suppressing them enough to move on may be helpful for entrepreneurs.

It's also crucial to keep in mind what is perhaps the most important rule of failure: don't fail alone. Failure is more palatable and success is sweeter when we have supportive people around us who share in the ups and downs.

And interestingly, people who have gone through adversity together

PASSION?

If you're about to start your own business, you've got to have a passion for whatever it is that you want to do. We can't teach passion; we can teach everything else. If you have passion and you do your homework, don't let fear of failure stop you from going into a new business. Fear of failure is the number one reason people don't go ahead in starting a business. They're just afraid to pull the trigger.

They start analysing what the fear means. There is the fear that the business won't succeed and the fear that their ego will be damaged. At least in your head, you've got to separate the two fears. Many people won't do things, like a sales call, because they're afraid they'll be turned down. Ego shouldn't be a concern. Every rejection is a learning experience. You deal with the fear of a business failing by doing all those things. There is risk in everything in life. Don't let fear of failure keep you from moving ahead.

Robert Reiss, Founder of R&R

LEARNING FROM FAILURE

According to Henry Ford, "The world was built to develop character." In a wonderful and very accessible little book, entrepreneurship researcher Dean Shepherd explains how failure can be—just as Henry Ford intimated—a positive learning and development experience if we know how to handle it.

Many people say they have learned more from their failures than from their successes. Yet how much we learn from failure depends on our ability to manage our emotional reactions to these disappointments, since our negative emotions will otherwise interfere with our opportunity to learn. Social support also helps a lot since the emotional capability of those surrounding us improves our own emotional regulation.

Ultimately, Shepherd reminds us that failure is not the opposite of success. Of course, failure hurts whereas success is fun. But failure in specific projects is not the same as overall failure because it provides learning opportunities that can be a vital ingredient for our overall success (Shepherd 2003).

tend to strengthen their bonds of trust and friendship. As the founder of Teledyne remarked, "My co-founders and I are blood brothers. We have been through failed ventures in the past."

David Shrank, the founder of PupCups, a promising startup that he was forced to close due to a cash crunch, said this about his entire team, "The PupCups alumni meet regularly and exchange memories and hopes. The question is not whether I would start another venture with them. I don't think I would start another venture without them."

And Bill Drayton, founder of Ashoka, is very careful to invest in people. He knows full well that any given idea might be a success or a failure. Regardless of the outcome, he wants to retain the learning. By making people "Ashoka Fellows," he ensures that the person can go from idea to idea, building the learning to

change the world in new ways with each iteration.

TAKEAWAY: FAILURE IS A BEGINNING, NOT AN END

The failure equations show us that some of the most common notions about failure are actually myths.

The most pernicious of these is that failure is, first and foremost, about the end of something. We urge you instead to think of it as a beginning. In Chapter 17, we will look at ICEHOTEL. The beautiful and popular winter destination created by Yngve Bergqvist was not the result of a flash of vision or insight, but rather an act of desperation by a man who

© Copyright Michiel Jonker 2006

had invited artists, press, and tourists to an ice-sculpting event that was washed out by rain. The rain could have put an end to Bergqvist's career as an entrepreneur and sent him back to the mines (literally). Instead, the fact that the ice could not be preserved led to the creation of the ICEHOTEL—something that had to be built anew every year.

Milton Hershey's numerous failures did not stop him from building the Hershey empire; in fact, they were integral to it; and the rejections of *Chicken Soup* did not stop the team from trying again and again. Apple's product failures did not stop it from being hailed by *Fortune*, in its March 2008 issue, as the most admired company in the world.

Research Roots

ADVERSITY MOTIVATES SUCCESSFUL UK ENTREPRENEURS

Personal adversity is a driving factor motivating successful UK entrepreneurs according to a survey by the Aldridge Foundation (2009).

The "Origins of an Entrepreneur" survey asked 370 of the country's successful entrepreneurs about their backgrounds, education, motivations, and personal characteristics.

Seven out of 10 (69%) said they had been motivated by adversity, including parental divorce, a car crash, cancer, and under-achieving at school. And the majority (56%) said determination is the most important characteristic for a successful entrepreneur, followed by passion (22%).

According to Glen Manchester, CEO of Thunderhead (CBI/Real Business Entrepreneur of the Year), "Adversity forged my independence and was a major influence over my drive for success in my career."

Laura Tenison said underachieving at school made her want to prove her teachers wrong, and she set up her acclaimed baby wear brand, JoJo Maman Bébé, after suffering a severe car crash in France.

Bar Hewlett said beating cancer gave her the determination to set up the weight loss business LighterLife.

Ten UK founder, Alex Cheatle, cited the breakdown of his parents' marriage when he was three: "A government minister once asked me how we can boost entrepreneurship in this country," he said. "My flippant response was, 'More misfortune.'"

DECIDING AND LEARNING

"Sir, what is the secret of your success?" a reporter asked a successful businessman.

"Two words."

"And what are they, sir?"

"Right decisions."

"And how do you make right decisions?"

"One word."

"And what is that, sir?"

"Experience."

"And how do you get experience?"

"Two words."

"And what are they, sir?"

"Wrong decisions."

If you can overcome the grief of a failed business and learn from it, then you have a fair chance of doing better (and smarter) the next time. In addition, failing can also tell you who you can trust and who will go along with you—those who stay with you when you fail will be valuable partners for your next venture.

Remember that the only real measure of failure is those companies that close down owing money to creditors, which represent only 8% of all the companies that close their doors. In fact, some may argue that you are a successful entrepreneur only if you have failed once and continue to want to risk failing again and again.

■ ■ ■

What Now?

Detail what you might lose if you fail versus what you will lose if you don't try. List five points for each option.

- What are your options after each situation? Which experience will put you in a stronger position?

- Think of failure as an option, as the norm. Paint the picture of everything consistently going wrong. How bad is it?

- In your current effort, what would you need to learn in order to be proud of a decision stop?

- What could be the next thing for you to try at that point?

So What?

By creating more companies, trying more often, your probability of success will increase because each experience will add to your learning. Think of yourself as an emerging chess master, learning new moves with each game and using them in the next.

Think It Through

How much does our ego get in the way of risking failure?

- Is the failure of a public firm different in important ways from the failure of an independently owned business?

- How do we deal with the cultural aspect of failure? Does it mean that it's easier to be an entrepreneur in some countries than in others?

CHAPTER 5

The important
thing is this:
To be able
at any moment
to sacrifice
what we are
for what
we could
become.
Charles Dubois

Plunge?

Wade?

Dip?

Entry into entrepreneurship is as
individual as the enormous range
of entrepreneurs themselves.

The plunge doesn't have to be a plunge at all

We have all heard of people who jumped ship and started their own businesses. Ask any group of students, whether undergraduates, or mid-career executives, if they want to start a venture, and two-thirds will say yes. Most, though, never go all the way.

The reasons we don't do it are varied. Some reasons are cultural (many Asian cultures have a high aversion to risk-taking, for example). Some are specific to the individual.

Most of us, faced with the decision of whether to take the plunge, instinctively compare what we know and have with what we think it will take to pursue an opportunity. Moreover, we look at our current job, salary, location, and comfort, and believe we can map our future. Then we look into the uncertainty of the entrepreneurial idea, and cannot discern a path. Even in a world where job security is a thing of the past, there is a perception that

IN THIS CHAPTER:

- **Four stories and four plunges**   *p. 47*
- **Anatomy of the plunge decision**   *p. 51*
- **Takeaway: Action trumps analysis**   *p. 54*

Research Roots

THE KEY TO HAPPINESS

Being Independent Is a Great Thing by Matthias Benz and Bruno Frey (2008) explores the role of happiness, and the subjective sense of well-being in the decision to become an entrepreneur. Their work highlights how "being your own boss" enables people to feel more in control of their lives and, therefore, have more of what they value, such as self-determination, flexibility and the ability to use their skills in what they think are the best ways possible.

Practically Speaking

THE MAKING OF SEARS

In 1886, when a Chicago jewellery company shipped some gold-filled watches to an unsuspecting jeweller in the Minnesota hamlet of Redwood Falls, it started a chain of events that led to the founding of an American icon.

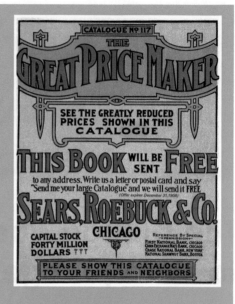

Watching out for opportunity

Richard Sears was an agent of the Minneapolis and St. Louis railway station in the neighboring hamlet of North Redwood. On the side, he sold lumber and coal to local residents for extra money. When the shipment of watches arrived, unwanted, at the Redwood Falls station, Sears went into action. He purchased them himself and sold the watches at a nice profit to other station agents up and down the line. It went so well that he ordered more. The following year Sears moved his business to Chicago and placed an ad in the Daily News.

> WANTED: Watchmaker with reference who can furnish
> tools. State age, experience and salary required.
> ADDRESS T39, Daily News.

Alvah C. Roebuck answered the ad, telling Sears he knew watches and showing a sample of his work to prove it. This began the association of two young men, both still in their 20s. In 1893, Sears, Roebuck & Co. was formally named and they were off.

Time for change

In that era, farmers in rural America were selling their crops for cash and buying what they needed from rural general stores. But when they laid their money on the line for goods, they were in the red. In 1891, the wholesale price of a barrel of flour was reported to be US\$3.47, while the price at retail was at least US\$7, a 100% increase. Farmers formed protest movements, such as the Grange, to do battle against high prices and the "middleman."

Going bigtime

Sears, Roebuck and Co. and other mail-order companies provided the answer. Through a combination of volume buying and making use of the railroads, the post office, and, later, rural free delivery and parcel post, they offered a happy alternative to the high-priced rural stores. Sears prospered in the 1890s, and over the next 100 years, the company built a huge product line, created countless successful brands, rolled out retail locations around the world, and added insurance and investment services, ultimately making a tremendous impact on the world of retail.

Practically Speaking *(continued)*

The right time

Was it market research? Deliberation? Luck? Opportunism? Richard Sears took advantage of a chance occurrence, and rather than focus on learning before doing, he learned while doing. Sometimes the best way to figure out whether an idea is really a good idea for a business, or the "right" opportunity for you, is to buy the box of watches and try to sell them. Richard couldn't envision what Sears would become, but the initial opportunity was one that he was able to take on, and he made good things happen from there.

certain situations (a full-time job in a stable industry, for instance) will lead to a comfortable future. We balk at the idea of plunging into the unknown or the unknowable, seeing it as a realm where we might fail.

What people (perhaps mistakenly) think about statistics on new venture success and failure (Chapter 4) could bias the decision. Other biases from this first section of the book could influence prospective entrepreneurs as well. Taking all the myths together, only overconfident, risk-seeking or mildly crazy people, it seems, would become entrepreneurs.

So, what kind of decision process leads potential entrepreneurs to feel comfortable taking the plunge? Researchers have spent a lot of time studying this question. The answer is important to governments and economic development organizations that spend large amounts of money trying to increase entrepreneurship. It's also important to the thriving industry of entrepreneurial educators who, either directly or indirectly, teach potential entrepreneurs how best to make the plunge decision. Over the next few pages, we will

It is not the critic who counts, not the man who points out how the strong man stumbles, or where the doer of deeds could have done them better. The credit belongs to the man who is actually in the arena, whose face is marred by dust and sweat and blood, who strives valiantly; who errs and comes short again and again; because there is not effort without error and shortcomings; but who does actually strive to do the deed; who knows the great enthusiasm, the great devotion, who spends himself in a worthy cause, who at the best knows in the end the triumph of high achievement and who at the worst, if he fails, at least he fails while daring greatly. So that his place shall never be with those cold and timid souls who know neither victory nor defeat.

Theodore Roosevelt

dissect the decision-making process behind the plunge decision. As you read the story of the creation of Sears, decide for yourself whether a plunge is really a plunge.

FOUR STORIES AND FOUR PLUNGES

Why plunge? The answer depends in large part on where you are in your life and on your entrepreneurial motivation. In this chapter, we offer four stories, each of which shows us an entrepreneur at a particular stage in

life and with a particular motivation. Contrast the story of Larry Hench (Boing-Boing) with that of Pierre Omidyar (eBay). Hench entered entrepreneurship at the end of a successful career; for Omidyar, entrepreneurship provided the start of a successful career. Contrasting those two stories, not all entrepreneurship is born of success. Judi Henderson-Townsend (Mannequin Madness) had time on her hands to try a new venture because her dot-com venture had gone out of business. And though she and Richard Sears (Sears and Roebuck) shared similar

WHY NOT PLUNGE?

Skip the delayed-life plan

Many people do things they don't like in the short term in the hope that one day they will be able to live their true-life plan. There are two major flaws with this approach. The first is that nobody is going to sit down and tell you when it's okay to stop doing what you don't want to do. The second is that we have limited time. If you plan to live forever, you can have as many life plans as you want. But given that you have only one life, why not use it to do the things you want to do, make the impact you want to make, and not wait another minute to do it?

circumstances around the founding of their respective ventures, Sears had clearly been looking for entrepreneurial opportunities and had already dipped his toe in the water, providing coal and wood outside of his day job as a railway station agent.

Clearly, there are more stages in life and more motivations for entrepreneurship than those we mention. The point is to see how the rationales change with context. Where would you situate yourself? What might motivate you?

Practically Speaking

SUSTAINING ENTREPRENEURSHIP

Back when I launched eBay on Labor Day 1995, eBay wasn't my business—it was my hobby. I had to build a system that was self-sustaining … because I had a real job to go to every morning. I was working as a software engineer from 10 to 7, and I wanted to have a life on the weekends. So I built a system that could keep working—catching complaints and capturing feedback—even when Pam and I were out mountain biking, and the only one home was our cat. If I had had a blank check from a big VC (venture capitalist), and a big staff running around—things might have gone much worse. I would have probably put together a very complex, elaborate system—something that justified all the investment. But because I had to operate on a tight budget—tight in terms of money and tight in terms of time—necessity focused me on simplicity: So I built a system simple enough to sustain itself. By building a simple system, with just a few guiding principles, eBay was open to organic growth—it could achieve a certain degree of self-organization. So I guess what I'm trying to tell you is: Whatever future you're building … don't try to program everything. Five-year plans never worked for the Soviet Union—in fact, if anything, central planning contributed to its fall. Chances are, central planning won't work any better for any of us.

Pierre Omidyar, eBay Founder

Practically Speaking

BOING-BOING

Larry Hench spent 40 years developing and commercializing a breakthrough in a life sciences technology called Bioglass—a successful, innovative material used in the repair of bone damage that has helped millions of people. Bioglass has also been the basis of numerous patents and even inspired science fiction writing.

Inventory of an entrepreneur's life

Nearly a septuagenarian, Hench wanted to extend his creativity into new areas, so he took stock of his means—the interests, knowledge, assets, and relationships he accumulated over his full life. One area was his understanding of core scientific research, particularly in the repair of human bone through his work with Bioglass. Another was his interest in making sure his grandchildren had accessible information about science. Hench was disappointed with what was available. And with more than 500 research papers and 22 books to his credit, he had strong writing abilities.

Assembling the pieces of an opportunity

So with this seemingly unrelated set of means, Hench created Boing-Boing, the bionic cat. Or, more specifically, he wrote fictional children's books about the adventures of Boing-Boing—tales that combine Hench's penchant for storytelling with his understanding of and passion for technology and his interest in educating children.

The bionic power of starting with means

It is easy to imagine dozens of other aspirations Hench might have had, given his means: a life sciences startup specializing in solutions for children with bone damage, a summer program for children wanting to get into medicine or clinical research, children's games built around science, etc. The fact that Hench's means could have generated various business options leads us to two insights into entrepreneurship. The first is that there is no one right opportunity upon which to take the plunge. The second is that by starting down the entrepreneurial path with his personal means, Hench had his own unique insight, a differentiated approach and a competitive advantage. By starting with his means, Hench was able to take an easy plunge with Boing-Boing. Boing-Boing started life as a robotic "cat substitute" for a boy with allergies, and has already gone on to wrangle with lion's claws and chase jewel thieves in subsequent adventures. Hench has also extended the product line to include Boing-Boing branded educational materials such as workbooks, experiment books, and hands-on kits for schoolchildren.

Bouncing ahead

What's next for Hench? Having added children's book publisher, brand owner, and children's science educator to his set of means, Hench has expanded his range of opportunities for the future. Imagine the possibilities ahead of Hench, who is in his 80s. More important, imagine the possibilities for you to combine your means into something novel.

Practically Speaking

A MODEL BUSINESS

Judi Henderson-Townsend had never worked in retail. She had done no market research on the demand for mannequins. In fact, she had never actually touched a mannequin prior to getting into the business 15 years ago. All she wanted was a creative art project—to mosaic a mannequin for her garden. But instead of buying a single mannequin, she impulsively bought 50 from a vendor who was closing his mannequin rental business and leaving the state. Cost of startup? $2,500.

Model concern

Though it didn't cost an arm and a leg for Judi to get into business, she then had to figure out the rest of the equation. After explaining to her husband Jay, that they would have 50 unusual guests in their basement, Judi went about creating the market. Her online marketing skills enabled her to attract customers all over the US and Canada. After acquiring 500 mannequins from a retail chain that was remodeling, it expanded her customer base from trade-show vendors to small retailers, artists, eBayers, event planners, and even to Industrial Light & Magic—the visual effects behind Lucas Films.

Practically Speaking (continued)

Faces and wallets

Her hard work has taken on a life of its own. Judi started running her firm, Mannequin Madness (www. mannequinmadness.com), at the end of 2001 after being let go from a failing dot-com. Today, she gets between $100 and $350 for a used mannequin based on its condition and style, and handles roughly 5,000 mannequins in a year. She sources most of her inventory from retailers that close or remodel and discard existing mannequins to bring in the latest styles. Mannequin Madness also repairs mannequins, has a blog about mannequins and recently became a distributor for new mannequins.

Alter ego

Creating a firm from an initial investment of $2,500, Judi clearly has a head for business. However, she has another persona—one that's remarkably green. Because while she is making money, she is also keeping used mannequins out of landfills. Mannequins are bulky and typically made of materials that do not biodegrade easily. Her business recycles more than 100,000 pounds of heads, limbs and torsos every year that would otherwise be waste. So in addition to a good living, she has earned a special achievement award from the US' Environmental Protection Agency.

Success on her terms

Judi has earned something else. Something less tangible, but perhaps more important. She has earned the right to do what she wants. She has much more contact with the creative people she enjoys. She works with her husband, who joined the business as it has grown. While Judi has not mastered the "four-hour work week" popularized by Timothy Ferris, she does have a flexible work schedule. And expanding with partners in New York and London, she works where she wants to work.

ANATOMY OF THE PLUNGE DECISION

There are at least four ways to think about the plunge decision, and ultimately, to take the plunge. They are closely related to the affordable loss principle, which we discuss in Chapter 12. Consider each to figure out which works best for the way you should think about the decision.

1 What you can lose

This is a twist on the textbook approach. Instead of calculating the opportunity cost of starting a business in terms of your current salary and future earnings potential, you calculate two relatively simple values. First, estimate the absolute maximum amount you are willing to lose. Second, decide on the absolute minimum you want to earn. Now evaluate only those opportunities you can afford with your maximum investment that will pay you at least the minimum earnings you need. This approach—called the min–max or max–min approach— provides a useful filter that reduces the number of ventures you can seriously consider and then leads you to a go/no-go decision on each of them.

2 Toes first (start small)

There are usually several plausible ways of pursuing an idea. One way to go about taking the plunge is to always choose the option that involves the least risk—for example, running a venture "on the side" while continuing to work at one's job, rather than launching a venture with all the associated costs right at the start. This is what Pierre Omidyar, the founder of eBay, did.

Research indicates that about 50% of entrepreneurs start this way.

3 Opportunity cost

Just as there are opportunity costs associated with starting a new business, there are opportunity costs associated with not starting one. People often overlook these costs. There are costs to staying in your current job and forgoing both the potential financial upside and the psychological returns of starting the new business venture. These costs, many of which are psychological or emotional, are often difficult to quantify. For someone who believes the costs of not becoming an entrepreneur outweigh the calculable costs of taking the plunge, it's critical to understand that you can start small and proceed step by step in the direction you have chosen. And remember, not starting at all guarantees you will never build a successful venture.

It is important to realize also that failing can have very positive side effects. For one, it helps you build relationships with people who are willing to walk through failure with you. If you don't try, you won't know who these people are. And there are larger implications. Many would-be entrepreneurs say they cannot fail because they live in a cultural setting that does not look kindly on failure. But research shows that in every country there are pockets of entrepreneurship and support groups. By refusing to take the plunge, would-be entrepreneurs turn their fears into self-fulfilling prophecies, encouraging the further stigmatization of failure.

4 Walk before you jump

Every company we know today was started by an entrepreneur. So, clearly, others have successfully created their own maps for an entrepreneurial journey.

The examples in this chapter demonstrate that the plunge decision is not about a sudden dive into unfathomable depths. It is a process that happens step by step, depending on your means and what you are willing to lose. It is actually not a plunge at all. It is just another way for you to achieve your objectives.

Practically Speaking

HOW TO LEARN TO LET GO

Moonlighting

Tom Fatjo was an accountant in Houston in 1967 when a meeting in his community challenged him to take up the garbage collection problem the neighbourhood was facing. He borrowed $7,000 for his first truck. Every day, Fatjo woke at 4 a.m. to collect garbage for two hours before changing into a suit to go to work in his accounting office. This went on for over a year before Tom sat down to make the hard decision of whether to go on his own.

Tax man or garbage man

The pressure just kept building. Even though it was cold, my body was damp from continuous perspiration. Since so much of what I was doing in the accounting firm had to be done by the end of the tax year and involved important decisions with key clients, I needed to spend time thinking through problems and consulting with them as they made decisions. I was caught in a triangle of pressing demands, and I felt my throat constricting as if there were wires around my neck.

(Fatjo and Miller, 1981)

Practically Speaking *(continued)*

Whatever it takes

That night I was exhausted, but I couldn't sleep. As I stared at the ceiling, I fantasized all our trucks breaking down at the same time. I was trying to push each of them myself in order to get them going. My heart began beating faster in the darkness and my body was chilled. The horrible thought that we might fail almost paralyzed me. I wanted to quit and run away. I was scared to death, very lonely, sick of the whole deal. As hard as I tried to think about my life and what was important to me, my mind was just a confused mass of muddled images … I remembered committing myself to make it in the garbage business 'whatever it takes!' I lay back on my pillow and felt a deep sigh within myself—'Good Lord, so this is what it takes,' I thought, then rolled over and got some restless sleep.

(Fatjo and Miller, 1981)

Coming to terms with letting go

When Fatjo let go of the security blanket of a white-collar profession to found the waste management giant Browning-Ferris Industries (originally American Refuse Systems), he had no way of knowing he would end up building a billion-dollar enterprise that shaped an entire industry. But what he did know was his worst-case scenario. For him, making the commitment to take the plunge meant understanding what he could lose, and coming to terms with that possibility.

Affordable loss

Fatjo's decision embodies the principle of affordable loss. Instead of considering the potential upside opportunity in waste management, the important information in Fatjo's decision was what the possible downside looked like, and whether he could tolerate it, should the worst happen. By focusing on the prospect of the negative, entrepreneurs effectively manage the risk inherent in a new venture down to only what they find personally acceptable.

Research Roots

WHO ACTUALLY PLUNGES?

A report on "The Startup Economy" compared startup interest, intentions, and actions across countries. The Dutch had the highest percentage of the population who expressed interest (83%) in entrepreneurship. Of those who said they intended to start a business in the next three years, the French were the top of the list at 25%. And when it came to actually doing something, the Australians, the Americans, and the Irish were the only three countries that exceeded 15% of the population that take action. The biggest difference between interest and action was Italy, with 68% of Italians interested in entrepreneurship, but less than 4% actually embarking on the entrepreneurial journey. (PricewaterhouseCoopers, 2013)

So What?

The plunge doesn't have to be, and usually isn't, a plunge. It's often a series of smaller steps, driven by your means and what you are willing to lose, rather than what you hope to gain. By this design, getting started is much less daunting.

TAKEAWAY: ACTION TRUMPS ANALYSIS

In general, we observe that expert entrepreneurs emphasize action rather than analysis. The history of entrepreneurship includes many examples of entrepreneurs whose ideas were not considered blockbuster opportunities but who went ahead and built successful businesses simply by doing the next thing and the next thing and the next.

Expert entrepreneurs are means-driven, not goal-driven in formulating their ventures. The more experienced they are, the better they become at using readily available bits and pieces of ideas to create new possibilities, including new strategies, new business models, rapid responses to changes in the environment, valuable new applications for mundane technologies, and even new markets no one quite knew could exist.

What Now?

Figure out your own max-min. What's the max you can afford to lose? Over what time frame? What is the minimum you need to earn to meet your needs?

▪ What can you do today to get started? It could be something as simple as coming up with a name for your venture and getting a business card printed.

▪ Is there anything you need to let go of before you can take just the next step?

Think It Through

If one starts with a toe in the water, rather than diving in head first, does it limit how "big" the venture can/will become?

▪ Is it "moonlighting" to start a venture on the side of a full-time job? Does it matter?

▪ If this approach to getting started makes it easier to take action, how might more formal planning get in the way of taking action?

PART II

How (expert) entrepreneurs think

Systematic study of expertise in areas that range from chess to taxi driving shows that experts are not different from the rest of us except in how they have learned to think about and solve problems. These differences are what enable the extraordinary performance we have come to associate with experts across domains. This section is dedicated to explaining those differences within the domain of entrepreneurship. Here, you should expect to find a clear explanation of what makes the entrepreneurial problem space unique, and fundamental strategies expert entrepreneurs have learned for operating effectively within that problem space. As you work through it, we hope you will begin constructing a clear and precise way of looking at the world, so you can see the world in the same way that expert entrepreneurs have learned to see it. In their view, the world is both uncertain and shapeable at the same time. Understanding this perspective helps explain the relationship between the effectual principles we introduce in this section, and the ways that expert entrepreneurs seek to control outcomes through their own actions.

I think a great entrepreneur is learning every day. An entrepreneur is somebody that doesn't take no for an answer—they're going to figure something out. They also take responsibility. They don't blame anybody else. And they're dreamers in one sense but they're also realistic and they take affordable steps when they can.

Daymond John

Risking their own time, money, and reputations, entrepreneurs are more conservative than bankers.

Security is mostly a superstition. It does not exist in nature, nor do the children of men as a whole experience it. Avoiding danger is no safer in the long run than outright exposure. Life is either a daring adventure or it is nothing.

Helen Keller

Prediction, risk, and uncertainty

■ ■ ■

Is risk taking an attribute—something people are born with? Or can it be taught and learned? Is risk inherent to all entrepreneurial ventures, or is it a characteristic of the environment in which entrepreneurship occurs? Are all risks created equal? If not, what metrics can we use to classify different types of risk? Do all people perceive the same "risk" in the same venture? If not, why not?

FACTORS OF PRODUCTION

Let's explore a framework that can help us tackle those questions. For that, we turn to one of the first and most exciting dissertations in entrepreneurship, published in 1921 by a doctoral student named Frank Knight.

Take any simple product—say, a pen. If you ask yourself, "Where does the value or price of this pen come from?" you will get at least three types of answers—these can be mapped onto the three "factors of production" that are listed in every Economics 101 textbook. They are as follows:

- The value of the pen comes from the raw materials that go into it—the factor of production here is "land," and the price of land is usually termed "rent."
- The value of the pen also comes from the people who actually produced it—their time, effort and skills. This factor is "labor," and the price of labor is usually termed "wages."
- The value of the pen also includes the ideas, creativity,

and design of the technologists who invented it and the machinery and business processes that were used to produce it. This is considered "capital," and the price of capital is usually termed "interest" or "return on investment."

If the market is "efficient," classical economists argue that these three factors of production—land, labor and capital—cover all the value that goes into the making of the pen, and the pen should cost no more and no less than the prices paid for the three factors. Ergo, when demand and supply are in sync with each other in an open, efficient market, "profit" should equal zero.

THE FOURTH FACTOR OF PRODUCTION: ENTREPRENEURS

It was this utopian view of microeconomics that Knight (1921) assaulted when he argued, in essence, that human capital (which includes entrepreneurship) is a necessary fourth factor of production, and that "profit" is the price paid for it.

What do entrepreneurs contribute?

So, what do entrepreneurs bring to supply and demand? And why do they appear to keep such a big share of the price of the products and services that, after all, are made up of the raw materials, labor, and investments belonging to their stakeholders? The answer lies in the simple fact that after the other three factors are paid for, there may or may not be anything left over. In other words, before new products or services are produced and sold, there is no guarantee that they can indeed be produced, nor is there any assurance that they will indeed be bought at a price above the cost of production. Someone has to bear the uncertainties involved in bringing new products and services to the market—and in creating markets where none existed before. In other words, demand and supply cannot always be known before the entrepreneur acts.

Why are entrepreneurs entitled to "profit"?

Most entrepreneurs have never even heard of Knight—and that's okay. But imagine you started an IT firm that needs to hire a chief technology officer. Most good technical people do not understand how the price of a product is determined. Not because they are not smart (they can often be smarter and perhaps more sophisticated than founding entrepreneurs), but because good technical people have been spending their time and energy on technical skills. And even the best technology education frequently does not include exposure to business concepts or the role of entrepreneurship in economics.

Hence, good technologists, even when they perceive the technical "value" of a product (or think they do), may wonder why products are priced so high, or why the marketing person often makes more money than the techie, or even why the founding entrepreneur gets the lion's share of the pie. Pointing to Knight's thesis not only makes a credible case to them but also provides an easy way to approach

otherwise delicate issues such as negotiating relevant and just compensation—not to mention the necessity to share in the risk.

Most people, not just technical folks, assume that price, customers, and markets can be analyzed and outcomes predicted. Or they go to the other extreme and fear vague and undefined "risks" associated with starting a company—based on the oft-repeated bromide "most firms fail." We have already tackled this combination of misconceptions in the first section. Which means that now we can return to Knight for a useful way to actually understand problems of risk in the entrepreneurial setting. We will explore important differences between prediction, risk, and uncertainty—terms that at first glance may seem very closely related.

A JAR FULL OF RISK

Imagine a game where you win if you pick a red ball. There are three jars in front of you. One has an equal number of red balls and green balls. The second contains balls, but you do not know how many are red. And you have no idea what the third jar contains. Which jar would you choose?

In 1961, Ellsberg used this jar game, described in Knight's (1921) dissertation, to investigate preferences and found that most people prefer the jar whose proportion of balls they know to the one whose proportion of balls they

"Wait a minute! This isn't your future...
it's Ken Lay's future."

Research Roots

FRANK KNIGHT

Frank Knight was born in 1885 in McLean County, Illinois. The son of Christian farmers, he never completed high school but went on anyway to American University in Tennessee in 1905. By 1916, he had completed his doctoral studies in economics with a dissertation entitled "Cost, Value, and Profit."

This was the start of a brilliant academic career. In addition to teaching many of the Nobel Laureates of the current era (Milton Friedman, Kenneth Arrow, and Herbert Simon among them), Knight was a prolific publisher. In his work, he creates the notion of entrepreneurship as the fourth factor of production; that in addition to land, labor, and capital, the entrepreneur manages uncertainty and in exchange is justified a profit.

don't know. That seems intuitive enough. But now, ask yourself, "Which jar would an entrepreneur choose?" Researchers speculated that entrepreneurs might prefer the unknown to the known—i.e. they are risk takers and hence might pick the second jar.

But all those years ago, Knight had already argued implicitly that entrepreneurs, by definition of operating in the unknowable, would choose the third jar; that there are so many dimensions to the entrepreneurial problem and each dimension is likely to

Research Roots

ADAM SMITH

Adam Smith was a key figure in the intellectual movement known as the Scottish Enlightenment. He gained international attention when his examination of societal ethics—The Theory of Moral Sentiments—was published in 1759. But it was his book An Inquiry into the Nature and Causes of the Wealth of Nations (1776) that secured his fame and went on to become a classic of modern economics. Widely acknowledged as the "father of economics," Smith is known for his explanation of how rational self-interest and competition can lead to economic well-being and prosperity. He also coined the metaphor "invisible hand of the market," which is a term economists use to describe the self-regulating nature of the marketplace. His work helped to create the modern academic discipline of economics and provided one of the best-known rationales for free trade and capitalism. And his writings on supply and demand encouraged academics and businesspeople to believe that many economic activities could be modelled and predicted.

vary in so many different ways, making the prediction problem impossible even to attempt, let alone solve.

To put this into context, few business situations are represented by the first jar. Nothing is cleanly predictable. Educators believe that most business situations fall into the second jar. All the forecasting, prediction and scenario analysis tools taught in school are approaches for determining the distribution contained in the second jar. But when you understand that entrepreneurs are drawing from a completely different jar, it's easy to see why a set of completely different principles apply to how they learn to make decisions.

Without arguing about whether expert entrepreneurs actually view the world through the lens of Knightian uncertainty, let us simply ask ourselves what some good examples of the three types of jars

would be. Once we describe, understand, and play with this notion enough, we can begin to think about how to make decisions and act in the face of true uncertainty. In fact, a substantial portion of this book is devoted to methods used to play the game in Knight's third jar.

PREDICTION, RISK, AND UNCERTAINTY

We will use the terms prediction, risk, and uncertainty to identify the types of problems that the three jars represent. It is important to understand the difference between the three concepts, because each calls for a different approach. When the future is predictable (i.e. we know the distribution of balls within the jar), we can use our knowledge of the past—of common recurring patterns—to predict the future. When the future is risky (i.e. when we are dealing with an unknown

distribution of balls), we can still use the past and our instincts about the future, but we also need to test the waters as we go, look out for new patterns, find ways to adapt to the new patterns wherever possible, and hedge our bets any way we can.

However, it is the third jar that is the most difficult, and maybe the most interesting. Representing a future that is truly uncertain, the distribution of balls in that jar can never be known, no matter how long you play.

> Prediction is very difficult, especially about the future.
> Neils Bohr

Prediction

Classical economists (and most business schools) teach us that markets exist, are predictable to a

YOU CAN'T PREDICT WHO WILL CHANGE THE WORLD

The American system of trial and error produces doers: black swan-hunting, dreamchasing entrepreneurs, with a tolerance for a certain class of risk taking and for making plenty of small errors on the road to success or knowledge ... It is high time to recognize that we humans are far better at doing than understanding, and better at tinkering than inventing. But we don't know it. We truly live under the illusion of order, believing that planning and forecasting are possible. We are scared of the random, yet we live from its fruits. We are so scared of the random that we create disciplines that try to make sense of the past—but we ultimately fail to understand it, just as we fail to see the future.

Nassim Nicholas Taleb (2007)

greater or lesser degree, and that sooner or later every market reaches a point of perfect equilibrium, where supply and demand intersect.

Since Adam Smith (1759) introduced the notion of the invisible hand of the market that helps allocate scarce resources to the best possible use through individuals who make decisions based on their self-interest, countless academics and managers have found ways to predict the behavior of that invisible hand. Underlying virtually every management tool today, from the sales forecast to expected value calculations to real options analyses, is the belief that Adam Smith's insight can be applied to estimate the future based on historical information of one sort or another.

In recent times, there has been a greater appreciation of the fact that not all elements of the market are known or even knowable in any meaningful manner. Therefore, our

models cannot rely on prediction alone; instead, they have to allow for risk—the idea that not all the actors would necessarily behave in a predetermined manner, nor would everyone even have access to the information necessary to make good decisions. Therefore, notions such as risk and imperfect information have become more common in economic analysis today.

The limits of prediction

We all know great stories of failed predictions. There are countless websites dedicated to failed predictions and end-of-world stories, the most famous one being the millennium hype prior to the shift from the last century to this one. Some other examples include:

"That idea is so damn nonsensical that I'm willing to stand on the

Research Roots

BLUE OCEAN STRATEGY

Kim and Mauborgne (2005) coined the term "blue ocean strategy" in their book Blue Ocean Strategy. The metaphor of red and blue oceans describes the market universe. Red oceans are industries in existence today—the known market space. In the red oceans, industry boundaries are defined and accepted, and the competitive rules of the game are known. Blue oceans, in contrast, represent all the industries not in existence today—the unknown market space, where standards, expectations, and competition don't yet exist. In blue oceans, demand is created rather than fought over. There is ample opportunity for growth that is both profitable and rapid. In blue oceans, competition is irrelevant because the rules of the game are yet to be set. Blue ocean strategies are about playing a different game—with the aim of creating markets. These strategies generate uncertainty in the environment. They can be contrasted with strategies that react to uncertainties in the environment, such as those posed by disruptive technologies.

bridge of a battleship while that nitwit tries to hit it from the air."
—Newton Baker, Secretary of War, 1910, responding to the suggestion that airplanes might sink battleships by dropping bombs on them.

"We don't like their sound. Groups of guitars are on the way out."
—Mike Smith, Decca Recording Co. executive, turning down The Beatles in 1962.

Research Roots

THE FUTURE THAT'S ALREADY HAPPENED

Highlighting an area where prediction is reasonably accurate, management guru Peter Drucker (1985) showed the reliability of demography predictions over the last 650 years, terming it "the future that's already happened."

The challenge to the entrepreneur? Take demographic information (or any other reliable predictive information) and use it to create the basis for opportunity!

"With over 50 foreign cars already on sale here, the Japanese auto industry isn't likely to carve out a big slice of the US market for itself."
—Business Week, August 2, 1968.

While these stories are funny only insofar as you haven't put any money, time, or effort into a business that is based on prediction, they are also good examples of why you would not want to predict in an uncertain environment.

THE DIFFERENCES BETWEEN PREDICTION, RISK, AND UNCERTAINTY

	Prediction An environment with enough stability that future events can be determined based on past recurring patterns.	**Risk** An environment characterized by general trends and local variance. The decision-maker seeks to model these data to tolerances that meaningfully inform decision-making.	**Uncertainty** A situation in which no historical data exists to help the decision-maker. Uncertainty cannot be modelled or predicted. It is a future that is not only unknown but also unknowable.
What matters	Data, information that was collected in the past	Variance and possibility	Expertise, influence, and control
How you move ahead	Refine prior efforts—strive for a perfect business plan	Robustness, preparedness—scenarios	Co-creation and affordable loss
Dealing with surprises	Quality checking (must have been my mistake)	Weather the storm, work to stay on track/on plan	Embrace and rethink: it provides new opportunities
Measuring success	Actual versus plan, execution	Actual versus plan, closeness to the vision, within margin	Valued novelty, getting to somewhere that has potential

Look at some of the predictions you have made in your own environment. How many of these came true? What did you lose when they didn't come true? Did they apply to uncertain environments?

Risk

Unlike problems of prediction, which require only extrapolation, problems of risk call for the estimation of likely changes under multiple scenarios over time. Decision-making under risk involves calculating the odds of a specific outcome using not only existing information but also trial and error, which yields additional information. In other words, whereas prediction allows only

defensive tactics, risk can be managed through more proactive measures.

Countries assess risk—for example, in the Cold War, the superpowers attempted to use scenario planning to assess a range of possible outcomes. This approach was picked up and improved upon by companies such as Shell, who used scenario planning to determine the risks associated with fluctuations in oil production and prices. It then made its way to financial derivatives (options, futures, and the like) before becoming a tool for all sorts of decision-making.

Influential business writers such as Clayton Christensen (1997) and Chan Kim and Renée Mauborgne

(2005) have looked at uncertainty in the context of innovation and new markets. Christensen focused primarily on how to help managers who are the "victims" of uncertainty, while Kim and Mauborgne have looked at how managers can turn the existing environment upside down, in effect creating uncertainty for others. While both approaches help us consider uncertainty as a given in the business environment, they do not provide an overall perspective on how to work with uncertainty as an opportunity.

Uncertainty exists with any new product, new market, or new technology, and it can happen at any level—from the macro (global warming, the end of fossil fuels) all the way to the micro (the CEO has a

Practically Speaking

THE UNLIKELY STORY OF FREITAG

In Zurich, Switzerland, Markus and Daniel Freitag started thinking about a new business from their apartment overlooking the main Zurich truck route at Hardbrücke. Dissatisfied with the durability of available bicycle messenger bags, the pair wanted to create a heavy-duty, water-repellent product. So in 1993 they started prototyping bags and formed Freitag AG. But instead of sourcing the latest high-tech materials, they formed bags from used truck tarpaulins, using second-hand car seatbelts as straps and used bicycle inner tubes for edging. Recycling materials keeps input costs low while taking advantage of the emerging environmental trend, and guaranteeing that every Freitag bag is as original, customized, and personal as the truck that hauled its skin in the first place.

A predictable success?

Freitag and its line of bags have done remarkably well. It currently sells about 200,000 bags per year online, in five Freitag shops across Germany and Switzerland, and in 300 stores around the world. Average price for a bag well exceeds US$250. But ask yourself this. If Freitag hadn't done it, would consumers pay high-fashion prices for bags made of commercial waste—or would such bags even exist at all? Likely not. Entrepreneurs do more than just meet existing market needs and discover business opportunities; they narrate novelty and uncertainty in the market.

RISK TAKING: COMPARING ENTREPRENEURS AND BANKERS

Which would you say is the most risk-averse profession? Until the financial crisis of 2008, most of us would probably have answered "bankers" (while secretly thinking, they had better be—after all, they are managing my account). We decided to test the risk aversion of bankers and entrepreneurs. A group of bankers and entrepreneurs were given a series of problems to solve, all in the context of managing a manufacturing plant. The problems included financial risk, risk to human life and health, and risk of a natural disaster. For each problem, we looked for similarities and differences in the ways bankers and entrepreneurs reacted.

When it came to purely financial problems (investing in a new product), the entrepreneurs and bankers seemed to have very different perceptions of what could be controlled: the entrepreneurs seemed to accept risk as a given—as a result, they worked on controlling the returns rather than the risk. Their approach was to pick an acceptable level of risk and then push for larger profits, selecting the project with the best worst-case scenario. They also expressed confidence that they could make the reality better than the worst-case probability. In contrast, bankers suggested many ways of controlling risk and practically no measures to increase returns. They seemed to believe that they could generate the highest possible returns and somehow work on minimizing the risks.

The next set of problems involved decisions around human life and health. The context was the following: the factory's industrial hygiene consultant recommended an investment of US$3 million to put a hood and special ventilation apparatus over the production area. The consultant concluded that a rupture of a pipe could spill an extremely toxic chemical, endangering the workers. When questioned closely, the consultant expected the pipe would rupture less often than once every 10 years, a rupture could cause the death of eight workers, and that putting up the hood and ventilation system would mean that only four workers would die if a pipe ruptured. A second option would require a US$10 million investment to put in special pipes and enclose the area so there would be a much lower chance of a pipe bursting, and there would be no worker exposure if the pipe did rupture.

In this situation, where the trade-off was between a US$3 million option that reduced but did not eliminate the risk to the workers' lives and a US$10 million option that eliminated risk but the firm could not afford it, all the entrepreneurs rejected the US$3 million option outright and came up with creative suggestions to pay for the US$10 million option. Besides possible technical suggestions, they also considered asking for volunteers and giving up equity, selling to a larger company, or cooperating with competitors to increase prices.

None of the bankers made a decision—their suggestions were doubtful and evasive. All of them said they would invest the US$3 million, because that was better than doing nothing. They did not make creative suggestions for raising the US$10 million. Their reactions focused on trying to delay or avoid the decision, suggesting that more information was needed. The way both groups saw their decision spaces can be schematized, as illustrated in the figure "Entrepreneurs and bankers have different approaches to risk."

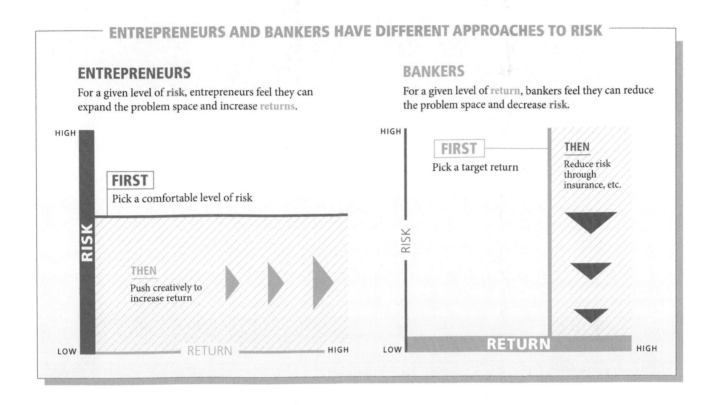

ENTREPRENEURS AND BANKERS HAVE DIFFERENT APPROACHES TO RISK

ENTREPRENEURS

For a given level of risk, entrepreneurs feel they can expand the problem space and increase returns.

FIRST
Pick a comfortable level of risk

THEN
Push creatively to increase return

RISK — HIGH / LOW
RETURN — LOW / HIGH

BANKERS

For a given level of return, bankers feel they can reduce the problem space and decrease risk.

FIRST
Pick a target return

THEN
Reduce risk through insurance, etc.

RISK — HIGH / LOW
RETURN — LOW / HIGH

heart attack). Who can predict the future of stem cell research today? Or of biofuels? When the price of oil dropped below US$10 per barrel in December 1998 it seemed unimaginable—barring any major damage to production or distribution capacity—that by the summer of 2004 the price would jump to over US$50 and keep going to reach a peak of US$100 a barrel in November 2007. Nor could anyone have predicted that Steve Jobs, the iconic founder of Apple, would be fired by his board in May 1985, only to come back in December 1997, or the impact that both moves would have on the company.

Keeping these examples in mind, it is clear that uncertainty is not confined to startups in budding industries. Consider the implications of the fact that one in every four firms on the *Fortune 500* list simply did not exist 30 years ago. That means that every 88 days, a new firm is created that will replace one of the existing *Fortune 500* firms. What new competitors, products, and business models that have yet to be imagined will burst onto the landscape without advance notice?

Research Roots

REAL OPTIONS

Faced with the problems of making investments in uncertain technologies and ventures, one intuitive approach is to think of yourself as making initial small investments in order to "buy" an "option" on making larger investments later. This approach helps manage the risk of failure by keeping initial investments small, and delaying significant investments until you have more information about how the initial steps worked out. One of the biggest upsides of starting with a small investment is that "options" may emerge in the process that you couldn't have imagined when you started (McGrath, 1999).

Research Roots

CAN ONE BE AN EXPERT IN FORECASTING?

Entrepreneurs who end up on the cover of business magazines are often hailed as visionaries who had an ability to see what the next big thing was going to be. However, such accolades fly in the face of everything we know from studying human beings' ability to predict, including the forecasting ability of people who are considered experts in their domains. In a painstakingly constructed multi-year study, researcher Phil Tetlock gathered data on thousands of predictions made by experts in politics and economics. The results showed that on average, the experts fared no better in their forecasting results than novices, and both were essentially no different to coin flipping. Moreover, people who successfully forecast extreme events have been shown to be, on average, poor forecasters who rank lower on forecasting than their peers. One can conclude that no one has an upper hand in forecasting the future, whatever claims are made retrospectively.

Such research suggests that claims regarding a particular entrepreneur's prescience as a forecaster may be misattributing the sources of their success. Alternative factors may better explain why they achieved what they did. The most important of these explanations may be the capabilities and skills in entrepreneurship that they developed. These are skills in the process of entrepreneuring. Having these skills may make expert entrepreneurs less dependent on making accurate forecasts. If this is the case, then prediction and forecasting abilities—which research shows to be a myth anyway—may have very limited relevance for explaining entrepreneurial success (Tetlock, 2005).

EXPERT ENTREPRENEURS DEAL WITH UNCERTAINTY, NOT RISK

Entrepreneurs face uncertainty. What have they learned through the accumulation of their expertise in this unique setting that is teachable and learnable?

To better understand, we not only studied experts themselves, as described in the sidebar comparing bankers and entrepreneurs, but also conducted follow-on studies with business novices and managers with expertise in large multinational corporations. We describe these studies in more detail later in the book. Here we briefly summarize what we found.

Research Roots

ENTREPRENEURS AND RISK: IT JUST AIN'T SO

Risk is a perennial topic of interest in entrepreneurship research with a long history dating all the way back to the very origin of the term "entrepreneur" in French. The early writings of the French economist Cantillon describe entrepreneurs as individuals who assume the risk of running a firm.

So, are entrepreneurs distinguished as having a higher risk tolerance than non-entrepreneurs? The usual practice in research on this topic is to compare entrepreneurs to a control group typically made up of managers. Miner and Raju meta-analyzed the results of 28 studies like this, concluding that the combined results indicate that entrepreneurs may not have a propensity for risk. However, the interesting result is that the studies split depending on how risk was measured. Studies in which entrepreneurs self-reported their risk proneness suggest that they are risk tolerant; whereas studies that measure entrepreneurs' behavior show them to be strongly risk avoidant. This makes it tempting to conclude that biased self-perceptions may play a distorting role in our image of risk taking in entrepreneurship. It may be that entrepreneurs perceive themselves as risk takers even though they actually score as more risk avoidant than managers. (Miner and Raju, 2004)

Practically Speaking

TRANSFORMING UNCERTAINTY INTO SUCCESS

In 1945, newly married and with barely US$5,000 in his pocket, Leonard Samuel (L.S.) Shoen and his wife, Anna Mary Carty Shoen, initiated a sequence of events that led to the creation of U-Haul.

In just four years, the duo had founded a company that made it possible to rent a trailer one-way from city to city throughout most of the US. When we examine these events, we find that this could not have been accomplished by using prediction or by trying to measure risk. In fact, when students today set out to write a business plan for this venture, they invariably conclude that the plan is financially infeasible, and even psychologically infeasible, since it requires a large and risky capital outlay, most of which gets locked up in relatively worthless assets such as trucks and rental locations. Moreover, the logistics of starting the business on a much smaller scale and growing it as fast as Shoen did overwhelms the analytical prowess of the best of forecasters. The lack of any entry barriers to imitators with deep pockets is seen as another insurmountable obstacle to success.

Means over prediction

Shoen, however, did not do elaborate market research or detailed forecasting and fundraising in the sense we generally use those terms. Instead, using who he was, what he knew and who he knew (what we call effectual means), he plunged into action, creating the market as he grew the business, working from the observation that people kept coming to his father-in-law's garage asking whether they could borrow the truck that was parked in the back. In his own words:

> Since my fortune was just about enough to make the down payment on a home and furnish it, and knowing that if I did this we would be sunk, we started the life of nomads by putting our belongings in a trailer and living between in-laws and parents for the next six months. I barbered part time and bought the kind of trailers I thought we needed to rent from anybody who happened to have one at a price I thought was right. By the fall of 1945, I was so deep into the trailer rental deal economically that it was either make it or lose the whole thing.

Building with partners

Shoen moved with his wife and their young child to the Carty ranch in Ridgefield, Washington. There, with the help of the Carty family, the Shoens built the first trailers in the fall of 1945. They painted them in striking orange with the evocative name U-Haul on the sides, and they used the ranch's automobile garage (and milk house) as the first manufacturing plant. Shoen often gave renters discounts on their trailer rentals if they would find a reputable gas station that would agree to rent U-Haul trailers in the cities to which they moved.

In the 1950s, the company established a fleet ownership program that enabled investors (including dealers and eventually employees) to purchase trailers for the U-Haul fleet in return for future dividends. Shoen established a dealer network by partnering with service stations across the country. U-Haul provided the trailers (trucks were added in 1959), and the gas station provided the unused land and labor to service U-Haul customers. U-Haul benefited from new business, and the service station owner benefited from a second source of income.

Practically Speaking *(continued)*

Blocking competitors with partners

Together, this vast network of stakeholders formed a substantial entry barrier to any imitator, who would have to risk a large capital outlay to compete. Advertising was entirely limited to the Yellow Pages and to the sudden and startling sight of growing numbers of distinctively painted vans driving the freeways of the country.

Managing affordable loss

At any given moment, U-Haul could have failed, but the resulting financial fallout would not have been a disaster since the investments were spread across so many stakeholders.

Looking at the story of U-Haul's creation, we see that Shoen dealt with uncertainty step by step, using effectual principles—starting from his means, developing partnerships, and setting a limit on the potential downside loss. Of course, we could rewrite history and suggest that he could have done market research, found out about the migration of populations in the US in the late 1940s, borrowed money from investors to set up locations, and so on. But as demonstrated by students' attempts to create feasible business plans around the idea, this approach probably would have killed the venture. Instead, because he could not and would not measure the risk, he managed the uncertainty as best he could.

The most important difference between the expert entrepreneurs and the other two groups was in their decision-making strategies. The novices and expert managers wanted desperately to predict. The expert entrepreneurs did not try to predict, but neither did they shoot from the hip or exhibit divine insight into the future. Instead, they had developed workable and sometimes even winning strategies for the game embodied in Knight's third jar. In terms of that jar, experts had learned something like the following: work with the first few things you draw from the jar and ignore the rest of what's in it; or add red balls to the jar so you are more likely to win; or rebuild the jar from what you have and persuade others to play a different game altogether.

In sum, expert entrepreneurs appear to have developed a set of techniques that effectively answers the question,

"How do I control a future I cannot predict?" This pattern of decision-making behavior is what we call effectuation. Throughout the third section of the book, we explore the principles of effectuation and understand how each works at different stages of the life cycle of new ventures as well as in a variety of other settings, such as large corporations and the social sector.

■ ■ ■

So What?

Prediction is a particularly challenging activity when creating new markets and new ventures. Handling uncertainty is at the very core of why entrepreneurs are able to create wealth, but betting on predictions isn't often how they do it. Instead, they look for ways to control the future so they do not have to predict it.

What Now?

- In your current job—how much time do you spend trying to predict versus trying to control. Is that mix of prediction and control a good match for the environment in which you are operating?

- Think about the last market research report you read. How useful would it have been for a company in that environment? How predictable or uncertain was that company's environment?

- How might the new venture opportunities you are developing more directly work to create the future?

- How critical are predictions to the moves you have in mind? If those predictions are wrong, does everything fall apart?

Think It Through

- How does one know what is and isn't predictable? That is, how do I know I'm operating in an unknowable situation?

- Choose your favorite new product. Is its market risky, predictable, or uncertain? Why?

- What have you learned over the years about HOW to create the future? Have you learned more about how to research and predict, or to control and create?

CHAPTER 7

If opportunity doesn't
knock, build a door.
Milton Berle

Opportunities are created as well as discovered

■ ■ ■

In the first chapter, we made the argument that entrepreneurship is about the very creation of new roadmaps. We did so with a bit of hesitance because the analogy of a roadmap is misleading in two ways. First, it suggests a clear destination. And second, with the help of the map and perhaps additional navigational aid, there might be an optimal way to arrive at that destination.

Before we talk about where opportunities come from, we would like to set the record straight in terms of how we view a map. Our view is not new. It is consistent with the map provided by the Bellman in Lewis Carroll's *Hunting of the Snark* (1874). We see a map not as a static image of a fixed environment but as

a dynamic reflection of your activities, with paths that are constantly changing and destinations shaped by your own actions. No two maps are alike, and the number of possible paths and destinations is infinite.

WHERE OPPORTUNITIES COME FROM

The question of where opportunities come from may seem abstract, academic, and about as useful as a blank sheet of paper. But it may help explain the way those interested in starting a business think about opportunity (maybe not even consciously) and offer insight into what they do as they pursue a venture.

OPPORTUNITY CREATION AND DISCOVERY

To be clear, there is no right or wrong answer to the question of whether opportunities already exist and if they can be discovered or if they must be created—that is, whether they are found or made.

OPPORTUNITIES ARE FOUND

Entrepreneurs operating under the "found" view start by looking at the traditional growth areas of a market and the largest unserved segments in that market. This information helps them select the best possible opportunity. Once they've made their choice, they develop a business plan based on extensive market research and detailed competitive analysis. They then look to acquire the resources and stakeholders required to implement the plan. Over time, the entrepreneurs adapt the venture to the environment, in an attempt to sustain a competitive edge.

The "found" view assumes that the budding venture is sufficiently similar to an existing business for historical information to inform decisions, and the environment is sufficiently stable for outcomes from the past to be relevant to the current situation and to the future.

The Bellman himself they all praised to the skies—
Such a carriage, such ease and such grace!
Such solemnity, too! One could see he was wise,
The moment one looked in his face!

He had bought a large map representing the sea,
Without the least vestige of land:
And the crew were much pleased when they found it to be
A map they could all understand.

"What's the good of Mercator's North Poles and Equators,
Tropics, Zones, and Meridian Lines?"
So the Bellman would cry: and the crew would reply
"They are merely conventional signs!

"Other maps are such shapes, with their islands and capes!
But we've got our brave Bellman to thank"
(So the crew would protest) "that he's bought us the best—
A perfect and absolute blank!"

Lewis Carroll, *The Hunting of the Snark* (1874)

Practically Speaking

BUILDING THE ROAD AHEAD

Off the top of your head (no looking at the receipts in your wallet), what was the name of the company operating the car the last time you took a taxicab? If you don't know, you represent the vast majority of passengers. Taxis are the kind of service that has become a commodity across the world. Standardized. Ubiquitous. Necessary. But undifferentiated.

Practically Speaking *(continued)*

Opportunity stoplight

Commodity is convenient for the user but, from the provider perspective, it is a keyword for an unattractive industry. Unless you're an entrepreneur who uses the existing situation as only a starting point and as something that can be changed based on what you have available and the actions you take. So what does this kind of forward thinking look like once it is in motion?

Green passengers

Those of you living in or travelling to London have certainly enjoyed the iconic black city cab. Distinctive in its chunky bulbous shape, it represents the commodity of the cab in the UK. But Nicko Williamson is driving change.

Building on his own environmental principles, he launched Climate Cars in 2007, offering a fleet of hybrid Toyota Prius taxis that generate the lowest CO_2 footprint of any UK model. They are also equipped with bike racks, ready to rescue stranded cyclists with eco-friendly motor transportation. On the leather seats, passengers trapped in traffic will find a bottle of mineral water and a copy of the latest glossy magazine should they need a little distraction. Williamson achieved revenues of £255,000 in his first year, a number that increased tenfold by 2010 and made the firm so attractive it was acquired by transportation giant Addison Lee in 2015.

Just for her

At roughly the same time, halfway across the world in Mumbai, India, Revathi Roy was facing a personal crisis. When her husband fell into a coma in 2007, she had no job to support her three children. Her solution? An avid rally driver who had raced cars for decades, she used her passion for driving to start ForShe (doing business as Forsche), a taxi service specifically for women passengers. With strong demand from women working in large cities in India, Roy has expanded to 65 cabs across Mumbai and Delhi, delivering convenience and confidence to tens of thousands of women.

But that's not the last stop. As much as Roy's venture serves the needs of female commuters, it has also grown to serve employees as effectively as customers. In 2008, Roy started her second venture, a training academy for women wanting to work for her as taxi

Practically Speaking (continued)

chauffeurs. The academy teaches driving safety, first aid, and the martial arts so that her employees can manage every aspect of safety while driving for ForShe. Roy even brokers micro-loans and arranges sponsorships into the academy for women who seek the same thing she enjoys from ForShe—income and personal independence.

Creating the road ahead

Both Roy and Williamson show us that it is the unique hand of the entrepreneur—starting with the unique set of things they have available and then taking action—that creates the road we later take. So the next time you hop into the back seat of a cab, consider what it would look like if you were in the driver's seat.

Practically Speaking

SOMETHING FROM NOTHING

While some entrepreneurs discover their business plans are unintentionally full of excrement, Tom Szaky's was designed around it. Worm dung, in fact. Inspired by his friends' success using red wiggler worms to process compost and feeding the resulting dung to plants, Szaky felt there could be a business in commercially producing and distributing a product he would call "Worm Poop." Emboldened by taking fifth place in the Princeton Business Plan Contest, he quit Princeton after two years to form TerraCycle and devote himself to delivering Worm Poop to households everywhere.

The smell of success

With $20,000—the proceeds of Szaky's bank accounts and credit cards—he purchased a worm gin and began shovelling Princeton University's food waste into it to feed an ever-growing colony of worms. A worm can consume twice its body weight each day, so Szaky was soon up to his knees in product. Committed to a fully sustainable offering, he packaged his prized Worm Poop in paper bags and took it to gardening stores inviting them to stock it. The polite response was that the product looked good, but the aroma was not consumer compatible.

Recycled idea

The answer already existed—used plastic bottles. The product was made from waste, so why not package it in waste as well? Szaky developed a process to mix his Worm Poop with water, strain out the solids to leave a nutrient-rich liquid, then fill recycled bottles with it and seal them with waste spray tops. The idea was so good that Szaky took top honours at the Carrot Capital Business Plan Challenge in 2003, recognition that came with a $1 million investment prize. A good thing, as TerraCycle had only $500 in the bank at the time.

Practically Speaking *(continued)*

Committed to waste

For some entrepreneurs, this would define the moment of success—validation of an idea combined with the financial resources to make it happen. For Szaky, it was a defining dilemma.

The investors wanted to direct TerraCycle into plant foods without the eco-friendly mission and change some management. Szaky refused the investment. Instead, he redoubled his efforts with big retailers and brought in a more benevolent form of capital. Revenue. By 2004, Walmart and The Home Depot were stocking his products in Canada, and he was negotiating to expand into the US.

Upcycling

Under Szaky's direction, more and more trash fed more and more worms, which fed more and more plants, and, with Americans throwing out 2.5 million plastic bottles an hour, packaging was also readily available. As TerraCycle grew, Szaky saw opportunities everywhere. Trash was something to be "upcycled" into an offering more valuable than the original product.

He started with seed starters and potting mix, made from and packaged in waste. Then he offered the Urban Art Pot, made from electronic waste. Then came plastic products, from kites to clipboards, all completely recycled. Partnerships with Target, Walmart, Nabisco, and Kraft have now closed the cycle. Today, these firms participate in "Sponsored Waste" programmes where TerraCycle pays "Brigades" of consumers to collect used packaging manufactured by and distributed by these firms, which TerraCycle turns into new products. And money. In 2014, the firm made $20 million in revenue.

Learning from trash

Szaky teaches us that opportunities are more a function of what you already have than a function of convincing a venture capitalist to invest large sums in your business plan. And that some people are paying to get rid of resources that can form the basis of new and valuable offerings. While building a business on trash might not top the glamour charts, it also offers one more lesson: the word sustainability can apply equally to the business and to the planet when spoken by an entrepreneur.

Search and select in music

The range of approaches used to find opportunities, generally referred to as search and select, is useful in explaining the success of new ventures in predictable environments. We know people listen to music on the move, and we know the Internet provides broader access to music libraries. So through the search and select process we come up with the software and a device, add some design, and we have the MP3 player. However, this does not explain the Walkman. There was no market and no historical data to guide its creation. The idea that possibilities are transformed into opportunities (opportunities are made) is useful in exactly those situations where the past cannot help predict the future.

OPPORTUNITIES ARE MADE

Under the "made" approach, the information available to entrepreneurs at the start of the venture creation process is both incomplete and overwhelming. The market cannot be defined. Consumers are not aware of their

Research Roots

NEW COMBINATIONS

Joseph Schumpeter (1934) theorized that demand could be created, proposing that innovations took the form of "new combinations" that combined existing things in new ways. These transformations could result in new markets, new production processes, new products, new ways of organizing, and new methods of distribution. Schumpeter defined "the carrying out of new combinations" as the essence of entrepreneurship.

future preferences. New technologies may emerge. Available data are confusing and conflicting. All this implies that entrepreneurs do more than simply recombine existing resources or transfer them from their current use to one that yields better returns. In reality, they create or transform, thereby generating new opportunities from mere possibilities.

Because new ventures are uncertain, effectual logic often prevails

Surprising as it may seem to aspiring entrepreneurs, the "made" view often prevails in the world of expert entrepreneurs. This view is guided

The Approach	The Market	The Logic	The Heuristics
Search and Select	Markets are fixed. Part of any given market may be served, underserved, or latent.	Explore a finite set of possibilities to find unserved, underserved, or latent areas of the market.	**Causation** Predict to identify a goal. Focus is on achieving that goal by accumulating the necessary means. Surprises are bad.
Create and Transform	Markets can be created. Creation can be intentional or an unanticipated consequence of people just doing things they think are possible and worth doing.	Knowing it is possible to create demand, let interactions give rise to an infinite set of possibilities, which can then be prioritized by self-selected stakeholders.	**Effectuation** Start taking action. Focus is on transforming a set of evolving means to generate goals that emerge along the way. Surprises are good.

by what we call the logic of effectuation—a logic particularly suited to moving forward in uncertain situations. To understand how we're using this funky word, let's think about the difference between cause and effect—or between causal and effectual. Search and select (the "found" view) is guided by a causal or predictive logic—the kind that is taught in MBA programs and ascribed to by managers around the world. The idea is that you start with a goal in mind, and you find the optimal way to reach it. Effectual logic, which adopts a create-and-transform approach, is the inverse: instead of beginning with a specific goal, you begin with a given set of means, and you allow goals, or effects, to emerge as you work with your means. (We outline the principles of effectuation in Chapter 9 and detail them in Part III.) We can see an effectual logic at work in the stories of many of the firms we admire—firms that started out doing nothing close to what they

Practically Speaking

CURRY IN A HURRY

Imagine an entrepreneur who wants to start an Indian restaurant. Using a search and select approach, she would start by doing market research in the restaurant industry in the city of her choice. On the basis of the market research, she would carefully select a location, segment the market in a meaningful way, select target segments based on estimates of potential return, design a restaurant to appeal to her target segments, raise the required funding, bring her team together and, finally, implement specific marketing strategies and manage daily operations to make her restaurant a success.

If our entrepreneur instead followed a create-and-transform approach, the outcome would depend on who she is, what she knows, and who she knows. For the sake of understanding the process here, let us say she is a good Indian chef considering starting an independent business. Assuming she has little money of her own, what are some of the ways she can bring her idea to the market? She might partner with an existing restaurant, participate in food fairs, set up a catering service, and so on. Let us say she decides to pursue starting a business and persuades friends who work downtown to allow her to bring lunch for their office colleagues to sample. Some of those people sign up for a lunch service, and she begins preparing the lunches at home and delivering them personally. Eventually, she could save up enough money to rent a location and start a restaurant.

Practically Speaking *(continued)*

It is equally plausible that the lunch business does not take off beyond the first few customers. However, using a creative and transformative logic, our entrepreneur could co-create other enterprises depending on whatever her customers are actually interested in, besides her cooking. For example, maybe it is her personality that is interesting; she could then produce a cooking video or maybe start a cooking school. Contingent on who is interested in what, our entrepreneur could go into any one of several businesses. Her eventual successful enterprise could be in entertainment, education, travel, manufacturing, packaging, retail, interior decoration, or self-help and motivation—to name just a few possibilities.

do today. Opportunities were made over time and through interactions with customers, partners, and employees. The "curry in a hurry" example gives us two ways—one "found" (causal) the other "made" (effectual)—to pursue the same possibility.

> Never doubt that a small group of thoughtful, committed, citizens can change the world. Indeed, it is the only thing that ever has.
> Margaret Mead

THE CENTRAL PREMISE OF EFFECTUATION

The "curry in a hurry" example illustrates what we describe as the "pilot in the plane" principle. Core to effectual logic, it conceives the entrepreneur as the person at the controls. The person who, to some greater or lesser degree, creates the course a venture will take. The course of the venture is just as likely to be created in the process of doing as it is to be preconceived. While Columbus set a course for discovering India, his mission was transformed when he was surprised by a new continent.

The Pet Rock is a particularly amusing example of a market that could not have been anticipated or preconceived. And it highlights another important aspect of effectual logic: success or failure does not hinge on how accurate the original vision turns out to be or how well the strategies crafted to deliver that vision are executed. Success is individually defined and may change as the process evolves. The relationships formed in creating new products, new ventures, or even new markets (such as the Pet Rock) also influence what those outcomes look like and how success is defined.

Practically Speaking

MAKING A MARKET OUT OF A JOKE

Gary Dahl was out one evening having a few drinks with his buddies when the conversation turned to pets. Dahl, a California advertising man, joined in by claiming he had a pet rock—an ideal pet with a great personality that was easy and cheap to care for. His friends laughed at the idea. Little did they know that a pop-culture fad was about to be born.

It was April 1975, and Dahl's initial idea was to write a book—The Care and Training of Your Pet Rock—a step-by-step guide to having a happy relationship with your geological pet. He spent the next few weeks writing the book, which included instructions on training the Pet Rock to do tricks, such as roll over (best taught on a hillside) and play dead (which the rocks love to practice on their own). As the book took shape, Dahl decided to add some props—an actual rock nestled in some excelsior and packaged in a little carrying case, equipped with breathing holes. Dahl found his Pet Rock in a builder's supply store in San Jose. At a penny apiece, it was the most expensive rock in the place.

After introducing the Pet Rock at the San Francisco gift show in August, and then later in New York, Neiman-Marcus placed an order for 500. Then, based on a homemade news release that showed a picture of Dahl surrounded by his Pet Rocks in their carrying cases, Dahl was able to attract some great publicity, including a half-page story in Newsweek. He was also invited to be a guest on The Tonight Show twice. By the end of October he was shipping 10,000 Pet Rocks a day, and by Christmas, when 2.5 tons of rocks had been sold, three-quarters of all the daily newspapers in the US had run Pet Rock stories.

Just a few months after unleashing his Pet Rock, he had sold more than one million units at US$3.95 apiece. Dahl—who, from the very beginning had decided to make at least one dollar from every rock—had become an instant millionaire.

CREATE YOUR OWN OPPORTUNITIES

Casual readers of history often see heroes, visionaries, and explorers as possessing superhuman qualities. This impression is reinforced by the larger-than-life descriptions of successful entrepreneurs we read about in the news. In this chapter, we separate these myths from reality. Entrepreneurs are not necessarily visionaries who are better, faster, or smarter than others are at seizing and exploiting opportunities that no one else can see. Instead, in many cases, they make their own opportunities using mundane means. While entrepreneurs have traditionally been described as discoverers, we view them also as creators— terraforming as well as map-making.

TAKEAWAY: IT'S UP TO YOU

What does this mean for you?

The answer is that you do not need to sit and wait for a unique opportunity to come hurtling at you from the sky. On the contrary, it is up to you to create that opportunity. This calls for a much more active role on your part and for you to feel comfortable with a blank map that you will fill in according to your tastes, abilities, and means, what you know and who you know. You're not alone. Our early explorers (and the Bellman) were in this situation. Entrepreneurship is what happens when you don't rely on luck.

■ ■ ■

So What?

Opportunities are created by entrepreneurs, not just found "out there" in the market. Often, the pilot in the plane actively and accidentally creates the roadmap, in addition to goals, partners, and products. Entrepreneurs rarely have a clear vision, clear goals, or a clear roadmap as they launch.

Think It Through

■ If you develop opportunities as the pilot in the plane, rather than a discoverer with a map, how might your actions and decisions differ?

■ What might be the unintended consequences of becoming an entrepreneur with no map and no rules?

■ Where does one begin without any roadmap at all?

■ Where does one start when hunting snarks?

What Now?

■ Look into four of your favorite companies and identify what aspects of their opportunities were made vs. found?

■ For those that were made, what were the key ingredients in how they were made?

■ Now that you can see where those companies ended up, i.e. their roadmap has been created, identify one complete alternative route to the same destination. How ELSE might they have more "efficiently" reached that same destination? This is similar to causation.

■ Conversely, now that you can see what those companies became good at, identify one alternative destination that they might have happened upon if a couple of moments changed in their history. This is more like effectual thinking.

CHAPTER 8

Only you can control your future.
Dr Seuss

Managing uncertainty through control

■ ■ ■

In this chapter, we explain how the concept of control fits with situations of prediction and uncertainty, exactly what is controllable and how entrepreneurs control the destiny of their ventures in uncertain environments.

As you read this chapter, consider how empowering the idea of control is in the context of starting a new venture, or generally taking action in uncertain situations.

WHY CONTROL?

The struggle for personal control is as old as humankind itself—primitive and innate. There is abundant evidence that most people desire control of the events in their lives, indeed over their lives, and that such strivings for control span history and cultures. The venues, mechanisms, and instruments for control-striving today are different than they used to be, but the issue remains. In fact, psychological research suggests that an enormous range of human behaviors relate to

> Complete adaptation to environment means death. The essential point in all response is the desire to control environment.
> John Dewey

control striving in some way and are intrinsically linked to healthy human functioning. For example, personal control is linked to the development of self-esteem and the reduction of stress, whereas loss of control increases the likelihood of feelings of helplessness and depression.

In other words, having a desire for control over your life doesn't make you a "control freak" (despite what your friends may say!). Instead, it is normal and healthy.

Many entrepreneurs instinctively recognize the importance of personal control: fundamentally, many chose entrepreneurship because they want to be their own boss and choose their own course. Control enables entrepreneurs to work on things they think are important, set their own schedules, and work with whom they want. Many entrepreneurs attest that they feel differently about running a business they own as compared with working for a wage, and that they value being in control. For them, the experience of personal control is closely associated with freedom, self-direction, and autonomy.

The strength of a person's desire for control can be thought of as an element of his or her means: "Who you are." While everyone has some desire for control, the intensity of that desire varies among individuals and over the course of a lifetime. For example, a high desire for control may motivate someone to become an entrepreneur, but the experience of working for himself may

IS THERE MORE PERSONAL CONTROL NOW THAN IN THE PAST?

Changing social attitudes in the latter half of the twentieth century have definitely influenced individual perceptions of personal control. These perceptions are embedded in broader social belief systems, such as beliefs about individual freedom and choice, which have been legitimized by social movements in Western democracies and political changes such as the collapse of communism in the former Soviet Union, and the spread of the free market system in China, India, and elsewhere.

Research Roots

ON THE IMPORTANCE OF CONTROL

People are highly sensitive to their world, particularly its causal texture. Although our efforts to specify the fine detail of this sensitivity—how it is acquired and represented and used to channel subsequent action—are ongoing, we nonetheless can say with confidence that people strive to appreciate what they can and cannot control. Whatever they learn is registered deeply and profoundly, influencing everything from physiological processes to world politics. (Peterson et al. ,1995: 305)

strengthen the desire even further—he may not be able to imagine working for anyone else again.

PREDICTION, RISK, UNCERTAINTY, AND CONTROL

The thousands of books about business strategy generally suggest two levers that enable decision-making. The first is prediction. If the future can be predicted, the decision-maker can steer the company toward a position where it will have an advantage. The second

lever is control. If the future can be controlled, the business leader can work to create a situation that provides his firm an advantage. These levers are not alternatives, but rather tools managers can apply to improve the chances of making good decisions. The diagram entitled "Strategies with respect to prediction and control" shows the relationship between the environment and the combination of suitable levers. Next, we lay out the logic for matching decision-making strategies with the environments represented in the different quadrants.

In the planning and adaptation areas on the left-hand side, companies have to either plan more (predict better) or be more flexible and faster in responding to changes in their environment (adapt better). Both approaches rely on the firm's ability to sense and make sense out of the environment, either in the longer term (planning) or in the shorter term (adapting).

In a mature, stable environment, planning, as the source of strategy making, can be effective. Planning assumes that information—particularly historical information from the environment—is reliable enough to provide a base for decision-making (prediction is possible).

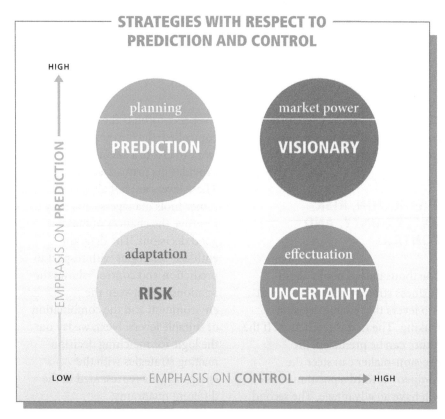

STRATEGIES WITH RESPECT TO PREDICTION AND CONTROL

HIGH

EMPHASIS ON PREDICTION

planning
PREDICTION

market power
VISIONARY

adaptation
RISK

effectuation
UNCERTAINTY

LOW   — EMPHASIS ON **CONTROL** ⟶ HIGH

Research Roots

YOUR STRATEGY NEEDS A STRATEGY

Martin Reeves and colleagues (2015) have applied the orientation of strategies along the dimensions of prediction and control to create an approach for choosing a strategy in a larger more established firm. Through their BCG research institute, they have released a book, an app, and a number of cases.

If strategy is based on adapting and learning, the ability to react and iterate quickly is key, with the intent of outpacing the competition in response to changes in the environment.

The visionary (market power) and effectuation areas on the right-hand side call for a more proactive approach to the environment. If a company has market power (government-regulated markets or quasi-monopolistic status such as that achieved by Microsoft in the 2000s), it can try to dictate what will happen in that environment, imposing its view (visionary) on the landscape and ensuring the position of the organization within that environment.

The effectuation area calls for a different approach. Because the company does not have market power, it needs to co-create (with partners, customers, suppliers, and other self-selected stakeholders) elements of its environment by, for example, developing a new product or market from which all the players involved will benefit. Effectuation assumes you can shape the environment by creating new elements using your means, partnerships, and actions.

Some may argue that managing uncertainty is possible through a combination of predicting better and adapting faster. But consider some examples you may already know. Because they were working on predicting better, Coca-Cola and Pepsi missed the opportunity that allowed Red Bull to create a new category and develop a new market in soft drinks—those who connect a high-caffeine beverage with sports. By contrast, trying to adapt to market research led to the spectacular failure and subsequent costly termination of New Coke.

ENTREPRENEUR'S CHOICE

The entrepreneur, or manager more generally, always has a choice about what kind of environment to operate in, and what kind of decision-making to use in that environment.

Choosing to offer a competitive product in an existing market means the environment is more predictable than creating a venture to introduce something completely new. As such, the choice to use prediction or control can be driven by the stage of the market or the stage of the company. During the early startup phase (of market or firm), there is very little that is predictable.

THEORY IN PRACTICE: KEEP180

Imagine a popular independent radio station, KEEP180, which plays a wide range of new music, from country and western to French rap. The station broadcasts locally and has a growing online audience. The station is funded by donations from listeners and it is facing a strategic decision about where to invest its limited resources as it moves ahead. Let's think about how the radio station would evolve in each of these environments:

- Planning. The station might carry out market research and predict an explosion in a new genre of French music. It could then invest in bringing that music to its audience and consequently capitalize on higher ratings.

- Market power. Alternatively, the producer at KEEP180 may simply love the French language and may build a format exclusively on French rap and other novel French music, knowing s/he will own the category if s/he can establish it.

- Adaptation. Given the high rate of change in technology and customer demand, the station might devote its efforts to watching other independent stations and talking with customers, ready to move quickly as new trends are identified.

- Effectuation. Finally, the station might partner with a French recording label and a current American music icon to create a French rap music scene, selling music online, where all the self-selected stakeholders profit from the new environment they create together.

While control strategies connect naturally with uncertainty and predictive strategies with maturity, entrepreneurial managers might also choose control strategies as a foundation for new ways of competing and innovating in mature markets.

CHANGE OVER TIME

Neither environment nor strategy is static. For example, as an entrepreneurial opportunity develops from nothing, VCs and other potential funders may ask for a business plan, reflecting their expectations of some degree of prediction (sometimes regardless of whether that expectation has any bearing on reality). Many successful new markets do become more predictable and stable over time and, therefore, more amenable to prediction and planning. When a venture reaches a more mature stage, it can become very reliant on prediction, and managers can choose to base decisions dominantly on predictive inputs. In this situation, it is easy for a firm to be surprised by uncertainty in its environment, making it vulnerable to innovative new products. Ironically, these surprise new products are created using the same (effectual) logic from which the large firm's foundation was constructed in the first place.

WHAT IS CONTROLLABLE?

Part of learning how to create new ventures is learning where the

more—and less—controllable elements are and how best to leverage them. While prediction and control have different roles at different stages in the life of a venture, our focus here is on the startup and what can be controlled as it launches into existence. There are many factors involved in a firm's success. Some can be directly controlled or managed by the firm, others can be influenced by the firm and some are completely out of the firm's control.

The diagram on the next page illustrates some elements institutional investors use to determine the "investability" or viability of a venture. Imagine you are ready to build a venture. Where do you start? What do you do on day one? Since you can't do everything at the same time, you need to prioritize.

Start with actions relating to elements over which you have the greatest degree of control.

Accept those you can't control.

At all times, be open to the possibility that your perceptions are wrong. There are probably more factors within your control than you imagine. But even if your perceptions are not accurate, starting with where you believe you have some control gets you going with manageable risk and accessible resources.

> Immense power is acquired by assuring yourself in your secret reveries that you were born to control affairs.
> Andrew Carnegie

CONTROL AND VENTURE SUCCESS

Success within an entrepreneurial venture is determined by the ability of the organization to define, shape, and optimize the elements shown in the following figure as industry, firm, market, and customers emerge and evolve. Think about how you will approach each—we discuss three examples here.

Competition

Should a new venture deal with competition using prediction or control? Decisions managers or entrepreneurs in other firms make about how they want to compete, particularly in new and undefined markets, are quite hard to predict. But does that mean you have no control? We place competition in the middle of our diagram to reflect that the actions of competitors are largely out of our control. At the same time, we do not place it on the bottom edge of controllability, as there are many competitive factors that are shapeable. Determining the differentiator(s) (technology, business model or distribution strategy) that make your venture unique provides you with significant latitude to determine the dimensions of the competition (and give you a chance to select ones where you have an advantage). As you start your business, think carefully about what makes you distinctive.

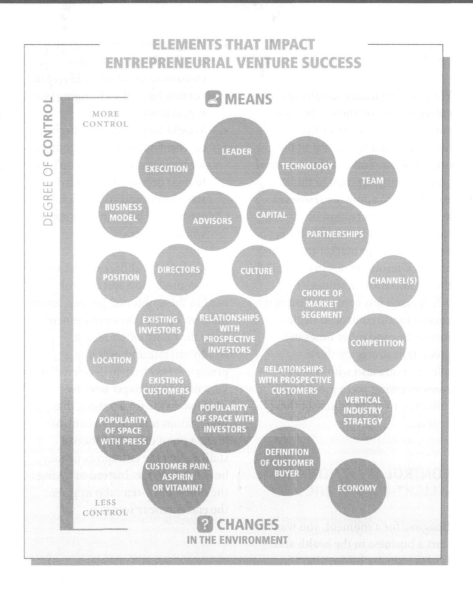

ELEMENTS THAT IMPACT ENTREPRENEURIAL VENTURE SUCCESS

Economy

Economic climate is relevant to the success of most new ventures for two reasons. In general, a good economy allows mediocre companies to succeed and helps good companies flourish. A rising tide lifts all boats. At the same time, there are some products and services that become more attractive in a bad economy (for examples, please see Chapter 16 on surprise). Unfortunately, neither prediction nor control is terribly good at managing the economy. That acknowledged, we generally observe offerings that help people make money perform better in a good economy. And those that help people save money perform better in a bad economy. So if you direct your efforts toward offerings that might support both value propositions, you give yourself more potential control in responding at least to the economy.

Leader: The meta-controller

We place the leader, usually the entrepreneur, on the top because you as a leader can steer the heuristics used by the rest of the organization. You can (for example) guide the organization to think about how to apply the resources available to the creation of something new (a control strategy) or to go perform market research and seek resources not in control of the organization (a strategy that offers much less control). You may choose to use control strategies sometimes and other times use prediction strategies; those selections are also within your control, giving you a great deal of influence over the course of the venture.

CONTROL IN ACTION: WEIGHT-LOSS CLINIC

Imagine, for a moment, you want to start a business in the health and fitness industry by opening a weight-loss clinic. You observe a big market in helping people lose weight but the fact is that nine out of ten people quickly regain that weight, ultimately making them unsatisfied. What are some ways you can use these data in your business? You could observe that there is a nine-out-of-ten probability of recidivism and decide that:

- Conventional weight-loss programs are a waste of time, and choose to start a venture in health foods instead.

- Weight-loss programs are an excellent business because customers inevitably will end up coming back, thus bringing you repeat business.
- Weight-loss programs offer an excellent opportunity to compete for business because all you have to do is decrease the recidivism rate slightly and your weight-loss centres will be a runaway success with customers.

Now, what's the difference between the way prediction and control are used in these options? Simply, in the first two options the entrepreneur takes the information on the recidivism rate and uses it in a predictive way to help decide what kind of venture to get into. By contrast, in the final option, that information is taken as a control lever, a point of intervention, a statistic that the entrepreneur may be able to change. Instead of taking the nine-out-of-ten ratio as given, the entrepreneur sees it as

something she might be able to influence in order to control the success of the venture.

The history of human action has proven time and time again the power of human beings to change the odds of events. Consider, for example, the odds of being crippled by polio. Globally, these odds are dramatically different now than they were 50 years ago owing to efforts by the World Health Organization and individual country organizations to eradicate the disease. In other words, we have collectively changed a child's probability of getting polio.

The weight-loss clinic example challenges us to think about what might be controllable and what truly is not. It also allows us to look at the relationship between prediction and control in a more "active" way. For controllers, understanding probabilities is valuable to the extent that you can find a way of changing them.

Research Roots

SELF-EFFICACY AND LEARNED HELPLESSNESS

One psychological trait that frequently has been shown to be related to people choosing to become entrepreneurs and to entrepreneurial success is self-efficacy. Albert Bandura (Bandura and Cervone, 1986: 92) describes the concept as follows:

> Perceived self-efficacy is defined as people's beliefs about their capabilities to produce designated levels of performance that exercise influence over events that affect their lives. Self-efficacy beliefs determine how people feel, think, motivate themselves, and behave. Such beliefs produce these diverse effects through four major processes. They include cognitive, motivational, affective and selection processes. A strong sense of efficacy enhances human accomplishment and personal well-being in many ways. People with high assurance in their capabilities approach difficult tasks as challenges to be mastered rather than as threats to be avoided. Such an efficacious outlook fosters intrinsic interest and deep engrossment in activities. People with high self-efficacy heighten and sustain their efforts in the face of failure, quickly recovering after failures or setbacks. They attribute failure to insufficient effort or deficient knowledge and skills, which are acquirable. They approach threatening situations with assurance that they can exercise control over them.

In important ways, self-efficacy is the inverse of learned helplessness. Learned helplessness occurs when individuals' predictions about cause and effect, about the relationship between inputs and outcomes, are repeatedly violated. After a while, they feel as if nothing they do can get control over their situation (Peterson et al., 1995).

Practically Speaking

THE POWER OF CONTROL

Close your eyes and imagine life without electricity. Entertainment and communications are generally what people think of first. No iPod. No mobile. No television or computer. It's very quiet. But electricity also drives more fundamental services we take for granted, such as running water (an electric pump is usually required) and lighting. Now multiply by 580 million. That's the number of people in India (more than half of the country's population) who live without electricity today. Sounds like the basis for a charitable effort that should command the attention of citizens in the world's wealthier countries.

Time for a switch

Now imagine you are Gyanesh Pandey, a young electrical engineer who learned he could generate electricity from rice husks, a waste product heaped along the rural roads of his native state of Bihar. Would you be tempted to apply for government grants, approach international aid agencies, and seek donations from private foundations? Maybe. But with the input of a couple of MBAs from the Darden School in the USA, Manoj Sinha and Charles (Chip) Ransler, might you consider the heretical notion that you could actually make money from this thing?

Practically Speaking *(continued)*

What profit?

With grants and donations, you could do it the right way—import gasification plants from the US, employ trained technicians, and set up a power grid, probably on a rationally justifiable five-year plan. But when you entertain the notion of "profit," you can only begin with what you have or, if you are clever, maybe build a working proof of concept with resources you can afford to lose. The specifications for your prototype are clear: the solution has to be cheap. Or free. Or cheaper than free. That means you have to make machinery locally and train local talent to put it together and maintain it. And you have to figure out how to get paid. It's just about possible. Except for a few small details. You are in Bihar, one of the poorest states in India. The local population is not educated, often not literate. And the notion of "paying" for electric power is not customary. Tapping into grids and stealing it is more the norm.

Twice illuminated

The team set out to design a business model based on village systems, not power grids. Small, cheap, and prepaid would describe it, like the mobile phones pervasive in rural Bihar. Make technicians, salespersons, and even business leaders out of local people—those hungry to learn, even if only to pay the bills. As the team spins out this unlikely tapestry, they learn that a community's emotional ownership in a business is a powerful thing. And that a functional business model is worth a thousand grandiose plans that gobble cash and go nowhere. It is the same lesson that so-called social entrepreneurs who dare to do it for profit are learning all over the world. Ask Muhammed Yunus, founder of Grameen Bank. Ask Matt Flannery, founder of Kiva. Ask Bill Drayton, founder of Ashoka.

Bright future

Today, Husk Power Systems serves around 200,000 customers in villages across Bihar. It won the prestigious Cisco–DFJ Global Business Plan Competition, and it has attracted approximately $2.5 million in investments from sources such as the Acumen Fund to finance expansion. Add another $800,000 from the Shell Foundation and it gets a little bit easier to imagine the possibilities. Husk has created thousands of local jobs. But the most interesting fact is in the fine print. Husk makes a profit selling power at $0.07 per kilowatt-hour. That's a bargain compared with buying kerosene for a lamp. And it's a bargain compared with buying electricity from the national power company. Could a social venture out-compete a state subsidized monopoly? If so, Husk could expand from social startup venture into social multinational firm. That, indeed, would be powerful progress.

Controllers thus use knowledge of probabilities differently than predictors do. For controllers, probabilities are opportunities to intervene, to manipulate events; for predictors, they are an opportunity to make a bet. While the predictor is working on the assumption that no one else will be successful in changing the probabilities, the entrepreneur is working on the assumption that other entrepreneurs out there, like them, are trying to find some way to change the world.

HOW CONTROL WORKS: YOU AND YOUR STAKEHOLDERS

Why should you work directly with stakeholders? Why do seasoned entrepreneurs say they prefer first-hand market input, derived from personally going out and trying to sell a product, rather than gathering data about the potential market?

The answer is that working with self-selected stakeholders enables controllability.

- You control who you interact with. Stakeholders select you, and you select them—the process is mutual. If you don't get along, you can decide to move on and do business with someone else.
- Any relationship that is to some extent negotiable is more controllable than a relationship that is not. Negotiations happen in many different ways, including bargaining, haggling, manipulating, influencing, etc.

These methods of interacting with other human beings involve some sharing of control.

- You can be confident your stakeholders also desire control. That means it makes sense to join forces with them and try to shape the future together, rather than spend your time trying to predict what everyone else might do. A large part of the method of control relies on the fact that human beings generally prefer control to prediction; therefore, they are willing to work with others to integrate their goals and plans.

It should be clear from the foregoing discussion that controlling with and through others requires an acceptance of a shared role for those stakeholders. It involves the entrepreneur and stakeholders working together, to co-create a non-zero sum game in which everyone benefits in the future together.

PERCEPTION OF CONTROL

Thus far in the chapter, we have addressed things you can do—actions you can take which will increase your level of control. But detailed research from psychology tells us that underlying your willingness to act is your perception of control.

One ship sails East,
And another West,
By the self-same winds that blow,
Tis the set of the sails
And not the gales,
That tells the way we go.
Ella Wheeler Wilcox

Perceptions of control are important only when we're considering outcomes that offer some resistance, outcomes that probably will not happen in the absence of human intervention. So, control, for our purposes, is about attempting to influence things contingent not only on what I do but also on what others do. Your influence might be 1% or 99%. Low-control activities are those with cause–effect relationships that you can't influence much; high-control activities are ones you have some significant influence over.

We focus our attention on what we will call effectual control techniques. In general, effectuation works with elements where a significant contingency relationship exists between you and the element. An example would be pre-selling a prospective product to a client, where your actions significantly influence how the sale turns out, i.e. the management of the client relationship and the delivery of the promised product, which is in your hands. Not everything is controllable, but the effectual entrepreneur focuses on what he or she can control.

This approach clearly contrasts with causal control techniques that work with elements where there is a low- or no-contingency relationship between you and the element. An example would be developing a business plan on your prediction of the results of an election: "I'm going to invest in a construction company because I predict that the government election will result in more government spending that will spur demand for construction." You can't control the election results; precisely for this reason, you have to predict them and then make a bet based on your prediction.

CONTROL OVER INPUTS AND CONTROL OVER OUTCOMES

To increase our understanding of how control is linked to action, we must consider not only control over outcomes but also control over inputs. For example, some people feel they could control outcomes if only they had the "correct" inputs. In contrast, effectuators act based on inputs within their control on environments they believe they can influence through their actions.

Limited control over outcomes

When people are unsure about how much they can influence outcomes, they may try to compensate with elaborate planning and calculated bets. This can lead to "analysis paralysis" if they are relying on prediction. Instead, the effectual principle of affordable loss can drive action, especially if actors are willing to change their goals as new stakeholders come on board.

Limited control over inputs

When people do not have the means they believe are required to achieve desired outcomes, they become susceptible to inertia induced by the "if onlys"—if only I had the money;

FOR YOUR INFORMATION, I AM ENGAGING THE ENERGY OF CHANGE AND COMPLEXITY TO CREATE THE FUTURE I DESIRE.

if only my personal circumstances were different; if only I had access to the technology; and so on. If they do decide to act under these circumstances, and choose a causal approach, they face the prospect of chasing resources outside their control. If they take an effectual approach, they need to be open to self-selected stakeholders because these stakeholders can increase the available means (inputs). They can act using either approach, but effectuation lowers the cost by reducing resource requirements to affordable loss levels.

Control over neither inputs nor outcomes

Perceiving both inputs and outcomes as unpredictable and outside one's control can lead to a state that psychologists call "learned helplessness." This is a serious danger associated with using prediction in uncertain circumstances, and it highlights why effectuators begin with the inputs they control—their means.

In sum, focusing on control strategies can have a positive impact on the likelihood of action because it does not rely on predictability, upfront investments in planning, and the pursuit of resources to deliver on the plans.

TAKEAWAY: CONTROL THE CONTROLLABLE

It is important to know both what you can control, or influence, and what you cannot. You can then tailor your strategies to the situation at hand:

- Control and influence what you can.
- Predict when it's more useful than control.
- Heighten the controllability of your situation by working as much as possible with factors you can influence. This reduces your dependence on prediction and puts you on an overall firmer footing.

People vary in their assumptions about the power of human action at all levels and in all domains to control processes and outcomes. Effectuators see themselves not as risk takers defying long odds but as active agents who directly intervene in the world.

Research Roots

OVERCONFIDENCE

Together with risk-taking, plenty of research has suggested overconfidence as an explanation for why some people become entrepreneurs despite the frequency of entrepreneurial failure. We already know the common perceptions about entrepreneurial failure are wrong (Chapter 4) but what about overconfidence?

Overconfidence can refer to overestimation of one's performance, overestimation of performance relative to others, or overestimating the precision of one's beliefs. In a series of critical papers, researcher Don Moore has shown that, in fact, people both underestimate and overestimate their performance.

On difficult tasks, people overestimate their performance but simultaneously believe they are doing worse than others are. On easy tasks, they underestimate their performance but think they are better than others are. This suggests that the way a task is framed and perceived (as either "easy" or "hard") is intricately linked to over- and under-confidence.

So, is it easy or hard to start your own business? Whatever your starting point, it gets easier if you know the right techniques and as you get more practice with them.

Summarized from Moore and Healy (2008: 502–17).

WHAT IS CONTROL?

To some extent, prediction will allow you a certain degree of control, as long as you are operating in a stable environment. But the type of control we discuss here is particularly useful in uncertain, entrepreneurial situations because it does not rely on the past to predict the future.

The control you exercise can be either exogenous (you shape the environment) or endogenous (you shape yourself).

Obviously, not everything is controllable, but the entrepreneur focuses on the elements he or she can control to create outcomes that he or she finds desirable.

So What?

- Action enables entrepreneurs to exert control on things that are otherwise impossible to predict.

- With control-driven strategies, you do not need full control—you only need sufficient control so that you can move on to the next step and the next stakeholder.

- Expert entrepreneurs don't often seek unilateral control of people or markets, but they work hard to control the controllable, often with partners (see figure on Elements That Impact Entrepreneurial Venture Success in this chapter).

What Now?

- For the opportunity you are developing, work through the figure in this chapter "Elements of Entrepreneurial Success" and detail where and how you are focusing your efforts to control.

- Now identify three moves you could make to exert control of additional elements in that figure.

- Actions enable control. Are your actions consistent with your ideas on what might be controlled? What important action are you postponing today that might enable more control of your future?

Think It Through

- Re-read this chapter. It might be the most important one in this whole book.

Expert entrepreneurs have learned to control or shape the future using these basic principles:

1. Start with your means.

2. Don't risk what you can't afford to lose.

3. Build the future together with partners.

4. Be open to surprise.

These enable control, so the entrepreneur need not rely on prediction.

CHAPTER 9

The effectual logic of expert entrepreneurs

So, entrepreneurs—even expert entrepreneurs—aren't any different from the rest of us. But they do operate in a unique problem space characterized by uncertainty. Without the ability to predict in that problem space, entrepreneurs seek to shape or control outcomes as much as they can, together with their stakeholders. We contrast this difference between their fundamental assumptions about the future with those of a novice:

- *Novice.* To the extent that we can predict the future, we can control it.
- *Expert.* To the extent that we can control the future, we do not need to predict it.

Research Roots

WHY STUDY EXPERT (ENTREPRENEURS)?

Psychologists have studied expertise for years, starting by watching chess experts play. What the psychologists learned is that experts develop unique heuristics for pattern matching and problem solving within their domains, but are otherwise no smarter or otherwise different from the general population (Ericsson et al., 2006). Studying expert entrepreneurs, we extract heuristics developed in making opportunities in uncertain environments.

IN THIS CHAPTER:

- **First principle: Start with your means** *p. 97*

- **Second principle: Set affordable loss** *p. 99*

- **Third principle: Leverage contingencies** *p. 101*

- **Fourth principle: Form partnerships** *p. 103*

- **Principles rooted in reality** *p. 103*

- **Takeaway: A different way of looking at the world** *p. 106*

Practically Speaking

MAKING A CLEAN START (MEANS)

What do you do when you wake up one day in San Francisco and realize you actually want to be living on a sparsely populated Estonian Island in the middle of the Baltic Sea? You make sure you will be able to support yourself by starting a company there, of course. That is what Stephen and Ea (pronounced e-ah) Greenwood did when they moved to the island of Saaremaa in 2004. But then come the details—what kind of company, where to start, and how to make it work?

Opportunity bubbles

The answers to some of those questions lies in starting with what you have. The Greenwoods took stock of their assets:

- A derelict farmhouse on 4 hectares on Saaremaa

- The island of Saaremaa with its numerous beaches and spas, and their town of Kaarma

- Access to €10,000 in seed investment, through a friend managing an EU entrepreneur incubator

- An appreciation of a sustainable, organic lifestyle.

While it may have been difficult to conceive new venture directions after the first paragraph of this story, looking at their means it is possible to imagine the Greenwoods in the organic farming industry, in the eco-tourism business, or in the promotion of Estonia to potential US visitors.

Natural ingredients

The Greenwoods knew that startup costs for their business could not exceed the €10,000 funding they might receive from the EU (as they had no more cash to put into the venture), and decided their business had to have year-round revenue potential. After taking the complete set of inputs into consideration, the Greenwoods decided to launch a business making organic soap. Potential customers needed to wash all year long, the business required no expensive equipment, and the product would meet their personal desires for a pure and healthy offering.

Warming the water

Once the basic idea was clear, the Greenwoods were able to put together a plan that enabled them to secure EU funding. With the money, they started renovation of the farmhouse (their production facility and first retail

Practically Speaking *(continued)*

location). They also started experimenting with soap manufacture (using less expensive non-organic ingredients for practice). Stephen learned computer programming so he could set up an Internet site for the company, and the Greenwoods named the firm GoodKaarma, after their town of Kaarma. Next, the couple began putting together partnerships. They approached local spas to see whether GoodKaarma could work with them to develop customized soap products that would enhance spa goers' experience. And they worked with local designers and printers to create packaging using organic local materials.

Scrubbing sensation

Today, all of GoodKaarma's soap production happens in the farmhouse kitchen using simple household equipment and wooden moulds the Greenwoods made. The soaps are created by hand (using certified organic ingredients) in small batches of about seven kilograms. Production is year-round with all 13 varieties available on the Internet and exported to retail outlets in Ireland, UK, Sweden, Finland, Denmark, and Germany. The soaps are also available throughout Estonia and under private label at many of Saaremaa's best spas. Over 5,000 people visit the GoodKaarma Talu (farm) each summer to buy soap; many of them also participate in the Greenwoods' second business, hands-on soap-making classes. GoodKaarma was recognized by Estonian President Toomas Hendrik Ilves as a model of sustainable entrepreneurship. And perhaps most important, the Greenwoods are now permanent residents of Kaarma.

The novice's view reflects a causal logic; the expert's reflects an effectual one. While causal reasoning may or may not involve creative thinking, effectual reasoning is inherently creative. And both can be taught and learned. In other words, everybody can learn to think and act like an entrepreneur. Our claim is not that we can produce entrepreneurial genius on cue, just that each and every one of us can learn to become a better entrepreneur if we know what principles to apply.

But how? As interesting, lofty or maybe even inspirational as the idea of controlling the future may be, it doesn't answer the question of where to start and what to do. In this chapter, we begin getting specific.

In addition to identifying the concept of control as central for dealing with uncertainty, our research also identified specific heuristics that expert entrepreneurs use for control instead of predicting. These are a set of common principles, which together with the "pilot in the plane" principle constitute the logic of effectuation. As we look closely at each, giving you a feel for effectuation, we hope you begin to populate your own roadmap with more detail.

FIRST PRINCIPLE: START WITH YOUR MEANS

When expert entrepreneurs seek to build a new venture, they start with their means. These means can be grouped into three categories:

- *Who I am*—my traits, tastes, and abilities.
- *What I know*—my education, training, expertise, and experience.
- *Who I know*—my social and professional networks.

Using a combination of these means, the entrepreneur begins to imagine possibilities and take action. Most often, she starts very small with the closest means and moves almost directly into implementation without elaborate planning (fire, aim versus aim, fire). With each action, possible outcomes are reconfigured. Eventually, certain emerging effects coalesce into clearly achievable and

Practically Speaking

ENTREPRENEURIAL MANNERS (AFFORDABLE LOSS)

Brett Nicol was an MBA student at the Darden School, studying with other sharp minds and interviewing with some of the world's most prestigious corporations. In the rush of classes, college social life, and job offers, his world froze for a moment. "I was going through a drawer and found a bunch of unfinished thank-you notes to potential employers," he says. "I thought about how disappointed my mum would be with me. I'd been taught to have good manners, but it was so hard to put into action." That observation suggested a broader issue. It wasn't just thank you notes to prospective employers; it was valentines, birthdays, and all sorts of well-mannered correspondence. And talking with his classmate Nathan Tan, it wasn't a problem specific to Brett, either. So the pair decided to build a business that would help men be less forgetful.

Intention into action

Turning entrepreneurial intent into action is just as difficult as realising gentlemanly intent. A venture called Forgetful Gentleman, providing pre-stamped, manly stationery, may sound intuitive but the implementation must be handwritten by the entrepreneur. "We had stationery printed, together with a small stack of 'Elephant Cards' as brief reminders," says Nicol. "We packaged them in cigar boxes, sold them to our classmates and made enough money to do another run, which we took to farmers' markets. Each time we sold a box, we learnt what people liked and how to improve it. We met more and more people interested in helping us and we thought to ourselves—we might actually have a business here."

Manly implementation

The pair passed on fancy job offers from large firms when they graduated in order to develop Forgetful Gentleman. They debuted at the New York Gift Fair in January of 2010 with three sample boxes and a promise from the factory of inventory in a few weeks. Neiman Marcus placed an order. Suddenly pastime shifted into process as Nicol and Tan scurried to serve the store's upscale retail clientele. A few months later, an online e-commerce site was up, and the company was nominated for best new product in the National Stationery Show.

A gentleman's venture

Building a venture by making only affordable investments offers two advantages. The first is feedback. Each time Nicol and Tan went back to make another small run there was a clear option for taking customer feedback and making improvements. The second is control. Neither had to gamble more investment than was affordable. And by waiting for a customer to finance a big production run, the pair didn't have to give up an equity position to a financial investor. These features make the process a little more civilized. Which is what they set out to do in the first place.

desirable goals—landmarks begin to appear on the blank map. The end goals are the combined result of the imagination and aspirations of the entrepreneur and the people she has interacted with during the process.

SECOND PRINCIPLE: SET AFFORDABLE LOSS

In much of the business world, the manager in charge of launching a new product analyzes the market and chooses segments with the highest expected value. It is a natural reflex that is the result of years of training around a single mantra: maximize returns by selecting the optimal strategy for your target.

Expert entrepreneurs turn this logic on its head—they think in terms of affordable loss rather than expected returns. They decide what they are willing to lose rather than what they expect to make. Instead of calculating up front how much money they will need to launch their project and investing time, effort, and energy in raising that money, the effectual entrepreneur tries to estimate the downside and examines what she is willing to lose. The entrepreneur then uses the process of building the project to bring other stakeholders on board and leverage what they can afford to lose together.

Research Roots

MEASURING EFFECTUATION

Beyond the initial work by the authors of this book, Chandler et al. (2011), Blauth et al. (2014), and Werhahn et al. (2015) developed and validated survey tools that help measure effectual approaches in the context of new ventures, new products, and corporate settings, and contrast effectuation with traditional causal approaches. Their work confirms that entrepreneurs tend to effectuate more when confronted with highly uncertain situations, and that effectuation performs well in these settings.

An estimate of affordable loss does not depend on the venture but on the person. It varies from person to person and even across his or her life stages and circumstances. In the Pet Rock example (Chapter 7), Dahl had time on his hands and enough cash to prototype his idea. For the Greenwoods (GoodKaarma), affordable loss did not permit the use of cash, but did include the use of their old farmhouse.

By allowing estimates of affordable loss to drive decisions about which venture to start, entrepreneurs stop depending on prediction. Instead, they focus on cultivating opportunities that have a low failure cost and that generate more options for the future. The combination enables cheap failure and learning that can be applied to the next iteration of the opportunity.

This does not mean that entrepreneurs choose projects that won't cost a lot if they fail—or that they do not expect to make a lot of money. It simply acknowledges that uncertain new venture opportunities are difficult to value up front, whereas the investment of time, money, and other resources is quantifiable, manageable and controllable.

Practically Speaking

SURPRISE IN A GLASS (CONTINGENCIES)

Think innovation, and whiskey isn't the first market that comes to mind. Yet in the moist cellars where distillers are patiently waiting for their current batch to reach a delicious age in exotic oak barrels, they are also dreaming up new combinations. For William Grant and Sons, that dream is the perfect beer-finished blended whiskey. Which is why the firm engaged Dougal Sharp, the head brewer at Scotland's largest craft brewery, to create a special brew that would infuse the oak barrels with a malty, hoppy flavour that could become part of a whiskey during the aging process.

Success and the drain

William Grant and Sons were pleased with the results. The Grant's Ale Cask Reserve whiskey that had rested in the barrels after the beer had been discarded had an exciting and distinctive taste. But as the ever-diligent distillery staff discovered during the process of emptying the barrels, so did the beer itself. So Sharp arranged a partnership with William Grant and Sons that enabled him to take the waste beer from the whiskey manufacture and bring it to market under a new label bearing the middle names of Sharp and his brother, Innis & Gunn.

Success from the drain

From there, things have gone well for Innis & Gunn. Starting with an advance commitment from Safeway and Sainsbury's in 2002, before the brand had even been introduced, the firm shipped nearly half a million cases of beer in 2009 that would otherwise have gone to waste. The product has also been a hit internationally and is now the leading British bottled brew in beer-loving Canada and the number two bottled import ale in Sweden.

Business surprise

The story of Innis & Gunn offers two insights into innovation. The first is that many innovations are not true inventions—created from scratch— but rather new combinations of things we already have. The second is the role of surprise. Had the employees of William Grant and Sons not sampled the waste beer, the world would have one less premium micro-brew. What is also surprising is how many of the products we know and love today came from accidents and unintended results of completely different ideas.

THIRD PRINCIPLE: LEVERAGE CONTINGENCIES

If you come across lemons, make lemonade! The third principle of effectual reasoning is at the heart of entrepreneurial expertise—the ability to turn the unexpected into the profitable.

Expert entrepreneurs learn not only to work with surprises but also to take advantage of them. In most contingency plans, surprises are bad—the worst-case scenarios. But because entrepreneurs do not tie their idea to any theorized or preconceived "market," anything and everything is potentially a surprise that can lead to a valuable opportunity.

To accompany the story of Innis & Gunn, consider these three beer-compatible products:

Crisp surprise

At the pub, you might enjoy a crisp with your beer. Legend describes these popular snacks as born of customer complaint. In 1853, tired of having fried potatoes sent back to the kitchen of Moon's Lake House near Saratoga Springs, New York, because they were soggy, a frustrated George Crum sliced potatoes as thinly as he could and then fried and salted them. The intent was to frustrate the complainers by making the potatoes too thin to be picked up with a fork. But the result has gone on to please beer consumers around the world.

Transparent surprise

Perhaps after a pint in the lab, French scientist Edouard Benedictus accidentally broke a glass container and observed that the shattered pieces remained bound as a result of a plastic liquid from another experiment that had formed a thin film inside the container. The year was 1903, and safety glass was born.

Romantic surprise

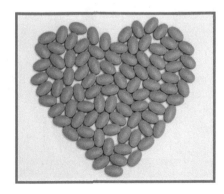

While we will leave the connection with beer to the imagination of the reader, Viagra was also discovered by accident. The active ingredient, sildenafil, never met its intended use against angina (chest pain resulting from insufficient blood flow to the heart muscle), but in clinical trials, new applications popped up. Viagra became the first oral treatment for men with erectile dysfunction.

The surprising entrepreneur

While we love to tell stories of divine inspiration, the actual origins of many products are surprises that an entrepreneur was able to transform into an opportunity. The implication is clear: those waiting for the perfect idea will have to be patient, while those taking action will likely create something interesting and then need only figure out how to make a business out of it. Maybe that will change the way you see your next surprise.

Practically Speaking

GOOD PILL HUNTING (PARTNERSHIPS)

Bright Simons began his career as an activist at an early age. As a secondary student in Ghana, he organized his friends to protest a change in the school menu with a mass appeal through a popular radio talk show. Upon graduation, he followed his early success by campaigning to drive political change that would open opportunities for people to migrate freely around the world. But, as glamorous as it sounds to be a card-carrying professional activist, governments proved difficult to influence, progress was slow, and Simons soon became interested in more impact, and maybe even a salary. So, reluctantly, he turned to business.

Phony pharmaceuticals

Unsurprisingly, he began to work on opportunities at the intersection of his home country of Ghana and his interest in creating positive social change. When he came across UN estimates that roughly half of the anti-malarial drugs sold in Africa are counterfeits, Simons decided that fake drugs might be an effort worthy of his attention. Phony anti-malarials generate £270 million per year in sales on his continent alone. Simons wanted to create a business to stop sales of fake pills. Worthy indeed—counterfeit drugs are responsible for an estimated 2,000 deaths a day globally and represent a grey industry estimated by Terry Hisey of Deloitte to be worth between £45 billion and £125 billion a year, touching Europe, America, and Japan as it does emerging markets. But how do you set up a business to stop people from selling things?

Possible partners

Clearly, legitimate pharmaceutical companies might be interested in curbing fake drug trade. But their willingness to listen to a retired activist with no technology, no product, and no experience in the industry was limited. So Simons started talking with more people. He talked with people in the laser hologram and RFID industries to see whether those technologies would enable him to tag genuine drug packages. He talked with pharmacists to understand the supply chain and the consumer buying patterns. But it was talking on his cell phone that showed him he already had all the technology he needed for a solution right in his handset.

Activist cell

In 2007, Simons set up a company called mPedigree. The idea was based on a simple service. Together with a pharmaceutical manufacturer, he would tag individual boxes of legitimate medications with a ten-digit non-duplicable code, covered by a scratch-off surface used on lottery tickets and prepaid cell cards. The end user could dial a toll-free four-digit SMS number

Practically Speaking *(continued)*

listed on the package, enter the medication code hidden under the scratch-off surface and, within a couple of seconds, receive a validation that the medication was authentic (or not), as well as information about when and where it was manufactured. Furthermore, the manufacturer could trace where and when the medication was sold and even the buyer's cell phone number. The system could close the loop on fake drugs and ensure authenticity to large numbers of patients at a very low cost, virtually anywhere in the world.

Legendary launch

Simons' first commercial pharmaceutical partner was May & Baker, tagging packages of Easadol, Loxagyl, and Artelum and validating them against a database set up in partnership with HP. Today, mPedigree collaborates with virtually all of the cellular service providers operating in Africa. The system proved so effective that mPedigree expanded from Ghana into Nigeria and Kenya, and it hopes to serve five more African countries before the year is out. Being in the business of stopping illegal business has enabled Simons to hire 12 associates, earned him an Ashoka fellowship and gained him an award from the African Leadership Institute. But, most importantly, it turned his activist aspirations into impact for real pharmacists, real manufacturers, and real patients. Who knows? Might entrepreneurship be the secret weapon of the idealist?

FOURTH PRINCIPLE: FORM PARTNERSHIPS

The final principle of effectual reasoning, which we touched upon in Chapter 2, is the focus on building partnerships rather than beating competitors. Since entrepreneurs tend to start the process without assuming the existence of a predetermined market for their idea, they don't know who their competitors will be, so detailed competitive analyses have little value.

Instead, entrepreneurs generally take the product to the nearest potential customer. Some of the people they interact with make a commitment to the venture, committing time and/or money and/or resources and, thus, self-select into the new-venture creation process.

The partnership principle dovetails well with the affordable loss principle to bring the entrepreneur's idea to market with very little cash expenditure. Obtaining pre-commitments from key stakeholders, suppliers or customers helps reduce uncertainty in the early stages of creating an enterprise. Finally, since the entrepreneur is not wedded to any particular market for his or her idea, the expanding network of strategic partnerships determines, to a great extent, which market or markets the company will eventually end up entering or creating.

PRINCIPLES ROOTED IN REALITY

Using effectuation, entrepreneurs begin with who they are, what they know, and who they know. From there, they set in motion a network of stakeholders, each of whom makes commitments that, on the one hand, increase the resources available to the network, but on the other hand, add constraints to the budding businesses because in exchange for their commitment to the venture, they expect something from the venture. As commitments collect, so do salaries, customer promises, supplier invoices, and the like. Effectual commitment impacts the process of creating a venture in important ways:

- It focuses on what is controllable about the future and the external environment.
- The entrepreneur commits only what he can afford to lose.
- The goals of the venture are determined by whoever makes commitments and what they negotiate.
- The key to the process is not the selection among alternatives but the transformation of existing realities into new alternatives.

Going back to our example of jars in Chapter 6, the entrepreneur using effectual logic says, "Whatever the initial distribution of balls in the jar, I will continue to acquire red balls and put them in the jar. I will look for other people who own red balls and induce them to become partners and add to the red balls in the jar. As time goes by, there will be so many red balls in the jar that almost every draw will obtain one. On the other hand, if my acquaintances and I have only green balls, we will put them in the jar, and when there are enough, we will create a new game where green balls win."

Of course, such a view may express hopes rather than realities, and many entrepreneurs do fail. At the same time, unpredictable markets are often an advantage for entrepreneurs because they believe they can shape the market through their own decisions and actions, working with pre-committed stakeholders and customer-partners. Together they use contingencies, the surprises along the way, as part of the raw materials that constitute Knight's jar (please see Chapter 6)

Research Roots

SUPERSIZING THE ENTREPRENEURIAL MIND

Cognition research is something that is usually associated with trying to understand what is going on inside people's heads when they say and do things. However, there is a growing awareness that this view is incomplete because it ignores one of the human brain's most powerful characteristics, which is its ability to take advantage of its physical environment, including the human body. Cognition, therefore, extends itself in three ways; it is:

- *Embedded in the natural environment.* For instance, much new product development involves hands-on tinkering with prototypes and mock-ups. These are not outcomes of previously formed ideas but instead examples of how entrepreneurs think by physically manipulating objects to "see" what works.

- *Embodied in the sense that our conceptual systems are at least partially indexed to our perceptual experiences in the world.* For example, our notion of "pivoting" a venture is based on our experiences of bodily movement.

- *Extended by being spread across multiple agents.* For example in a new venture, different team members provide specialized cognitive resources to one another, thus enabling the venture to "think."

The upshot of these insights is that entrepreneurs are adept at supersizing their minds by opportunistically co-opting aspects of their material, physical, and social context (Dew et al., 2015).

Research Roots

ENTREPRENEURS MADE THROUGH EDUCATION

Vivek Wadhwa and colleagues (2009) looked at 549 successful entrepreneurs and did not find a connection with even the few things prior research had suggested might be associated with successful entrepreneurs—entrepreneurial parentage and early entrepreneurial activity. In his study, he found that 52% of successful entrepreneurs were the first in their immediate families to start a business. Furthermore, only a quarter were interested in entrepreneurship in college. Half didn't think about it and had little interest in it when in school. Wadhwa's main finding was that education was the biggest predictor of success. Education enabled a huge advantage. Interestingly, the source of that education was not important. Firms founded by Ivy League graduates and those started by graduates of other universities experienced reasonably similar success.

Research Roots

THE SURPRISING DIFFERENCES BETWEEN EXPERT AND NOVICE DECISION-MAKING

To make a decision, generate several options, and compare them to pick the best one.

Obviously true, right? Gary Klein has spent his career researching such obvious claims and indeed, when Klein surveyed 160 students, managers, and military officers they strongly endorsed this claim. Such claims are not only widely accepted as appropriate but also form the basis of formal, rational decision theory. What could be wrong with that?

But in one study, Klein tested this claim, asking 26 highly experienced firefighters how they actually make decisions when fighting a fire. The firefighters insisted they didn't compare options. Commanders with an average of 23 years' experience fighting fires—experts in firefighting—said that when they look at an incident they just recognize what to do, handily upending the conventional wisdom about the roots of effective decision-making.

Why is this? Klein points out that this result is in fact typical. The more skilled a person is at a task the less they have to consider options. Experienced people immediately recognize familiar situations and apply an option that they already know is a good one. In contrast, novices juggle options precisely because they don't have the experience to know what works well.

Such examples show us that many conventional norms about how to make decisions are at best situational, and at worst, get in the way of effective decision-making processes. We can do better by learning from how experts in a domain actually make decisions in that domain (Klein, 2009).

Research Roots

TALENT IS OVERRATED?

Asked why some people succeed in their endeavors while others fail, one explanation commonly offered is that the successful people had a talent for it. The notion that some people are just born into the world with certain natural gifts that, once discovered, gives them superior abilities is a deeply entrenched and socially endorsed answer to why some people do extraordinarily well. It could be in sports, in music ... or in business.

Fortune Magazine's senior editor Geoff Colvin wants you to wholeheartedly reject this story about the roots of extraordinary performance and replace it with a different story based on the notion that people develop superior abilities by deliberately practicing them. Colvin reminds us that talent researchers have a surprisingly difficult time explaining what natural factors actually make someone a world-class brain surgeon or chess player, leading some researchers to argue that the idea of innate talent is simply fiction. Instead, the idea that people develop talents by practicing deliberately seems much more plausible, and a great deal of research supports this view by examining in detail what exceptionally talented people actually did to get, and stay, on top of their game.

Then what is the role of talent in entrepreneurship? Despite the simplistic appeal of explaining entrepreneurial success in terms of natural born talents, it seems more likely that entrepreneurial talents are developed the same way that talents in other areas are developed: by deep experience and practice in the domain. Being very good at the specific tasks that are needed to start new ventures successfully is more likely to come from putting in the hard work and effort to learn these skills than by hoping that it's something you were born with (Colvin, 2008).

to build the future they are constructing.

Unlike causal reasoning, which comes to life through careful planning and subsequent execution, effectual reasoning lives and breathes action. Plans are made, unmade, revised, and recast through action and interaction with others on a daily basis. Yet, at any given moment, there is always a meaningful picture that keeps the team together, a compelling story that brings more stakeholders and continues the journey that maps uncharted territories. By consciously disregarding the past, the entrepreneur effectually creates the future of his dreams.

TAKEAWAY: A DIFFERENT WAY OF LOOKING AT THE WORLD

Beyond mapping the future, effectuation carries certain assumptions about the world. Effectual thinkers:

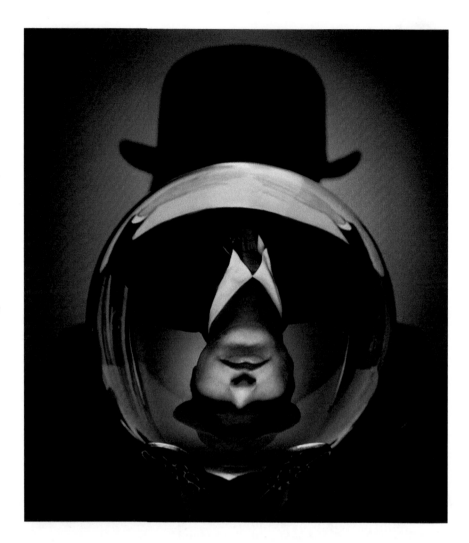

- See the world as open, still in the making. They see human action as having a genuine role. They see firms and markets as human artefacts.
- Do not see opportunities as given or outside their control. On the contrary, they believe in creating, as well as recognizing and discovering opportunities.
- Do not have an instrumental view of the world. On the contrary, they see companies as tools that allow them to create novelty for themselves and the

world; they see markets as made rather than found; and consider stakeholders to be partners in co-creation rather than simply customers or suppliers.
- Work on making success happen rather than trying to avoid failure. They see failing as a normal part of venturing. Because they are willing to fail, they often create portfolios of ventures, knowing and learning to kill those that will lead nowhere and nurture those with potential.

Now you have a complete overview of the logic underlying effectuation. The next section of this book will dot the "i"s and cross the "t"s of the principles outlined here and explicitly relate them to the nitty-gritty details of starting a new venture.

■ ■ ■

So What?

Start with your Means.

Set your Affordable Loss.

Leverage Contingencies.

Develop Committed Partners.

Expert entrepreneurs regularly turn our MBA lessons upside down.

What Now?

☐ Think about the companies you admire. To what extent did the principles in this chapter contribute to their creation/success?

☐ For the opportunity you are working on, detail your thoughts on the use of each of the principles. Where do you have momentum?

☐ Is the opportunity you are developing an expression of YOU?

☐ Do others understand how your means and the opportunity deeply connect?

☐ Do you know in detail how much time/money you can afford to lose in its pursuit?

☐ What has surprised you as you've developed the opportunity? Did it change you or your approach?

☐ What partners have truly joined the cause? Have you asked them for concrete support of the cause?

Think It Through

☐ What are the consequences of using only one or two of the effectual principles?

☐ How do the principles outlined in this chapter reinforce or undermine the concept of control in the prior chapter?

☐ What might be the consequence of using these principles in a setting that is very predictable?

The nuts and bolts of venturing: Effectuation in action

This section is the heart of the book—the point where the venture gets started. We hope you notice the change in tone from one that is more thoughtful in the first two sections to one that is more action-oriented in this section. Each of the effectual principles is laid out in detail in the even numbered chapters, while the odd numbered chapters explain how to put the principles to use. So whether you use this section to organize yourself for your venture, or you navigate through the section as you navigate through the first steps of starting up, we wish you fair winds and following seas.

PART III

We have come to think of the actual as one among many possible worlds.

We need to repaint that picture.

All possible worlds lie within the actual.

Nelson Goodman (1983)

The bird-in-hand principle: Start with what you have

■ ■ ■

After years of anticipation, huge investments, and months of preparation, the ancient mariners had to face the day of reckoning: the day they cast free of the dock where their vessel was safely tied, and ventured forth into the uncertain sea.

When facing the prospect of entering the entrepreneurial world, you may feel the same sense of leaving a safe harbor. But it need not be so.

So far, we've dispelled several myths about entrepreneurship—myths that make creating a venture seem like a much more daunting endeavor than it is. We've seen that opportunities are not lying around waiting to be found but are created by the entrepreneur and his or her

partners, so it's not critical or even necessary to have the perfect idea when you leave the dock. The idea will more likely be created as a result of setting out on the journey. We've learned that entrepreneurs aren't looking to take huge risks, nor are they genius forecasters; instead, they risk only what they can afford to lose and they seek to control and shape the future rather than making futile predictions. We've learned that many entrepreneurs don't necessarily "take the plunge"; they set out gradually, constructing the business in components while preserving the ability to return to the dock. Finally, we've seen that success and failure are a matter of perspective—how you define those terms depends on what you and your partners want to do.

Expert entrepreneurs, we've seen, follow a logic of effectuation, working with readily available resources and taking small steps into uncertainty, thus shaping the future as they go. Several principles guide the effectual entrepreneur.

In this chapter, we explore the first principle—working with the means at your disposal. We call this the bird-in-hand principle after the old saying that "a bird in hand is worth two in the bush."

We begin by looking at how effectual entrepreneurs start with means, while causal entrepreneurs start with goals, and the difference between the two approaches. We then explore the idea of means in greater detail, helping you work with what you already have (but may not be aware of).

WHAT DO WE MEAN BY "START WITH YOUR MEANS?"

People focus so much on whether they will be successful or not, whether their idea is a good one or not, that they forget about all the things they could be doing with what they already have—their means. There are three categories of means available to all of us: who we are (traits, abilities, attributes), what we know (expertise and experience), and who we know (social networks).

For the effectual entrepreneur, the fundamental question is, "What effects can I create, given who I am, what I know and who I know?" He or she begins by imagining several possible courses of action, the consequences of which are, for the most part, uncertain. The entrepreneur evaluates these courses of action in terms of what

resources need to be put at risk to pursue each. Any course of action needs to have the possibility of becoming valuable, but rather than select on an expected upside, she prioritizes them according to which possibility is associated with the most acceptable downside.

The entrepreneur's decision about what to pursue is also co-determined by stakeholders willing to commit resources. As they contribute various resources, according to their own means and affordable loss, stakeholders set immediate agendas and generate new sub-goals for the venture, thus helping shape it.

This effectual approach stands in stark contrast to the causal approach. The crux of the difference between the two is how you think about goals and means. As the diagram on the next page illustrates, with the causal

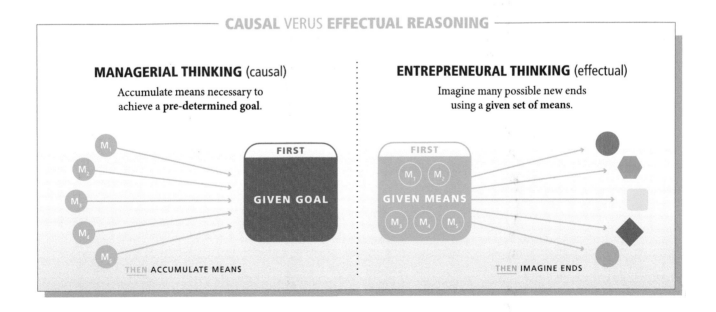

CAUSAL VERUS EFFECTUAL REASONING

MANAGERIAL THINKING (causal)

Accumulate means necessary to achieve a **pre-determined goal**.

M₁ M₂ M₃ M₄ M₅

FIRST

GIVEN GOAL

THEN ACCUMULATE MEANS

ENTREPRENEURAL THINKING (effectual)

Imagine many possible new ends using a **given set of means**.

FIRST

GIVEN MEANS

M₁ M₂ M₃ M₄ M₅

THEN IMAGINE ENDS

Practically Speaking

POWER OF PERSONALITY

Born Josephine Esther Mentzer, Estée Lauder created a cosmetic giant in the first half of the twentieth century by unabashedly leveraging both what she loved and hated about her heritage to reinvent herself. Starting with her name, which she changed from Esty to Estée and her married name of Lauter to Lauder, she reached out to other women, helping them see that they, too, could be whoever they wanted to be.

A beautiful mind

Even in her early days in business, instead of greeting potential customers with the usual, "May I help you?" the self-created Estée Lauder would approach women in beauty parlors and say, "I have something that would look perfect on you, madam. May I show you how to apply it?" Later, in places like Saks Fifth Avenue and Neiman Marcus, she would say, "Try this. I am Estée Lauder, and these are the most wonderful beauty products in the world."

A beautiful approach

Because Lauder did not have the kind of money her competitors, such as Revlon, were spending on ad campaigns, she gave out free samples—a practice unheard of in the industry at the time and jeered at by professionals as a recipe for disaster, tantamount to "giving away her whole business." However, Lauder averred this was "the most honest way to do business," and it turned out that people who trooped into the store to get free samples ended up not only buying products but also acting as word-of-mouth evangelists—something no ad budget could buy.

Her approach to her retailer customers was also driven by her distinct personality—who she was. Stanley Marcus, head of the Texas-based department store, described her as "… a very determined salesperson; she pushed her way into acceptance. She was determined—and gracious and lovely through it all. It was easier to say yes to Estée than to say no."

approach, you begin with clear goals. These goals may be externally imposed (e.g. maximization of shareholder value in a public corporation), or self-imposed (e.g. I want to make US$10 million before I am 40 years old). In both cases, the goals are given, so the only real decision is how to accumulate the resources necessary to achieve them. Often, this question leads to the formation of a vision that will induce the stakeholders who possess those resources to come on board. The accumulation of resources becomes the predominant purpose of the venture, and stakeholders are seen primarily as resource providers.

So, effectuation is means-driven and the causal approach is goals-driven. But aren't entrepreneurs highly goal-driven individuals?

Yes. And the important thing to realize is that goals exist in hierarchies. It is not that effectual entrepreneurs have no goals; indeed, they may have quite ambitious higher-level goals. But when push comes to shove and the choice is to be tethered either to means or to specific lower-level goals, they are more likely to change those goals rather than chase means they have no control over. Understanding that goals exist in hierarchies leads to two important insights: (1) higher-level goals, such as wanting to be a millionaire by age 40, do not tell you what you should do on the first day of your new venture; and (2) tying yourself down to specific lower-level goals, such as starting an upscale restaurant in a high-income neighborhood, focuses your

entrepreneurial actions on pursuing resources you currently do not possess. Starting with what you can do with your readily available means is a practical approach, helping you take action now toward building your new enterprise without giving up your higher-level, longer-term goals, such as becoming financially successful or being your own boss.

What are some of the advantages of being means-driven rather than goal-driven?

- You are not chasing investors.
- You are not waiting for the perfect opportunity or the perfect set of resources.
- You are working with your strengths without having to overcome your weaknesses first.

- You attract co-creative stakeholders, who want to shape goals, not just provide resources.
- You are increasing the possible slate of stakeholders who can self-select into your venture.
- You are increasing the probability of innovative surprises.
- You are increasing the likelihood of finding or creating opportunities that are a better fit for you.
- You are decreasing the cost of possible failure, as you only risk means that are affordable to lose, and by doing that:
- You are increasing the likelihood that failures will be learning experiences that you can recover from faster and build on when you are ready to try again.
- You are forcing yourself to get creative with meager resources, including slack resources and even waste.

Practically Speaking

WORKING WITH WHAT YOU HAVE

Barbara Corcoran runs a real estate empire worth US$4 billion. In her book *Use What You've Got* (Corcoran and Littlefield, 2003: 6), she recounts a crucial piece of advice her mother passed along: If you don't have big breasts, put ribbons in your pigtails. She learned this during her job as a waitress, when she felt her life was going nowhere fast. One day she came home complaining to her mother that the other waitresses were getting all the attention because they had big breasts and she did not. Her mother replied, "You're going to have to learn to use what you've got. Since you don't have big breasts, why don't you tie some ribbons on your pigtails and just be as sweet as you are." Which is exactly what she did . . .

Lesson: Forget about what you don't have and focus on what you have.

WHO I AM: THE UNBEATABLE COMPETITIVE ADVANTAGE

We do not usually think of ourselves as the primary source of valuable new opportunities or as the basis for unique competitive advantages. Yet a little reflection will show this can indeed be true and often is.

One of the most beautiful things about entrepreneurship is that there are probably as many high-potential opportunities as there are individuals. Unlike other professions, such as medicine, accounting, dance, or sports, there is no one particular set of skills, abilities, or personality types necessary and sufficient for entrepreneurial success. An accountancy-based enterprise, such as H&R Block, can co-exist with an athletics-based firm, such as Nike, on the list of the most successful companies ever built. Similarly, a flamboyant risk taker, such as Mark Cuban, and a prudent calculator, such as Daniel Snyder, can both build thriving entrepreneurial careers resulting in eventual ownership of sports teams (the Dallas Mavericks in the case of Cuban and the Washington Redskins in the case of Snyder).

If we begin with the premise that who we are and what makes us unique could be not only the starting point but also the basic ingredient of the venture and market opportunity we set out to create, we throw open the door to courses of action we would otherwise be blind to. In fact, the success of many enterprises can be traced to the idiosyncratic circumstances and eccentric quirks of their founders.

WHAT I KNOW: BRINGING LEARNING TO THE VENTURE

Think about all you know, the facts, wisdom, and insight you've gained from your idiosyncratic life experiences. Now consider that

Practically Speaking

MANY HAPPY RETURNS

Entrepreneurs begin the venture creation process with a body of knowledge, but their knowledge grows along the way and shapes their course of action. Ann DeLaVergne started with a very small idea—one the size of an envelope. While looking at the stack of used envelopes in her recycling bin, it occurred to her that a lot of small envelopes could have a big impact.

Back of the envelope math

Through further investigation, Ann learned that at least 81 billion return envelopes are produced and sent through the US mail each year. This is tough on the environment—using 1.8 billion tons of wood, generating 1 billion pounds of greenhouse gases, and requiring more than 71 trillion BTUs of energy to process and transport. It's tough on the bottom line too, as return envelopes represent between 15% and 45% of a business' direct mailing costs.

Bulk post

An organic farmer with a philosophy of reuse, Ann already saved large envelopes to send out again herself. But what if she could apply that thinking to 81 billion return envelopes? With that idea, Ann founded EcoEnvelopes, a firm built on the simple goal of using one envelope instead of two for round-trip business mail transactions.

Practically Speaking *(continued)*

Pen pals

Figuring out how to transform her small idea into an opportunity that would have a big impact, however, was not obvious. So Ann, who had also worked as a graphic designer, sat down at her kitchen table with some office supplies and a sewing machine (to make perforations in paper) and prototyped her reusable envelope idea. Her first effort yielded 10 envelopes, which she mailed off to friends around the country. When all 10 came back, she knew she was on to something.

Direct mail community

Partnerships and communities can provide the critical mass for an entrepreneurial idea. Ann began extending her community beyond her friends to include businesses that both use the mail and have an environmental mission. The first were the Land Stewardship Project and the Minnesota Landscape Arboretum. In addition to feeling better about their direct mail efforts and saving money, these organizations increased response rates to their direct mail campaigns to as high as 8% (roughly 10 times the average) using EcoEnvelopes.

The check in the mail

Today, EcoEnvelopes produces and markets a range of patented zip-close reusable envelopes, manufactured with paper from managed forests and containing up to 100% post-consumer waste content. In January 2008, EcoEnvelopes received a US$570,000 investment from TC Angels—the largest single investment the group had made to date—to help Ann hire employees, secure patents, and take her invention to companies around the globe. Just a month later, the US Postal Service granted Ann a National Consumer Ruling, making EcoEnvelopes the first reusable envelope certified for standard mail. From there, her returns have continued to grow.

Practically Speaking

NEW VENTURE RECIPE

If you were going into the restaurant business, you'd probably want to be Claus Meyer. His Copenhagen-based eatery Noma, was hailed as the best restaurant on the planet from 2010 to 2014 by Restaurant Magazine. Featuring Nordic cuisine that includes fresh seafood, local herbs, and radishes in edible "soil," Noma draws superlatives from critics that go way beyond delicious and mouth watering. So what are the ingredients behind its success?

Without a recipe

Meyer grew up in Denmark, an environment where food was neither pleasure nor luxury, but necessity. Intending to become a banker when he was a student, Meyer spent a year in the south of France. There, the purpose of food took on new meaning. It was more than nutrition—it was beauty. At the age of 21, he returned to Denmark and "knew deeply inside that I wanted to change Danish food culture … and I believed I could do it." It was a grand vision for someone yet to finish university, and one with no clear starting point.

From the fridge

Cooking meals and starting new ventures have a lot in common, as Meyer himself points out. One way is to start with a tried and tested recipe, get the necessary ingredients, follow instructions carefully, and produce a company. The other is to open the refrigerator, peer inside and create something—a new dish—an unexpected business model—an entirely innovative venture no one involved could have predicted in advance. Meyer took the second path, capitalizing on the availability of the university kitchen to launch his first venture, a catering and delivery business for students run with the benefit of his Raleigh bicycle.

Into the kitchen

Like many meals, new ventures often start like Meyer's: a function of what is available and who wants to tie on an apron. Indeed, cooks of every kind and even non-cooks have since joined with him and contributed their own ingredients and flavors to the mix. The result is that Meyer and his partners have launched nearly a venture a year over the last 25 years. The Meyer Group imports chocolate to Scandinavia with partner Søren Sylvest, a relationship that cooked up ventures in coffee importing as well as cafés. With Mette Martinussen, Meyer created a theater-like restaurant and also built a factory to manufacture soy cakes. He has hosted a television cookery show and yet more collaboration has taken him into the hotel business, corporate catering, food consulting, and a non-profit food laboratory. And that's not all. Meyer has established a micro vinegar brewery, an organic commercial orchard, and a boutique bakery. He has authored several cookbooks, gives lectures,

Practically Speaking *(continued)*

and he is active in health and wellness research. Even the famed Noma, which has dealt a fatal blow to jokes about Nordic cuisine being an oxymoron, is a partnership with kitchen chef René Redzepi.

Venture à la mode

In many ways, Meyer has come full circle. Twenty-five years later, he can fairly claim a recipe for his vision. Not through any one of his ventures, though, but through the process that led to the accumulation of them all. Whether it's changing Danish food culture or changing the world, real entrepreneurship kneads together an enormous amount of information culled from the experiences of large numbers of people such as those who contributed in some greater or lesser way to the runaway success of Noma. The vision imbibes the resultant flavors into a heady blend that appears to have always been part of the recipe. Entrepreneurship is not an all-or-nothing heroic act associated with the unique insight of a single chef. It is about learning, interaction, and application combined through acts of continual co-creation. It starts with Meyer taking the first step and then pushing onward step after step, partner by partner—not informed by a plan, but by the previous step, the people around him, and the available resources at each stage. So now that your appetite is whetted, what's in your fridge?

everyone has their own distinct stock of knowledge, informed by their own experiences. It's no wonder that two entrepreneurs, at the same starting point and in the same environment, will come up with two completely different ventures.

Because of the corridor principle, entrepreneurs may be better off simply getting started and developing opportunities as they walk down the corridor. And getting started is easier with the advantage of resources, information, and knowledge you already have.

WHO I KNOW: SIX DEGREES OF SEPARATION

Expert entrepreneurs build firms by building stakeholder networks— adding other people's means to their own.

Research Roots

THE SIX DEGREES OF SEPARATION

A 1929 short story by a Hungarian writer (Karinthy, 1929) suggested that all individuals are connected to all others by a maximum of six other individuals. Human relationships are both fascinating and important to understanding how we interact, and in 1967, Stanley Milgram (1967: 61–67) addressed the idea of how interconnected human beings are in an academic publication.

Countless studies have since been conducted to measure connectedness. While the exact number of links between people differs depending on the population and the types of links, it is generally found to be relatively small. So whether you want to call it "six degrees of separation" or the "small-world" phenomenon, your network and the network of your network extends to everyone on the planet.

Research Roots

THE CORRIDOR PRINCIPLE

Robert Ronstadt (1988: 31–40) developed the Corridor Principle to describe how new and unintended opportunities often arise for entrepreneurs when they are launching a new venture. Picture yourself standing at the entrance of a corridor. Until you proceed down the corridor, it is impossible to know what it holds, but as you move along you gain knowledge and insight. The Corridor Principle explains how entrepreneurs, simply by opening a door and pursuing one opportunity, create other opportunities (other corridors) they otherwise would not or could not have imagined.

In thinking about creating such a network, consider three sources of stakeholders. The first source is the people who are directly and perhaps immediately accessible to you: friends, family, and acquaintances.

The second is people you meet serendipitously, by chance or accident. And the third source is those you don't know directly, but they are linked to you through people you do know. We all exist in a network of connections: we know people who know people who know people (and on and on) who could become helpful partners. If you believe the "six degrees of separation" theory, you'd need to move only six steps out to be connected to everyone in the world. Distant contacts can be some of the most valuable because they may offer perspectives and ideas you've never encountered before. This is what's known as "the strength of weak ties."

HOW IT WORKS

To see how this means-driven process works, consider examples from the history of entrepreneurship. The entrepreneurs who founded Sears, Staples, Starbucks, CNN, and many other companies used their means to shape, step by step, their opportunities. Their enduring ventures mostly started small, without elaborate market analyses.

INVENTORY YOUR MEANS

Who you know		What you know		Who you are	
Your Rolodex (LinkedIn, Facebook)		Your prior knowledge and education		Tastes, values, and preferences	
Classmates, alumni		Knowledge from your job		Passions	
Serendipitous encounters		Knowledge from your life		Hobbies	
The strangers in your life		Informal learning, hobbies		Interests	

ONE TECHNOLOGY → EIGHT ENTREPRENEURS → EIGHT DIFFERENT IDEAS

Consider a study of eight entrepreneurs who sought to commercialize a 3DP (three-dimensional printing) technology when it was being developed at MIT. All eight entrepreneurs heard about 3DP technology from someone directly involved in its development. None of the entrepreneurs contacted MIT's Technology Licensing Office. And none of the entrepreneurs contacted each other. The fascinating thing is that each of the eight entrepreneurs envisioned a different idea for what to do with three-dimensional printing—differences that could be traced back to unique knowledge or experiences specific to each of the individuals (Shane, 2000).

The entrepreneurs wove together the mundane realities of who they were, what they knew, and who they knew into projects that they believed were worth doing. They then continually added to their projects, pushing them outward, reshaping them to work with new stakeholders, stretching themselves—just a bit at a time to reach higher and farther—until eventually they transformed both their means and ends into unimagined new possibilities.

MAP YOUR MEANS

Start by printing off a one-page version of your resume. Then start adding things. Be creative about what you consider; it needn't be things you would normally include in a resume. To get started, look back at your life. What means did you acquire or build:

- As a teenager
- At school
- At university
- In your first, second . . . job
- In your private life
- With your hobbies, activities
- From your parents?

Practically Speaking

PICTURE PERFECT

Now that everyone with a cell phone is by definition carrying a high quality camera, picture taking is seeing enormous growth. But what will you do with all those precious images? You could email them, post them on Facebook or Instagram, or just let them accumulate on your hard drive.

Picture delivery

Deb Whitman has an alternative: a way to make those photos magically appear on the screens of close friends and relatives who want to enjoy your pictures again and again. Instead of them searching for your latest, you decide which pictures will automatically be displayed on their onscreen photo frame. Regardless of whether this idea appeals to you, Photo Mambo (the name of her new company and service) and Whitman embody two useful aspects of entrepreneurship.

Mambo means

The first is where ideas come from. Though entrepreneurship lore celebrates the "aha moment" (which generally occurs in the shower—hopefully without a camera), the story of Photo Mambo is less picture perfect, and more consistent with how most new ventures come to be. Before appointing herself founder and CEO of Photo Mambo, Whitman worked at Adobe with responsibility for digital imaging software such as Photoshop. Rewind further and she worked in digital media presentation at Microsoft. Her experience with

Practically Speaking *(continued)*

consumer software goes back to the 1980s, when she was responsible for marketing the personal finance package Quicken, at Intuit. So the idea for Photo Mambo represents a combination of experience and interests of a mother born in the Midwest who wants to share her daughter's photographs with non-technical family members.

Action shot

The second interesting point that this story raises is where action comes from. Because Whitman worked in software, she knew the idea was feasible and what level of effort it would take to create it. Because she knew people who understand digital photography, it was easy for her to find advice and collaborators. Someone with experience in direct mail might have taken the same idea and created a monthly post card service. But Whitman used what she knew, got up in the morning and started taking action. Which is really what makes her an entrepreneur.

How would your friends, colleagues, family, or acquaintances describe your means?

Be as broad as you can. You will certainly need more room than we provide in the "Inventory Your Means" table, but we hope this gives you a place to start.

SLACK AND OTHER RESOURCES YOU DON'T EVEN KNOW YOU HAVE

Sometimes unusual opportunities and the successful ventures built on them are forged from resources you don't even recognize as resources in the first place. Truth is the world is full of "slack"—resources left over from other uses or simply lying around because nobody has paid attention to them.

Slack can include anything from waste to empty space to loopholes in the law to buffers created for emergencies. Consider the story of billionaire J.R. Simplot, the founder of potato processing plants and creator of the first frozen french fries. He began his career by collecting hogs set for slaughter by farmers who feared a pork surplus. Simplot fed the hogs until demand returned and when he sold them to the meat companies, made enough money to buy an electric potato sorter. Throughout his career, Simplot was quick at picking up slack resources that he transformed into valuable products, often appearing to snatch opportunities right from under the noses of his competition.

Practically Speaking

DESTINATION UNKNOWN

The story of Airbnb illustrates how not having any means can even provide the basis for a new venture. Born of the need to pay their rent, Joe Gebbia and Brian Chesky started offering lodging on air mattresses and breakfast in their apartment in order to fund their own living situation. To their surprise, three people showed up, and an idea was born. But in order to achieve the success that Airbnb enjoys today, the pair employed many of their other means, from their effort to launch the venture at SXSW, to their ability to nicely photograph listed houses, to the people they knew and brought into the venture.

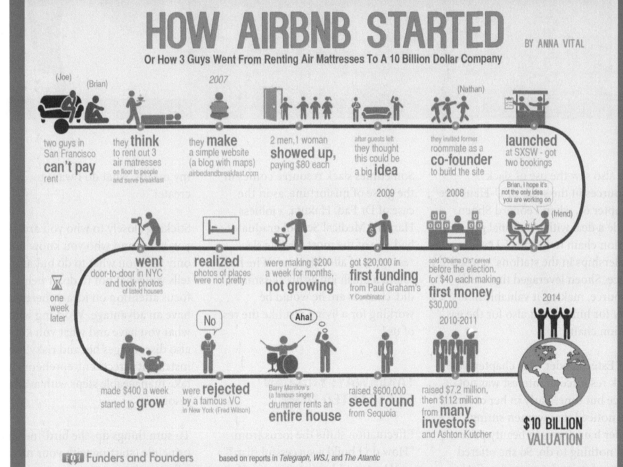

Practically Speaking

UP THE WALL

Dr Fad started out as Ken Hakuta, a Harvard Medical School graduate who was disgruntled by the fact that his classmates all seemed to have better job offers than he did. As he mulled over his situation, he nonchalantly threw around a slimy, sticky, octopus-shaped rubber toy that his mother had sent from Japan for his children. In 1982, they were the only toys that could climb down walls. Ken bought US$100,000 worth of the toys, thinking that if his venture failed he could go back to Japan. He started selling them to small gift shops and toy stores in Washington, D.C., where he lived. And then one day CBS evening news did a feature on them, turning the Wacky WallWalkers into an overnight hit. Over 240 million Wacky WallWalkers were sold, making it one of the biggest selling fads ever. Dr Fad ran his own shows about fads and published a bestseller called: How to Create Your Own Fad and Make a Million Dollars (1989).

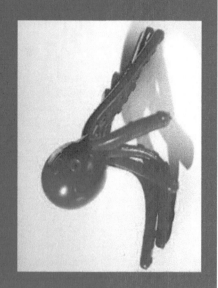

We also saw the use of slack resources in the story of U-Haul (see Chapter 6), when Leonard Shoen made a deal with a national gas station chain to locate U-Haul dealerships in the stations' unused space. Shoen leveraged that slack resource, making it valuable not only for himself but also for the gas station chain.

For Estée Lauder (this chapter), the slack resource of interest was not space but time. Early in her career, she noticed that women sitting under hair dryers in beauty parlors had nothing to do. So she offered them a free makeover using Estée Lauder creams and lotions. Most would accept, and many would end up buying some of the products to use at home.

Sometimes slack resource comes in the guise of misfortune, as in the case of Dr Fad. Hakuta, a jobless Harvard Medical School graduate had one of the most flexible slack resources of all—his time. If he had found a plush job as his classmates did, chances are he would be working for a living just like the rest of us.

TAKEAWAY: YOU CAN GET STARTED NOW

Effectuation shifts the focus from "How do I build a successful firm?" or "How can I become a successful entrepreneur?" to "What types of ideas and opportunities should I pursue, given who I am, what I know, and who I know?" and "Given

my means, what do I want to create?"

Sticking closely to who you are, what you know and who you know not only tells you what to do but also tells you what not to do. It helps focus attention on ideas where you have an advantage. Working with what you have and what you know also discourages big and risky leaps; instead, it directs entrepreneurs to take manageable steps with available resources.

To sum things up, the bird-in-hand principle (starting with your means) tells you that you can get going inexpensively, and that your means form the basis of your own competitive advantage. Combined with your partners' means and commitments, the venture you create will be both feasible and unique.

When you use the bird-in-hand principle, starting a new venture is no longer an incredibly risky act of heroism. It is something you can do within the constraints and possibilities of your normal life. You can start a new venture anytime you want. You can get started now.

So What?

Everyone has means—and everyone is different—which explains how even starting with the same idea, each person who begins taking action toward it creates something that is in some way unique.

Don't focus on what you don't have, find ways you can take advantage of who you are, who you know, and what you know.

What Now?

- ☐ If you are having trouble deciding on an idea, how about starting with more than one idea at once and let the dominant path self-select in the process through stakeholder commitments?

- ☐ Create an elevator pitch for yourself—if you had to sell stock in yourself, what would your prospectus look like? Think means not goals.

- ☐ Who are you? What sorts of things do you do and work on when you can do anything?

- ☐ Whom do you know?

- ☐ What sort of slack resources might you use together?

- ☐ What do you know? It's not just expertise in doing things, it can also be knowing about people, and who needs what, or how to combine slack resources in new ways.

Think It Through

- ☐ In goal-oriented societies, how can you develop a means-oriented mindset?

- ☐ In what ways might having specific goals for your venture impede your progress?

- ☐ Without goals, how can you know if you are successful?

- ☐ What if you can't imagine anything worth pursuing from your current means (hint: that's what Chapter 11 is about)?

An entrepreneur is a person who is willing and able to convert a new idea or invention into a successful innovation, simultaneously creating new products and business models largely responsible for the dynamism of industries and long-run economic growth.
Joseph A. Schumpeter
(1942)

Innovation is not mysterious.

There are simple approaches that can be easily learned and applied.

Transforming means into something valuable

■ ■ ■

You've taken stock of your means—you know who you are, what you know, and who you know. But how do you turn all that into something valuable—into a new product, a new venture or even a new market? Clearly, there is a critical step involved, but it's not magic. It's transformation.

How do entrepreneurs transform mundane means into valuable results? To answer that question, we created an experiment— Venturing—that we describe in this chapter. The Venturing experiment allowed us to watch entrepreneurs transform ideas into opportunities. And in doing so, we were able to remove some of the mystery that surrounds entrepreneurs.

From the Venturing experiment, we observed general types of transformations. In this chapter, we describe the Venturing experiment, describe each type of transformation, provide real-world examples of each and look at how you can create your own transformations.

As you work your way through the chapter, stop at each transformation type and look at the things around you—everything from the features of the chair you are sitting in to the water you are drinking. Imagine the transformations that are at the heart of the things you use every day. What pieces came together to join hydraulics with office furniture so it's easy to scoot your chair up and

THE VENTURING SCENARIO (EXACTLY AS IT WAS PRESENTED)

Introduction

In the following experiment, you will solve two decision problems. These problems arise in the context of building a new company for an imaginary product. A detailed description of the product follows this introduction.

Although the product is imaginary, it is technically feasible and financially viable. The data for the problems have been obtained through realistic market research—the kind of market research used in developing a real-world business plan. So far, the entrepreneurs who have participated in this study found the project both interesting and feasible.

Before you start on the product description and the problems, I do need one act of creative imagination on your part. I request you to put yourself in the role of the lead entrepreneur in building this company—i.e. you have very little money of your own to start this company, and you have your experience.

Description of the product

You have created a computer game of entrepreneurship. You believe you can combine this game with some educational material and profiles of successful entrepreneurs to make an excellent teaching tool for entrepreneurship. Your inspiration for the product came from several reports in the newspapers and magazines about the increasing demand for entrepreneurship education and the fact that a curriculum involving entrepreneurship, even at the junior high or high school level, induces students to learn not only business-related topics but math, science, and communication skills as well.

The game part of the product consists of a simulated environment for starting and running a company. There are separate sub-simulations of markets, competitors, regulators, macroeconomic factors, and a random factor for "luck." The game has a sophisticated multi-media interface—for example, a 3D office where phones ring with messages from the market, a TV that will provide macroeconomic information when switched on and simulated managerial staff whom the player (CEO) can consult in making decisions. At the beginning of the game the player can choose from a variety of businesses and the type of business s/he wants to start (e.g. manufacturing, personal services, software, etc.) and has to make decisions such as which market segment to sell to, how many people to hire, what type of financing to go for, etc. During the game the player has to make production decisions such as how much to produce, whether to build new warehouses or negotiate with trucking companies, etc.; marketing decisions such as which distribution channels to use, which media to advertise in, and so on; management decisions involving hiring, training, promoting and firing of employees, and so on. An accounting subroutine tracks and computes the implications of the various decisions for the bottom line. The simulation's responses to the player's decisions permit a range of possible outcomes—from bankruptcy to a "hockey stick."

You have taken all possible precautions regarding intellectual property. The name of your company is Entrepreneurship, Inc. The name of the product is Venturing.

down? How did sports equipment and kitchenware merge to put that designer re-useable water bottle on your desk?

Once you start looking, you will see transformations everywhere, because, of course, everything was created from something.

THE VENTURING EXPERIMENT

The Venturing experiment presented people with an uncertain business situation that allowed a wide range of possible strategies and outcomes. We asked people to talk their way through how they would develop an imaginary company preparing to offer an imaginary entrepreneurship game called Venturing.

Based on the description of the idea, people were asked to answer a set of questions pertaining to the development of an initial market for the product and think aloud continuously during the task. Their comments were collected on tape and transcribed for coding and analysis.

In order to see strategies unique to expert entrepreneurs, we carefully identified three groups of participants so we could compare the differences. Expert entrepreneurs had, either as individuals or as part of a team, founded one or more companies, remained with at least one company they founded for more than 10 years, and taken it public.

Research Roots

SO, YOU WANT TO BE A CREATIVE GENIUS AT WORK?

Many factors have been associated with a person's creativity, including intrinsic motivation, aspects of personality, degree of external communication and supportive work environments. Teresa Amabile pioneered research on creativity in organizations over three decades ago. Her recent work has turned to the immediate drivers of creativity, in particular the role of mood.

In one study, Amabile and her colleagues tracked the relationship between moods and the creativity of individuals working on new product development and process innovation projects. Over 200 subjects participated from seven firms in three different industries. Subjects gave daily reports regarding how they were feeling about work that day as well as the events that happened that day. Findings indicated that an individual's creativity at work was preceded by positive feelings the day before. The researchers suggest this relationship occurs because positive feelings facilitate more variation in thoughts; therefore, they enable individuals to make new, creative associations. This process seems to be played out overnight, with sleep performing an important role in enabling the creative process (Amabile et al., 2005).

We compared the expert entrepreneurs with a sample of MBA students and with a sample of expert corporate managers who had spent a minimum of 10 years operating in a multinational organization consisting of more than 500 individuals.

A BIG DIFFERENCE: TRANSFORMATION TYPES

The results of the Venturing experiment clearly showed that expert entrepreneurs had acquired a unique set of decision-making strategies that form the basis of the effectual logic described in this book.

In addition to those strategies (means, affordable loss, partnerships, and contingency), the experts were very creative in the way they used the strategies to transform situations into opportunities. Let's look at the four most common transformation types we observed from our expert entrepreneurs (we'll offer a more complete list later in the chapter).

Deleting/supplementing

In the context of a new venture, deleting/supplementing involves looking at a product or service and thinking about which features you may want to remove or add in order

to increase its attractiveness. There is really no limit to the possibilities for adding and removing product or service features in order to transform an offering. New elements can be related to the original offering in some way or from a completely unrelated domain.

Ruth Owades (Chapter 15) provides a good example of deleting. Her company, Calyx and Corolla, weeded out florists from the fresh flower delivery process by mailing flowers direct from the growers to the customers via Federal Express. By doing so, she not only eliminated the intermediary but also provided her customers with fresher, longer-lasting flowers.

Composing/decomposing

Reorganizing material that is already there (in contrast with the first approach, which takes away or adds material to or from the existing set) is what we mean by composing and decomposing.

In the context of a new venture, this means taking stock of what you have to offer—a product, a service, a process—and pulling it apart to recombine the elements in a new way. It's a process similar to pulling apart Lego blocks and putting them together to create something new.

As you read the story of Mr Manon and his Chocolate Magic, appreciate how he composes and decomposes with ideas ranging from confectionary to tourism to magic.

Practically Speaking

CHOCOLATE MAGIC

Tucked in a quiet Brussels suburb behind an unassuming garage door is the workshop of Manon Chocolatier. As easy as it is to miss the small sign, once inside the garage it expands into Christian (known as Mr Manon) Vanderkerken's sanctuary of chocolate. The operation, founded in 1935 by Manon's grandfather, handcrafts 80 different types of bonbons using all natural ingredients, some of which come from Manon's own garden. The treasured confections are offered at an equally unassuming retail location in downtown Brussels and those chocolates that are not too delicate to travel are exported to international destinations that include Europe, Japan, and the US.

Exclusive Excursion

Around 17 years ago, Manon received a call. The caller was not someone asking to have a shipment of Manon's creations express delivered for a special occasion, as was usually the case; instead, he was looking to gain admittance to Manon's refuge—he wanted a private tour of the workshop. Interested to share his expertise and intrigued by the possibility of some direct marketing for the company, Manon agreed.

Enchanted recipe

Combining his vast knowledge of chocolate with a bit of magic learned from an old Chinese man, Manon created a tour that involved hands-on education, tasting, vintage chocolate-making equipment and a surprise ingredient thrown in for good measure. The result was such a success that word got out, and Manon began offering regular tours.

Mr Manon says:

When I did my first tour, it was for fun. Twelve years later, I still do the tours for fun. I never really imagined it as a business, but a chance to get paid for something I like doing anyway. In addition to eating 250 grams of dark chocolate per day (for health), I think that everyone should know how chocolate is made, and that is my real goal.

Supernatural supplement

Roughly, 3,000 people visit the enclave each year. At €12 per person (€10 for groups of 15 or more during the week), Manon is not in much danger of getting wealthy and retiring from tour proceeds. However, in creating a complementary business with little incremental cost (making the tour income highly profitable) he has also managed to get paid to do his own marketing. Most visitors purchase his handiwork at the tiny factory shop near the garage door following the tour, and word-of-mouth has placed him among the top 30 attractions in Brussels on TripAdvisor.com.

Practically Speaking *(continued)*

Conjuring up a venture

Is Manon in the business of selling chocolate? Certainly. Is he also in the business of education and entertainment around chocolate? Without a doubt. And by supplementing education he expands the scope of what constitutes a chocolate business and effectively differentiates himself from the numerous other excellent (many larger and better funded) truffle traders in Brussels. He also teaches us where to look for unique insights. They come from things we already have and support things we already do. Manon has 100-year-old chocolate recipes and Chinese card tricks. His story prompts us to ask what business you could be in. Chances are excellent that you have something equally magical to offer.

Practically Speaking

CHARGING AHEAD

Today, there are more cell phones than people on the planet. Every one of these has to be charged at least every few days in order to keep its faithful user connected. That means a lot of little chargers to get lost, forgotten or broken. But what if you could charge these devices wirelessly? Sound like Star Trek? Surprisingly, the core technology (magnetic resonance) has existed since before the first Star Trek episode was aired. All that needs to be done is to bring the technology to the altar of the user.

Get me to the church on time

But technology can sometimes prove the reluctant groom. Wireless charging of mobile devices requires equipment to send the power and equipment to receive the power. It requires integration so the system functions as intuitively as a wedding ring. It requires consumer awareness and adoption. From a business perspective, that means bringing power adapter suppliers, telephone and laptop manufacturers, standards and certification bodies, and countless other industry players on board. Not easy for a single entrepreneur to accomplish.

Practically Speaking *(continued)*

Designing relationships

Undaunted, Maija Itkonen set out to make this opportunity her own. An industrial designer from the University of Art and Design, Helsinki, her instinct was not to look for a technical answer but to redesign the user experience in a way that intuitively integrates the technology into people's daily lives. When she thinks about user experience, she starts with frustration, like that moment when you still have two hours in the terminal to wait for your flight and you realize you forgot to charge your cell phone. Itkonen is right there with you in your moment of pain, and so is her product. When you put your dead phone down on the table next to you, the phone magically comes alive. And you sit up to notice: It's getting charged!

Forming relationships

Approaching the problem from the perspective of design led Itkonen to partner with Martela and Isku, two of Finland's largest and most established furniture manufacturers. To her delight, she found these traditional, typically stolid firms excited by the prospect of transforming their age-old product lines into active elements powering today's mobile lifestyle. A table was no longer just a table. And so the romance was on. Working with these first partners, Itkonen built a prototype as well as more relationships with local cafes so that she could pilot test the technology. In 2009, users in downtown Helsinki sipped coffee, talked with friends, and chewed on pastries while their cell phones, lying naturally on the table, were equally recharged. A perfect union, by design.

Happily ever after

The initial introduction generated much attention for Itkonen and her 12-person startup, Powerkiss. Itkonen found herself CEO as well as chief matchmaker, and was recognized by EUWIIN when they selected her 2009 Woman Innovator of the Year. In 2013, the matchmaking continued as Powerkiss was acquired by PowerMat Technologies, so the two could join to deliver wireless charging. Pretty powerful stuff.

Research Roots

CREATIVE TEMPLATES

Jacob Goldenberg (Goldenberg et al., 1999: 200), who researches creativity and innovation, writes about creative templates, similar to the transformation types we discuss in this chapter. He describes five templates, which his research indicates are the basis of about 70% of all new product ideas:

- Subtraction, multiplication, and division, each of which is a specific approach to deleting and supplementing we have described here.

- Task unification (making some aspect of an artefact do more than one task) and attribute dependency change (changing a linkage between the artefact and the environment), which are both similar to exaptation in that they involve changing what a product or component is capable of doing.

So, regardless of what you call them, it is useful to know that scholars consistently observe the systematic nature of idea generation. It's not magic; it's method.

Exaptation

Exaptation is a term evolutionary biologists use to describe the use of something for a purpose for which it was not originally designed or intended.

In the new venture setting, exaptation involves employing existing technologies, products, services or elements thereof, for a use they were not intended to serve.

Consider the humble aspirin tablet. In 1897 researchers at Bayer, a drug company, found acetylsalicylic acid to be an excellent painkiller and fever reducer. They decided to call it aspirin, and by 1899, a brand was born. The product was immensely successful, particularly once its effectiveness was demonstrated during the Spanish flu pandemic of 1918. When the patent expired in 1917, copies populated the market. But the product's popularity fell with the launch of paracetamol (1956) and ibuprofen (1969). It seemed as though aspirin was doomed.

But in the 1970s, clinical trials showed the product's efficacy as an anti-clotting agent—it reduced the risk of clotting diseases. Aspirin sales grew once more, spurred by its use as a preventative treatment for heart attacks and strokes—far from its original use!

For another example of exaptation, make sure you read the nearby story . . . "Charging ahead."

Re-weighting

Re-weighting involves increasing or decreasing the emphasis of features or attributes of a product or market.

BMW, for example, has gradually increased its emphasis on "driver appeal" as it launches new product designs, emphasizing "The Ultimate Driving Machine." Volvo, in contrast, emphasizes the safety features of its cars. "Dust, Sweat and New Ventures", consider how Polegato re-weights the importance of perspiration in the footwear purchase decision.

Research Roots

ADAM SMITH AND NOVEL COMBINATIONS

Many improvements have been made by the ingenuity of the makers of the machines, when to make them became the business of a peculiar trade; and some by that of those who are called philosophers or men of speculation, whose trade it is, not to do anything, but to observe everything; and who, upon that account, are often capable of combining together the powers of the most distant and dissimilar objects.

Adam Smith (1776)

ONGOING TRANSFORMATION

The previous sections outline only some of the ways expert entrepreneurs transform their means into ideas. If you need inspiration on more, the following table lists some additional transformation types we observed expert entrepreneurs using in the Venturing scenario.

TRANSFORMATION TYPES

Transformation type	Description	How our expert entrepreneurs use this transformation in Venturing
Deleting / supplementing	Subtracting from or adding to an existing offering.	Adding features to use the software to teach skills beyond entrepreneurship such as marketing and sales.
Composing / decomposing	Reorganizing material that is already there; decomposing and recomposing it.	Looking at just the negotiation aspect of the experiment to focus on that.
Exaptation	Transforming existing artefacts by converting them to new uses.	Using the software instead of as a game, as a self-assessment tool for prospective entrepreneurs.
Re-weighting	Increasing or decreasing the emphasis of features or attributes.	In Venturing, re-weighting was preceded with a statement such as "What we're really talking about . . ." and then focusing in on one aspect of Venturing.
Manipulation	Inverting, mirroring, twisting, turning an idea or artefact inside out.	Instead of marketing to people who might want to become entrepreneurs—market to those who **don't**, a group one person called "Pretendsters."
Deformation	Deliberately deforming the original idea or concept; analogous to melody deformation in jazz.	Use Venturing not as a product, but as a platform for a family of different products that might range from crowdfunding to distribution software.
Localization / regionalization / globalization	Changing the scope of the market by proposing smaller or larger markets.	Ideas ranged from selling Venturing to regional development agencies to use in global entrepreneurship competitions.
Ad hoc associating	Drawing on prior experience and memory by associating the current venture with some previous problem or opportunity.	One entrepreneur who had experience in licensing worked through the process of turning Venturing into a cross-licensed product.

Research Roots

DESIGN THINKING

Perhaps formally originating in the Bauhaus Movement (1919), there is an expectation that design requires a specific way of thinking. That perspective has generated a great deal of related academic work (Simon, 1969), the creation of a global industrial design firm named IDEO, and the establishment of an entire school at Stanford University that teaches "design thinking" (it is called the d.school). There is good overlap with effectuation and design thinking, particularly as it relates to the topic of this chapter. Current research is beginning to explore those relationships, looking at very specific theories of design (Agogué et al., 2015), and we expect to see more work in the future that brings these ideas together.

Research Roots

HOW TO FLY A HORSE

In a recent book, Kevin Ashton summarizes his insights on innovation as:

> What determines whether we will succeed as creators is not how intelligent we are, how talented we are, or how hard we work, but how we respond to the adversity of creation.
> (Ashton, 2015: 90)

Research Roots

EXAPTATION

How did feathers evolve, allowing birds to fly? One explanation is that they initially served to regulate temperature in some creatures and were later "exapted" for a different purpose—flight. This is the notion of exaptation, a term that was originally coined by the evolutionary biologists Gould and Vrba (1982: 4–15). These researchers noticed that biologists paid a lot of attention to the adaptation of species, which makes them better suited to their environments. However, they had paid less attention to the features of organisms that had initially evolved for one reason, or for no identifiable reason, and were later used for a new purpose. In entrepreneurship, the same idea can be used to describe the process of converting an artefact (which could be anything) from one use to another. Therefore, entrepreneurs faced with a hammer ask themselves not only, "What can we do with a hammer?" but also, "What else can we do with a hammer besides hit nails on their heads?" The process of exaptation, of asking "what else?" over and over again, is natural for many entrepreneurs.

TAKEAWAY: COMMITMENT TRANSFORMS AN IDEA INTO A GOOD IDEA

The notion of turning "something into something" can be found at the heart of Schumpeter's definition of entrepreneurship from his 1911 book, *The Theory of Economic Development*: "Our assumption is that he who makes new combinations is an entrepreneur."

But while making new combinations is easy because there are an infinite number of possible new combinations, it is immensely difficult to find valuable new combinations, for exactly the same reason. Most scholars of entrepreneurship, including Knight (1921), Schumpeter (1911), and contemporary researchers conclude that entrepreneurs have some kind

Practically Speaking

DUST, SWEAT, AND NEW VENTURES

In 1992, you would not have called Mario Moretti Polegato an entrepreneur. He was a vintner, bottling wines from Italy's Treviso region. In that year, business took Polegato to Reno, Nevada, for a meeting of international wine producers. Seeking to make the most of his visit to the US' scenic west, he took a hike in the mountains and found himself with sweaty feet from the summer heat. His solution? Cut holes in the soles of his shoes so his feet could breathe. He did this on the spot and still has both the shoes and a scar to show for it.

Not a sole sufferer

Polegato was simultaneously delighted and dissatisfied with his innovation. On the one hand, he could not be the only person in the world afflicted with the discomfort of sweaty feet. Surely, his idea would be of interest to a potential consumer audience. On the other hand, the innovation had an obvious defect. What was fantastic in the dry desert would be downright damp on a rainy London street. He still had work to do before he could leave the winery and pursue his newfound mission of making feet around the world more comfortable.

Novel combinations

Then Polegato started doing something often seen in the world of new ventures. He put things together that had never been put together before. Two of his more fruitful, though not initially obvious inputs came from NASA and academia. Anxious to find a material that would let sweat out, while keeping rainwater from getting in, Polegato headed to NASA in Houston, Texas, where he found a material developed to perform exactly that— but for space suits. And, at the universities of Padua, in Italy, and Trondheim, in Norway, he found researchers in materials science working on membrane technology to manage water transfer. Making the connection to his own needs, Polegato engaged them in development of his new shoe. Combining these unusual partners with a bit of investment money and some assistance with footwear design from a small ski-boot company, Polegato stepped out with something truly novel—a shoe that breathes.

Stepping up the pace

Polegato's story offers three useful tips for any entrepreneur. The first is that opportunities abound, and the second is that an easy way to create opportunities is simply to look for problems people need solved. The third is that innovation is more often a process of combination than invention. Everything Polegato needed to create breathable shoes existed—but nobody had put the pieces together to create a shoe.

Best foot forward

Apparently, Polegato was not the only foot-sweater in the world. In 2014, his breathable shoe-producing firm Geox posted net revenues of just under $1 billion, employed 30,000 people worldwide, and operated 1,200 retail stores. Polegato himself is a billionaire and, perhaps more importantly, has had dry, comfortable feet for years.

of intuition or judgment that enables them to instinctively pick good combinations from the infinite set of all possible combinations.

In this chapter, we have outlined the clinical mechanisms behind this process, but thus far, we omit one element common to them all—the importance of interaction.

The interaction sequence is a relatively easy one: I have an idea, I talk to someone about it, and together we transform it into something meaningful. So while the transformation types here may allow you to generate ideas on your own, they also allow you to transform ideas collaboratively with others.

Also critical to interaction is the importance of commitment. While you may be able to generate many ideas with these transformation types, what separates ideas from good ideas is whether key stakeholders such as employees, partners, and customers are willing to make a commitment to them. Expert entrepreneurs make transformations based on stakeholder commitments, not merely new combinations pulled out of a hat. Transformations, as mathematicians know, require interactions in space—in the case of expert entrepreneurs, this interaction happens in the space where stakeholders reside.

■ ■ ■

So What?

Entrepreneurs who use transformational processes produce more new market ideas than those who search and select for an existing opportunity. If you're struggling to create an opportunity, you don't have to invent something from nothing. Instead, transform something or several somethings into something else.

What Now?

- For an opportunity you have in mind, use the transformation concepts from expert entrepreneurs, and imagine three new ways to create value for different audiences.

- Decompose what you've got into its most basic elements, and imagine different audiences that could connect to those elements.

- Imagine that a component of your idea, which you consider to be the most irrelevant, turned out to be the most valuable. How would you adjust?

- Develop a way to describe some of these new ideas to someone who might actually value what you assumed to be irrelevant.

- Borrow the idea from a product you most love. How might you make it valuable to the audiences you imagined in points 1 and 2?

Think It Through

- Is it possible to create something genuinely new by transforming things that already exist?

- If you're just recombining things, are your efforts really transforming the world? Examples?

- In the venture you dream about, are you adapting to the world or is it adapting to you?

CHAPTER 12

Managing risk like a seasoned entrepreneur means basing decisions on the acceptable downside rather than guesses about a potential upside.

The affordable loss principle: Risk little, fail cheap

■ ■ ■

To explore the affordable loss principle, the second principle we see at work in the decision-making approach of expert entrepreneurs, we're going to start with a thought experiment.

Imagine you are an entrepreneur. During your 12-year tenure as an engineer at a major computer manufacturer, you work on your own time to invent a device that recognizes and responds to eye movements. You imagine it might make a great alternative to the computer mouse. You can make it rest on the user's head much like headphones and set it up so that point-and-click navigation is accomplished with even the most minor head and eye movements. You are convinced the device has huge potential. But when you attempt to interest your current company in licensing the idea from you, they don't bite. There are no firms currently offering anything similar to this device, and you possess all the technical skills needed to create the product effectively and efficiently. You quit your job to develop this idea further by, among other things, conducting initial market research on selling the device through the retail channel as an upgrade to existing or new computers. You win a business plan competition and develop a prototype. And then you face a big decision.

A VC who was one of the judges in the business plan competition likes your idea and believes that with an initial investment of US$10 million you could realistically capture 1% of the personal computer market worldwide. She believes your product should sell for US$30 and generate a 20% net profit margin. In return for her investment, the VC would expect to own 40% of your company.

In the meantime, you have been speaking with a friend of your father who runs a large manufacturing facility. He is willing to pay you US$1 million to adapt your technology to create a hands-free device that enables blue-collar factory workers to control industrial manufacturing systems from secure, protected work areas. The adaptation of your product, integration with the factory systems, and commercialization will cost you about US$950,000. He is willing to pay you up front.

CHOOSING THE BEST OPPORTUNITY

Because of the time required to develop these opportunities, you cannot do both simultaneously. You must choose. Here are some questions you might reasonably ask in order to make this decision:

- Which is the bigger opportunity?
- What is the net present value of each opportunity?
- What would you be personally investing into each alternative?
- What is the downside risk of each alternative?

As you look at these questions, you will probably recognize that the first two are the more causal, or predictive ways of thinking about the decision, and the second two are more in line with the logic of effectuation, which we have been discussing in this book. Let us look at each question in turn to get a better grip on what might—and

what might not—help you make a good choice between the VC and the father's friend.

Which is the bigger opportunity?

This seems like an obvious question to ask, but how can you possibly know the answer? Take the case of the absurdly unlikely venture 1–800-AUTOPSY, discussed in Chapter 3. Until 1988, the world got along without a company that provided autopsies on demand. However, in light of the growing success of and increasing demand for private autopsy services since the company was founded, one could argue that there was latent demand that simply went unnoticed until Vidal Herrera came along. But if we wind back to 1988, what would his elevator pitch have been to potential investors? Or, for that matter, what would Starbucks' pitch have been in 1980, when US coffee consumption had been declining for 20 years straight?

WHAT GOES INTO MAKING A NET PRESENT VALUE (NPV) PREDICTION?

A lot of forward-looking details. Let's unpack some of them.

Most NPV calculations are anchored with a demand forecast. This typically involves gathering information to form a consensus on the high side and the low side of demand for the product, given certain price assumptions. The price assumptions, similarly, rely on predictions about product features and competitors' actions.

The next step is to estimate the costs it takes to deliver. Costs must be organized into materials and labor, and again according to which are fixed and variable. Each of these costs as well as margins change over time, impacted by your own actions (improving the product or scaling quantities up or down), and your competitors' actions.

Atop those assumptions, you need to discount the cost of capital and assess the variability in the forecast. Put this together, and you can see all the dimensions in NPV that introduce variance and the consequent wide margins of error when forecasting the activity of an uncertain new venture.

Practically Speaking

DELIVERING A VENTURE

It only takes a minute of Steve Kiruri's story to see where entrepreneurial opportunities originate. A recent university graduate in his native Kenya, Kiruri was quick to inventory the things he didn't have: a job, cash or any assets that might be used to secure a loan. Instead, in his own words, "I didn't sit back and moan. I focused on things right there in front of me." These he established to be: his education, relatives asking him to take care of their errands, available space, a government with bureaucratic and time-consuming processes, voluntary labor from high-school graduates and dropouts who were jobless, friends willing to give him a chance and a national media willing to broadcast his story to the world. Transforming this assortment of resources, Kiruri launched a venture called "Petty Errands." His value proposition assured his clients (initially friends and relatives) that he would take care of the small tasks that consume a lot of time because of Kenya's developing infrastructure.

Unplanned route

Instead of a business plan and $5 million in venture capital, Kiruri started right away using what was readily available. And the venture developed as a function of the next resource he added to his list—his clients. Once he had renewed a driver's licence for a client they might ask him if he could pay a bill—a task that can still require a personal visit in Kenya—or courier a package across Nairobi, a chore that could easily cost a morning amid traffic, confusion, and construction. New requests grew into new business opportunities, and Petty Errands became more than a petty business.

Next stop

That was 1995. Since then, the firm has added corporations, non-governmental organizations (NGOs), and government bodies to its client base. Petty Errands is licensed by the Communication Commission of Kenya (CCK) as an Intra-City Operator, and Steve has been recognized as the "Most Inspiring Business Person" by Kenya Television Networks. Today, the firm employs more than 50 people and handles over 15,000 "errands" in a year. But Steve's story isn't over, and neither is the story of where opportunities originate. Because today, Steve's list of things to work with is much longer than it was in 1995. In addition to certifications, clients, and

Mr Steve Kiruri, in blue jacket, of Petty Errands at his firm's offices.

Practically Speaking *(continued)*

employees, he has also added things such as a respected brand, knowledge of the current needs (and issues) of clients, operations and motorcycle transportation expertise, extensive contacts within the Kenya courier industry, and good relations with bankers. Indeed, the story of creating opportunities is one that starts again and again as new resources are found, acquired, used and lost through business activity, meeting new people and learning new skills. Similarly, Steve's own story is still very much in the writing.

Expanding the path

As Petty Errands becomes a business of scale, new opportunities abound. Should Steve take his expertise with the light motorcycles the firm uses for its couriers to offer service, spare parts or leasing of the machines to the general public? Could Steve advance into the cargo business, taking advantage of his operational knowledge to better serve his client base? Or might Steve best create ways to fully use his resources, such as delivering wedding or event invitations on Saturdays when the errand business is slow? These businesses have yet to appear, but the insight into the source of opportunity is already here. Taking what is readily available and transforming what are seemingly mundane resources into something valuable is the ongoing errand of the committed entrepreneur.

Common sense suggests that while you might be able to calculate what you could lose by investing in a venture (namely, everything that you put into it), it is much harder to calculate the potential upside—that is, the size of the opportunity.

What is the net present value of each opportunity?

Just because calculating the upside of an opportunity is difficult doesn't mean people don't try. Net present value (NPV) is a formula widely used in the business world to predict the current value of a future project. To calculate the NPV of your two options, you'll need to answer several questions: What is your forecasted demand? What is your

product cost? What are your overheads? How will these costs change over time?

Put this together, and you can see the interrelated system of prediction involved in trying to assess the value of an opportunity. And you can also see how, as the assumptions accumulate, the calculation becomes much closer to guesswork than science.

What would you be personally investing into each alternative?

Both options, the one from the VC and the one from your father's friend, require you to invest a variety of resources. Spend a moment

thinking about how the options differ in terms of the following:

- Your time commitment.
- Your reputation.
- Your opportunity cost.
- Your knowledge.
- Your emotional commitment.
- How would you measure these? How would you decide what constitutes an appropriate level of investment? These are highly subjective and personal assessments that change over time, just as tangible costs do.
- What is the downside risk of each alternative?

Let's assume you choose the venture capital option. Here are some possible scenarios:

ASSESSING AFFORDABLE LOSS

	Venture Capitalist	My Father's Friend
Time		
Reputation		
Opportunity Cost		
Knowledge		

- The market is not there, and the VC pulls the plug on the company.
- The market is there, but the VC takes control of the firm and fires you.
- You don't get along with the VC, but you can't buy her out.
- The market ends up being 25,000 units per year, just enough to break even, but leaving you managing a firm turned into the "living dead."

Now, assuming you have decided to work with your father's friend, consider these scenarios:

- You miss a critical deadline that costs your father's friend a week's manufacturing output. Your father's friend is unhappy with your father.
- You deliver something defective, and an employee is hurt as a result.
- It costs you twice as much to implement the solution as you estimated.
- While you are working with your father's friend, a new company releases a product very similar to yours, and it is a runaway success.

For each option, which scenario is the worst and why? Which scenarios are within your control? Which are not? What do you do next in each case?

Starting by organizing the issues in this way is the first step in assessing "affordable loss."

Affordable loss and its use as a decision tool

NPV offers useful projections in situations where the information that goes into the calculation is relatively stable. Managers in mature markets ranging from energy to carbonated soda make frequent use of NPV. But in the uncertain setting of new venture creation, the information necessary to perform an NPV calculation is either unavailable, or the ranges are so broad that results are not helpful in planning or running a new venture.

The research upon which this book is based suggests that instead of trying to calculate the upside of an opportunity, using NPV, expert entrepreneurs take what we call an "affordable loss" approach. Fundamentally, affordable loss is based on things they know and can control, whereas NPV is based on predictions they don't trust and can't control.

Like the other principles of effectuation, affordable loss turns traditional business practice on its head. Instead of deciding whether to pursue an opportunity based on potential returns, effectual entrepreneurs look at potential losses. They base their decisions on what downside risk they find acceptable rather than on what they guess the upsides might be. So instead of calculating up front how much money they need to launch their project and then investing time, effort, and energy into raising that money, effectual entrepreneurs determine what they are willing to lose. As they pursue the opportunity, they bring stakeholders on board, reducing resources the entrepreneur and the stakeholders need to commit to the venture and better controlling risks through the effort, commitment, and resources of self-selected stakeholders.

As we walk through how to think in terms of affordable loss, the important point to remember is that affordable loss puts the entrepreneur front and center. Traditional business planning puts the venture front and center, asking what financing the venture needs to get off the ground independent of the entrepreneur's available means. Affordable loss starts with the entrepreneur's concrete situation,

not abstract estimates of venture financing needs. As such, the emphasis is on taking the entrepreneur's context into account. Big decisions like taking the plunge into entrepreneurship depend a lot on your family, your stage of life, and the social norms around you —for example, attitudes toward failure in your community and industry.

To figure out your affordable loss, you must consider your life situation, current commitments, aspirations, and risk propensity. It is helpful to think of this as a two-step process.

The first step is to ask how much you really need to start your business—the less you need, the less you need to worry about losing. You can greatly reduce your upfront cash needs by getting creative about different ways of bringing your idea to market using all the means that are available to you. The vast majority of new businesses are started with small sums of money, and rely heavily on nonfinancial contributions, such as the entrepreneur's time and (often) family support as well as slack resources from partners.

Research Roots

MENTAL ACCOUNTING

The notion of mental accounting was first developed in a paper by Thaler (1985: 199) and later summarized in another of his papers (Thaler, 1999). Mental accounting emerges fairly straightforwardly from the idea of bounded rationality: creatures with limited cognitive processing capabilities (human beings, that is) require ways of keeping track of their money. Thaler theorized that people do so by categorizing their resources, as accountants do. For example, they create separate mental compartments for long-term savings (such as retirement and children's education) and short-term expenses (such as entertainment and leisure activities). A key implication of mental accounting is the violation of the fungibility premise of economics— i.e. that resources are automatically arbitraged across accounts (Thaler, 1999: 183). A simple way to think about this is that for Homo economicus, "Money by any other name is still money" but for most Homo sapiens, "Money in one mental account is simply not the same as money in another account." Because of this non-fungibility characteristic, mental accounting suggests that consumers may borrow at high interest rates in some accounts even while they save at much lower interest rates in others.

Practically Speaking

OPPORTUNITY IN THE TRASH

Academics in general, and economists in particular, are not known for their sense of humor. However, there is an old joke about an economist strolling down the street with an entrepreneur when they come upon a £50 note on the ground. As the entrepreneur reaches down to pick it up, the economist says, "Don't bother—if it was a real £50 note, someone would have already picked it up." The entrepreneur shrugs his shoulders, puts the bill in his pocket and says, "You're right—someone just did."

But seriously . . .

The entrepreneur in the joke is probably Brooke Farrell. The £50 note? Not exactly real currency, but likely more valuable. It's trash. Farrell spent eight years consulting to US waste conglomerate Waste Management, and saw how many £50 notes cross the kerbside every day. "You look around and you see waste absolutely everywhere," she says. "If you loaded the annual waste generated by the US into trucks, the convoy necessary to carry it all would circle the equator of the earth 600 times. But look around again. What you're seeing are opportunities. Everywhere."

Matchmaker

In 2009, Farrell quit her job and, together with her brother-in-law, co-founded a firm called RecycleMatch. The idea was an online exchange where firms trade trash. From a recycling perspective, it is a natural recombination of her experience in the waste business with his software expertise creating business-to-business marketplaces. But having a good match in the founding team does not guarantee the same with the clients.

Moneymaker

The pair self-funded the venture on the shoestring they were willing to invest and spent the first six months creating a prototype they could show potential clients. Most executives in large firms do not spend their days looking for a market for their waste, so Farrell went looking for them. The first was a large international corporation with 180,000 pounds of window glass that had been damaged in a hurricane. Covered in a thick

How it works

 Sellers posts waste or recyclables
- Company is confidential
- Specify conditions & requirements
- Invite buyers you know to bid

For Sellers

 Buyers bid on materials
- Receive alerts on new materials
- Buyers can ask questions of sellers
- Consider reputation of sellers when making offers

For Buyers

 A Match is made
- Escrow service protects both buyers and sellers
- Save money and the environment
- Materials stay in closed loop system instead of landfill

For Pricing

Practically Speaking *(continued)*

plastic coating, the glass was deemed unrecyclable and was headed for a landfill. "We told them we could make them money listing their material on our marketplace," says Farrell. "We thought we were offering upside, but actually they signed with us because they had nothing to lose. Our service is confidential, and we don't get paid unless the market clears. We found another company that wanted to crush the glass and 'upcycle' it into countertops. The market was born."

A market for the market

RecycleMatch launched in February 2011. Already, the firm has enabled trading of waste polyester from paint roller production to an automobile manufacturer, and consumer product returns from an interior decorator to a textile producer that upcycles the unwanted upholstery. It has attracted outside investors and a seasoned CEO. Farrell, not one to let an opportunity go to waste, is already working on a new offering from RecycleMatch. In addition to the public marketplace where any company can list waste and bid on it, she is creating an enterprise product—software that helps large companies and supply chains manage, track, and monetize waste streams and industrial by-products across their distributed locations. "I would go to a big firm, and tell them what we are doing," she says. "They would tell me it's fantastic, but that their trash isn't like that. It took me a little while, but what I realized they were saying is that they have absolutely no idea what they waste. We're going to give them the information they need about themselves to be more sustainable and make more money." Apart from showing how business can do good for the world, the lesson is where opportunities originate. It isn't the theories from the economist, or the inevitability of the market. It is the dirty hands of the entrepreneur who picks up £50 notes.

The second step is to ask what you are really able and willing to lose to start your business. This means taking an inventory of your available resources and gauging your risk tolerance.

DECIDING ON YOUR AFFORDABLE LOSS: SOME GUIDELINES

Once you have gone through the process of doing everything possible to lower the amount of money you need to get your venture off the ground, you are left with the question of what downside risk is acceptable to you. Here, the key thing is to ask yourself the right questions. It's helpful to think through both what you can afford to lose and what you are willing to lose. We'll look at each of these in turn.

Different kinds of losses

People "mentally account" for different resources in different ways. For example, many individuals are willing to invest loads of time in a new business but carefully limit how much cash they put into it. Evidently, people account for their time differently than they account for their cash. Similarly, some resources are mentally accounted for in ways that preclude them from being put at risk. A good example is savings that parents accumulate to fund their children's education. These monies are often considered "out of bounds" for risking on a new business venture.

To figure out what you can afford to lose, you have to know what your resources are, and you have to make some decisions about what belongs in the category of "riskable" and what doesn't. As you are thinking about this, remember that some psychologists have argued that

DETERMINING AN ACCEPTABLE LEVEL OF RED INK IN THE NEWSPAPER INDUSTRY

Consider the launch of the USA Today newspaper. The newspaper's owners did substantial financial analysis on the launch decision. But all the analysis did not change the fact that the paper's success was critically dependent on advertising revenues (70% of the revenue base), which were driven by the reactions of several key competitors to the new paper—that is, the success or failure of the venture hinged in part on the interaction between the different actors in the marketplace. However good the analysis that went into the launch decision, the paper's financial future couldn't be controlled by its owners—it was in the hands of its competitors.

USA Today was launched in 1982. It was estimated to have lost US$400 million in its first five years, and continued to lose money for its first decade. It reported its first year of profits (US$7.5 million) in 1993.

---

rational people never put at risk what is truly valuable to them.

Consider the following categories of resources as you think through what you can afford to lose and what is "out of bounds" for you.

Time

The time entrepreneurs put into a new venture is often referred to as "sweat equity." A good proportion of entrepreneurs sweat it out over long periods. However, this may make sense to them because time is a different "currency" from cash and, therefore, it is often accounted for in a different way. Moreover, because time is perishable, people feel differently about contributing it—after all, they might have wasted it anyway. Therefore, you may be able to afford losing time more than you can afford losing money.

Windfalls

As Fred Smith was creating the business plan for FedEx, his father died, leaving US$8 million to Fred and his sister—money that was used to fund the new company. This seems like a rather high level of affordable loss, but it's not surprising. Many people put inherited money into a different mental account than earned income—they are willing to risk the former but not the latter. Other kinds of windfalls that can significantly increase an individual's affordable loss are lottery winnings and big upswings in the value of assets such as stock.

> You can't always control the wind, but you can control your sails.
>
> Anthony Robbins

In retrospect, Fred Smith's decision to invest his and his sister's inheritance into the fledgling FedEx looks prescient. But had he been a seasoned entrepreneur, he might have first tried to start the firm with US$0 of his own money.

Long-term savings

Research suggests that most people apply rules of thumb to borrowing against or spending certain resources that are mentally accounted for as belonging to other parts of their life. Examples include funds set aside for their own retirement and for the care of dependents, e.g. children and parents.

Practically Speaking

PARTNERS' AFFORDABLE LOSS

It would be fair to say that Marius Tudosiei was longer on aspiration than more tangible resources. Growing up in the northern part of Romania, his childhood was spent in and around a big kitchen, where traditional food was cooked using fresh and natural ingredients. But when Marius arrived in the capital city of Bucharest, the availability of such artisanal cuisine was very limited. So in 2009, Marius quit his job in the media industry to build "something dedicated to good food"—though he had no idea what that something might ultimately look like, and no capital to fund the project.

Aspiration to action

So he started with what was available and free. He built a Facebook page and asked his friends to tell him about food and about what his business should be. Soon, he had 1,000 friends advising him to open a restaurant. But he said no. Not enough money, not enough expertise. Instead, he decided to offer his friends good food from his small network of suppliers—opening a small and highly specialized grocery store as a means of distribution.

Action to interaction

Though less expensive to start than a restaurant, a grocery store still required capital Marius didn't have. Until a mentor asked him how much he needed. "10,000 euro," he replied, "and I do not have any idea where I could get that much money." To which the mentor responded, "But do you have 10 friends to give you 1,000 euro each?" Before he was done, he had raised a total of 25,000 euro in small bits and pieces from a number of friends.

Interaction to creation

Marius founded Bacania Veche (The Old Grocery Store) in 2010 and it is already one of the most popular small food enterprises in Romania dedicated to good and healthy food. From that starting point he has gone on to open a restaurant (which is also a Charity Shop for Hospice), and a TV cooking show. He delivers food daily for 200 children in five nurseries, has a corporate catering business, and employs 20 people.

Secret ingredient

There is no way to get the recipes which generated this comment on Tripadvisor: "It is the greatest shop that I have ever seen. Cookies and bread cooked on the spot give the flavour and enchant the visitor." But the secret that enabled Marius to get going is understanding his partners' affordable loss. While an investment of 10,000 euro is a meaningful sum for many individuals, providing 1,000 euro to a friend starting the business changes the proposition. If the business fails, losing 1,000 euro is not a crushing loss. But if the business is successful, the 1,000 euro will return a profit and perhaps all sorts of other benefits. A good recipe for bringing people into a venture.

The family home/home equity

There are many instances in which people use home equity loans to fund a business startup. However, some individuals are unwilling to put their home at risk, as the loss would not be "affordable."

Credit cards

We've all heard stories about companies initially financed on credit cards—EDS and Home Depot come to mind.

There is some evidence that people mentally account for credit card expenses differently from other expenses because credit cards weaken the link between making the decision to purchase something and actually paying for it.

Loans from family and friends

Other examples of weak links between purchasing and paying may include loans from family members that have flexible or unspecified payback terms. Descriptions of family business, for example, refer to the relatives' money as "patient capital." Such funds may seem more affordable to use and to lose than funds with heavy pressure to repay at specific deadlines.

What am I willing to lose?

Once you have decided what you can afford to lose in general, you still need to decide what you are willing to lose on this particular venture. Figuring this out will mean assessing the degree and intensity of your desire to start this particular venture. It will also mean creating thresholds, since if the downside case for your venture hits a key threshold you have set, this will dictate your course of action. Ultimately, the question you have to ask yourself is, "Is the venture worth doing even if I lose what I invest?"

Regardless of whether your motivation to become an entrepreneur is largely pecuniary or non-pecuniary, there are several ways reasoning through the plunge decision using the idea of affordable loss is likely to increase the chances that you'll decide to go ahead:

- It reduces the financial risk. Going through the exercise of minimizing startup costs lowers the risk of starting your venture.
- It allows you to focus on things within your control (the downside loss) and proceed in spite of things outside your control, which increases your confidence.
- It makes explicit that the upside potential for the venture is in large part contingent on your actions and the actions of your stakeholders,

"We've considered every potential risk except the risks of avoiding all risks."

HARDIN

Research Roots

AFFORDABLE LOSS

The economist George Shackle refers to the concept of affordable loss in a paper in which he postulates that the entrepreneur might characterize each venture opportunity according to the possible gains and possible losses and suggests that the latter can help the entrepreneur evaluate which opportunity to pursue.

It is practical and reasonable to regard the focus-loss, in absolute terms, as depending on the nature and scale of the enterprise concerned. Thus, by choice of an appropriate kind, or an appropriate size, of plant or enterprise, he can adjust the greatest amount he stands to lose, that is, his focus loss, to the amount which, given the size and character of his assets, he can afford to lose.

(Shackle, 1966: 765)

In short, using the principle of affordable loss will provide you with more reasons for taking the plunge into entrepreneurship and fewer reasons for saying no.

TAKEAWAY: UN-RISKY BUSINESS

Statistics would seem to suggest that budding entrepreneurs would have a bias against starting new ventures, simply because a large number of new firms fail. Affordable loss lessens the impact of failure—it makes failure clearly survivable by constraining the loss to something the entrepreneur is in fact willing to lose in order to pursue the venture. If the entrepreneur reduces the downside risk to an acceptable level, he or she is likely to lose less in the event of failure than an entrepreneur who invests based on his or her guess about the venture's upside potential.

which again increases the perceived controllability of the venture and, therefore, its attractiveness.

- It encourages you to consider an opportunity from the perspective of what matters

to you in ways beyond the economic upside. Bringing in factors that lie beyond financial calculation makes the decision more realistic, and in tune with how most people actually make major decisions.

■ ■ ■

So What?

Using affordable loss to reason through the plunge decision helps you see how to get started right now, while managing your risk. The decision to start a business doesn't have to be about predicting whether the upside is big enough; instead, it can be about whether the downside is "life threatening."

What Now?

For the opportunity you are developing, work these through from the perspective of affordable loss:

- [ ] Do I hire at all? Whom specifically should I hire? How should I hire them?

- [ ] How much, if any, do I invest in longer-term investments such as research and development?

- [ ] Can I quantify the levels of time, reputation, money, and other resources I am willing to lose to advance my idea to the next step?

- [ ] Who benefits from my idea, and how can I bring them on board to share the expense and risk as well as the benefit?

Think It Through

- [ ] How do notions of affordable loss differ in different parts of the world?

- [ ] How might affordable loss encourage or discourage commitment?

- [ ] If investment in an opportunity is constrained by affordable loss, can it lead to a "homerun"?

CHAPTER 13

Bootstrapping

There were others who had forced their way to the top from the lowest rung by the aid of their bootstraps.
James Joyce, *Ulysses*, 1922

Never buy what you can rent.

Never rent what you can barter for.

Never barter for what you can borrow.

Never borrow what you can get for free.

Using slack for bootstrap financing

■ ■ ■

As we saw in Chapter 3, "I don't have enough money" is a common refrain among aspiring entrepreneurs. Lulled by the stories of VCs and angel investors who pour millions of dollars into small startups with barely a business plan to their name, the budding entrepreneur naturally assumes that the first step is to look for money, preferably a lot of it. But before you embark on that quest, think about the following:

• How much do you want?
• How much do you need?
• What do you need money for?
• What can you do without money?
• What does money cost?
• What are you willing to give up in return for money?

This chapter and Chapters 18 (ownership) and 19 (business plans) will help you answer those questions and offer alternative views on startup financing—views that reflect the effectual logic we observe among expert entrepreneurs.

In this chapter, we look at bootstrapping—that is, starting a business without taking on external funding (or taking on as little as possible). It's a practice that embodies the principle of affordable loss, discussed in Chapter 12.

To explore the nuts and bolts of bootstrapping, we'll consider in this chapter a real-life case of a young couple who decided to launch their own business. At each decision point in the story, think back to the questions listed here and how you,

as the founder of this business, would have answered them.

The base assumption throughout the case is, not surprisingly, when you start a business, the amount of cash coming in has to be greater than or equal to the amount going out (the idea of money matching, described in Chapter 3).

GRAPHICAL PRACTICALLY SPEAKING
STACEY'S PITA CHIPS

Who I am, what I know, who I know (Chapter 9)

The year is 1996. Stacy and Mark are a couple, living in Boston. Mark is a psychologist and Stacy a social worker. They both have experience in the Californian food industry, having worked in restaurants. They know trends in the US often move from west to east. They believe Boston might soon acquire an appetite for Californian style food. They are strong believers in the healthy diets they experienced in the West. They know they want to be their own boss. Together they have debt of US$370,000.

Mark and Stacy are attracted to the food/restaurant business. Ideally, they would like to start a healthy bistro, but that dream is squelched by their debt and the lack of enthusiasm by their immediate family to support the venture. So they start selling sausages and hot dogs from a pushcart in the streets of Boston. It isn't exactly the healthy diet they had in mind, but it is a profitable and cash positive living.

What should they do next?

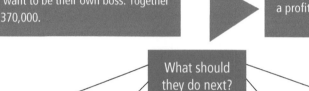

Keep selling sausages from the pushcart: it's making money?	Quit selling junk food and look for jobs?	Make healthier sandwiches Californian style?	Do something else (remember Curry in a Hurry, Chapter 7?)
Not consistent with values	Not consistent with goals	Interesting—what's the cost?	Possible—guided by partners

The opportunity cost of time

Spending money versus spending time are perceived differently. The value of time (or sweat equity, as it is sometimes called) is more ambiguous and perishable because time can't be saved for future use. Therefore, losses paid for in time may be experienced as more affordable than losses paid for in money because they can be accounted for more flexibly and are, therefore, seen as being more affordable than ventures paid for in money.

WHAT IS THE BALANCE SHEET FOR SELLING HEALTHIER SANDWICHES?

Income	Expenses	Money questions
From their first venture into hot dogs, they know there is demand.	Ingredients	Do you want fresh ingredients? Could you get yesterday's bread cheaper? Could you cut a deal with a pita manufacturer?
	Pushcart	You already have one, but are you willing to lose the revenue you might have generated selling sausages?
	Time	How do you account for your time?

The couple decides to make pita wrap sandwiches to sell on a pushcart in Boston's financial district. The date is 1997.

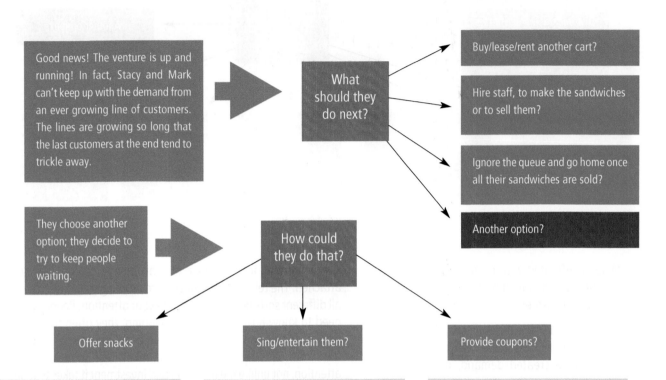

Good news! The venture is up and running! In fact, Stacy and Mark can't keep up with the demand from an ever growing line of customers. The lines are growing so long that the last customers at the end tend to trickle away.

What should they do next?

Buy/lease/rent another cart?

Hire staff, to make the sandwiches or to sell them?

Ignore the queue and go home once all their sandwiches are sold?

Another option?

They choose another option; they decide to try to keep people waiting.

How could they do that?

Offer snacks

Sing/entertain them?

Provide coupons?

BALANCE SHEET FOR SNACKS	
Income	**Expenses**
More sandwiches if people stay to buy the sandwich	Additional ingredients
If I sell the snacks, maybe some income	More time, and maybe loss of customers, cost of snacks

BALANCE SHEET FOR ENTERTAINMENT	
Income	**Expenses**
More sandwiches if people stay and buy more	Additional ingredients
	The time it takes to learn and provide some form of entertainment

BALANCE SHEET FOR COUPONS	
Income	**Expenses**
Some more business from the people who don't leave	Loss of income due to lower price, and additional ingredients
	Time to print the coupons

Mark and Stacy decide to offer snacks. But they cannot buy something off the shelf. Instead, each evening they take the left-over pita bread, dust it with spices—cinnamon, garlic, etc., and the next day they hand these "chips" out to the customers waiting in line.

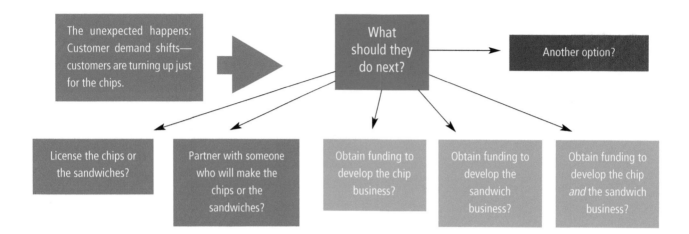

The unexpected happens: Customer demand shifts—customers are turning up just for the chips.

What should they do next?

Another option?

License the chips or the sandwiches?

Partner with someone who will make the chips or the sandwiches?

Obtain funding to develop the chip business?

Obtain funding to develop the sandwich business?

Obtain funding to develop the chip *and* the sandwich business?

When it's partners you need

When confronted with choice, there is always another option. Sometimes, it's not money you need but a partner.

For Mark and Stacy, this is an easy time to bring on a partner. They have two opportunities, which have created demand, more demand than they have the resources to handle. A partner could add all sorts of resources to their set of means, ranging from broad distribution (a high-end grocery store interested in offering sandwiches), to factory capacity (a bread factory, idle during the day as most baking is done at night).

In addition, money is not always the only motivation for launching a partnership. As these two examples highlight, you may have investors interested for other reasons than money. And in turn, these partners can both offer resources that go beyond money and can also enable the pursuit of new opportunities that were not previously imagined (for example, flavored pita bread produced by the bakery partner to make the sandwiches more unique and exciting).

When it's money you need

It is important to remember that all money comes with strings attached. The relationships you create as you gather investments of all different sorts reasonably require your attention. People involved need to know how things are developing, they often have specific legal rights to be updated, and have a say in some of your major decisions. This relationship work takes real time and sincere attention, not unlike the attention and investment it takes to manage your relationship with a great customer. More money means more of this type of relationship management.

Like all relationships, it's a two-way street: People involved don't just listen to you, you also learn from them and include their resources in your portfolio. We made the case for the value of taking advantage of contingencies earlier in the book and we will look at it again in detail when we talk about contingency. The listening and cooperating involved in working with your investors/lenders/other sources of money can limit the degrees of freedom that you have in dealing with contingencies. Even with great sources of capital and shrewd big thinkers that trust you, the process can slow you down.

Finally, more money often leads to customer interactions that are relatively more directive than collaborative. Imagine you are in the business of selling garlic chips and you find an interested customer. He loves your garlic chips, but will only buy from you if you can modify them into cinnamon chips. If you are sitting on US$10 million in cash, you are imminently less inclined to say yes to that possibility than if you are sitting on US$1 in cash. As a result, you turn the customer away—your business is garlic!

Mark and Stacy are unsure what to do. They stop and think. They speak to other people in the industry, read trade journals, and talk to colleagues and competitors.

As a result of their conversations, Mark and Stacy decide to drop the sandwiches and make chips. The market seems to say that they could get bigger faster that way. But they want to do it without asking for funding and without going into a partnership. With their debt still looming, Mark and Stacy look for ways to make chips while spending as little as possible. But they need some things:

- An oven in which to bake the chips
- A space in which to make the chips
- A machine to slice the bread
- Ingredients

What should they do next?

Where do you find money?

Obvious sources

- Friends, family and fools
- Angels
- Venture capitalists
- Banks
- Government and grant sources

Not-so-obvious sources

- Factoring (customers)
- Suppliers
- Professional advisors
- Media
- Non-monetary resources

How to get around the money hurdle:

When dealing with your suppliers, think of negotiating the following:

- delayed payment terms
- payment as a percentage of revenue
- direct capital investment
- paying them in direct services (make them customers)
- using their process/assets/talent during their downtime (use their slack resources)
- getting them to guarantee a line of credit for you at their bank.

When working with customers:

- pay first purchase order (PO) in cash upfront for better pricing
- get a solid PO and then connect to a lender that will accept that as collateral
- use their commercial bank and piggy back on their line of credit (slack resource)
- get them to guarantee a line of credit

- pre-sell them the first year's worth of their purchases.

When going to investors:

- borrow money from them, don't just take investment
- pay them back as a variable cost against a percentage of revenues (not against time)
- get them to guarantee a line of credit
- take investment but negotiate for a "clawback" where you can earn back ownership if things go well.

When hiring employees, think about offering:

- options rather than cash
- percentage of sales rather than base salary.

All of these options can lower the cash-based entry barrier. And when all else fails, use your credit card!

They rent space from a bakery—using the bakery's down time to bake their chips in the bakery's oven. This solves the space, oven, and machine problem. But it does not allow for large-scale production.

By January 1999 revenue from the sales of chips reaches US$450,000. But the bakery space is becoming too small.

What should they do next?

Look for another space? Their own space? Or another one they can share?

Bite the bullet and get the cash that will allow them to expand in the way that they choose?

Another option?

Mark and Stacy decide to look for a space where they can manufacture their chips. But cost is an issue. They look at each cost very carefully. Going back to the previous page, what could be a variable cost? Where is the real cost?

An oven

- Mark and Stacy can get a new one for US$160,000.
- They can also partner in developing one with an oven maker. If two ovens are made, each will only cost US$80,000.
- If they find a bakery selling a second-hand oven they could pay as little as US$13,000.

Ingredients

Stacy and Mark have always been keen on using the freshest ingredients. But if you are making chips, would yesterday's bread do just as well? Could they get leftovers from a pita manufacturer?

Slicing machines

- A bread-slicing machine costs US$100,000 and is available immediately.
- A second-hand carrot-slicing machine could be found for US$18,000.

Staff

At this point, they have 15 staff. Should they hire additional people to make more chips?

Packaging machines and supplies

With the business growing, they can no longer pack and send all the chips by hand. But this machinery seems impossible to buy second hand.

What should they do next?

Mark and Stacy expand the chip business

- They make Stacy the majority owner of the company so that she is eligible for funding from BankBoston, which has a loan program that assists women in business. They ask for a US$60,000 loan to buy automated packaging equipment and supplies. Six months later they apply for US$500,000. But in exchange for that amount, the bank wants equity, which the couple is not willing to give. They settle for US$300,000.

- They partner with an oven manufacturer to make the oven they cannot find, paying US$80,000—half the original price.

- When they realize they need a second oven, and that the banks will not lend them any more money, they buy a used oven from a bankrupt bakery. They pay for it with their credit card.

- Since they cannot find an automatic slicer at a price they can afford, they buy a 40-year-old carrot-cutting machine from Campbell Soup, which Mark modifies.

- They rent a suburban warehousing space from a contracting company. They spend nothing furnishing it, getting furniture for free from friends and family or making their own.

- They hire Stacy's brother into the company in exchange for a share of the profit.

- When they need more staff than the 15 they have, they hire temporary employees.

- They spend nothing on advertising—instead they give samples away in person at trade shows, cooking demonstrations, public appearances, and grocery stores everywhere across the US.

- They partner with Babson, a Boston area business school focused on entrepreneurship, to hire summer interns to design their website in exchange for them speaking at the school.

The story of Stacy and Mark illustrates the timeless rules of new venture bootstrapping:

- Never buy what you can rent.
- Never rent what you can barter for.
- Never barter for what you can borrow.
- Never borrow what you can get for free.

By 2000 Stacy's Pita Chips is a profitable business with US$1.3 million in revenues (double that of 1999).

Five years later Mark and Stacy sell their pita chips to PepsiCo's Frito-Lay. By then, they are the top-selling maker of pita chips in the US, with revenues of US$60 million and 100 employees.

Research Roots

EARN VERSUS BURN

We analyzed all the private firms acquired by public firms in the US over a 10-year period. Twenty-seven percent of the acquired firms were created, grown, and acquired on total investments of less than $50,000. Yet when we looked at the data, we did not find a significant discount on the total valuation of those firms with little invested capital, with respect to their terminal valuation at acquisition. Money in did not predict money out.

The big variable that changed with respect to the amount of investment money is the time between founding and acquisition. Investment money accelerated growth and time to liquidity. The finding was so clear in our data that we were able to separate the population into a group of "earners" who created value through revenue and cash flows, and "burners" who fuelled growth with investment money (Wiltbank et al., 2015).

SELECTING A FUNDING APPROACH

Bootstrapping limits the money entrepreneurs put into fledgling ventures, but that doesn't mean it's without risk. Clearly, bootstrapping entrepreneurs risk underinvesting in a promising opportunity. They may underestimate the upside potential of the market or choose to pursue only one aspect of it, leaving a chunk for someone else.

But entrepreneurs shouldn't look for external funding just because they're afraid of missing out on something.

As normal people, we tend to be overly optimistic in our predictions. Our startups, we believe, will grow rapidly, and so we assume we need a large infusion of cash. The risk is that we will have built a business with more space, more people, more patents, more marketing, and more sales channels than we can sustain with actual revenue.

For most new ventures, bootstrapping is a better fit than outside funding, because of the reduced risk and the obligation of proving the business before a large investment is made. And because of the simple odds against attracting large tranches of institutional investments.

TAKEAWAY: MAINTAIN CONTROL BY DOING THE MOST WITH THE LEAST

Aspiring entrepreneurs wondering how they'll finance their ventures need to remember that there are countless ways, beyond investment money, to grow a business.

In general, experienced entrepreneurs prefer the cheapest option, so they come up with creative ways of doing things at little cost and risk to themselves. When they do have to seek outside investment, they think carefully about what and whom they need.

By figuring out how to do the most with the least, they are also rewarded with control over their ventures.

■ ■ ■

So What?

Most startups can find creative ways to avoid external funding. Done right, they retain control and flexibility without betting everything on big predictions.

What Now?

For one of your opportunities, before you go looking for money, ask yourself:

■ When do you need it?

You probably don't need it all at once. Identify at least three points when you would need a chunk of money. Can you prioritize them? Which point can you reach first for the least resources?

■ When does cash flow into this business relative to when you need to pay your largest bills?

Create three ideas for how you can make cash flow in sooner. Create three ideas for how you can delay expenses. Even if it means paying a little extra, or getting a little less, matching ins and outs can be very worthwhile.

Think It Through

■ What would have happened if Mark and Stacy had chosen different options at each decision point?

■ What are the cultural aspects of financing that affect entrepreneurial startups in different communities?

The crazy quilt principle: Form partnerships

■ ■ ■

Think you can go it alone in starting a business? Think again. We're not saying you must have a cofounder, but you do need other people. More important, your business needs other people. In fact, other people—a supplier who can provide raw materials you need, a customer who's interested in what you have to offer, an acquaintance who introduces you to new potential partners—may end up having a more profound impact on your venture than you'd ever imagine.

We've described how the effectual logic that guides expert entrepreneurs turns traditional causal business logic on its head. This is certainly true when it comes to partnerships. What distinguishes effectual partnerships from causal

partnerships is the belief that those who choose to engage with the venture in some way, those who self-select into it, ultimately make the venture what it is.

If you start with certain goals in mind, as causal thinkers do, you select partners who help achieve them. The venture will dictate the partnerships. But if instead you start with a given set of means—who you are, what you know, who you know—and let various ends emerge, the partnerships create the venture. You'll see a partner as someone with another set of means to add to the mix, someone who may end up transforming the venture in a way you could not anticipate. You'll think of a partner not as a partner but as a stakeholder.

The effectual process involves interacting with any and all stakeholders willing to make actual commitments to the project, even though some interactions may result in commitments while others may not.

THE PATCHWORK QUILT AND THE PUZZLE

Metaphorically, we contrast effectual and causal approaches using the image of a quilt and a jigsaw puzzle. Making a patchwork quilt differs from putting together a puzzle in at least four ways:

- Unlike the puzzle solver, the quilter determines the pattern. Even when he begins with a basket of random patches, he can choose which patches to use and juxtapose them in a way that is personally pleasing and

Research Roots

THE INTERSUBJECTIVE

For hundreds of years, philosophers have argued about whether we see the world objectively (fact-based and measurable) or subjectively (interpreted or perceived). But recently, Donald Davidson (2001) proposed a third alternative—that we see the world intersubjectively. What he means by this is that it is nearly impossible to observe anything in isolation and that as human beings we make sense of the world by developing shared understandings. The concept of the intersubjective acknowledges that we are deeply social beings, and when projected onto the problem of starting new ventures, it explains why partnerships, particularly effectual partnerships, are so important.

meaningful. A puzzle can come together in only one way.

- Large quilting projects are usually communal: a good quilter works with others who bring their own baskets of patches along with their tastes and talents. In the process, the quilter must decide who to work with and why, manage various coordination issues, and deal with the unexpected. The puzzle solver may work with others, but this means only that the puzzle may come together more quickly, not that it will be transformed in any way by the contributions of others.
- The uncertainty of what the quilt will look like when it is done, is resolved one commitment at a time. Whether it is the quilter making a decision, or a group that decides on a color scheme, a stitch or a border, unlimited possibilities are gradually managed down to a finished result.

Research Roots

PARTNERSHIPS AND SOCIAL MEDIA

Fischer and Rueber (2011) looked at how entrepreneurs use online social media, such as Twitter, to connect to stakeholders. What they found is that effectuation is clearly enabled by these new tools and that entrepreneurs use them to develop their businesses. The primary outcome of using social media was to expand the means an entrepreneur has to work with, but for the tools to be productive, the entrepreneurs had to adopt a community orientation and adhere to community norms.

- The quilt must be not only pleasing and meaningful, but also useful and valuable—ultimately, it has to keep human bodies warm or embody their aesthetics. The puzzle just needs to get finished; all the pieces must be in place. The completed picture may be pleasing to look at, but it serves no other purpose.

An effectual logic for building a new firm or a new organization or any type of collaborative institution incorporates similar subjective, intersubjective and objective elements that make it more analogous to stitching together a patchwork quilt than solving a jigsaw puzzle.

HOW EFFECTUAL PARTNERSHIPS HAPPEN

Once the entrepreneur has taken stock of her means and affordable loss, she starts to reach out to other people to obtain advice, inputs, knowledge or help. We term this "the ask" and devote the entire next chapter to it because it is such a central part of effectuation. It is also one of the activities where new entrepreneurs have the most difficulty. Based on who she knows, potential stakeholders could be friends, family, work colleagues or random people she meets in the course of daily life. As she finds people who want to participate in the effort to build something (at this point, the "something" may be vague or concrete, but it is always open to discussion), she moves

toward obtaining commitments from the people she interacts with. What counts here is the willingness of stakeholders to commit to the construction process—not their fit or alignment with some preconceived vision or opportunity. Each person who concretely stakes something to come on board contributes to shaping the opportunity. As you read the story of how Anil Parajuli (Practically Speaking, this chapter) blurs the distinction between doctors, tourists, and clients to bring together the stakeholders who run Himalayan Health Care, you will begin to get a flavor for the kinds of creative combinations that emerge.

Whatever each stakeholder commits becomes a patch in a growing quilt whose pattern becomes meaningful only through the continual interaction that brings new stakeholders on board. In other words, stakeholders commit resources in exchange for a chance to re-shape the goals of the project and influence the future that will ultimately result.

Thus, the process of interacting with stakeholders has two contrasting effects: On the one hand, with each new partner, the means of the venture increase (again, we are not talking only about financial means), enabling new possibilities. On the other hand, as commitments accumulate, the goal of the venture crystallizes and the direction becomes more specific.

At some point, stakeholder acquisition ends, and there is no

more room for negotiating and maneuvering the shape of what will be created. As the structures of the market begin to take visible shape and consistent information becomes available, decision-making naturally shifts from a focus on control and shaping the venture, to one that makes increasing use of prediction in operating the venture.

As we begin to bring this all together, it is useful to see that the interactions between effectual stakeholder partners are based on the other three main principles of effectuation:

- **Each stakeholder brings new means to the venture (Means).** Each interaction seeks to combine individuals and their various means to create something novel and valuable. In this way, the entrepreneur and the stakeholder select each other.
- **Each stakeholder strives to invest only what he or she can afford to lose (Affordable Loss).** Since it is not clear at the early stages of the effectual process what the pie will be, let alone how much each piece will be worth, stakeholders cannot effectively use expected return as their immediate criterion for deciding what resources to invest. Instead, stakeholders have to reconcile within their own minds whether they can live with the loss of what they are contributing to the enterprise. Here, as well, the selection process goes both ways.

Practically Speaking

A MOUNTAIN OF PARTNERS

It seems so straightforward. Companies generate revenue and—ideally—
return a profit to their owners. Charities, by contrast, do not generate
revenue, and certainly not profit. But enter the creative entrepreneur. The
word is actually a concatenation of two: in French, "entre" means
between and "preneur" means taker. Which makes an entrepreneur
literally someone who takes from between.

Steep trail

On a trek in the mountainous country of Nepal, Anil Parajuli met porters
from the northern Dhading district. The porters asked for medicine to take
back to their village. Curious, Parajuli undertook his first medical
assessment trek in 1991. That experience clarified the need to bring medical expertise to the villages of Nepal.
Parajuli then talked with a friend in New York who offered to establish a non-profit and solicit funds in America.
He met doctors who had come to Nepal on vacation but were willing to offer their expertise to locals needing
medical attention. Pharmaceutical firms with medication to donate found their way to him. And gradually, an
entity that is known today as Himalayan Health Care (HHC) emerged.

Collaborative cure

The model for HHC is a reflection of its partners. Parajuli runs "medical treks" that bring foreign doctors into
remote villages to treat the sick, train local healthcare workers, and build awareness about the needs of his
country. Oh—and did we mention?—generate revenue. If you are a doctor with itchy travel feet and want to
perform medicine "in the wild," the rate is about £1,800 for a two-week trek (you pay for airfare, moleskin for
blisters, and any other personal expenses—himalayanhealthcare.org).

Self-selection

Parajuli offers us a unique insight into how entrepreneurs can do so much with what seems like so little. They
are not only unconcerned by artificial distinctions, they encourage the people around them to help create
opportunities that bridge those distinctions. By letting a volunteer self-select into also being a paying customer,
letting a trekker also share her medical expertise, Parajuli opens up the range of people, time, and money
resources available to him and his healthcare initiative.

Distinguished entrepreneur

Parajuli just celebrated 20 years of running HHC. In that time, he has run over 80 medical treks into the Dhading
region (the north part that borders Tibet) and the Ilam region (the eastern part bordering India) of Nepal. He has
provided primary healthcare services to tens of thousands of rural Nepalese and runs the Parajuli Community
Hospital, offering 24-hour service and employing Nepalese medical doctors and 40 staff. Furthermore, he has
bridged the gap between hundreds of international doctors and local healthcare providers, and is advancing
into education as well as income-generating programs for the people of Nepal. Customers? Partners? Creators
of a venture? Yes.

Research Roots

MARKETS ARE CO-CREATED

Explanations for how markets come into existence cover the entire field of social studies from psychology and sociology to economics and marketing. However, none of these fields agree or offer a comprehensive explanation for the generation of new markets.

In the field of marketing, some researchers have started to adopt the view we use in this book, which is that markets are co-created by supplier and consumer interactions. Vargo and Lusch (2004: 1–17) propose that in developed economies most markets are for services, not products, and that products be viewed as valuable for the services they provide. In either case, the value of the services provided is realized by customers interacting with the service. The ultimate point at which value is created is when customers interact with a service. Therefore, there is no such thing as firms creating value without interaction with customers. Markets have two active sides to them: they are co-created.

- **Every interaction contains unexpected contingencies (Surprise).** If you don't allow contingencies to influence your venture, you end up with purely transactional relationships aimed at reaching a predetermined goal. Contingencies don't only undermine the value of current means in achieving given goals; they also provide opportunities to create new value through those means in pursuit of new goals.

If your takeaway from reading this chapter so far is that effectual partnerships encourage you and your venture to go in directions you couldn't have possibly imagined when you started, that's good. Effectuation does not seek to find a single optimal solution. Instead, you and your partners create a new venture that is the result of sufficient conditions as opposed to necessary conditions—one that is the right venture for all of you.

BI-DIRECTIONAL PERSUASION

Working in an uncertain environment, with a product or service that is yet to be defined, you have to be persuasive—and—be able to be persuaded. In talking about being persuasive, we don't mean that you have to be a sales shark. And in talking about being able to be persuaded, we don't mean either that you should be wishy-washy, vague or opinion-free.

What we do mean is that if you can't convince anyone to work and create with you—be it potential customers, suppliers, etc.—then you have no business. Being persuadable so you can co-create with others is important as well.

Creation, then, is the outcome of interaction between stakeholders.

Practically Speaking

A MESSY COLLABORATION

When was the last time you enjoyed a glass of orange juice from a Tetra Pak carton? Made from a mix of plastic, paper and aluminum, those containers do a great job of keeping natural beverages fresh. They're also likely to end up as non-biodegradable waste that burdens landfills, costs money, and puts the squeeze on the environment.

Natural solution

You may be thinking this story is about recycling used cartons, and perhaps making a business of it. But it's not. That has already been done. Across Europe, the system for collecting and recycling cartons is well developed. Every year, around 25 billion containers end up at recycling plants, where the paper fiber is extracted and remanufactured into new packaging such as cereal boxes.

Residual problem

Which is terrific . . . as far as the paper portion of your drink carton is concerned. But what about the plastic and the aluminum? You're not likely to see those in a cereal box. The reason is that the gooey muck left over from the paper part of the recycling process gets dumped into landfills. For a large recycler such as Stora Enso in Barcelona, that means 30,000 tonnes a year of sludge, costing about £1.3 million to "tip" into the Earth. Messy however you look at it.

Practically Speaking *(continued)*

Residual opportunity

Unless you are Hans Cool or Gijs Jansen, that is. Where we see mess, they see potential in extracting value from the plastic/aluminum soup left over from Tetra Pak recycling. After talking about this potential in an MBA class, their classmates introduced the pair to Carlos Ludlow-Palafox, a Ph.D. in chemical engineering from Cambridge University working on pyrolysis, a process that gasifies plastic. The partners formed Alucha, a company whose name combines the word aluminum with the Spanish verb luchar, meaning to struggle. The next step was to manage the struggle by engaging as many committed partners as possible.

Partner soup

Cool and Jansen's first stop was a visit to Stora Enso in Barcelona. After hearing their idea of converting sludge into value, the manager of the recycling mill walked the pair out to a shuttered building in the compound and showed them a dormant machine—a previous attempt at a system for processing plastic/aluminum waste. Could they use the space to try again with a new technology? Cool and Jansen then met with the German aluminum processor Konzelmann. Would they be interested in the grade of aluminum Alucha could extract from packaging? In Austria, the pair talked with GE Jenbacher, maker of generators that run on specialized gas. Might they be interested in co-developing machinery that would burn the gas that results from extracting plastic waste from aluminum waste? As the yeses mounted up, the struggle turned into a business.

Clean evidence

Since starting in 2004, Cool and Jansen, together with their partners, have faced technical, regulatory, and operational struggles. But together with their partners, their efforts yielded a functioning plant that today runs five shifts, 24 hours a day, seven days a week. Their compensation comes in many forms, from revenues that should reach £1.8 million (2011), to an award from the EC as one of the best LIFE environment projects of 2010, to the satisfaction of seeing trucks loaded with aluminum headed for production instead of sludge headed for landfill. Not to mention the knowledge that they provide Stora Enso with 20% of its steam needs by burning the gas generated in their process. Future efforts may direct that gas directly to a special generator that produces electricity for the plant or even for sale on the grid. From the grunge of entrepreneurial struggle, they show us how partners combine to form the glamor of an entrepreneurial venture that creates both profit today and a cleaner environment tomorrow.

CREATING MARKETS THROUGH PARTNERSHIPS

Effectuation emphasizes commitments from stakeholders as a way to manage, reduce, and/or eliminate uncertainty in the environment. Each committed stakeholder expands the means available to the venture, making the venture more viable. And each committed stakeholder steers the concept of the venture to one that more people have bought into—increasing the likelihood that the idea is one that presents good validity.

Partners can come in different shapes and forms—what matters is that they commit to a future in which they all find a stake, and they influence one another's ideas about what shape that venture should take. In an effectual partnership, what matters is that all parties find something in it for them.

Practically Speaking

HUNTING WITH THE PACK

Baloo Patel was born in Uganda in 1939, but the tracks to his entrepreneurial career had already been laid; laid by hand, in fact, by ancestors who had been brought from India to work on the East African Railway. Starting out as a bank teller in Kenya, Patel soon began working in a tour operating company. Believing he could improve the business, he participated in a management buy-out of the operator, and with the stroke of a pen became an entrepreneur.

Individual growth

With responsibility for the tour business, Patel started to imagine new services and new offerings. Clients enjoyed seeing the Kenyan landscape and wildlife from the ground, but might they find the view from the air to be even more dramatic? In 1981, he bought a plane and entered the aviation business. And in 1986, he bought a balloon and offered silent aerial excursions above the Masai Mara. Business soared, and Patel used the proceeds to expand into real estate, printing, insurance, and mining.

With every step of expansion, Patel had the benefit of knowing the clients and the market, so he could be comfortable with demand, but he took the risk associated with buying hard assets on his own. This risk was underscored in his printing venture with his cousin Nayan. In 2002 Patel observed that only about 300,000 physical phone lines supported Kenya's population of 35 million people. The cellular industry was poised to take off. He was going to benefit by printing prepaid cellular phone cards. So he invested in specialized equipment for secure card printing. But the cellular phone operators in Kenya had existing partners, and Patel was on his own. His equipment lay dormant for years, until disruptions in Kenya's transportation system left the operators without foreign printed cards, putting Patel in business—finally.

Shared growth

The experience added to Patel's sophistication, which enabled him, together with his son Rohan, to expand the business into Wilderness Lodges, their high-end hospitality offering within the boundaries of Kenya's national parks that use properties leased from the government. Their latest venture, Sankara Hotels and Resorts, a hotel management company, will hold no hard assets, but partner with owners to operate contemporary five-star hotels for business travellers in Africa's key growing cities.

> Our new business, Sankara, is based on the Sanskrit word meaning "causer of tranquillity." Appropriately named, our goal is to develop refined hotels that offer functional yet tranquil guestrooms whilst simultaneously offering vibrant recreational and entertainment facilities that will become the center of daily urban life. On a personal note, it has a special meaning for me; I find that the more I spread risk and reward with my partners, the more tranquil I am in running the business.
>
> Baloo Patel

Practically Speaking *(continued)*

Entrepreneurial growth

As you venture out into the savannah of entrepreneurship, it is worth thinking about who might share risk with you. Not only will these people or companies lower the amount of money you need, they will also have an incentive to help you succeed. Perhaps the real entrepreneurial lesson from Kenya is that hunting is more effective when you're part of a pack than when you're on your own.

But the result created something new for both parties, something beneficial to both, and something neither could have created on their own.

Getting started on building a stakeholder commitment could be the hardest part. Once the conversation has begun, the possibilities begin to unfold.

TAKEAWAY: BUY-IN IS BETTER THAN SELLIN'

We close this chapter with a practical answer to the philosophical question of how you think about the effectual interaction. The answer is simply that buy-in is better than sellin'. In other words, effectual interaction comes together at commitment. So as nice as it is to have someone who is willing to make a transaction with you, what you really want is that concrete and rational commitment to co-creating an idea with you.

■ ■ ■

So What?

Partners self-select into new ventures and commit different means to the effort. Without commitments, you don't have a partner; you have merely a potential partner. Committed stakeholders co-create ventures that don't always look like the original venture you had in mind. You influence them, and they influence you.

What Now?

Time for some personal reflection:

■ Are you persuadable, willing to reshape your venture with partners in order to gain their commitment to it?

■ What are you unwilling to change? Why?

■ What potential partners would like to see you succeed? Why?

■ How, specifically, will you know if potential partners are actually committed to the relationship in some way?

■ Now . . . go and talk with potential partners. What would it take for them to commit to working with you?

Think It Through

■ How does viewing everyone as persuadable change your view of the world?

■ When "co-creating" an opportunity . . . who is the entrepreneur? Why?

CHAPTER 15

Most people never pick up the phone and call. Most people never ask. And that's what sometimes separates people who do things from the people who just dream about them.

Steve Jobs

Asking potential partners to make commitments

■ ■ ■

An entrepreneur's first steps with a new idea, the first things she does in taking her idea for a test drive in the real world, almost always involve a partner—someone, as we saw in Chapter 14, who makes a commitment, large or small, to join the entrepreneur in shaping her venture. How do these partnerships come to be? How does an entrepreneur turn a disinterested bystander into a true stakeholder?

By asking.

Consider the last time you asked someone for something—a date, a favor, some tangible or intangible resource. Chances are you were a bit uncomfortable. Maybe you didn't know how to begin or how to handle the conversation or how to recover from a no.

Many of us cringe at the thought of such situations, while others, especially expert entrepreneurs, become very adept in them. They are not only comfortable asking people for things but also asking in ways that lead to productive relationships. Instead of focusing solely on their own immediate need—the thing they're asking for—they continually seek common ground, inviting the other person to ask for what he wants. They take the occasion to learn about the other person—how his means and level of affordable loss might dovetail with their own—so they can co-create the future. In short, they look for ways to turn the person they are interacting with into a stakeholder of some kind.

Entrepreneurs are famously fond of taking action rather than planning and cogitating. Effectuation, the approach we've observed among expert entrepreneurs, is in part a mindset, a way of viewing opportunity and uncertainty. But ultimately, it's a series of actions. Asking is one of the very first actions, one of the first things you can do to practice effectuation.

And you never stop asking as you grow your ventures and become an expert entrepreneur yourself.

Asking—for advice, for help with an idea, for resources, for introductions to other people, for money—is so central to effectual entrepreneurship that we decided to give it a fancy name—"the ask."

Practically Speaking

A PRETTY COLLABORATION

Entrepreneur Ash Sood imports technical mountaineering equipment for Indian soldiers patrolling the mountainous northern borders India shares with Pakistan and Afghanistan. Sood travels the world sourcing the best gear he can find. One such trip took him to Taiwan where his business partner showed him an unexpected innovation: a device that could rapidly print graphics on to individual fingernails. The machine was not expensive, so Ash brought two back to his home in Delhi.

Pretty uncertain

But what does a person, whose clients defend India's borders against incursion for months at a time, do with a high-technology manicure product? The answer depends on the person. Someone with covert operations experience might load the device with camouflage colors to prepare troops for complete secrecy. Someone with cartography experience might print map information on to soldiers' nails for a remote mission in unknown territory. Ash had access to a different kind of expertise. His wife Monika had previously been an entrepreneur in the fashion industry, and she suggested they create a unique consumer manicure kiosk.

Parlour room

"We went to the only mall in Delhi and asked for space," Monika explains. "When we described what we wanted to do, they looked at us as though we were crazy. But they offered us a small, unwanted location between the cinema and the food court. The terms were clear. No rent up front. If we did well for a month, we would discuss a fee. And if we didn't make money, we were to take our table and never return." Almost immediately, mall-goers were fascinated by the possibility of instantly having photos, graphics, and custom colors printed on their nails. Ash and Monika were happy to have to negotiate rent.

Fashion flaw

Sadly, the entrepreneurial life is not all glamor. So good at attracting customers, the high-tech machine wasn't as good at retaining them. It sometimes failed to finish a nail, or printed misaligned graphics. The printing ink and materials it used were expensive and ran out fast. So the Soods hopped on a plane to China to talk to the manufacturer about improving the machine, and to see about sourcing wholesale ink and printing materials. Their travels took them to the interior of China where in the open market, amidst vendors of ink and printing supplies, they found sellers of fashion accessories and faux jewellery. Monika envisioned an alternative offering for her customers when the manicure machines weren't working. She filled her bag with sparkles and returned to Delhi.

Practically Speaking *(continued)*

Makeover

After only four months in the custom manicure graphics business, Ash and Monika were selling so many fashion accessories that they moved the machines out. The new business was named Youshine, and was so successful that the owner of the mall suggested they consider a second outlet in his newest mall. By the time they opened their third location in a competing mall that had just opened across the street from their first location, Monika was travelling to China every three months. The couple have gone on to open eight more kiosks across India plus an internet retail site (youshine.in) in less than two years.

A look in the mirror

Aside from highlighting the importance of transforming the things and knowledge you have, working with the people who choose to work with you, taking affordable risks and using surprise as an input to new possibilities, the Soods offer us one more entrepreneurial lesson. "If you're going to go into business with your husband, make sure responsibilities are clear," says Monika. "As head of procurement, if I make a bad decision, it is my problem, not something Ash is going to second guess. Respect and tolerance are critical for board meetings at the breakfast table. But the result is that I get to do what I want to do, when I want to, and with the person I choose." Beautiful indeed.

Asking should not be a mystery. Each of us likely started asking for all sorts of things from a very young age, yet most of us have probably not mastered the art of "the ask." We can, but first we must learn what "the ask" is—and what it is not. Then we can set out to master the effectual ask.

ASKING IS NOT SELLING

In the popular imagination, entrepreneurs are the consummate salespeople. They are individuals with a compelling vision, who have the communication skills and forceful personalities that get other people to "buy" into their ideas. As we discussed earlier, however, entrepreneurship is less about selling a vision, which is a one-sided exchange, and more about co-creating a vision with others, building a mutually beneficial partnership.

Yet, as we saw in Chapter 14, although you do not need to be an exceptional salesperson to be an entrepreneur, you do need to understand something about the art of persuasion. You need to know how you might persuade others to join you in your adventure. And, just as important, you need to be persuadable yourself. You must know how to communicate what is most compelling and interesting about your initial idea but then be open—eager even—to incorporating other people's means and affordable loss, to let other people transform your project and even your vision. It is through such openness to co-creation that entrepreneurs create value. And it is through asking that fruitful partnerships are born.

To understand the difference between selling and asking, consider the difference between a traditional causal approach and an effectual approach. A causal approach is about gathering the specific means you need to reach a predetermined

Research Roots

INFLUENCE

In his bestseller *Influence: The Psychology of Persuasion* (2006), Robert Cialdini looks at what he calls "weapons of influence." We summarize them here.

- *Social proof.* Human beings imitate each other.

- *Authority.* People tend to obey authority.

- *Liking.* People are more likely to be persuaded if they like the person doing the persuading.

- *Scarcity.* Perceived scarcity creates demand.

- *Reciprocation.* If someone does you a favor, you tend to return it.

- *Commitment and consistency.* Once a person has committed, they tend not to back out.

These insights can be applied equally well to "the ask" as they can to more transactional sales kinds of interactions.

Practically Speaking

IS A COST ALWAYS A COST?

As an executive at diversified mail order retailer Avion Group, Ruth Owades saw an opportunity in the amateur horticulturalist segment, a group that was easy to reach, was extremely loyal if well served and most important, had a pressing need: These consumers did not have easy access to specialty gardening equipment. She proposed the idea of building a mail order business around this need to executives at Avion, but they had no interest. Her next step was to ask if she could develop it on her own. Surprisingly, they agreed.

After a brief investigation, Ruth, who had never worked outside the comfortable confines of the corporate world, discovered that investment money for an unproven entrepreneur with an unproven idea was not exactly forthcoming. Ruth's best offer came from a group of four private investors, who were asking for 49% of the company and would require Ruth to provide 25% of the money for the venture from her own bank account. Determined to make it work without the investors' money, she plunged into business, naming her venture Gardener's Eden.

Planting the seeds

Ruth's first stop was the printer. For a mail order company the single largest expense is printing and mailing the catalogue—this item can account for up to half of the total costs. Ruth needed both a fantastic print job and good financial terms—two elements that are usually mutually exclusive. So she proposed a scheme in which the printers would bid on her first two catalogues rather than just her first one. This showed the printers that she was willing to make a commitment to them, in exchange for favorable treatment. Her suggestion—a novel one in the industry—was well received. So when she went in and said, "Gee, the other printers are offering me 90-day terms. Can't we do better than that?" the printer gave her six months to pay.

Practically Speaking *(continued)*

Gardener's Eden needed more than catalogues, however. Ruth asked her utility providers for long credit terms so she did not have to tie up her cash with deposits for electricity and telephones. She asked for long credit windows with the manufacturers of the exotic gardening items she intended to sell. She asked both her landlord and her credit card company for unusually low terms, and got them. She even pursued her local post office branch, visiting the postmaster again and again until he found a forgotten regulation that enabled her to collect her daily mail without any service charge.

Ruth's strategy was simple: figure out who would benefit from her success, tell them the story about what she was trying to accomplish, and explain to them why they were essential to the venture and how they would be successful when she was. She asked everyone for everything she needed and found she could do much better than she might have expected. Without using the terminology, she was successfully applying "the ask" and affordable loss to her venture, finding creative ways to reduce her startup costs so she could reduce her risk to only what she could afford to lose. The box below compares what her costs would have been (using a pitch) versus what they ended up being.

Watching them grow

Ultimately, Ruth built an environment where everyone around her had a reason to do something special to make her successful, an environment where she had transformed suppliers to the venture into partners with the venture. Ruth's revenue well exceeded US$1 million when stylish retailer Williams-Sonoma acquired Gardener's Eden less than four years after its launch.

RUTH OWADES' CAPITAL EXPENDITURES

Startup Expense Item	Using the pitch	Using "the ask"
Catalogue printing and mailing	US$100,000	Negotiated for two catalogues and six-month payment terms
Mailing list rentals	US$30,800	US$30,800
Payment for merchandise	US$75,600	Negotiated long credit windows
Miscellaneous utility and other deposits	US$4,000	Negotiated no deposit
Other working capital, e.g. mailing supplies, employee, rent	US$15,000	US$15,000
TOTAL	**US$225,400**	**US$45,800**

goal. Effectuation, in contrast, is about working with a set of evolving means and seeing where you end up. Both approaches require asking for things, but in very different ways.

The causal ask is like a traditional sales pitch:

- You develop a vision.
- You figure out the resources you need to achieve that vision.
- You identify the individuals or organizations who can provide those resources.
- You craft a pitch that can induce them to give you what you want.
- You deliver the pitch, and you either get the resources you're looking for—or you don't.

The effectual ask is the start of a conversation. Your ask may be a "pitch" of some sort, but ultimately you want to get others to give you their pitch in return:

- You decide what you can start doing based on your means and your level of affordable loss.
- You identify individuals and organizations who may be interested in co-creating the future with you. They may be potential customers or suppliers, or they may just be interesting and talented people whose possible role in the new venture is entirely unclear at the start.
- You craft a variety of asks.
- You deliver "the asks" and perhaps end up with commitments—of talent, money, ideas, time—from new stakeholders, whose means may transform your idea. Those

stakeholders may then bring on yet other people, who, in turn, will shape the project with their means.

Whereas the causal pitch can succeed or fail—you either get what you're asking for or you don't—the effectual ask is flexible enough to not really fail. And unlike the traditional sales pitch, it's not necessarily a one-time thing, you can go back to the same person multiple times with different kinds of asks. Maybe in an initial conversation you find a person that loves your idea and is willing to help design an offering. Having established a relationship you can make follow-on asks, such as asking if she can introduce you to any potential customers.

At the end of an effectual ask, you've "sold" yourself as someone others want to collaborate with. But you've probably been doing less talking—especially the sort associated with aggressive selling—and more listening, learning about what potential stakeholders have to offer, *their* visions of your idea and what they are willing to commit to make those happen.

Outcomes of the effectual ask go beyond what you set out to ask for. In fact, the outcome usually is one that neither party to "the ask" may have had in mind at the beginning of the conversation. One example is when someone changes roles. Your landlord may become your customer. Your customer may become your investor. The company next door may become your provider of Internet access or manufacturing

Back in the 1790s Adam Smith (1798: 493–494) writes that:

> Different genius is not the foundation of this disposition to barter which is the cause of the division of labour. The real foundation of it is that principle to persuade which so much prevails in human nature . . . We ought then to mainly cultivate the power of persuasion, and indeed, we do so without intending it. Since the whole life is spent in the exercise of it, a ready method of bargaining with each other must undoubtedly be attained.

capacity. The effectual ask almost guarantees surprises. After all, you can't know what the other person will say or what his circumstances are. He might respond to your ask with an ask of his own—maybe he's following his own passion or is considering a career change and has started thinking about what he could do with his own means. Just as he has ideas and resources that he did not realize were valuable to you until you came along and asked for them, you might have something to offer him that you had never dreamed he would find value in. The goal of "the ask" is to get others to put skin in the game. You may end up gaining and making commitments to a game you never could have envisioned at the outset.

Research Roots

ADVICE

Recently, experimental economists have looked at the role of advice in decision-making. In a presentation of experimental games incorporating advice, Andrew Schotter remarks, "Despite the prevalence of reliance on advice, economic theory has relatively little to say about it . . ." However, he found that, "Experimental results . . . indicate that word-of-mouth advice is a very powerful force in shaping the decisions that people make."

Schotter's (2003) key findings:

* Subjects tended to follow the advice of advisors with hardly more expertise at the task than the subject, and this led to better decisions than acting alone.

* Advice does change behavior: subjects played games differently after receiving advice.

* Given a choice between information and advice, subjects tended to opt for advice.

* The process of giving and taking advice tended to foster learning because people tend to give better advice for others than they do for themselves.

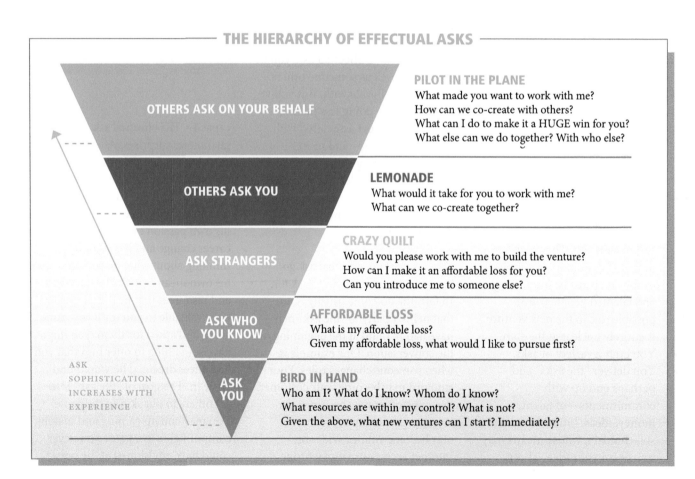

THE HIERARCHY OF EFFECTUAL ASKS

OTHERS ASK ON YOUR BEHALF

PILOT IN THE PLANE
What made you want to work with me?
How can we co-create with others?
What can I do to make it a HUGE win for you?
What else can we do together? With who else?

OTHERS ASK YOU

LEMONADE
What would it take for you to work with me?
What can we co-create together?

ASK STRANGERS

CRAZY QUILT
Would you please work with me to build the venture?
How can I make it an affordable loss for you?
Can you introduce me to someone else?

ASK WHO YOU KNOW

AFFORDABLE LOSS
What is my affordable loss?
Given my affordable loss, what would I like to pursue first?

ASK SOPHISTICATION INCREASES WITH EXPERIENCE

ASK YOU

BIRD IN HAND
Who am I? What do I know? Whom do I know?
What resources are within my control? What is not?
Given the above, what new ventures can I start? Immediately?

THE HIERARCHY OF ASKS

The effectual process begins when entrepreneurs ask themselves what means they have at their disposal and what they're willing to put at risk: "What do I know?" "What do I know that might not appear on my resume?" "Who do I know?" "What can I afford to lose?"

They then turn to potential partners—generally people they know—asking for advice, feedback, assistance of various kinds. These asks give the other person an opportunity to discuss his or her ideas and aspirations. Along the way, the other person may end up asking you for something, asking you to make some sort of commitment. This is how the crazy quilt of committed partners is pieced together.

Ultimately, as your network of committed stakeholders expands, others may make asks on your behalf—a sign of true commitment and partnership in a venture.

BARRIERS TO ASKING

Asking is not necessarily easy. It does not come naturally to many of us. Numerous obstacles—some internal, some external—make it difficult to approach other people for assistance. Here are some of the doubts, insecurities, nagging impressions, and fears that make it easy to chicken out or procrastinate. If you're aware of them, it's easier to overcome them.

Research Roots

YES IS CLOSER THAN YOU THINK

Social psychology researchers studied asking for favors from people. For example, in a series of six studies, Francis Flynn and Vanessa Lake (2008) asked students at Columbia University to go out and ask for help from the general public. The tasks included asking people to fill out questionnaires, asking for the use of another person's cell phone, asking people for directions, etc. One of the studies also examined people in a real situation, asking donors for money for a non-profit organization. In each study, before they embarked on asking for favors, the subjects were asked to estimate the likelihood of success. For example, they were asked about the time and effort it would take, or the number of people they would have to ask before someone would do them the favor they were asking for.

In all the studies, people overestimated the difficulty of getting other people to do them a favor. In other words, more people are more willing to help than most people believed at the outset.

- **Asking will make me seem weak**. It's true: in a culture that values independence and self-reliance, asking for anything— even for directions when you're lost—can be seen as a weakness, an admission that you can't do it all on your own. But the

simple truth is that we can't do it all on our own, and why would we want to? As the quote from Steve Jobs at the beginning of this chapter shows, the expert entrepreneurs we've studied understand that they need other people's ideas, insights, expertise, contacts, and other resources to create value. They are comfortable admitting what they don't know and don't have. That understanding is not a weakness but one of their greatest strengths.

- **Asking will make me seem pushy.** What to some people seems pushy will seem brave or creative to others. Especially when you ask for permission to pester without being a pest. Most people usually find humor in such candor and are likely to tell you how much "pestering" they are willing to tolerate. The great thing about asking is that you don't necessarily have just one shot at it. If you sense that the askee is put off or offended by your request, you can step back and engage in a more open-ended conversation about the askee's interests and goals. Ultimately, the askee may end up asking you for something.
- **How can I ask for something when I have nothing to give in return?** Try to let the other person be the judge of that. You may think you have nothing to offer, but you aren't in the other person's head, so you don't know how they will respond. We know an MBA student who summoned the courage to contact a prominent

professional for advice about breaking into his industry. She got his advice, but she also ended up agreeing to help his niece navigate the business-school application process. She could never have guessed at the beginning of "the ask" that she did have something of value to him. It was "the ask" itself that led to her learning that. The effectual ask is not necessarily a quid pro quo situation, but approaching each interaction openly and truly engaging with the other person will often lead you down unexpected paths and

present opportunities for mutual benefit.

Even if the other person is simply generous and you currently have nothing to offer them in return does not mean you cannot return the favor in the future. Or pay it forward to another entrepreneur.

- **I'm afraid the person will say no.** If the answer is no, don't lose heart. Instead, change direction. Rather than ask a yes or no question, try asking open-ended questions that invite conversation and draw on the person's imagination: "How

might we be able to work together?" "What would it take to persuade you to collaborate with me?" It's also important to recognize the difference between a flat-out no and a "No, but. . ." as in "No, I cannot help you with that, but I know someone who might be able to" or "No, I am not particularly interested in that idea, but here's what I am interested in." Sometimes a valuable yes may be hiding within a no.

- **I'm afraid the person will say yes!** If a conversation with a potential stakeholder seems to be heading toward some sort of commitment, even a small one, you are deep into the effectual process. Congratulations! But of course, your work is not over—it is probably just beginning, and it's natural to feel a bit nervous. You will now need to honor this budding partnership by following through on shared commitments and staying open to surprises.

BECOMING AN EXPERT ASKER

The best way to get better at asking and to overcome any fear or anxiety surrounding "the ask" is to practice asking. You can practice asking even if you're not actively building a business. Try to find opportunities in your daily life (asking someone to join you on a fun project or to contribute time and money to a worthy cause) or do a practice run with a friend. Here are some tips to keep in mind as you master the art of "the ask":

- **Tailor a narrative.** Try to create a story that connects your interest with the individual in front of you. That story should be geared toward your possible overlapping interests but broad enough to let her determine how she might become your collaborator. In creating this story, consider why this person is willing to talk to you in the first place and how her experience aligns with your interests.
- **Start specific.** Go into the conversation with a concrete ask in mind (e.g. for an investment, mentorship, introduction to other people) but keep a mental list of backup asks. Maybe the person doesn't have the time or interest to be an active mentor but would be delighted to introduce you to some of his colleagues. Don't

focus so much on what you think you want that you miss what the other person is offering.
- **Be a good listener.** Sure, you'll need to do some talking, but the listening is just as, if not more, important. To be truly open to what another person has to offer, you must listen with your full attention.
- **Don't expect a linear path.** It's usually not as simple as asking for something, getting it, going away until the next need arises, and then asking for that next thing. You must allow your vision to be co-opted and be receptive to the other person's vision and means. Remember, it's about building relationships with committed stakeholders, not about getting what you think you need at a given moment.

- **Develop a repertoire of open-ended questions.** "What would you think of. . .?" "What would it take for you to. . .?" "How could we work together to. . .?" "Could you tell me how to. . .?" "Can you think of a way we could. . .?" "What do you think is the best way to. . .?"

- **Set the tone—and then follow through.** Let the other person know at the outset the sort of conversation you'd like to have: "I'd love to be able to tell you a bit about my idea, and I'd be interested to hear about what you've been working on." And then make sure you live up to that promise.

- **Be open to more than money.** You may think that what you really need is money. But in fact, you probably need money to buy something, and it may be easier for someone to give you that something than to give you money. For example, after a successful entrepreneur gave a presentation in one of our classes, two of the students asked him to invest in their venture. They needed money, they explained, to fly around the world to promote their idea. Instead of writing a check, the entrepreneur offered the students his many (unused) frequent flyer miles.

- **Think about the exit.** Ideally, the person you're speaking with will make some sort of commitment to your venture. If not, that's okay. Remember that asking is an iterative process. You can end the conversation by asking if it would be possible to talk again in the future (at which point you'd make a different ask) or if the person can suggest someone else you could talk to.

TAKEAWAY: IT'S ABOUT BUILDING, NOT GETTING

Ask and you shall receive? Yes, but what you receive might be something you had not anticipated. The goal of the kind of asking effectual entrepreneurs do isn't receiving per se but building by integrating others' means and aspirations with their own and seeing where that leads.

With this in mind, it's time to update the old axiom to something more effectual:

Ask and you shall learn,
Ask and you shall co-create,
Ask and you shall open doors,
   and . . .
Practice and you shall learn
   how to ask.

■ ■ ■

So What?

Partners can only select into new ventures when asked. In the early stages of your efforts, open-ended conversations are about building partnerships, not just getting what you want. Help others see what you see, LISTEN to what they want to be a part of, influence each other, and ask for action that seems mutually beneficial. Practice. It's not just selling, it's building.

What Now?

- Are you comfortable with making "the ask"? Are you good at it? Spend some time considering when/where/how you do well asking for advice/money/ideas/introductions.

For an opportunity you are developing:

- Consider some things you imagine you need, who might you ask for them? Now step up your game: how might you build a conversation with them that goes beyond just asking for a yes/no for things you need?

- Consider the "whom you know" of your means . . . reach out to some people; develop three different possibilities of how to ask them to engage with you.

- What "ask" are you most nervous to make? Why? Don't hide from it. Develop your next three ideas for building your way toward that ask.

Think It Through

- Without "asking" how else can a venture proceed?

- How do you know when you should make an effectual ask and when you should make a causal ask?

- How could you build partnerships that can explore both kinds? Or must they be mutually exclusive?

CHAPTER 16

There is no question about whether the unexpected will present itself in the new venture creation process.

The question is when and whether you will take advantage of it.

Both optimists and pessimists contribute to our society.

The optimist invents the airplane.

The pessimist invents the parachute.

G.B. Stern, Novelist

The lemonade principle: Leverage surprise

As we will see in the story of ICEHOTEL (next chapter), contingencies can mark important turning points for a venture. In the case of ICEHOTEL, rain on ice sculptures was an unpleasant surprise. It wasn't what was meant to happen. But the ICEHOTEL story illustrates that contingencies—even negative ones—can be leveraged in positive ways. Instead of fighting the rain, Yngve Bergqvist did something a little less obvious: in his words, he "invented a new feeling." Rather than trying to preserve something against the forces of nature, he leveraged the natural process, letting the sculptures be destroyed and making something new in their place.

This response epitomizes the lemonade principle, named for the bromide, "When life gives you lemons, make lemonade." It's the idea that in entrepreneurship, as well as in other areas of life, you can often do well by acknowledging and appropriating the accidental events, meetings, and information that the environment serves up. Traditional

A pessimist sees the difficulty in every opportunity.

An optimist sees the opportunity in every difficulty.

Winston Churchill

Practically Speaking

PRINTED SURPRISE

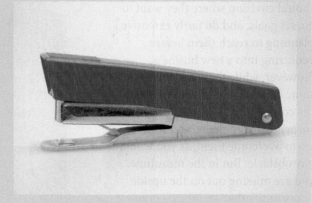

A terrific example of the role of contingency in a new venture can be found in the history of Staples, the discount office supplies superstore. It was 1985, the Thursday before the July 4 holiday weekend in the US. Having recently lost his job working for a supermarket, Thomas Stemberg was formulating a business plan for a supermarket chain when he ran out of printer ribbon for his Apple ImageWriter. When he went to local stores to buy a new printer ribbon, he found either they didn't have the ribbon he needed or the store had closed early for the holiday weekend. The simple information that printer ribbon was unobtainable triggered an idea for Stemberg. In a later interview with CNN, he said, "It dawned on me that not only could small entrepreneurs not get stationery at the rate of bigger companies—sometimes they couldn't get it at all." Because he didn't have the printer ribbon, Stemberg couldn't finish his business plan over the weekend, but it didn't matter. Out of the contingency was born an idea for a venture he wanted to start—a chain of office supply stores currently valued (start of 2016) at more than US$6 billion.

Practically Speaking

SILLY SURPRISE

Perhaps one of the best-known stories of a new venture founded on a contingency is Silly Putty. The substance was actually the result of a failed experiment to create synthetic rubber during World War II in General Electric's New Haven laboratory. General Electric bounced the idea around for years in search of a practical use, but it wasn't until 1949 that Peter Hodgson, an unemployed advertising agent, encountered the compound as part of the entertainment at a party. Finding the stretchy material was an accident, but Hodgson did what he could with that contingent event. Unemployed and US$12,000 in debt, he saw potential opportunity and borrowed US$147 to produce a batch of the stuff. He renamed it Silly Putty and used his public relations skills to get it featured in Doubleday bookstores, Neiman-Marcus, and The New Yorker magazine. To everyone's amazement, sales took off, and Peter Hodgson laughed all the way to the bank. When he died in 1976, his estate was worth US$140 million.

Photo provided courtesy of Crayola LLC, used with permission. © 2010 Crayola. Silly Putty® is a registered trademark of Crayola LLC.

models suggest the entrepreneurs should envision where they want to go, set goals, and do fairly extensive planning to reach them before venturing into a new business. However, while these activities offer some benefits, it is easy to overlook the costs. Rigid plans tend to frame surprises as problems, and so you try to overcome them, as you would any obstacle. But in the meantime, you are missing out on the upside opportunity that surprises—even negative ones—can represent.

Instead of looking at the unexpected as a problem, it can be looked at as a new building block—a resource—for a young enterprise.

Some of the materials the venture will be constructed from will become known to the entrepreneur only after the venture gets started. Using these new building blocks, expert entrepreneurs exercise control over the unexpected by considering how they might provide a foundation for a new opportunity.

In many ways, the lemonade principle lies at the heart of entrepreneurial expertise. It says that the unexpected is not a cost but a resource that, in the right hands, may become something valuable. Surprises may be few or many, come early or take their time and be good or bad. But whatever form they take, whenever they come along, and however frequently they occur, they can be used as inputs into new ventures. Entrepreneurs can't predict surprises, and they can't design them, but they can try to exploit them by building their venture to use them.

Practically Speaking

VEGETABLE SURPRISE

Contingency often takes the form of unexpected people arriving on your doorstep. Consider the history of J.R. Simplot. Simplot built a business storing and sorting potatoes and onions during the Great Depression. As David Silver (1985) recounts:

> [I]n the spring of 1940, Jack Simplot decided to drive to Berkeley, California, to find out why an onion exporter there had run up a bill of US$8,400 for cull (or reject) onions without paying . . . The girl in the office said that the boss wasn't in. J.R. said that was fine; he would wait until the man arrived.

> Two hours later, at ten o'clock, a bearded old man walked in. Assuming this was his debtor, Simplot accosted him. But he turned out to be a man named Sokol, inquiring why he was not getting his due deliveries of onion flakes and powder. They sat together until noon, but still the exporter failed to arrive.

> As the noon hour passed, Simplot was suddenly struck with an idea. He asked the bewhiskered old trader to a fateful lunch at the Berkeley Hotel. "You want onion powder and flakes," said J.R., "I've got onions. I'll dry 'em and make powder and flakes in Idaho."

Thus, through a chance meeting with Sokol, Simplot found an opportunity. He went on to develop one of the largest agricultural businesses in the US.

UNDERSTANDING DIFFERENT KINDS OF CONTINGENCIES

In general, a contingency can be thought of as something that is a mere possibility, something that may or may not happen. Contingencies are, therefore, unnecessary; they are not a logical requirement. Instead, they fall into the realm of pure chance, something that happens without a specific known cause.

But these chance events come in many shapes and sizes, so it is helpful to have a rudimentary way of categorizing them. For instance, though the stories just told are all instances of contingency, in fact they are examples of three very different kinds.

Unexpected people

One category of contingency is accidental interactions with other people. Either you might meet a particular person by pure chance, or the content of your interaction with someone is unexpected and perhaps feels a bit random. Both kinds of contingency are at work in the encounter between Simplot and Sokol: The two met completely by accident, and they struck up an unanticipated conversation about onion powder and flakes. Research in entrepreneurship suggests that meetings like the one between Simplot and Sokol are far more likely than you might think.

Unexpected events

Historians talk frequently about unexpected events—so much so that there is a new genre of counterfactual history, which asks what might have been if such-and-such hadn't happened. Classic examples of the important role accorded to contingent events can be found in military history. Rain on the battlefield bogged down Napoleon's troops at Waterloo, allowing Wellington to carry the day. And a savage storm scattered the Spanish Armada, saving Elizabethan England from invasion.

Practically Speaking

$10 SURPRISE

Sometimes contingent events come in unfortunate form. In the case of Steve Mariotti, a mugging at the hands of six teenagers was the chance event. In September 1981, Mariotti was walking on the Lower East Side of Manhattan when a group of youths surrounded him, slapped him, knocked him to the ground, and threatened to throw him into the East River. Their target: a US$10 bill he was carrying. Traumatized by the event but determined to make something positive out of it, Mariotti decided to become a high school teacher in a New York City neighborhood in an effort to do what he could to improve the lives of young people in the inner cities. His experiences teaching high schoolers about making money led him to see the potential in entrepreneurship as a tool for changing people's lives, and he went on to found NFTE (the Network for Teaching Entrepreneurship), which is dedicated to educating kids about the possibilities for using entrepreneurship to better themselves.

Practically Speaking

RAILROAD SURPRISE

Like many of the stories we recount in this book, Railtex leans toward the mundane—after all, short-haul railroading is not exactly the newest or most exciting business venture one could get into. The Railtex story starts in 1977, when Bruce Flohr put US$50,000 of his own money together with US$50,000 from investors to launch a railcar-leasing firm in San Antonio, Texas. Railcar leasing turned out not to be a particularly great idea: five years later, the business was still not profitable and was struggling to stay afloat. The situation forced Flohr and his team to start doing consultancy work with small railroads as a way of pulling in some extra cash. The consulting work proved to be a stroke of luck: what they accidentally discovered was that small railroads were badly in need of competent management and marketing. This contingency proved to be a turning point for the firm. Instead of consulting for small railroads, Flohr started buying them, improving their operations, and growing them by marketing freight services to local businesses. Starting with San Diego & Imperial Valley Railroad, the firm went on to pick up dozens of short-haul lines, going public in 1993 and growing into the largest short-haul railroad operator in the US.

Research Roots

ACCIDENTAL INNOVATION?

Despite the fact that managers do everything possible to reduce the scope for accidents to happen in the process of developing new products and services, it is well known that "Lady Luck" plays an important role in innovation. Entrepreneurs seem to show more imagination in granting a role for luck in their business ventures. How, then, does an entrepreneur increase the likelihood of favorable surprises occurring on their entrepreneurial journey?

Clues can be found in a recent paper by Robert Austin and colleagues, who examined how innovators integrate the accidental into their work using 20 case studies ranging across a variety of industries (from shoes to aerospace to Broadway productions). The researchers found that some innovators not only were open to accidents but also intentionally designed their environment and processes to tempt accident. In one case, a pottery artist showed the researchers the beautiful artwork he made, describing how he would whack his pots with a stick in order to produce an accidental outcome, saying to himself "Ooh, that's quite wonderful."

The researchers concluded that the biggest driver of innovators being open to accidents was the cost of unproductive accidents. Subjects said that most of the accidents they experienced were not beneficial and that the affordability of the downside dictated the degree to which they could invite the accidental into their work (Austin et al., 2012).

POSITIVE OR NEGATIVE, SURPRISE IS A RESOURCE

Company	Contingency	Changed means	New things to do	Novel outcomes
Unexpected Event				
Zopa	2009 financial crisis	Lock of credit markets	Expand person-to-person (P2P) lending	Growth in new areas
NFTE	Mugged by inner city youths	Personal fear	Take steps to overcome personal fears	Become a high school teacher in a tough inner city neighbourhood
Unexpected Information				
Silly Putty	Failed development of synthetic rubber	Pliable putty	Create a toy	A product that has lasted 60 years
Contour	Limited demand for rear-view motorcycle cameras	Use of camera for "selfies"	Sports camera	A larger market for the video camera
Railtex	Losing money in short-haul rail	Information about why short-haul rail fails	Consulting	A new business model for short-haul rail
Staples	Unable to easily obtain office supplies	Knowledge of non-availability of products for small businesses	Sell office products to small businesses	Development of Staples retail chain
Unexpected People				
Simplot	Accidental meeting	Knowing someone with a specific need	Produce powdered onions using existing equipment	Opportunity in dried fruits and vegetables
Honda	Sears wants small Honda scooters	Demand in an unexpected area	Sell scooters	Entry into the US market

Steve Mariotti's mugging is a good example of a bad contingent event at the personal level, while Zopa is an example at the level of the economy. Either way, the entrepreneur has turned the event into something novel and valuable.

Unexpected information

A third type of contingency is the unexpected arrival of new information. One example of this is information that changes your expectations about the "market," as we see in the Honda example. New information might arrive in many different ways: in the Staples story, Thomas Stemberg's inability to find printer ribbon was a critical bit of information about the potential for an office supply chain in the US.

In the table above, we organize the eight stories in this chapter according to what was unexpected. When you see them together, you may find that some of the surprises are positive and some are negative. When surprises initially look positive, people often refer to them as "serendipitous" events—good things that happened by accident. If at first glance they appear negative, people often refer to them as examples of "Murphy's Law," the notion that anything that can go wrong will go wrong. In the next section, we describe how you might think about leveraging contingencies regardless of whether they appear positive or negative.

LEVERAGING CONTINGENCY: THE PROCESS

In the examples, we have considered so far, it's important to realize that the contingencies themselves did not automatically shape the direction of the venture. Instead, the entrepreneurs had to leverage them—they had to behave in a certain way in response to the contingency. Indeed, entrepreneurs are adept at seizing surprises in an instrumental fashion and figuring out ways to imaginatively utilize them to create new possibilities in the world.

There are several generic ways to think about how to handle contingencies. Consider two common ways and then a third, entrepreneurial, way:

- An adaptive response involves changing yourself to fit the contingency. For example, Thomas Stemberg could have taken the non-availability of printer ribbon to be a constraint that he would just have to cope with and resign himself to printing his business plan the following weekend.
- A heroic response involves changing the world into a state that you prefer. Stemberg might have treated the non-availability of printer ribbon as an obstacle to overcome and—determined to print his business plan—he might have gone on an all-out campaign to find printer ribbon, spending the whole of the July 4 weekend combing every store within a 50-mile radius of his home until he found one that carried the printer ribbon he desired.
- An entrepreneurial response involves a different approach— using contingencies as resources, as inputs into your entrepreneurial endeavors. Instead of adapting to or overcoming the contingencies the world throws at you, you see contingencies as assets with which you may be able to do something creative. Whereas the adaptive response involves thinking "inside the box," and the heroic response involves thinking "outside the box," the entrepreneurial response is somewhat more subtle—it involves realizing that the "box" has changed and then doing something creative with this new box.

Here, the colloquial "box" is seen as an input to the venture.

Sometimes contingencies will be obviously good things; in those cases, the entrepreneur's job is to jump on them and try to milk them for all they're worth. But the most challenging contingencies are those that come in unfortunate or negative forms—such as the mugging of Steve Mariotti in New York City. As that example shows, it is almost always possible to leverage a contingency in some kind of positive way—if you are creative enough. As we've noted, the critical point about contingencies is what entrepreneurs do with them.

The diagram entitled "The Contingency Path to Novel Outcomes" sketches out the process of leveraging contingencies.

The first step in the process is the contingency itself, which, as we've discussed, generally takes the form of an unexpected meeting, an unexpected event, or unexpected information.

The second step is seeing that a contingency usually changes the entrepreneur's means (who I am, what I know and who I know), the immediately available resources with which the entrepreneur begins building a venture.

Meeting someone new changes "who you know," while new information and contingent events change "what you know" and perhaps "who you are." In fact, every one of us can be thought of as partly constituted by a long list of contingencies that—in the

Practically Speaking

SCOOTER SURPRISE

When Honda entered the US motorcycle market in the 1960s, the company thought it would be in the business of selling big motorcycles. In the meantime, its sales team rode mopeds to get around Los Angeles. It was an unexpected call one day from a Sears representative who had seen one of the mopeds in traffic that informed Honda of the potential to sell mopeds in the US. Honda subsequently leveraged that contingency into a significant market opportunity.

long run—help form our personality, knowledge, and personal networks. Think about your own life and all the events, people, and information that have shaped you. Contingencies play a significant role in forming most individuals' means. Therefore, when contingencies occur, entrepreneurs should consider how they alter their means, as a first step toward thinking through how they could be leveraged.

The third step in the process is forming possible actions in response to the contingency. The general approach to leveraging contingencies that we outline here fits with some of the most important findings from research on creative problem solving. This research shows that, in general, there are two keys to being more creative when solving problems.

The first is to consider a lot of solutions. In general, the more potential solutions you consider for a given problem, the more likely you are to find one that's creative. For entrepreneurs, this means imagining lots of different things you might be able to do in response to an unexpected meeting, event or piece of information.

UNEXPECTED RESPONSES THAT CHANGED THE WORLD

In the course of this chapter, we have emphasized that the real source of value in contingencies is the novelty of entrepreneurs' responses to them. The same principles that apply to entrepreneurial ventures also apply to creating value in society as a whole. A powerful example of this may be found in the story of Indian nationalist Mahatma Gandhi. While still in his 20s, Gandhi travelled to South Africa, seeking work as a lawyer. There, to his surprise, he experienced the full range of discrimination directed at Indians in South Africa. In a series of contingent events, triggered by his race, he was thrown off trains and stagecoaches, and beaten and barred from hotels. These experiences of racism deeply influenced Gandhi and, though he apparently never intended it when he went to South Africa, they led him to begin working as a social activist there. When the Transvaal government began forcing the registration of Indians in 1906, Gandhi concocted a novel response to the demand: instead of advocating violent resistance, he turned the approach on its head and began promoting the method of nonviolent protest for which he subsequently became famous. He urged Indians to burn their registration cards or refuse to register, actions that expressed the deeper novelty in Gandhi's approach, which involved defying the law and suffering the consequences for doing so. Public outcry over the harsh response of the South African government to peaceful Indian protests eventually forced the authorities to compromise. It was an important symbolic victory for Gandhi and his supporters and proof that unexpected responses can change the world.

THE CONTINGENCY PATH TO NOVEL OUTCOMES

? CONTINGENCIES

People   Information   Events

CHANGE YOUR MEANS

What you   Who you   Who you
know   know   are

GIVES YOU NEW
MEANS TO LEVERAGE

"Now what can I do with my revised means?"

WHICH MAY GENERATE
NOVEL OUTCOMES

i.e. new venture directions

SURPRISE 6 →

Very often, there are immediate, obvious, spontaneous responses, such as partnering with someone you just met (as in the case of Simplot and Sokol). In other situations, there is no obvious thing to do, and so the entrepreneur may take some time to imagine various

Practically Speaking

CREATING DURING CRISIS

From all the news stories of economic collapse during the 2009 financial crisis, a casual reader might conclude that at some point society might be reduced to only the most primitive trading activity. With blocked credit markets, corporations and banks could not function effectively, and sometimes the only way to find credit was between individuals, taking us back to the millennia preceding Adam Smith.

Old ideas, new opportunities

Crisis? Not to Giles Andrews. He is not a caveman or even a Luddite. But, as managing director and co-founder of Zopa (short for the negotiating term Zone Of Possible Agreement), he is stealing an old idea from our medieval trading ancestors to create a modern business that flourished as a result of the credit crisis and has been growing since. The old idea is person-to-person (with a hip new moniker: P2P) lending. Zopa, founded in 2005, provides a simple online market to connect individual lenders with other individuals who need money. It works a lot like eBay, in that potential borrowers can post their capital needs, be rated on prior transactions and, with luck, be funded by one or many people in the Zopa community.

The power of people

What makes Zopa tick is that it's everything a bank is not. Here's how it works: say Jamesrw (his Zopa username) is looking to borrow £10,100 to pay off an existing loan and invest in his advertising consultancy business. He receives money from a large number of people, such as finkerxyz1 (his Zopa username), who lends £20 at an annual rate of 12%. Finkerxyz1 distributes tiny loans to many individual borrowers, and spreads lending risk across them all. Andrews knows that most defaults happen on bigger loans, so Zopa limits transactions to £15,000. So far, the default rate is just 0.1% of total loans, which is less than the banks' default rates.

The business of the solution

Some people might say that the middle of an economic crisis is not a good time to start a venture. Yet such venerable companies as Sony and Procter & Gamble were launched in down financial markets. One of the approaches observed in expert entrepreneurs is the ability to invert a problem and imagine how even unpleasant surprises can provide the foundation for new opportunities. In the same way that Andrews is succeeding in the banking industry as the very result of bank failure, crises ranging from energy to malnutrition present opportunities to both make a positive impact and make some money. Which crisis are you going to turn upside down?

courses of action. For example, Steve Mariotti didn't have to make an instantaneous decision to become a high school teacher—that alternative emerged from his need to face his fears about being mugged.

The second key for improving creative problem solving is to change the way the problem is framed. Entrepreneurs generally do this by inverting the way a contingency presents itself: instead of looking at it as a problem, they turn it on its head and look at it as a (badly disguised) opportunity. For example, Bruce Flohr applied what he learned from the difficulty in his short-haul rail business to other similar businesses, and created an opportunity from that realization.

The final step in the contingency leveraging process is the novel outcome that may be generated. We say "may" because, as with all creative processes, there is no guarantee that a novel, value-creating outcome is going to be forthcoming—it's just a possibility that may occur. Contingency leveraging is about seizing the unique possibilities that may arise from the interaction between the entrepreneur—with his or her unique attributes, prior experience, networks, personality traits, etc.—and a particular contingency. These interactions tend to be unpredictable because different people will interact differently with different contingencies. Think about it: something unexpected happens to you, and then you concoct an unexpected response. There is a double novelty in such interactions, which is precisely why they sometimes result in creative moments in the history of entrepreneurial ventures.

Research Roots

CONTINGENCIES AS RESOURCES IN THE STARTUP PROCESS

In a series of papers, Susan Harmeling (Harmeling and Sarasvathy, 2013) has argued that a distinguishing feature of entrepreneurship is the way contingencies are treated by entrepreneurs. The notion that chance happenings, accidents, and serendipity may play an important role in new ventures has a long history. But Harmeling's point is that the key issue is not whether contingencies occur in the course of starting a venture (because they always do) but what entrepreneurs do with them. The entrepreneurial stance is one that is resourceful regarding contingencies. This stance involves leveraging the contingencies that come along (both "good" and "bad") by incorporating them as inputs into the process of entrepreneuring.

The notion of responding more or less entrepreneurially to contingencies is grounded in the observation that individuals vary in their personal beliefs about the impact of their own agency. Some people perceive more control over their destiny than others do (Harmeling and Sarasvathy, 2013).

Practically Speaking

TWISTS AND TURNS

If you've ever had a motorcycle helmet on, you know that it's hard to see, particularly behind you. Too bad, because seeing is useful when you ride a bike on the motorway among cars, trucks, and buses at high speed. So Marc Barros did what any normal college student in Seattle, Washington, would have done: he took his student loan money and formed a company with some classmates to put a little technology to work. They attached a video camera to the back of a bike, and connected it to a small LCD display that riders could attach to their motorcycle gas tank. Perfect rear view mirror—perfect product.

Wrong turn

Unfortunately, it didn't turn out to be the perfect business. While some serious interest among motorcycle retailers was encouraging, sales were generally slow. Interestingly, though, Barros started seeing his customers watching their rear view LCD screens while doing something he didn't expect. They weren't using the video camera for safety, they were using it for fun—recording their friends do wheelies or competing to pull off perfect knee-dragging fast turns.

Lane change

Barros and his partners had a chance to take advantage of this surprise. But rethinking the product from the perspective of entertaining videos, as opposed to safety, meant numerous changes. The camera needed to be "hands-free" to operate on a motorcycle, but also wearable on the body, or other equipment, and it had to be simple to share the edited video online. With a local design firm, the team reinvented its product.

Building speed

With the VholdR camera, demand accelerated so quickly that the company had to stop allowing pre-orders so their small team could catch up on production. The launch at the 2008 Consumer Electronics Show led to their first CES Innovation Award, orders from around the world, and a litany of new ways their customers used the camera: they strapped it to a harness to capture their rock climbing ascent, taped it to a football uniform to see games as the players see it, mounted it on goggles to ski an epic powder day.

Entrepreneurial view

Barros gives us a general and a specific view, from behind the camera, of a smart entrepreneur. Generally, he shows us that new products, firms, and even markets are often not a function of vision, but instead a co-created result of working with customers. Specifically, he shows the potential for taking advantage of surprise, growing Contour from a dorm room production in 2003 to a booming creative consumer product company, by doing something completely different from what he originally intended, as a result of surprise.

Practically Speaking *(continued)*

Next journey

But the story doesn't end there. Barros and his team continued to innovate, delivering their first 1080px camera, their first HD camera, and their first combination of HD and GPS, all from their insight into their customers' desire to simply show their friends what they do. Will their insight prove correct? Maybe, but the real question is whether Barros and his team will continue to act entrepreneurially—creating new products interactively with users and taking advantage of surprise—or whether their success will encourage them to begin trying to force their vision into the market. We'll only know when we get a chance to look in the rear view video camera.

MAKING SURPRISES WORK FOR YOU

It may sound paradoxical, but you can prepare for the unexpected. Indeed, there are several things you can do to improve the odds you will experience contingencies that can be leveraged in positive ways. These are activities or ways of thinking that experienced entrepreneurs seem to have internalized and often do more or less automatically.

Social networking

New information often arrives through people you know. Therefore, there is an important linkage between social network activity and position and access to new information. To the extent that experienced entrepreneurs have richer social networks, their network connections may expose them to information flows that make them more likely to encounter contingencies. This suggests entrepreneurs may be able to engage in social networking behaviors that make it more likely contingencies

happen to them. Sony's "wandering chairman" brings this to a personal level. It was his wandering between different development teams that connected the two disparate projects that ultimately created the speaker system for the Walkman. So as an entrepreneur, you may be able to increase your exposure to contingencies by deliberately engaging in networking behaviors.

Openness to experiences

Access to contingencies may also be related to certain personality traits. These may play a role in receptiveness to contingencies and, therefore, the likelihood of leveraging them. Studies of entrepreneurial psychology have found that in general entrepreneurs score higher on the measure of "openness to experience" than comparable managers. Openness to experience is defined as intellectual curiosity and the tendency to seek new experiences. Individuals who exhibit those qualities may be more receptive to, and welcoming of, contingent events and information

and thus more likely to view them as opportunities for action. In a sense, these individuals display a taste for surprises. Therefore, another way to increase your exposure to contingencies is to deliberately cultivate a taste for new things.

Opportunity framing

Some research suggests that entrepreneurs are more likely to see the world in terms of the opportunities it presents rather than the attendant threat of changes. This tendency is the opposite of what we generally find among corporate managers, who are overwhelmingly more likely to see threats rather than opportunities in any given scenario. These different responses are probably related to the way entrepreneurs frame situations and, therefore, what information they tend to see as important. It's unclear what drives people to frame things differently, but one explanation may be that people differ in how they perceive the world and their place in it. If you view the world as particularly difficult to shape, you are more likely to respond to contingencies by seeing them as a threat and trying to adapt yourself to them. Alternatively, if you view the world as open to transformation, you might see contingency as some kind of cue to shape the future.

TAKEAWAY: HAVE CONFIDENCE IN YOUR OWN ABILITY TO MAKE A DIFFERENCE

Many entrepreneurs have "survival" stories that illustrate how even unfortunate contingencies are not only survivable in the short run but the genesis of new business opportunities and can be the source of long-term success. Thus, entrepreneurs who have successfully leveraged contingencies in the past justifiably have more confidence in their own agency and, therefore, may have less anxiety about their ability to face the unexpected in the future. The implication here is that another way to increase your exposure to contingencies is to cultivate your self-efficacy, recognizing and having confidence in your own agency in the world— your ability to make a difference (however small that difference might be).

So What?

You will be surprised. There is no way around it. The creative use of a surprise is part of being an entrepreneur. Find ways to learn from surprises, use them as new means, and consider fundamental changes in direction.

What Now?

For an opportunity you are developing, identify the surprises that you've taken advantage of. If none, consider the possibility that you aren't actively engaging with your market/partners.

- [ ] Ad-lib: Imagine one new expertise in your means. Describe one ask you're developing and flip a coin to "determine" the outcome. And add six months of time commitment to what you can afford to commit. Now create three ideas for how to change your opportunity as a result of these surprises.

- [ ] Reduce your affordable loss to $500. Adjust.

- [ ] Win your biggest "ask" and then create an entirely new direction for your opportunity as a result of the means that resulted.

- [ ] Consider whether any of these created new directions might be pursued directly.

- [ ] Consider whether you are giving luck a chance as you develop your opportunity.

Think It Through

- [ ] How can you tell if what you're seeing is just "noise" or is an actual signal of something you hadn't anticipated?

- [ ] If you pursue all surprises things may be a mess; how can you choose when to stay the course or deviate?

- [ ] How does affordable loss reinforce leveraging surprise?

- [ ] What makes a given surprise seem negative rather than positive? Are these things inherent to the surprise?

CHAPTER 17

Any of the effectual principles can be used on their own. Combined, the principles form a logic for creating an infinite set of new artefacts in the world.

Putting it together: The effectuation process

■ ■ ■

This chapter is devoted to explaining the process that connects means, affordable loss, partnerships, and contingencies. There are as many paths as there are entrepreneurs, but effectual entrepreneurs share a common flow as they co-create new ventures with stakeholders.

As we narrate this process, you will recognize each of the steps—each of the principles. The new element to consider in this chapter is the seemingly contradictory set of outcomes that result from a chain of effectual commitments. On the one hand, the process increases the resources available to the venture. On the other hand, it constrains the

venture by crystallizing its goals and helping it converge toward something specific.

Here you see the natural tension between effectuation and causation. As the effectual network grows to include more and more of the external world, it tends to become less effectual, slowly turning into a distinct new market.

Up to a certain point, changes in the environment can provide the venture with new means and thus kick-start the cycle again. And any interactions that fail to gain the traction of commitment are put on hold, at least for the moment. But enough successful iterations result in enough commitments that there is room for no more. The goals have emerged and the idea is now a venture.

The venture that results may or may not be what the entrepreneur had in mind at the beginning, and the process may take many or few iterations, so think of the process less as a map and more as an engine.

THE EFFECTUAL PROCESS

We laid out the chapters in this section of the book according to the way entrepreneurs generally work their way through the process. The entrepreneur's means provide the starting point. The action begins in earnest when the entrepreneur begins interacting with people. Sometimes the starting point of that interaction is an idea, a provisional goal the entrepreneur uses to initiate the interaction. Sometimes the interaction is specifically initiated in the terms of "what can we do?" as the entrepreneur determines possibilities together with the person she interacts with. Regardless, each interaction can terminate without a commitment. In that case, the opportunity, as the entrepreneur and that specific person she interacts with envisioned, is on hold. Alternatively, that interaction might result in a commitment. As we described upfront, those commitments have two effects. One effect of adding a stakeholder to the venture is the addition of that stakeholder's means—the possibilities those means suggest. At the same time, new goals also accompany the commitment, adding to the constraints accumulated by the venture and converging it toward a specific direction. At any time in this cycle, unexpected events, information, and meetings can change the environment the

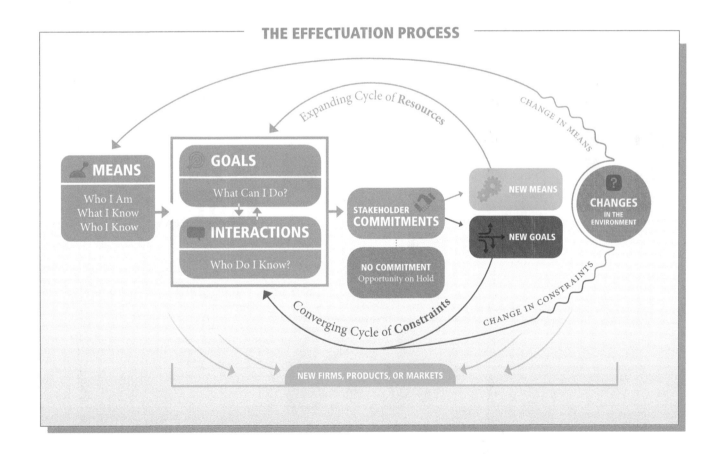

venture is developing. Those contingencies have similar effects to commitments. On one hand, they present new resources—new means the entrepreneur can use to expand the possibilities of the venture. On the other hand, they present new constraints also, perhaps sending the venture in a more specific direction.

ITERATIONS OF THE EFFECTUAL PROCESS

This process may cycle once or many many times. If there are no stakeholders willing to make commitments, it may not even complete a single cycle. But given the room to operate, the process will generate all sorts of different possible and unexpected outcomes. On our diagram, we indicate new firms, markets, and products as possible forms of outcomes. And by now it should be easy to see how once a sufficient number of constraints have accumulated, the venture is formed and operational, with all the people, resources, clients, and partners needed to deliver on the commitments that determine its direction. But the process can also generate new knowledge, new aspirations, new likes, and new dislikes. These too are iterated into future cycles, as the entrepreneur completes the delivery of a venture or product that results from a set of iterations and goes on to create their next product or even their next venture.

GRAPHICAL PRACTICALLY SPEAKING: EFFECTUATION IN ACTION: ICE MAN COMETH

After five years working for a mining company in Kiruna, Sweden, Yngve Bergqvist realized what he did not

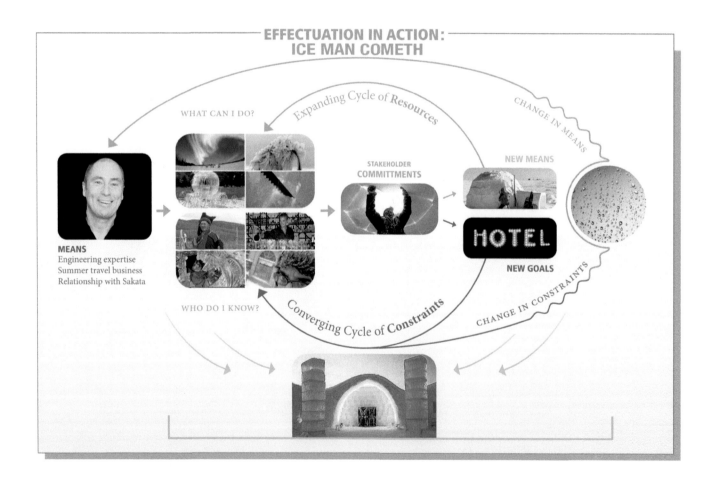

want to do with his life—work for a big company. His colleagues' lack of enthusiasm for the job grated on him. And he found it impersonal and unpleasant having people refer to him by his employee number. But Yngve was an outdoorsman, and as an outlet from his job, he took up river rafting. One day a tourist asked Yngve for a ride on the river. Suddenly, he was in business. He began going to the tourist office on weekend mornings and nearly always found clients. Yngve ultimately resigned from his mining job and gradually expanded the rafting business to 40 summer employees and 30 boats.

But summer in Sweden is short, and rafting on the Torne River in winter is impossible. For starters, the river is frozen solid. Yngve needed to find a winter business to complement his summer earnings. He had heard about Japanese tourists visiting Alaska in winter to see the Northern Lights (Aurora Borealis) and wanted to learn more. In 1988, he travelled to Sapporo and Hokkaido, Japan, for the Snow Festivals, and there he met an ice sculptor from Asahikawa. Over beer, the two men planned a winter ice-sculpting workshop in Sweden. The workshop received a lot of press, as numerous international artists, spectators, and local people flocked to Jukkasjärvi.

In recalling the event, Yngve described the evening before as cold and clear. His family was there watching the beautiful ice sculptures take shape, and they were so impressed. The local people in the village were taking photos.

But then, as Yngve recalled, "The next morning when I woke up, at six, I heard something strange. I couldn't believe it . . . it was raining, and it was plus seven degrees." The ice workshop was scheduled to start at 11, and the sculptors wanted to know what to do. Rather than trying to preserve something that belonged to nature, Yngve said, "Let it be destroyed and make something new when it is destroyed." What they made new was the ICEHOTEL. It is a business that is the embodiment of Yngve. It is constructed each winter

using ice from the Torne River, where he runs rafting trips, and employs skills learned during his ice-sculpting workshop. Yngve's friends at the Swedish tourist board then introduced him to Sakata, the owner of a Japanese travel agency named Northern Express. A natural partnership ensued in which Sakata generated interest in Japan for travel to Jukkasjärvi and Yngve provided Sakata's clients with a wholly unique experience in Swedish Lapland, including ice fishing, getting married in an ice chapel, or simply

marvelling at the art that is the ICEHOTEL itself.

When it rained on Yngve Bergqvist's ice sculpture exhibit, there was more than one way to deal with the unpleasant surprise. Yngve could have gone back to the mines or to the summer canoe job; his employees could have seen the madness in a project that was so weather dependent and cut their losses. Instead, some of them picked up their ice-sculpting tools and turned to the guests and press people who had come to see the sculptures. Some chose to learn the art of ice sculpting; others chose to make igloos. When night fell, the group that had been busy building igloos invited others to come and try to spend a night in their creations. Contrary to what they had imagined, it was not cold in the igloos. And it was not dark: in fact, the light coming through the ice made it shimmer in a translucent manner that was almost magical.

It is this partnership between ice sculptors and guests that truly launched the ICEHOTEL. There was no money involved, no big VC cash deal—nothing but a group of people who came back the following year to build another group of igloos. To illustrate the effectual process in the context of ICEHOTEL, we map out the sequence of effectual partnerships and actions in the diagram on p. 196.

Yngve Bergqvist did not stop with the success of the ICEHOTEL. This first round of business building

provided him with new means. Even from the original ice-sculpting exhibit, Yngve wanted his own Swedish icon to be associated with another Swedish icon, the premium vodka brand Absolut. He wrote to Absolut, suggesting a partnership. Initially, Absolut was not interested in partnering with a tree hugger building igloos in the far north of Sweden. Yngve persisted. And as often happens, he was helped by a little serendipity.

The ICEHOTEL featured a sculpture of a giant Absolut bottle as the centrepiece of its bar. As a result of an ICEHOTEL press release, a picture of the bottle made its way back to Absolut. At first incensed (the sculpture had not received their approval), the company started seeing the potential in a partnership. But their aspirations were much greater than ICEHOTEL.

Together, the tree hugger and the world's fourth largest spirit brand

came up with the idea of launching ICEBARS in major cities around the world, using the ice from the Torne River—the very same ice that was used to build the ICEHOTEL.

The bars are kept at a constant temperature of minus 5°C. A selection of international artists and designers are invited to design the bars, which are transformed every six months. As with the ice hotel, everything is sculpted from ice—the bars, the stools, the glasses, the walls. While the original ice bar sits in the ICEHOTEL, today there are ICEBARs in dozens of cities, from Copenhagen to Tokyo, Las Vegas to Dubai.

Ice in space?

Thanks to the partnership between ICEHOTEL and Absolut, ice is now the largest export product of that part of Sweden. The success of both ventures could have encouraged

Yngve Bergqvist to stop there and focus on running the existing business. But the most unexpected partnership was yet to come. ICEHOTEL has decided to partner with Virgin Galactic to sell space travel. Kiruna is the home of an ESA Space station and trips into space will start from this base, once Virgin Galactic commences operation. The trips will allow travellers to experience the Northern Lights in the winter or the midnight sun in the summer. Virgin had been looking for accredited space agents to take in bookings, and ICEHOTEL was looking to add new trips to the list of excursions available to guests. And so a new partnership, and a new business venture, was born. Who knows what is next?

TAKEAWAY: THE CONSEQUENCE OF COMMITMENT

The ICEHOTEL example helps us understand how stakeholder commitments shape ventures. The mutual commitments between the first stakeholders (Yngve and the tourist office, the sculptors, the press, the travel agents) forge a network that eventually transforms a budding reality into a new market. Neither Yngve nor any of his early partners knew what the end product would look like or whether it would be worth anything. Instead, the market was an outcome of the interaction among them. It emerged gradually, as they started making things happen. Through their actions, the stakeholders negotiated the very existence and shape of what would be.

This kind of negotiation proceeds as though everything and anything is possible until the last minute. There is always room for the actual transformation to surprise everyone involved. This is effectuation in action.

■ ■ ■

What Now?

- For an opportunity you are pursuing, describe your process so far using the effectual process map.

- How many times around the loop have you travelled?

- What dead ends have you reached?

- What new means have joined?

- What parts of your efforts thus far just don't fit this effectual process?

- Which of the effectual principles have you used the least in your efforts?

So What?

The effectual process comes together in this chapter. You need to thoroughly understand the process described by the two figures in this chapter.

Think It Through

- In hindsight, how might one revise the ICEHOTEL creation story with a causal approach?

- Does that (causal) story sound more familiar? Often, looking back, everything all seems so clear/direct/obvious. Entrepreneur hero, visionary forecasts, and the like, often hide an effectual process.

- Using the effectual process, can really large new ventures be created? Or does it lead to small incremental ideas?

PART IV

I am an entrepreneur now: How far can I go?

The chances of injury, expensive damage, and even loss of life increase exponentially with respect to the length of the boat, the distance sailed, and the number of crew on board. This is precisely what makes racing sailboats across the open ocean as complicated as it is exciting.

Summarized from a commentary on The Proving Ground (Knecht, 2002), a factual account of the 1998 Sydney to Hobart race where 115 boats started and just 43 finished. Six sailors perished and 55 were rescued as the fleet was decimated by unforecast hurricane winds and 80-foot-high waves.

Having successfully navigated the rocky waters of entrepreneurship, you face new challenges. Will you want to stay with your venture as it grows? Will your venture want you to stay as it grows? Though not surprising, the very heuristics that help you create new ventures, markets, and products are something of a liability in a larger firm, a bigger operation, serving a mature market where prediction prevails. This explains why so many entrepreneurs scale up and then exit the venture for new opportunities. Exiting may mean that the founder resigns from an ongoing operation, or may involve selling the business. Either way, the founder entrepreneur who leads the firm once the firm has advanced into maturity, such as Bill Gates at Microsoft, is something of an anomaly. Clearly, Gates was able to make the transition from employing non-predictive strategy at the outset to effectively utilizing prediction as Microsoft grew. But most founders leave or are thrown out. These represent two of the three main paths taken by serial entrepreneurs. The third involves starting again at the first chapter of the book. The point is that successful entrepreneurs have dramatically expanded the means available to them. And so, while some may feel trapped having to run "their baby," the truth is that the range of options available to the successful entrepreneur is not only broader than that, it is significantly broader than when they started "their baby" in the first place. So whatever direction you point your successful venture and your own success, we hope to have an appropriate section for you.

CHAPTER 18

Essentially you are valuing things that have not yet happened, and the likelihood of the CEO and team being able to make them happen. Finance people find this appalling, but investors who do this well can make a lot of money.

Marc Andreessen shares investment tips on Twitter

Ownership, equity, and control: Manage stakeholders

■ ■ ■

As you consider setting up a business and involving various kinds of stakeholders in it—particularly those who will become formal investors in the venture—it is critical to understand the difference between ownership and control. Most people think they are the same. As a result, the natural reaction is to focus on how to retain equity (ownership) in order to retain control. In this chapter, we challenge you to think more deeply about what you really want from the venture. Do you want ownership? Do you want control? How are they different? Where does each come from? And how does the combination help you design partnerships that work well for everyone involved?

On the surface, the connection between ownership and control seems clear. If you own more than half of the company, you control it, from the day-to-day operations to the overall shape and direction of the new venture—in theory, at least. VCs know better. They understand that decision rights are a negotiable matter they establish with the entrepreneur and the terms they build into the contract. For example, they may negotiate specific rights on how the assets of the firm will be distributed in case of liquidity. They can specify when and where the venture can raise subsequent rounds of funding and even the conditions under which they can fire the founding CEO and members of the top management team. Additionally,

WILL THE DOGS EAT THE DOG FOOD?

Testing your idea and getting it funded at the same time

Sometimes it's easier to grow your business with customers and suppliers than to raise investment capital. Why can't you just go sell what you're doing to buyers instead of raising money? You might find that you can do exactly that, lending great credibility to your business idea and to your own capabilities. A yes from a potential customer does not come easy. But a yes from an investor does not come easy either. And the yes from a customer is less likely to demand equity and more likely to generate demand.

COMMON AND PREFERRED STOCK

Both forms of equity provide ownership of a company. They differ in that preferred shares generally a) receive dividends at a higher rate, and b) are repaid before common shares in the event of insolvency or liquidity.

they have seats on the board with voting rights on a variety of issues. And they can do all this with only a minority ownership share in a venture.

Thus, ownership does not necessarily mean control.

This chapter is intended to help you explore the variety of alternatives you have available in terms of ownership and control. These options give you more choices for structuring partnerships that are low on friction and high on productivity.

WHAT DOES OWNERSHIP BUY?

If ownership does not automatically give you control and decision rights, what does it buy you? The answer: residual claims.

Residual claims are claims to anything of value that remains after

Steve Jobs, who exercised great control over Apple, owned less than 1% of the outstanding shares of the firm when he passed away in 2011.

all contractual rights and obligations have been fulfilled. In plain English, this means the owners of a venture possess anything that remains after the firm's contracts are met and bills are paid. For example, if the firm is being liquidated, a variety of creditors, debt holders, preferred shareholders, and others, who have specific rights written down in contracts, get paid before the common shareholders.

WHEN AND HOW TO USE EQUITY

Even the example of Castor & Pollux shows why the game is not simply

about trying to hold as much equity as possible. Instead, you need to think through the subtleties of how to use equity—when to give it away and how much, how to design contractual provisions, and so on. What the mastery of colors and knives and brushes is to the artist, the mastery of the role of equity, decision rights, time, and cash flows is for the expert entrepreneur. Let's start with some examples of how you can use equity (common or preferred) beyond simply selling shares in your venture:

1   Through appropriate contractual provisions, you can share ownership of the financial returns of the venture without giving up decision rights. In other words, investors and other stakeholders can be entitled to receive a percentage (large or small) of earnings—while having no rights in making management decisions.

2   You can provide equity on a temporary basis, with the right

to buy it back if specific milestones are met. This condition is frequently associated with short-term debt or loans.

3   You can offer equity in order to attract high-potential partners, using equity to align everyone's interests while keeping day-to-day management control through contractual provisions. It is up to you to decide, at any given point, exactly what you want and need in building your venture. Sometimes you might

REAL LIFE: WHAT ELSE COULD CASTOR & POLLUX HAVE DONE FOR FUNDING?

Imagine you are the founder of Castor & Pollux, looking for capital to expand a growing idea. Think about the following questions and see how many options you can come up with:

• Where might you find other potential sources of funding?

• What do you have to offer them?

• How would you approach them?

• What would they want from you?

Practically Speaking

SHARING THE TREATS AMONG INVESTORS

Castor & Pollux is a successful organic dog food company. Founded by entrepreneurs with expertise in the pet food business, they chose to bring in a significant amount of angel investment to expand what they saw as a great opportunity. It cost them about one-third of their business, board seats, and the sharing of some decision rights.

Puppy love

They doubled revenue for the first several years, putting the early capital to great use. Over the course of five years they moved, added facilities, hired more people, changed packaging and increased marketing.

At a certain point, the early investors wanted to cash out their ownership. At the same time, the venture attracted later stage private investors, with additional expertise, who were willing to buy the ownership of those early investors at an attractive price. The entrepreneurs' portion of the venture continued to shrink.

Big dog

Today, the entrepreneurs own much less than half of the business, yet they maintain substantial control of the day-to-day operation. Decisions about additional rounds of financing, new board members, new executives, strategic changes to the operation, and major capital expenditures are made with an extended range of stakeholders that includes new investors, original investors, lenders, customers, suppliers, and employees. The founders would add, of course, that all of this activity takes place under the strict oversight of culinary-minded canines.

find the ability to make decisions in the face of unpredictable contingencies more valuable than the ability to control the daily management of the venture. Depending on the direction of the venture, the right to a larger share of the return may be more important than a hold on the day-to-day control of operations. And yet, at other times, you might want to give away equity to get great people on board and share pieces of the larger pie you co-create with stakeholders.

Ultimately, it is up to you. You can make specific judgments as you build the venture and ensure technicalities are taken care of by good advisors. But it is crucial to understand the subtleties of ownership versus control before you take the plunge.

Food for thought

There are many alternatives to equity that will encourage people to join you in creating your venture, market or product. You can offer investors a fraction of revenue or even discounted products instead of equity. You can offer cofounders a sliding scale of salary rather than stock. You can even offer new employees a better title or a nicer office. If you are intent on holding on to equity, you can, provided the alternative keeps the stakeholder engaged in the venture.

However paranoid you might feel, most outside stakeholders, even VCs, do not want control over your venture—even if they want equity. They want protection from downturns and optimal participation in upturns—the slice of the pie that matches their appetite to invest.

CONTROL WITHOUT OWNERSHIP AND OWNERSHIP WITHOUT CONTROL

We consider control to be the ability to direct the use of any particular resource. When can control be utilized? To what extent? To what end? By what processes? Control is never absolute. Different types of decisions involve different players. Sometimes you have a say in a matter, sometimes, you have the say in a matter. Control is rarely simple.

Ownership is connected to control, but it is not control. A clear example is ownership of public companies: if you own a mutual fund, you own a bit of some public companies, but you have very little control over them. There has been an entire body of academic research around agency theory, which asserts that owners explicitly don't control the operation of the firm but instead subcontract control to agents, such as the CEO. So, it is possible to control a large firm with relatively small amounts of ownership, if any at all. Then again, what does it mean to "control" a firm? Clearly, if you own 100% of a firm, you have significant control, but even then you do not have 100% control of the entire venture; you simply have control of how you will lead the venture in reaction to the actions of other stakeholders.

Consider customers versus lenders versus investors versus cofounders and the ownership and control they enjoy in exchange for their commitment to the venture.

"Congratulations on becoming a partner - your share of company losses are £200,000."

THE PURPOSE OF OWNERSHIP

Ownership is primarily about two things: rewarding risk takers and providing incentives for success. A key difference between these ideas is that the first is about the past and the second is about the future. Ownership tends to go to the people who assume risk when they commit resources to your venture. Obviously, it doesn't have to—people are often compensated directly for their commitments with salary, purchase orders, etc. But early in the life of a venture, sharing ownership is often a way to reward the risk takers.

Customers might have no ownership of your organization, yet exert a lot of control in the form of influence and leverage, especially early on in the life of the organization.

Lenders might not have any ownership of the venture, but they exert significant control in how you use cash and probably little control over anything else. However, should financial problems arise, lenders can take complete control of the organization, without taking complete ownership. Investors have a range in the extent to which their ownership, purchased by providing cash to you, translates into control. In fact, venture investors are nuanced in the nature of their ownership and the specific rights and situations over which they retain control. And that's the point—there is a suite of options in the structure of ownership and the delineation of control.

Research Roots

AGENCY THEORY

The incentive difference between an owner and a worker has long been appreciated, at least since the days of land barons and feudal farmers. It is the incentive of the worker to be paid as much as possible by the owner to do as little as possible. And it is the incentive of the owner to pay the worker as little as possible and get as much productivity as possible.

Management scholars refer to the owner as the "principal" and the worker as the "agent." The agent works on behalf of the principal. Land barons tried to resolve the incentive difference, the agency problem, by taking only a fraction of the crop that farmers produced. Thus, farmers had some incentive to be productive—the more they produced, the more they benefited. The same is true today for the sharing of equity. It is the goal of the owner of a venture, be it the founder or the investor, to provide incentives to the agents to be productive. Equity offers a strong incentive, as the agent benefits directly from any value created. There are many other approaches to overcoming the agency problem, ranging from financial rewards, such as raises and bonuses, to less tangible rewards, such as promotions, more interesting work assignments and public recognition of accomplishments.

EARLY STAGE INVESTORS

How early-stage investors learn about entrepreneurs before making an investment:

- *Referrals.* Investors rely on referrals from people they trust who have known the entrepreneur for some time, to understand the ability and motivation of the entrepreneur.

- *Interaction.* Investors meet time and again with entrepreneurs. Personal questions are fair game. Do you want to get rich? Do you want power and control? What kind of leader are you? How do you respond to disaster? How do you know?

How early stage investors think about investing in new ventures:

- *Time.* While you are in a hurry when you're raising money, investors are not. Why hurry? It regularly takes 6 to 12 months to raise investment money, and over that time they can see whether you're delivering on promises and remaining committed to the effort.

- *Committee.* Investors learn from the judgment of other investors, partners in venture capital firms, and other entrepreneurs.

Early investors will generally not buy the entrepreneur out of a venture entirely. While they may want to capture as large a share of the rewards as possible, they know it's more important to maintain the entrepreneur's motivation and commitment. There are a lot of rules of thumb about the proper distribution of ownership as a venture grows up. You can search Google for the latest opinions, but we offer one basic, not too unusual, and reasonably fair approach as food for thought: one-third to the founding team, one-third to venture investors, and one-third to the employees of the organization. It doesn't have to be that way—you don't have to spend two-thirds of the equity of your venture to attract resources—but it's not outlandish.

BUILDING EQUITABLE PARTNERSHIPS

If everyone contributes an equal amount, and receives an equal share of the pie, there is no issue. But what if some partners bring more money, skills, credibility or contacts than others? How do you divide the equity?

The secret: There is no right answer at the level of detail most entrepreneurs are seeking. What we know is that the split needs to reward people sufficiently for the risks they've taken and motivate them sufficiently to continue to risk their time, talent, and resources on the venture. Notions of fairness can get mixed into this discussion. Feelings can get hurt. Lawyers can get involved. But in the end, what's most important is stakeholders' level of satisfaction with the agreement.

EXPLAINED: LIQUIDITY PREFERENCES

Often, shareholders will establish a claim on who gets paid first. A one-time liquidation preference means that shareholders get the amount of their investment paid to them first and foremost in the occurrence of a liquidity event. For example, if they invested US$1 million and the business sells for US$10 million, US$1 million is paid to them before any sort of allocation of capital according to ownership percentages is made. A two-times preference would mean that the first US$2 million would go to them, and the remaining US$8 million would be shared among others who participate in the general ownership of the venture.

Practically Speaking

A PIECE OF THE PIE

Kenny Burts is a man devoted to key lime pie. Introduced to this regional specialty by his grandfather at the age of nine, he refined his own key lime pie recipe in the mid-1980s and nearly everyone who tasted his pies told Burts he should sell them. When Burts was working as a bartender, he began making pies part time in his apartment. He did marketing, sales, manufacturing, and delivery to individuals and restaurants who raved about his product and kept coming back for seconds.

> I was making pies, I was delivering pies and I was tending bar. I was getting two hours sleep a night, setting three alarms and keeping the lights on so that when I woke up I wouldn't go back to sleep. I knew at that time that nobody in their right mind was willing to do this but that was my competitive edge. I used to make deliveries as far west as Birmingham, Alabama, 150 miles away, with 1–2 cases of pies. Nobody would have done that—nobody.

Ice or oven

Working like that, Burts had to make a decision. Should he quit his bartending job and commit to squeezing the most out of the key lime pie business? One a stable income, the other his passion. The answer came in a phone call. Through a friend, Burts met executives with California Pizza Kitchen, a national restaurant chain. They liked his pie so much that they wanted to offer it in all their restaurants.

> I knew right then I was ready to take the plunge. I ran down the street to my dad's place and he said, "Son you've got to be careful with big customers—they can make you or break you." He was right. With strong commitment on their part and strong delivery on our part, they made us.

Taste for investment

Prior to the call, the venture had been completely self-funded. But to serve California Pizza Kitchen, Burts began to consider raising capital for a more professional facility than his apartment. Almost immediately, he faced another decision more difficult than selling or making pies:

> I did not have the luxury of financial backing, which forced me to be sure I had a market (and income) before I could do anything. Now I needed to be crystal clear—what was I willing to part with for an investor? If I make a mistake—I had to make sure it would not wipe me out.

Practically Speaking *(continued)*

Burts built a partnership with an angel investor. An individual who shared (and invested in) his vision, his time horizon, his plans for growth, and his taste for key lime pie. Based on shared vision and objectives, the relationship has remained sweet for more than 20 years.

Expanding the pie

Kenny's recipe has worked. In addition to California Pizza Kitchen, Burts was able to build an early partnership with Longhorn Steakhouse before they went public, and grow with them as they expanded across the country. Burts' pies are now available on both sides of the Atlantic and he has the capacity to produce 6,000 pies a day. Not to worry, though. In spite of the success, the firm, now called Kenny's Great Pies, celebrated its 25th anniversary in 2014, and it is still making key lime pies according to exactly the same recipe and using the same fresh-squeezed key lime juice that earned his early rave reviews.

Where to start

Start by sitting down with a potential stakeholder (investor or key hire—anyone with whom you are negotiating ownership or control) and mutually agreeing on the skill sets and other factors that will be required to make the venture successful in a specified period—say, three years at the most. You'll be listing things like technical capability, sales, raising money, making contacts, running the operation, etc.

Weight the factors on a 0 to 10 scale. Do this together. If you disagree, talk it through until you agree. The conversation need not get emotional—you are understanding the business, its key success factors, and the skills you have available.

Next, take your list of weighted success factors and rate each of you on your ability to bring them to the

business. Rate them on the same 0 to 10 scale. When you're finished, multiply these scores by the weighted factor and you'll have a mutually agreed upon measure of each person's relative contribution to the success of the business. And hopefully you'll have done it without any black eyes or injured egos. If you can't agree on what each of you brings to the business, you might want to reconsider whether you have the makings for a successful partnership.

Splitting the pie

Dividing ownership is a stress-inducing topic. It can be legitimately thought of as fighting over a fixed pie—more for you is less for me. And, at some point in the future, if you are successful, real cash will change hands in line with these decisions, highlighting that every percentage point of ownership is

connected to a material amount of money. However, even if greed were your only motivation (which we have yet to see), ownership percentage is not what you're trying to maximize. Cash is what you're trying to maximize. Sharing ownership wisely can create more cash than hoarding it. In new ventures, the pie is not fixed. You want to share ownership with talented people, partners, and providers of great resources in order to increase the size of the pie.

THE LANGUAGE OF VALUATION, TRANSLATED INTO CONTROL

With investors, valuation and the distribution of ownership are more explicit than with partners. There are many nuances to the discussion of valuation, and we seek only to mention the main issues here and suggest a dedicated new venture

EXPLAINED: DILUTION PROTECTION

Existing investors may try to protect themselves from dilution of ownership when new investors bring more cash into the company. The most straightforward anti-dilution protection is the right of first refusal (also called pre-emptive rights, or "pro rata"). These establish the right of an investor to invest in the company before new investors, and they may be capped at the amount of investment that would keep their ownership percentage the same (i.e. if they own 20%, they have right of first refusal on whatever shares in the new round it would take to keep them at 20%, but no more). Sometimes they are not capped, meaning an investor has first rights to all future rounds. A special version of this is called a ratchet, which protects existing investors in the event of a "down round" (when the value of the firm drops over time) by maintaining their ownership percentage even if new investment is brought in at a lower valuation. Anti-dilution enables early investors to retain control as the ownership expands.

PROTECTIVE COVENANTS

These are specific rules about what types of votes, and by who, determine specific decisions in the venture. Decisions about new board members, changes in the size of the board, new rounds of financing, executive compensation, stock option plans, major capital expenditures, and so on can be detailed in such a way that the voting rights on a particular topic are not represented by the ownership percentages overall.

HOW ADVISORY BOARDS ARE DIFFERENT FROM BOARDS OF DIRECTORS

An advisory board is most useful in providing strategic ideas or feedback on increasing revenue and building your business, with the members not involved in the details of your company. You go to them, as you would to an old high school friend whom you don't see often, to catch up and pick their brains—for a view of your landscape from 20,000 feet.

The members of your board of directors, by contrast, are more like your parents, the people you go to when you are up against it and you need not so much advice, but guidance on a day-to-day basis about how to navigate choppy waters: a lawsuit, for example, or the sale of your company. These people give you the view of your business from 200 feet.

Hoffman (2003)

finance book when you need the details.

To start with, we need to be clear about the difference between the value of the venture before and after an investment. Pre-money valuation is simply the value of the venture before the investor puts his or her cash into it. Post-money valuation is simply the pre-money valuation plus the amount of cash the investors put into the company. Ownership percentages are determined using post-money value as the denominator. For example, if an investor puts US$1 million into a venture with a pre-money value of US$2 million, the investor owns US$1 million worth of a

THE YELLOW SARI

In Bollywood movies, when the heroine wears a yellow sari, it usually signifies that something big is about to happen. If there is a yellow sari moment in the entrepreneurship classroom, it has to do with learning how to use equity as a tool in building new ventures. Students confuse equity with (a) control—or the right to make and implement key decisions; (b) piece of the pie—rights to the returns earned; or (c) compensation—for inputs brought into the venture (such as ideas, technical knowhow, money, effort, reputation, etc.). Equity can, and of course should, be used as all of the above. But the important point is that it is not the same as any of these. Equity is like the trump card in a card game. It can substitute for any card in the deck. The key is to know when to use it and as what. By assuming in advance that it is any one card, even the Ace of Spades, we may be jeopardizing our chances of winning the game. Furthermore, in the case of equity in a new venture, as opposed to a trump card in a card game, we can play the trump card again and again and sometimes just temporarily lease or even pawn it with the possibility of redeeming it under circumstances we negotiate. So mastering the use of equity is key to how the story of the new venture will turn out. Like the yellow sari—whenever it shows up, the plot is about to change—and the fate of the new venture is literally at stake.

US$3 million business, or one-third of the company (but remember, this doesn't mean the investor controls one-third of it). Investors may want anti-dilution protection to guarantee that they always own their fraction of the business.

A lot of time can be spent negotiating the pre-money valuation of a venture and the terms of the investment. This is understandable, because the higher the pre-money valuation, the less the investment dilutes the current owners' stake, but the less attractive the deal is to new investors. In that regard, it's just like buying a house: A higher price is great for the sellers and worse for the buyers. But, in this case, the seller and the buyer have to cooperate extensively after the deal has closed. In fact, their ability and desire to cooperate effectively is part of what expands the pie, making consequences of valuation less clear cut than "higher is better" for the seller.

Consider the consequences of a high valuation for future fundraising. An empirical fact: The average series A pre-money valuation for a venture taking on formal venture capital investment is approximately US$6 million. If an entrepreneur is able to raise an angel investment at a valuation of US$12 million, it is significantly more difficult to raise that series A money from formal venture capitalists. This is the case for two reasons: 1) The angel investors who paid a premium to invest in the seed (first) round will expect a significant valuation increase in the Series A to maintain a good portion of their ownership, and as a result 2) the VCs will find the company overpriced compared to the norm for a Series A; it complicates things and can be an easy excuse to say no and move on.

You can Google a litany of advice concerning what the "right" pre-

"I'll agree to a fifty-fifty split, but I get the hyphen."

money valuation of a venture should be. These are mostly rules of thumb about how much a patent should be worth or what the value of having a completed product is, along with various milestones that can serve as a guide for valuation. We won't summarize them here.

Two issues dictate valuation in early-stage ventures. The venture needs X amount of cash, and the investor is willing to invest only if he or she can own Y percent of the venture.

For example, an entrepreneur needs to raise US$500,000 to complete a prototype and win her first major customer. An angel investor prefers to invest in opportunities where he can own around one-third of the business, so long as he has a seat on the board of directors and a say in the hiring of executives. If they were to execute the transaction, the valuation is essentially deduced rather than negotiated: US$500,000 is one-third of US$1.5 million, thus the post-money is US$1.5 million, and the pre-money is US$1 million.

This may lead the entrepreneur to say, "I don't want to sell my stock at that valuation—US$1 million is way too low." Thus, she might like to sell less stock at that valuation; maybe she'd want to raise only US$250,000. However, the angel investor would still want to own about one-third of the company. The entrepreneur may have to find a different angel investor to accomplish the goal of selling less stock, because the investment isn't being determined by the valuation. It's often the other way around; the valuation is being determined by the separate preferences of the entrepreneur and the angel investor.

WHAT THE INVESTOR SEES IN YOUR VENTURE

Venture investing is difficult and risky. Investors look at many deals and invest only in those on which they are incredibly bullish. In spite of this, they are wrong more often than they are right and are more likely to lose money than make money on any venture investment. Angel investors lose money in nearly two-thirds of their investments. The wins have to cover all the losses and take into account the dilution in ownership over time.

You may believe you will sell the business for US$100 million in five years because the opportunity is incredible. An early-stage investor can invest US$500,000 for one-third ownership, creating a US$33 million return in only five years. Seem obscene? You do the work; they make US$32.5 million.

Reality check. Most likely, you will return less than US$500,000 to that investor. Even if you are successful, in order to grow the company to where you can sell it for US$100 million, you will raise additional capital, and the initial investor might see ownership percentage go from one-third to one-tenth, meaning that they would get US$10 million of the US$100 million exit, a very nice return, 20 times their investment, but nowhere near US$33 million. Reduce that by the risk that the entrepreneur will not achieve targets, competitive entry, and difficulty of liquidity, and you see why the investor is slow to write a check.

Practically Speaking

INVESTING IN PEOPLE

Felipe Vergara was a unique student. Not a lot of people born in Barranquilla, Colombia, wind up studying management at the University of Pennsylvania's prestigious Wharton School. Vergara's path was one of education and entrepreneurship. From an early age, he tutored others in math, science, and languages and, after completing his university studies in Bogota, he founded a firm providing strategic and financial planning services to small businesses. Mixing education and business with his first-hand understanding of the financial difficulties of attending Wharton, Vergara asked himself a question: why, if someone could invest in the future value of a firm, could they not invest in the future value of him?

Equities r us

Governments and banks already offered student loans. But loans came with borrowing limits and fixed payments, and often had to be backed by parents' assets or income, all of which challenged applicants from Barranquilla, Colombia, to Columbia, North Carolina. And students' need for broader access to capital was increasing: the cost of education has outpaced the cost of living in the US over the past 20 years, and today a year of undergraduate tuition and room and board at a private college averages £16,600. When Vergara met Miguel Palacios from the Darden School, the answer came in the form of Lumni, a firm that pays a student's current tuition bills in exchange for a percentage of future earnings. Just like a share of stock, only it's stock in you and me. And the future is our careers.

Tomorrow's markets

A marketplace is the foundation of exchange. In its earliest form, it's a farmer with too many carrots wanting to trade some for a chicken. More recently, it's someone willing to pay money in return for getting a haircut or a lawn mowed. Today, markets enable us to not only trade what exists on the shelves, but also buy and sell future values of everything imaginable, from orange juice to the right to pollute. Markets deliver humanitarian aid—witness UNHCR's Kashmir Relief Note, which provides a return on investments made to reconstruct Pakistan-administered Kashmir following the 2005 earthquake (see also pp. 287–288). Markets also enabled David Bowie to sell the future value of his song royalties. And, with Lumni, that same alternative is open to individual students.

The circle of light

To date (2015), Lumni has worked with more than 7,000 students, and Vergara is in talks with investment banks in anticipation of creating a securitized portfolio of investments and earnings streams, so he can fund more of the best and the brightest. Looking ahead to when his investees turn into his investors is when the future will indeed be bright—for Lumni and the rest of us.

There is a lot written about valuation, and you should read some of it before you start thinking about a term sheet for raising venture investment.

TERM SHEETS: EVERYTHING IS NEGOTIABLE

If investors and entrepreneurs are able to come to an agreement, the specifics are written down on a term sheet. Not all term sheets use all the elements we discuss here. Angel investor term sheets tend to be less complicated than formal VC term sheets. As the venture grows and goes through multiple funding rounds, different rights are often assigned to different series of preferred stock issuance and to common stock. All the terms are subject to the golden rule: whoever has the gold makes the rules. When a venture must raise more cash or die, the negotiation power clearly lies in the hands of incoming investors. All terms are then subject to re-negotiation. Broadly speaking, good terms align the objectives of the investors and those of the entrepreneurs while protecting the investors from entrepreneurial recklessness (it isn't the entrepreneur's money, so agency risks come into play) and protecting the entrepreneur from investor intrusiveness (because too many chefs spoil the broth).

There are hundreds of actual term sheets to be found floating around the internet or at universities, think tanks, law firms, etc. These term sheets can provide a black and white

FACES AND WALLETS

Wallets always come with faces. So why not target faces instead of wallets? Luckily, faces often come with wallets, too, so by starting with your means, particularly the means of who you know, you may generate good leads for investment. And having a relationship with people who invest in you will also make it easier for you to anticipate what kind of interaction your investors will want. Early-stage investments are rarely at arm's length, so no matter what, you get the face with the wallet.

SUMMARY: OWNERSHIP AND CONTROL IN TERM SHEET TERMS

As you face a term sheet, think about trade-offs along the dimensions of ownership and control:

Ownership

- Ratchet. If there is a down round (valuation lower than the previous), early investors may protect against dilution by adding a "ratchet" to their anti-dilution to adjust the price of their previous investments to the new round.

- Right of first refusal. Major investors get the right to maintain ownership percentage on future financing.

- Liquidation preferences. Major investors get paid first in a liquidity event.

Control

- Directors. The ability to add a person to the board in conjunction with an investment.

- Information rights. Monthly or quarterly internal statements—or annually reviewed or audited statements.

- Voting rights. Preferred vote with common shares, except as required by law.

picture of how ownership is separate from control, and even how ownership can apply to different things. For example, ownership can change at different levels of upside or downside liquidity events, and can even change over time. The details will pile up as your venture grows. Google away on these topics, and seek legal advice.

INVESTOR PERSPECTIVE: ANGELS

Angel investors often provide the seed capital for startups. They will invest less and earlier than VC firms.

Typically, they will ask for 20% to 50% of firm ownership. They may invest as little as US$1,000 and more than US$5 million.

Angel investors often feel that the valuation of a company is less than what the entrepreneur has proposed, and given the early and uncertain nature of the opportunity, it is hard to measure and even harder to figure out how to measure. Investors will work with the entrepreneurs' financial projections and use various valuation methods such as transactional value, market value, and return as a multiple of investment. The valuation methodology most frequently used is backing into exit value. For example, if the company is expected to be worth US$50 million in five years, the company needs to raise a single round of US$1 million to reach that valuation and the investors will require a 10 times

cash-on-cash return upon exit— that is, the investors' share must be worth US$10 million in five years. Thus, the investors would need to own 20% of the company, which implies a US$4 million pre-money valuation and US$5 million post-money valuation (this presumes that no further dilutive capital is needed).

It is often said that because angels invest early and small, they miss out on the home runs. But based on our research, that appears not to be true. While the downside of an angel investor is less (from making smaller investments), the upside is as limitless as it is for the VC, who must invest much larger amounts at later stages in the venture's life. Because angels invest smaller amounts, they can make more investments and increase the chances of a home run.

TAKEAWAY: GOOD PARTNERSHIPS MAKE GOOD VENTURES

Regardless of whether your objective is to become obscenely wealthy or to create something of enduring value to society (or perhaps both), partnerships are critical. Structuring partnerships with investors, employees, board members, customers, and even lawyers demands a detailed understanding of the softer side—what each party values in the interaction. And it demands technical proficiency with structuring deals along the dimensions of control and ownership. The key aspects that underpin the negotiation of any arrangement include determining and articulating the appropriate level of risk, the appropriate amount of control and equitable provisions for ownership and liquidity.

It is important to realize that the spirit on both sides of the agreement is probably more important than the actual text of the agreement. As the venture, the environment, and the constellation of partnerships change, there is much opportunity for re-interpretation of the terms of the agreement, and it is useful to be able to fall back on a shared spirit. Further, if lawyers have to get involved to sort out differences in understandings of control or ownership, the likely outcome is that nobody wins, so it is good to be able to establish a shared foundation at the start.

■ ■ ■

Think It Through

- Who really owns the firm (customers, investors, management, society)? Why does ownership matter?

- Where does control come from (how much is earned and how much is bestowed)?

- What is the role of the entrepreneur—to control or to own?

- What is the real cost of money?

So What?

Control does not equal ownership—you can get a whole lot of control without ownership, and control rights can be assigned very specifically to different aspects of what your venture is working toward.

Ownership can be used to enable the alignment of incentives around the creation process.

What Now?

Consider your own venture or one you know well:

- What do you need to have control rights over in order to make this venture succeed?

- Can you gain any level of influence or control over those areas without owning anything? You might be surprised how far you can get on this front.

- How will you use equity to align interests and encourage everyone to give their all?

- Who needs equity, and who doesn't?

- What can you do for stakeholders who don't want equity?

- What terms do you really care about if you are going to take an investment? Do you have to be in charge? Are you willing to sell the business?

- Do you need a board of directors? Why? What value do you want to derive from that board? What will it take to build a board that you truly value? How will you attract and reward them (think beyond money)?

WHAT YOU NEED TO KNOW ABOUT BOARDS

Why do I need a board in the first place?	If you have a broad-reaching business concept and you want your business to mature, you should consider having a board. You will not possess all the functional skills necessary. . . . Nor, most probably, will you be able to afford the expertise with all those skills in the early stages. Having a board of advisors with balanced skills and experience will come in handy. The board can help you with financing and finding new customers. It will provide specific advice, offer wisdom of prior experience, keep you focused on strategy and provide credibility to outside parties such as bankers and investors. Most important, it will be there to ensure you make fewer mistakes. Everyone needs to be accountable to someone, and as founder, you will be accountable to the board. As one entrepreneur said, "I needed the board to save the company from myself."
Who should be on my board?	Initially, the board can be made up of insiders if you do not have outside investors. But it is better to have some members on the board whose skills are complementary, not identical, to yours. So, if you have questions, instead of calling professionals such as attorneys and paying them US$250 an hour, you can pick up the phone and call your board member. You try to find people for your board who have been there and done it before.
When do I need the board—at what stage?	Consider having a board from inception. If not, you must have one by the time you want to raise outside capital. In general, the board is there to help with current and strategic issues, but each stage in the development of a new venture calls for different kinds of expertise. **Stage** → **Expertise/need** Seed → Financial, legal, business development Emerging management → Industry expertise, market, financial, legal, management Growth → Similar to emerging, add in strategic Mature → Strategic, market, financial, management
Do I need a board of advisors or a board of directors?	An advisory board works fine at the outset. But once you start bringing in cash, it is time to create a board of directors. The members should have specific responsibilities and should be compensated; they can also be fired. In choosing board members, setting expectations up front is important. Your directors constitute your company's governing body and have fiduciary responsibilities for which they can be held legally accountable. Your advisors, by contrast, are high-level strategists or mentors. For small companies, directors are generally shareholders and thus already have an incentive to spend their time on your company. Many companies might compensate advisors with a small token of stock, but most advisors are motivated not by money but by the ability to mentor an entrepreneur.
How do I find people who can sit on my board?	Start with people you know and people who already care about and are deeply involved in your enterprise or industry. Do not take rejection personally. Good people have options, commitments, and not much spare time. When you find someone worthy, share your passion and candidly explore how he or she can add value to your organization. Appeal to someone who would like to help you. Self-selected stakeholders willing to make real commitments of time and interest are best. The key is to find those you want to work with and get them to want to work with you—not by "selling" them on the deal, but by persuading them enough so that they sell themselves.
How do I know whether I have the right people?	Carl F. Frischkorn, a successful entrepreneur, angel investor, and board member at many young companies, talks about his three criteria for choosing which boards to participate in—"I have to like the CEO as a person. I need to believe that the person has good ethics and integrity—a person who would listen and also argue. If she wins the argument, then she wins, but if she doesn't, she has to make a change. I think it's fantastic to stand up for what you believe in, but you also need to respond to feedback and then make the changes. I have to like the product, understand the concept and think that the product has good market acceptance and growth opportunity. I have to think that I can add value being involved as an advisor."

WHAT YOU NEED TO DO WITH YOUR BOARD

What are the duties of directors?	You should create job descriptions for members of the board before bringing them in. In general, the major responsibilities of a board are to: • Participate in policy formulation and financial and strategic planning • Serve as a sounding board for the CEO in major decisions • Evaluate the performance of senior management • Determine the compensation of senior management • Ensure the adequacy of financial controls and monitor compliance with laws and regulations • Advise on succession planning.
How engaged should my board be?	Boards can have varying degrees of engagement. For some companies, boards are passive, functioning at the discretion of the CEO. They only ratify management's decisions. At the other extreme are operating boards, which make all key decisions; management is simply present to implement them. A properly engaged board will provide insight, advice, and support to the CEO. It will oversee both the CEO's and the company's performance and add value to decisions by providing necessary expertise. Good board members will not hesitate to pick up the phone and call people for you or call you on their own initiative when they come across information or possibilities—both positive and negative—important to the survival and health of the business.
What is the best use of my time with the board?	Boards function best when they are tightly managed and have enough diversity of experience. You should bring in people who are neither afraid to question your judgments nor uncomfortable with your right to make final decisions. It's important to communicate with board members as much as you can. Hold four to 10 meetings a year. Talk to directors by phone whenever you are in doubt or need a certain expertise. Prior to every meeting, preview key issues with each director and provide a written agenda and information package at least a week in advance. Give your directors bad news quickly and be measured with good news. Taking care of key issues will ensure that your board remains focused and comes to your assistance. Otherwise, you may start seeing your board meetings as a waste of time.
How do I compensate board members? What's in it for them?	Signing on as a director is one thing; contributing is another. So, you must keep your board members interested. With advisory boards, the problem is that you can never pay them what they're worth. One way of keeping them interested is to pamper them. Send them free company products, pay for dinner at the best places in town and, if possible, arrange out-of-city meetings and pay for spouses to attend. The best way to keep them interested is by communicating regularly. What's in it for them? It is the pride in helping a promising entrepreneur. To some of them, it will be like a second chance. If you have a formal board of directors, make sure they have some skin in the game. Use stock, warrants, options, and cash to keep their interest. Often, the entrepreneur believes that board members serve simply because they like to. But ultimately, all of us want to be paid for our time. If your advisory board transforms into a real board and you want it to work properly, set aside 3% to 10% of the company as compensation for what they are doing. Do not assume that there is a standard package for compensation. People care about different things, and they often work for strange rewards. This is where it is important to spend sufficient time recruiting board members and to set expectations at the outset. You are building a long-term relationship. Take the time to get to know what each director cares about and why and to share your own passions and motivations.
What are the common conflicts that I should be aware of?	If the board is informal in structure, and it is time to make a real board of directors, compensation issues may arise. The first conflict usually happens over valuation of the director's time and expectations. As the founder, you will be working 365 days a year; your advisors will probably give 5% of their time. So when there is a question of sharing the pie, you may think they are asking too much. The solution is to be up front about the issue. The second conflict usually comes if, as founder, you are unable to grow with the company. Running a company at the startup stage requires different skills than running it when it is big and mature. Conflict arises if you are unable to change and your board thinks you are unfit to be the CEO. The only solution is to learn to manage your company well. As long as you are making good decisions, your board members and investors will not want to take the company away from you. They would rather spend 5% of their time on the company and not be involved in day-to-day affairs. Remember, they have other businesses to run, too.

WHAT YOU NEED TO KNOW ABOUT LAWYERS

Do I need a lawyer to incorporate?	Technically, no. A person can incorporate a business without the help of a lawyer. Check your government web sites for information; a simple incorporation (called an "S corporation" in the US) with one owner and no shareholders might take 20 minutes to register, with minimal fees applied. But it is always better to use professional help when you are not an expert. Good professional advice will save you from making mistakes that may prove costly down the line, especially if you anticipate having investors or selling your company later. There are even online services that take the place of live attorneys. They gather information from clients and automatically draft and customize the articles, bylaws, corporate minutes, stock certificates, and federal forms for each individual business. But because of the automation, it is sometimes difficult to completely customize. For example, creating specific bylaws within the Articles of Incorporation is not possible using most of the online services.
How do I find a lawyer?	Ask the people you know and like—your professors, your friends, or someone who is doing business locally. Those people should be able to point you to one or two good lawyers. Talk to at least a couple of people before you decide on the person or firm to go with.
What is the first meeting with a lawyer like? What do I say?	Usually lawyers will not charge you for the first meeting. This is the time to see whether that particular lawyer will be a good fit for you. Remember, the lawyer will also be trying to learn about you and decide whether he or she wants to do business with you. The first meeting involves bringing the lawyer up to speed on your business. What is the product? Who are the customers? What does the future of the business look like? And so forth. Have a set of questions ready for each lawyer. That way, you will be able to compare them before choosing. You should be asking the lawyer's opinion on: • What type of business entity you should choose given the business and its future vision • Any other issues such as patents, copyrights, and other intellectual property rights (depending on the nature of the business, you may need other clearances).
What if I cannot afford to pay the lawyer? Do I offer him or her equity?	To the greatest extent possible, treat a lawyer as a professional service that you pay for. Good and understanding lawyers usually cut startups some slack because they think of working with you as an investment. They expect future returns—repeat business, referrals—when you grow.

CHAPTER 19

Plans are worthless.

Planning is everything.

US President
Dwight D.
Eisenhower

Business plans and business models

■ ■ ■

The business plan is one of the most "taught" aspects of entrepreneurship. As a work project, it provides a learning platform that forces entrepreneurship students to spell out all functional areas related to the venture. Everything from financial plans and budgets, assessments and assertions of market need, the four P's (price, product, promotion, and placement) of marketing, key talent needs, risk assessments, competitive details, comparisons, etc., need to be included in a business plan.

WHAT IS THE ROLE OF BUSINESS PLANS IN BUILDING A VENTURE EFFECTUALLY?

The very idea of a business plan may seem contradictory to an effectual

approach to building new ventures. Yet the business plan is difficult to escape in a world of causal investors and the ubiquity of business plan contests. The difference between causal and effectual use of a business plan, therefore, is that in the effectual case, it is not a plan—it is merely a communication tool written over and over again as the venture develops and written differently for different stakeholders. Honesty demands that effectuators do their best in building predictive models but explicitly clarify that the aim is not to deliver on the plan but to do what it may take to co-create value for everyone involved.

As such, this chapter will not teach you how to write a business plan. You can Google the term and find all the outlines you need; there are whole books dedicated to the topic.

THE OBJECT IN YOUR BUSINESS PLAN

One of the key aspects of business plans is the fact that they are used not only by you (the entrepreneur) as an internal management tool but also by your outside stakeholders, in particular your bank (or other financial services firm), your investors, your accountant, your lawyer, business partners (for example, your suppliers) and sometimes even your employees (in ventures that have an "open book" policy). Thus, what business plans do can be much more than just what they do as an internal management tool, which is the standard way they are portrayed in textbooks.

Sociologists coined the term "Boundary Objects" to describe the fact that objects like business plans are important bridges across the boundaries between different professional worlds, such as entrepreneurship and banking. Seen as boundary objects, business plans occupy a special place in communicating and collaborating with stakeholders. Researchers have pointed out that many kinds of objects, both tangible and intangible, can act as boundary objects, with some favorite examples being maps, PowerPoint presentations, business models, and stories. Such objects are intermediaries in the collective work that entrepreneurs and their stakeholders put forth in building new ventures. Much more, potentially, than just a plan. (Nicolini et al., 2012)

One particular classic is entitled *How to Write a Great Business Plan* by Bill Sahlman (1997: 98). Instead, this chapter is dedicated to the principle of substance over form in thinking through a new business.

THE SUBSTANCE OF THE BUSINESS PLAN

Substance over form is essential because the business plan is largely a marketing tool. We don't mean this in any pejorative sense. You may need a business plan to pitch your venture to various resource providers, and so it must communicate the perspective, insights, and guidance that will help others evaluate and categorize the opportunity. As with any marketing communication, you must know your audience and the objectives you want to accomplish. Audiences for business plans might include lenders, private investors, potential employees and board members, customers, upstream suppliers, or downstream channel partners. The form of a business plan really depends on what you intend to do with it—how you plan to address the various desires of these diverse audiences. Here we'll focus on substance and leave it to you to fine-tune the form.

Each audience you're pitching to requires different information and uses the substance of the business plan—the information that's actually in it—to different ends. Talk to them and find out what they really want to know. Our suggestions in this chapter can help you get started, but we claim no encyclopaedic knowledge on the needs and preferences of all those audiences. All have shorthand rules and screening procedures that help them process the information you provide much more quickly than you might think. They often have requirements involving minimum revenue levels, industry/technology/sector preferences, different risk factors they are willing to take on, team member details and relationships, or primary customers and marketing channels. In many instances, you can learn the details of how your audience "screens" and how they rule out plans right up front. Ask what different resource providers want and listen to them—some will fit your venture, some won't. For example, most banks will not deal with new ventures, most VCs won't deal with pre-revenue businesses, and most angel investors won't invest in ventures valued at more than US$5 million pre-money (often less). Ask and listen.

MANAGING RISK

Our starting premise: business plans are not about selling the upside of your venture. Instead, they are about sharing your mastery of the opportunity, which involves upside, downside, inside, outside, and blindside. One of the most under-addressed topics in business plans is risk management. No one wants to "spook" potential partners with frank discussions of negative possibilities while in the midst of selling the winning potential of a venture. Yet if we take to heart ideas about influencing and being influenced, staying committed to means more than goals, working with affordable loss, finding committed partners and leveraging contingencies, then we must also take to heart that things will go wrong. Things we want to happen don't. Things we don't want to happen do. Murphy's Law applies.

Consequently, your business plan must reinforce your ability to deal with problems, change, disappointment, and so on. Business plans that sell the upside with a mere nod to the risks are considered naive by good investors and useless by expert entrepreneurs. Yes, your graphs should go "up and to the right," as Guy Kawasaki (a popular industry pundit and author) jokes about the hockey stick revenue projections entrepreneurs create. But if you stop there, you will be unprepared to deal with the inevitable beatings coming your way. Additionally, if you show only "up and to the right" information, you leave the risks to your audience's imagination and miss the opportunity to influence their assessment and learn from their honest feedback about the actual risks.

We've seen countless business plans in which the "worst-case scenario" is still a completely acceptable business, simply with lower sales growth, or the short-term customers go away but you're still okay in the long term, or the whole plan is simply an average of the best case and the worst case. Don't laugh—this is commonplace, and you'll likely do something similar unless you deliberately choose something better. Think through your Murphy's Law plan. Deal with the consequences of receiving a no from everyone you hope will say yes. For example:

Yes:

- Yes, the technical milestone was hit on time.
- Yes, the customer wants to set up a test and then scale out.
- Yes, we just hired the savvy and well-known marketing person we've been chasing.
- Yes, we just brought in an investor who has a lot of relevant expertise.

No:

- If you assume no, what will you do?
- Are there good fallback positions?
- Can you prioritize the pain from different failures?
- Can you take steps to shore up the highest priorities?
- Have you completely bet on one solution that could ruin you?
- Can you minimize the damage from any one particular no?

- In what ways have you kept things to an affordable loss in order to help minimize that damage?

Your Murphy's Law plan will not be entirely elegant. Sometimes, the answer to a problem is simply that you will have to work twice as hard to survive. Sometimes, the answer will be that you in fact have no response—and winning that particular yes is mission critical. Lose it and you lose. Okay. At least you see that. It should also mean that if you win it, you have made a great step forward. Attract more resources with that win. Manage the expectations of investors, and demonstrate your expertise, by considering these topics.

You won't share your Murphy's Law plan with everyone. Different versions of business plans are appropriate for different audiences. It may be that you use it with key leadership, board members or potential employees in their last decision steps, but not with prospective lenders, members of the press, or potential business partners. It is up to you, but having worked out your thoughts on managing risk is genuinely useful for whatever form of business plan you choose to create.

MANAGING BOTTLENECKS

Potential bottlenecks are also rarely addressed in business plans. You can learn a lot about bottlenecks from ideas in operations management. The kinds of questions that operations people ask include:

Research Roots

NEW TOOLS: THE BUSINESS MODEL CANVAS

Co-created by a huge international team of collaborators, Osterwalder's business model canvas is another recent example of a popular business book that has made its way into entrepreneurship education for the simple reason that people find it very useful.

What is it that makes the business model canvas such a helpful tool? One can point to several features. It gets users to focus on the key elements of their venture (i.e. who are the customers, what are the key resources that are needed, etc.). Therefore, it is a good tool for working through the basic activities entrepreneurs need to accomplish in many new ventures. The canvas also helps people see a venture end-to-end, seeing how everything fits—or doesn't fit—together. In other words, it is a useful way of detecting big inconsistencies. It also seems to have just the right amount of structure to help direct users without constraining their ideas too much.

However, the heart of the business model canvas, and what has made it popular, is undoubtedly the fact that it is a visual tool. It literally brings us a canvas and invites us to physically work on it. In doing so, it helps us to better think through problems by drawing on our powerful visualization skills. In short, the business model canvas works because it's a canvas. The idea of business models has been around for a long time but Osterwalder and colleagues put it into a format that turns something fuzzy into something that can be clearly visualized, hacked-together, worked and reworked, argued about by teams, and ultimately pinned to the wall (Osterwalder and Pigneur, 2010).

Research Roots

SEAT OF THE PANTS

People will tell you that before you launch a company, you have to write a business plan. So how come so many Inc. 500 CEOs skipped that sober exercise? Research on founders of firms in the Inc. 500 determined that only 40% of the firms in that sample had created a business plan. And of those who had created a plan, 65% said they were doing something significantly different from their original idea. Remarkably, only 12% of the group reported doing formal market research before launching their firms (Bartlett, 2002).

These data are consistent with other research conducted by Amar Bhidé (2000) who investigated a broader sample of new ventures and found that 41% of the founders had no business plan at all, 26% had a rudimentary plan and only 28% had a formal business plan.

In this regard, notable entrepreneurs that include Bill Gates, Sam Walton, and Jann Wenner are not unique. None of them started with a detailed business plan.

What is going to be truly difficult about your venture? When? How will things change over time? Where will things get stuck? Where are they stuck right now?

Cash is quite often presumed to be the bottleneck for entrepreneurs. This is generally misguided. You must keep asking "why" questions: Why can I not get cash? Chase those causes, dig a little deeper. Those are your real bottlenecks. And once you have gotten to the cause, you may realize that either a) there is something about your business that makes it unappealing to an investor, or b) you don't really need cash at all—you need a machine or a person or a distribution relationship, and finding those resources directly is often easier than finding the cash to go out and buy them.

BUSINESS PLANS

Difficulties, problems, and risks of a venture are consistently overlooked in business plans. Business models are rarely overlooked, but are consistently misunderstood and underspecified. While well-done business plans are primarily useful for potential resource providers, well-designed business models are primarily useful to guiding the entrepreneurial team into action.

There is no one pure definition of what a business plan is, so we'll proffer our own. A business plan consists of four components:

- *Revenue model.* What actually generates cash? What does a

Practically Speaking

THE CUBE WITHOUT A PLAN

It's hard to believe that the blockbuster toy that frustrated our childhood and sold almost a hundred million units between 1980 and 1983 is already practically an antique. But what was behind the product that created the first millionaire entrepreneur from the Communist Bloc?

Birth of the cube

The father of the Cube, Erno Rubik, was a sculptor, an architect, and a teacher of interior design. Spatial relationship problems were his business, and realizing them in three dimensions his specialty. In class, he would often build a physical design in order to make a point—as he did with the Cube. Rubik's Cube was not originally intended to be a blockbuster, or even a toy. It was the presentation of a solution to a structural design problem of surfaces in three dimensions that could be manipulated in any direction.

Inventor turns marketer

Technical creations come along all the time. Making a market for them is the job of the entrepreneur. And without such explicit intentions, Rubik started the process by sharing his puzzle with his students and friends. Their attraction to it indicated opportunity. So, when Rubik met Tibor Laczi, a salesman from an Austrian computer company, Rubik was open to what happened next.

Rising to the challenge

Laczi took Rubik's Cube to the Nuremberg Toy Fair, where he met British toy specialist Tom Kremer. Kremer shared Laczi's attraction to the cube, and the pair negotiated an order for a million cubes with the Ideal Toy Company in New York. Rubik set up production in his native Hungary, to feed the escalating demand for his toy. But trying to manufacture high-quality consumer products behind the Iron Curtain in the early 1980s was an insurmountable challenge. Ironically, the wild success of the cube, compounded with the expense of returned defective cubes, ultimately led to the collapse of Ideal Toy Company.

Practically Speaking *(continued)*

A block of benefits

The interesting thing about entrepreneurship is that value created in the process finds many homes. Rubik himself came away with about US$3 million. Laczi did well. The Chinese factories that picked up the manufacturing that the Hungarians could not handle did well. The event organizers who held Rubik's Cube solution competitions did well. Retailers selling the product did well. So, even though Rubik himself is the obvious entrepreneur in this story, the other players contributed to the process, and many benefited from it—they are all entrepreneurs.

Solving your own puzzle

Fortunately, entrepreneurship is not a Rubik's Cube puzzle. There is only one correct answer and 43 quintillion wrong ones for Rubik's Cube. Perhaps quite the reverse is true for an entrepreneur. Starting with what you know and using the partnerships you build may offer 43 quintillion possible paths to success. Rubik had no business plan. The chances of being able to plan what would happen with his cube were about 1 in 43 quintillion. And even if he had, nobody would have believed him until it was all history.

Rubik application questions:

- What was Rubik doing instead of writing a business plan?

- What level of business planning might have helped Rubik?

transaction look like?

- *Operating approach.* How do you do the things it takes to accomplish those transactions?
- *People approach.* What skills and talents are critical? How will you tap into them?
- *Differentiators.* What is unique about what you're doing? Why will it attract resources?

Business plan rules

- *Rule number 1.* A business plan is not any one of those components; the business plan is all of them. Underspecified business plans generally detail the revenue model and touch on differentiators, but they overlook the approach to operations and people/talent.
- *Rule number 2.* The map is not the terrain. A business plan is merely a map; it's not supposed to detail every nuance of what your venture is doing. It needs to focus on your key intended activities, on the primary drivers of your business success. If you can't be terse, you haven't yet made your map.

Practically Speaking

DISPOSABLE INCOME

gDiapers makes completely biodegradable and flushable baby diapers. The company's business plan:

- Revenue model. gDiapers generates sales revenue by selling products to grocery and apparel retail chains and to consumers from its website gdiapers.com. Retailers order crate-size shipments with return rights; consumers order starter and refill packs.

Practically Speaking *(continued)*

- Operating approach. The company focuses on the design and marketing of the product and packaging, sourcing the components from focused suppliers that ship a finished, boxed product to the main office.
- People approach. Critical talent needs are design, creative marketing in two different arenas (channel marketing and online marketing), and supply chain management. These skills are all in-house, and the company accesses additional talent in technical design through partners.
- Differentiators. The key differentiation is the 100% eco-friendly disposable diaper with style. It is one of a kind. The company has also cultivated relationships with a large group of remarkably passionate users online who help manage channel opportunities and sell products online.

This is clearly a summary of the business, a glimpse at the critical components gDiapers must master in order to be successful in its current endeavors. However, it offers a clear idea about the risk and opportunities facing this company. Business plans are design exercises, involving intentional design choices as well as emergent insights that result from working with different people. The business plan items (revenue, operations, people, and differentiators) can be considered variables in the equation, and can take different values as you play with the design. Business plan design involves imagining alternatives and getting ideas for alternatives from potential partners. For example, consider alternatives for gDiapers:

Revenue model

- Selling store-branded product to chains
- Selling through a wholesaler network; no direct relationships
- Exclusively online distribution

Operating approach

- Full integration, design to product to marketing to sales
- Exclusively use online marketing and order taking
- Drop shipping only to retailers, no direct handling
- Sourcing from similar operation in different country

People approach

- Online marketing in-house
- Outside reseller network to retailers
- Open-sourced pants design (product exterior)
- Technical expertise around the liner (product interior)

Differentiators

- Custom pant designs online
- Store branding to encourage channel adoption
- Differentiated focus on "Earth friendly"
- Heavy on style and functionality
- Position against cloth diapers rather than disposable

Practically Speaking *(continued)*

The list of possibilities is immense and inherently creative. These are merely examples of other legitimate choices that could detail the gDiapers business plan, but don't. These choices about what are and aren't part of the plan are the critical ones. We hope the earlier parts of this book will help you make these choices in ways that are coherent and actually connected to the preferences and aspirations of your potential customers, partners, and employees.

Attracting resources through metaphor and analogy

The process of attracting resources to new ventures is rife with contradictions. One of these is the desire to demonstrate that the venture is truly innovative and the need to provide evidence that it will work. New + proven = really tricky (oxymoronic, really).

Well-designed business plans help deal with this challenge. They allow you to use metaphors and analogies to other companies and industries as evidence to support the value and feasibility of your novel offering. What industries and companies provide metaphors and analogies? The ones that share important features of your business model.

What industries or companies would be relevant to gDiapers?

- Branded apparel (children's, specifically)
- Non-food products for sale in grocery retail (e.g. other baby products or video rental)
- Design/marketing outfits (e.g. Nike)
- Companies with a complicated mix of online and offline sales (e.g. Barnes & Noble or BMG)
- Companies that use suppliers for technical innovation (e.g. Dell)
- Companies positioned as eco-friendly (e.g. Seventh Generation)
- Obviously, other diaper companies (e.g. Huggies and Pampers).

Some of these will provide more robust analogies than others. Certainly, you can imagine more. Come up with a list to provide analogies for your company; let's call this your peer group. Now, you can study these companies, looking for evidence to support what you're trying to do.

What evidence does your peer group provide that . . .

- Customers will adopt a product like yours?
- Your venture can grow as fast as you want to show in your plan?
- Your particular business model choices are "state of the art"?
- Your business model is robust enough to endure mistakes?

Practically Speaking *(continued)*

If you were to tell the story of your peer companies, their key mistakes and successes, what would be the important learning points? If you've done a good job of connecting key components of your business model to those of the peer group, you'll be surprised by how much you can learn. Adjust your strategy and share some of what you've learned in your business plan.

Traction trumps everything: How to win a business plan competition for gDiapers

Of course, there is no evidence quite as good as your own successes to prove that the novelty of your business venture is valuable. This evidence is commonly referred to as traction. Traction is what connects the power of a car engine to the road—it's what leads to forward motion (in this case, you and your team are the horsepower). Every yes you win is a point of traction. Without traction, the effort you put into executing your business plan is akin to spinning your wheels. No one wants to put resources (time, money, relationships or talent) into a business that's going nowhere.

Business plan competitions can be outstanding learning experiences. The winners of these competitions consistently have genuine traction that differentiates their efforts from hypothetical plans, and they demonstrate their potential for success—they aren't just spinning their wheels.

Conjecture

- We'll make disposable diapers you can flush down the toilet.
- We'll sell these diapers in Whole Foods.

Sound interesting?

Traction

- Watch as I flush this diaper down the toilet.
- The local grocery store paid us cash for the 1,000 diapers they sold last month.

You win.

Sometimes, you can't get traction until you've attracted certain resources. You might need an engineer to finalize the prototype. You might need cash to order 1,000 diapers for your first store test. Traction can be a serious chicken and egg problem. Remember affordable loss? You need to prioritize and pursue accomplishments, within your levels of affordable loss, which constitute traction. This is an art, and so it takes practice, but keeping this concept in mind will help you focus on progress and make sense of the small victories you accumulate as you proceed.

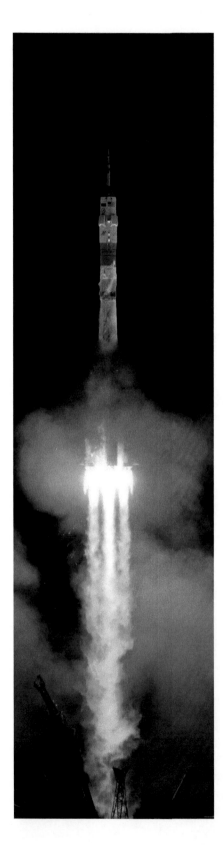

THE ROCKET PITCH

Entrepreneurs have long been challenged to reduce the description of their business to something someone could understand in an elevator ride, and it was called the "elevator pitch."

The world has gotten faster, and version two of that challenge is the "rocket pitch," something one could understand in the 30 seconds that it takes a rocket to launch. Imagine your business on a single slide, in 30-point font, with a total of four or five bullets. As you look at that condensed summary, ask yourself:

- Who are you pitching?

- What are you saying?

- What is that person hearing?

- What is the one thing you want the person to walk away with?

- How do you want them to describe it to the next person?

Remember that every pitch that fails gives you an idea for how to make the next one better. You should never make the same pitch twice as pitching is as much about your learning as it is about gaining commitments.

MANAGING PREDICTIONS

Another necessary element in most business plans is a demand forecast. This assumes you have described what customers seem to want, you've learned about other relevant companies and what they were able to accomplish and you've learned about the size of different markets. This builds an answer to the question: What do you think you can accomplish with your opportunity over the next few years?

How you build your prediction logic, starting at the top or starting at the bottom, is a matter of opinion. Top-down forecasting is simply estimating the overall size of the market, looking at what might be feasible in terms of market share and customer adoption, and doing the math. In our opinion, this sort of predictive work all too often leads to grossly high demand forecasts. Top-down forecasts lead to statements like this: We only need to get a 1% market share and we'll be really successful. These statements leap over the important logic of how the venture will obtain 1% market share and undermine the credibility of entrepreneurs.

Bottom-up forecasts look at things in a more micro fashion. What customers can you actually reach this year, by name? How many customers can you keep in your sales process simultaneously? If you add four salespeople, what happens to that number? Can you list the prospects you need to hit for each year you're forecasting in order to make those numbers real? What is the revenue from what you can actually produce right now? What are the bottlenecks keeping you from doubling your sales over the next 12 months? Can they be eliminated so your sales forecast is legitimate? These types of forecasts are consistently lower and more credible, but many entrepreneurs don't feel that it gives justice to the true potential of their opportunity.

Here is the painful reality: both types of forecasting typically lead to demand forecasts that simply don't get hit. Many investors, and all bankers, barely pay attention to forecasts made by entrepreneurs. Early-stage investors will use them to broadly characterize the overall size potential of the venture—small, medium, and large, if you will.

More important than either top-down or bottom-up forecasting is the more direct analysis relating to your business model. It's not the macroeconomics of the top-down approach or the micro level of the bottom-up forecast. It is the economics of your business model,

constructed with an understanding of the contribution margin of a typical transaction. To build your own, answer each of the following questions:

- What kind of marketing/sales investment is required to win a customer?
- What type of inventory will you have to build to attract sales?
- What drives your product costs?
- Are your gross margins fragile?
- What are the potential service requirements after you make a sale?
- Over the course of a year or two, what kind of cash are you netting overall from your lead customers?
- How many customers do you need to land in order to break even?
- How many transactions are needed to break even?
- Are there business model changes that can materially change these transaction-level economics?

If you can get clarity at this level of analysis, the needs facing your venture will be significantly clearer, and because this type of analysis involves less prediction (not zero prediction, just less prediction), it is less risky to use in your decision-making. (Of course, keep in mind that garbage in equals garbage out. You have to do real work to identify your product costs, selling costs, and service costs, and validate your pricing.)

ESCALATION OF COMMITMENT

A well-specified business plan that includes interesting thoughts and strategies for dealing with risk and surprise, and emphasis on traction and gaining ground with customers, partners, employees, and investors can materially change how you proceed as an entrepreneur. It can increase the emotional commitment you have to the work you've done thus far. This increased commitment to your plans, to the goals you now have in mind, and to delivering on the yeses you may have won from customers, partners, employees, and investors can prematurely pull you away from the principles of entrepreneurship we've been discussing in this book.

Your willingness to think of new ways to use your means, leverage contingency, stay connected to your affordable loss, and truly focus on committed partnerships can wane if you don't watch out. Timing is everything. As your venture develops, you will need to focus on goal-driven activities more and more, on delivering what everyone has agreed to deliver.

This is different from the notion of "escalation of commitment." Escalation of commitment involves an emotional response to the material resource investments that constrain your ability to change direction. Beware of this.

Entrepreneurs often become less willing to pursue the opportunities that reveal themselves through their work with customers, partners, employees, and investors.

Venture capital investors are a common example of this.

Venture capital investors get involved because they intend to execute on the vision, strategy, and opportunity championed by the entrepreneurs. With new cash resources available, the entrepreneurs focus on exploiting the opportunity. If the opportunity turns out to be valuable, the additional funds enable the entrepreneurs to develop it faster and give the entrepreneurs an advantage over competitors. On the other hand, if the opportunity does not materialize, it is hard for the

Research Roots

REWARDS TO ENTREPRENEURS WITH VENTURE CAPITAL INVESTORS

Only a tiny fraction of new ventures ever raises venture capital, but those that do sometimes turn into very valuable firms. Economists Hall and Woodward analyzed almost all the US firms funded by venture capital from 1987 to 2008. There were 22,004 cases in total. Of these 2,015 (9%) held initial public offerings of their stock, 5,625 (26%) were acquired, and 7,572 (34%) exited with zero value. At the time the study was done 6,792 (31%) still existed as independent businesses.

The study is interesting because it documents what rewards entrepreneurs receive from seeing a firm through from VC investment to exit. In the typical venture funded firm, the entrepreneur receives a submarket salary and keeps a substantial ownership interest in the firm. In 75% of cases, that ownership interest was worth zero at exit, while 1% received over $100 million. Venture capital funded entrepreneurship is, therefore, a low-probability/high-return game. This is epitomized by Google, which delivered the largest single entrepreneurial payoff in Hall and Woodward's (2010) sample of firms at over $1 billion.

Practically Speaking

THE WIND AND THE PLAN

"New-age traveller" is a euphemism for a hippie, a house trucker or even a vagrant. It's not the community typically associated with the next generation of business leaders. But then again, solutions to climate change don't seem to come from typical business leaders. This may explain part of why Dale Vince, an ex-traveller himself, is among the most influential "green" entrepreneurs on the planet today.

Measuring the zephyr

Committed to a low-impact lifestyle, Vince's journey into business began with building small-scale windmills to serve his personal energy needs and limit his dependency on commercial power. One of the most complex pieces of the puzzle was reliably measuring the environment in order to identify a location that provides consistent wind to drive turbines. Not finding adequate solutions on the market, Vince started crafting wind-monitoring towers in 1991 and, in 1992, founded Western Windpower. Though Vince has continued his own expedition, Western attracted orders from clients like Scottish Power and is now Nexgen Wind, the UK's market leader in wind monitoring equipment.

Practically Speaking *(continued)*

A powerful gust

Armed with knowledge of wind measurement and power generation, Vince applied for permission to establish a wind farm in the UK and in 1992 gained approval. Just three years later, he founded Ecotricity (originally the Renewable Energy Company), offering the radical alternative of "green" electricity to both household and business customers. By the end of 2007, Vince's firm was operating 12 wind farms, representing 10% of England's wind energy, 46 GWh/year of renewable electricity, and savings of around 46,000 tonnes of CO_2 emissions as well. His accomplishments have been duly recognized. Vince has been presented with an OBE for services to the environment, a Queen's Award for Enterprise and an Ashden Award for sustainable energy, and he made the list of the world's Top 100 Eco-Heroes. But this is really just the start of the story.

Contingency in the air

Fewer new-age travellers roam Europe today, and green energy is no longer a radical idea. With the external environment, Vince himself has changed. His networks, his knowledge, and even his assets have changed. And as is often evidenced with serial entrepreneurs, he is reconfiguring what he has in order to create his next opportunity. His current effort is a prototype electric sports car based on the Lotus Exige, which makes sense not only in light of Vince's relationship with sustainable energy, but also because Lotus is already an Ecotricity customer, building a wind-powered automobile factory in Norfolk, England.

> The one thing I have learned is that you have to be flexible, you have to continually reappraise that which you hold to be true because things change internally and externally.
>
> Dale Vince

Regeneration

And what lies ahead? Certainly, no specific business plan. A vegan, a keen advocate of organic farming, and still committed to a low-impact, self-sufficient life, Vince is currently experimenting with approaches to micro-generation at home. And not being constrained to a plan means Vince can stay open to options that range from creating software that manages home power consumption to working with Tesla's Elon Musk to sell the Powerwall home battery technology. Maybe he is also the creator of something else—the plan to not have a plan.

Research Roots

A GREAT DEBATE: BUSINESS PLANNING

Business planning is one of the most ubiquitous aspects of entrepreneurship education, but researchers have not agreed about the benefits of planning for the performance of new ventures. Over many years of research, studies have generated inconsistent results with some indicating a negative relationship between planning and firm performance, while others a positive relationship or no relationship. The benefits of planning are thought to occur from using resources more efficiently and from making better-informed decisions. Critics counter that entrepreneurs can put their time to better uses than planning (e.g. establishing relationships with new customers) and that planning introduces cognitive biases that limit an entrepreneur's flexibility.

Recent research by Brinckmann and colleagues sought to cut through the confusion by analyzing the combined results of 46 previously published studies involving over 11,000 small firms in total. Results indicated that on average planning does have a positive relationship with performance. However, the benefits of planning are significantly lower for new firms than for established firms. This may be because new firms face a more uncertain environment than established firms do, as well as more ambiguity about exactly what products they will offer and customers they will serve. These factors may limit the returns to planning.

Overall, these results suggest taking a contingent view of business planning where the right question to be asking is, "What is a business plan useful for in my venture?" and tailoring your planning approach accordingly (Brinckmann et al., 2010).

Practically Speaking

A MODEL FOR HEALTHY CHANGE

Kiran Mazumdar-Shaw is something of a modern business folk hero. She started her own life-sciences firm in a garage at the age of 25 on a shoestring of 10,000 Indian rupees (about £128). At that time, the idea of a woman CEO in India was as remote as the idea of a competitor to Pfizer coming from the country. Today, her venture, Biocon, is a multinational publicly listed pharmaceutical provider in Bangalore. The firm employs more than 5,500 people, offers more than a dozen therapies in areas from cardiology to oncology and is hot on the trail of breakthrough oral insulin. Mazumdar-Shaw has won just about every entrepreneurial award on the planet, and she is recognized as the wealthiest (self-made) woman in India.

Business change

But that's not what this story is about. It is about what happens next. It is easy to script romantic endings for business legends. She might retire to a private island. She might fancy art or theater and create a charity with her enormous wealth. Or she might do something as surprising as creating another successful firm. Indeed, she did start again, taking what she had learnt about business—and what she had learnt about wellness—and applying them to one of the most pressing social problems facing India today: the lack of available healthcare for the 40% of the population (nearly half a billion souls) that fall below the poverty line, earning less than 80 pence a day.

Practically Speaking (continued)

Business clarity

It would be easy for someone like Mazumdar-Shaw to simply throw money at the problem. With shares in Biocon currently trading around £175, she has plenty to throw. But she is a self-titled "compassionate capitalist," who spent the last 30 years learning that profit can be a solid foundation for impact, sustainability, and progress. And so when she turned her sights to social purpose, she meant business. "Innovation and commerce are as powerful tools for creating social progress as they are for driving technological advancement," she says. "The only difference is that when they are put to use for social progress, the implementation is a lot cheaper, a lot more people benefit, and the effect is more lasting."

Business impact

Mazumdar-Shaw created two platforms to enable caring capitalism. The first is a foundation called Arogya Raksha Yojana (translated as "Health Help"). Its mission is to run small rural clinics that serve a local radius of the population. The second is the Mazumdar-Shaw Cancer Center, a state-of-the-art facility in Bangalore. Each delivers quality healthcare using a uniquely social business model.

Micro insurance

India has neither socialized medicine nor government-backed health insurance. Without those mechanisms, any significant treatment of injury or illness for a member of a poor family would mean financial ruin or, more likely, foregoing treatment. But for 150 rupees a year (about £1.90), an individual can buy health insurance from Arogya Raksha Yojana and secure a year's worth of healthcare.

Social pricing

At Mazumdar-Shaw's high-tech cancer center in Bangalore, fixed costs are substantial, and micro insurance would not cover them. So she created a "subsidized convenience" pricing plan, enabling her to serve (wealthy) patients at full price between the hours of 8 a.m. and 5 p.m. (middle income) patients with more flexibility than money between the hours of 6 p.m. and 10 p.m. at half price, and offer the services of the center to the poor for free in the middle of the night.

Business health

By creating healthy patients and healthy profits, Mazumdar-Shaw also shows us the path to healthy change. For her, business is not good or evil; it is merely a means that can be applied to many purposes—and even at the same time. She shows us the cycle of the entrepreneur, continually creating with everything and anything available at hand. And she challenges us to improve the health and purpose of our own work.

entrepreneurs to change direction because the escalation of commitment to the specific opportunity associated with the venture capital investment limits flexibility.

We don't know one right way to resolve this tension. There is value in focus sometimes. There is value in flexibility at other times. We do know that if you don't explicitly deal with escalation of commitment bias, you likely will not make a fully informed choice, and may both overinvest in a failing path or fail to move to a new path—either way constraining your ability to succeed.

TAKEAWAY: WHETHER YOU PLAN OR NOT, TAKE ACTION

We hope you are both more confident in how to create a business plan if you want to, or to operate without one if you want to. Clearly, there are plenty of failed businesses both with and without business plans. And there are many successes with and without them as well.

Regardless of whether you have a plan, nothing takes the place of action—of accomplishing something with your venture. Whether it's closing a deal with a customer, shipping a product, or merely getting the sign up over the door, nothing happens in a new venture unless you do it. And doing it is what generates the traction that makes businesses happen.

Aside from acting as a marketing tool for raising institutional investment, one of the best uses of a business plan might be to help you take action. Not everyone needs the support of a plan in order to get going, but if it is something that helps you do so, then take advantage of it. Remember that, ultimately, the business plan is nothing more than a tool to help you get your venture going. If it is not helping you do that, then forget it. Forge ahead.

■ ■ ■

So What?

Great business plans are different for the different purposes to which they are put to use. One size does not fit all. Above all, they need to be compelling, not legalistic or focused on your divine predictions of the future. If you are doing it right, you will learn about your venture as you create different versions of your business plan.

Think It Through

■ What things can you really plan?

■ Is there something else that a business plan might provide—confidence to the entrepreneur?

■ How do the ideas of escalation of commitment and business planning intermingle?

What Now?

■ How simply can you explain your current opportunity?

■ Translate your current plan down to, "What do you sell? To whom do you sell? Why do they buy from you?"

■ Detail one transaction for your current business model; the timing, costs, pricing, and customer decisions around a typical transaction. Does your business plan effectively communicate this level of mastery, or is it focused only on big ideas and bold predictions?

■ Identify the audiences that will need to see a plan from you. What will you emphasize differently to each of those audiences? What do you want each audience to believe as a result of understanding your plan?

CHAPTER 20

When the ID badges show up, it's time for me to leave.

Cam Clarke
Serial Entrepreneur

The venture grows up: Create an entrepreneurial culture

■ ■ ■

It is the relentless business paradox: entrepreneurs dream of building a venture that becomes successful, enduring, and large. And yet executives from successful, enduring, large firms flock to business schools with the objective of somehow making their organizations and themselves entrepreneurial. There are enough large firms out there to reassure us that the entrepreneurial dream is possible. But will executives be forever unfulfilled in their quest?

It is important to acknowledge at the outset that the deck is stacked against large firms that aspire to be entrepreneurial. There are three positive attributes of big companies and their people that directly conflict with the approaches employed by expert entrepreneurs:

- *Prediction.* Firms become large typically because they are able to successfully create markets for their products or services. This success generates all sorts of positive reinforcement, like reliable revenue, a known brand, and a large client base. It also generates history. Successfully selling the same product year after year enables, encourages, and reinforces the use of prediction based on that history. Throughout the value chain, from raw material providers to distributors, the patterns generated from a history of success offer useful planning tools for further refining and expanding the business. Ironically, the reliance on prediction undermines managers' ability to pursue new opportunities—the uncertain ones that enabled them to grow in the first place.

- *Structure.* Scale must be managed. When a startup is selling only a few units, a single entrepreneur or a tight team can oversee the whole operation. But as the firm adds volume, moves into more geographic locations, supports more clients, works with more suppliers and seeks to standardize delivery, the operation grows. As it grows, the organization develops into specialized units within a hierarchy or a matrix, building structure under a small number of decision-makers at the top. Structure separates decision-making from action taking—the tasks expert entrepreneurs perform quickly, concurrently, and iteratively.

- *Process.* Process is a word with both positive and negative connotations. It is a natural result of the successful growth of a new venture and an asset to a large firm. Not everyone can interact with everyone else, so there is a want and a need for rules, policies, and procedures that enable the structure to function smoothly. Yet many processes design newness—the source of opportunity—out of the system.

A potential entrepreneur reading this might look at these attributes of large firms and be reassured by the reasons they chose NOT to work for a big firm and, instead, become an entrepreneur in the first place. But these are some of the mechanisms that enable firms to become large and successful. Surely, capitalizing on a market the firm worked to create cannot be undesirable. What the entrepreneur implicitly objects to is that these attributes do not generate novelty. They do not free the organization to create. And the reason for the entrepreneurial disdain of prediction, structure, and

> What we need is an entrepreneurial society in which innovation and entrepreneurship are normal, steady and continual.
> Peter F. Drucker

process is that these elements emerge in more mature environments, while entrepreneurs operate in the uncertain setting of venture, market, or product creation.

Our research identified the effectual principles expert entrepreneurs use for creating new ventures in uncertain situations. As we outline those principles throughout the book, we contrast effectuation with the predictive approaches better suited to mature organizations. For clarity, we sometimes describe effectuation and causation as either/or. But many situations have elements of both uncertainty and maturity. And as the venture grows and the market matures, the use of causation or prediction becomes more prominent in the decision-making around the firm.

Our objective is to take the best of expert entrepreneurial thinking and redesign prediction, structure, and process in a large-firm setting in order to free parts of the organization to work on creating the next market, product, or service—creating the longer-term future of the large firm.

THE POWER OF PREDICTION

When we present a business problem to expert entrepreneurs, one of the things we notice is how little they use prediction to try to solve it. In the course of creating new ventures, entrepreneurs learn not to rely on history for making decisions. Confident (wrongly or rightly) that they can change the environment, they focus instead on actions that will create a future where they will benefit.

Of course, entrepreneurs are not the only experts out there. There are expert doctors, chess players, taxi drivers, and even expert corporate executives. The same logic applies. Over the course of time (at least 10 years) and practice, expert corporate managers learn heuristics that work well in a large-firm environment. One of those is prediction.

Institutionally, prediction is forced on corporate executives. From forecasts to budgets, from personal objectives to customer satisfaction levels, historical data are used as a base line for planning and goal setting. And well it should be. It works. Plotting the sales growth over past years to predict sales this year in order to plan staffing levels and production gives a good and useful result. So the institutional mandate is reinforced by the fact that prediction is sufficiently useful, and it is what corporate executives learn.

In fact, corporate executives learn prediction so well that it becomes the hammer they use in any situation, regardless of whether the

CONTRASTING PERSPECTIVES: EXECUTIVES AND ENTREPRENEURS LOOK AT OPPORTUNITY

	Executives in a large corporation	Entrepreneurs in a new venture environment
View of opportunities	*Defined and narrow.* Corporate policies restrict options. Typically, only opportunities adjacent to or supporting the core business are considered.	*Diverse and negotiable.* Everything from product offering to target market is negotiable. Investors can consider investments unrelated by business area, size, customer, or nature of product.
Potential funders	*Few and restricted.* New opportunities often have a single point of approval. This limits both the ability to get a project started and to change the direction of a project as the opportunity unfolds.	*Many and flexible.* The diversity in the investor population gives entrepreneurs a market of potential funders.
Financial criteria	*Impact on the bottom line.* For a US$20 billion company, a minimum meaningful impact might be US$1 billion, precluding consideration of smaller opportunities, and forcing the firm to make a few large bets.	*Positive return.* Investors invest in a small fraction of the business plans they review. Level of investment can be scaled to the size of the opportunity, so the range of "interesting" can be broad.
Outlook	*Supportive and measured in quarters.* Large public firms answer to the stock market and inevitably manage toward quarterly earnings reports. Once funded, a project is typically supported unless faced with overwhelmingly negative results.	*Acted in moments and measured in years.* A venture capitalist-funded startup might raise four to six investment "rounds" prior to liquidity. Each new investment requires that significant milestones be achieved with the last investment and offers a checkpoint to adjust direction.
Value added by funder	*Offer infrastructure and build synergy.* The large enterprise offers distribution, brand, manufacturing, and administrative support to the venture. These assets are typically helpful only after the opportunity has been created.	*Offer a network and build a portfolio.* An investor brings relationships that might generate customers, partnerships or future investors to their portfolio firms.

problem is a nail or not. In an experiment, we presented senior corporate executives with a decision-making scenario. It started in a very mature industry and involved strategic decisions over multiple years for a fictitious refrigerator manufacturer named Frigus. For half the executives, the company and the industry stayed mature over time. Little changed. The same competitors made the same products, and the same consumers bought them. For the

Research Roots

EFFECTUATION AS BUSINESS

Several scholars have employed effectuation as an ingredient to their own businesses. Thomas Blekman built a consulting practice around effectuation, and contributes his insights in books that explain how larger corporations can be more effectual (Blekman, 2011), and more specifically, how to organize for effectual behavior (Blekman and Konijnenburg, 2012). Michael Faschingbauer built a coaching practice around effectuation and has distilled many of his insights regarding effectual action and decision-making (Faschingbauer 2013). Fashingbauer and Rene Mauer have also collaborated to deliver intensive private seminars on effectuation, helping people create and implement projects over time—work that has generated a number of new insights into the different ways effectuation encourages people to think differently (Mauer, 2015).

of what to do next, defaulted to the predictive tools they knew best.

Are corporate executives destined to deploy the hammer of prediction in any situation? No. The key is awareness. The understanding that prediction is but one of many possible tools helps. Enabling executives to see their own decision-making bias helps as well.

In addition, we analyzed two elements in our refrigeration company simulation that meaningfully influenced the ability of corporate executives to venture beyond prediction when faced with

other half of the executives, the environment became uncertain: competitors merged, new competitors entered, new technologies appeared, new consumer segments and new distribution channels arose. In both situations, we measured the extent to which executives based their decisions on prediction. As you might expect, in the mature environment, executives used prediction more and more as the scenario unfolded and they realized it was a useful tool. What you might not expect is that as soon as executives were presented with the uncertain situation, they chose actions based on prediction even more than their peers making the decisions in the mature environment. Despite the obvious disconnect between what had happened historically and what was happening, expert managers, unsure

Research Roots

CONGRATS, YOU'RE A SUCCESS! SORRY YOU'RE FIRED.

Noam Wasserman teaches a course at Harvard Business School on the conflicts founders encounter on their entrepreneurial journeys. His research and learnings from teaching the course are summarized in his award-winning book on Founder's Dilemmas. Wasserman argues that entrepreneurs often face a choice about whether they want to be "rich" or be "king." To grow a company to the point of becoming very valuable, founders usually need outside money, but bringing in outside investor means surrendering control of the firm. The alternative is to go it alone without outside money, in which case the founder can maintain control over the firm. However, it's rare to be able to do both: founder CEOs such as Richard Branson and Phil Knight are exceptions to the general rule. In a survey of 212 US startups that made it to IPO, fewer than 25% of founders led their firm to IPO. In fact, 50% of founders were no longer CEO by the time the firm was three years old. Most of these founders were pushed out of the firms they created in ways they didn't like, well before they thought it was their time to go. Wasserman points out that many outside investors (such as venture capitalists) will often insist on bringing in a professional CEO to run firms they invest in. It is part of "professionalizing" the firm by putting in place a management hierarchy and formal processes such as financial controls (Wasserman 2015).

Research Roots

THE ELEMENTS OF THE INTERNAL MARKET

Three core elements can be used to make any company more market-like:

- *Autonomy*. Give employees the freedom to pursue what they perceive to be interesting ideas.

- *Rewards*. Make sure that whoever creates an innovation derives some benefit.

- *Psychological safety*. Offer the assurance that if an employee has an idea, explores it, and it fails, the employee won't be fired or penalized for it.

In a recent study, we looked at around 6,000 firms representing some 2.5 million employees. We found these three elements—autonomy, reward, and psychological safety—significantly related to innovation. But the element that stands out, for which the relationship to innovation appears to be twice as significant, is psychological safety.

It seems the most important factor in creating a culture that promotes innovation is supporting employees and allowing them to weather the storm of failure. People should feel safe trying out innovative, experimental ideas without fear of being penalized for doing so.

Looking again at the difference between a hierarchical organization and an internal market, this also has an impact on decision-making and the progression of ideas. The traditional hierarchical system is like a monopoly— if you come up with a good idea and your boss doesn't like it, it goes no further.

The real question is how companies can institutionalize using failure as an opportunity for organizational learning. After all, not every project will result in a positive financial outcome, but there will always be a positive knowledge outcome (Read et al., 2013).

uncertainty. The first was how they viewed the situation. When they found the company's industry and competitive environment threatening, they resorted to prediction even more heavily. But when these factors were viewed instead as an opportunity, executives were able to shift more quickly to approaches similar to those used by our expert entrepreneurs. The other factor comes back to expertise. Those executives who had experience in uncertain situations (new locations, new products, new markets) were able to shift more quickly to non-predictive

approaches when they saw prediction wasn't working. So helping corporate executives reframe threats as opportunities and rotating them through positions where they will face uncertainty seems like a good way to keep people in large firms open to entrepreneurial heuristics.

THE STRENGTH OF STRUCTURE

How we think and how we organize are intimately connected. So it is natural that managers comfortable

with prediction would build structures that reinforce and streamline the repetition of activities. But that can come at a cost. Consider the following situation:

There is a proposal for a new product on top of the stack of papers on your desk. You left it there last night, knowing how important it is for the company to generate new opportunities. Before you even look at it, questions enter your mind. How will you get this approved by the division president? Are the numbers in the proposal big enough to get her attention? Are the numbers in the proposal so big the team can never achieve them? If it is approved, can the team execute fast enough to beat competitors? If it fails, will you lose your job? If it is so successful it eats into the margin on the firm's existing profitable products, will you lose your job? Beside it sits a budget for a small marketing outlay on an existing product. Your gut tells you to pick up the marketing budget and ignore the new product idea for yet another day. Too many financial hurdles. Too much personal risk. Too much uncertainty. You reach, and . . .

Restructuring structure

What is it about the organizational structure of a large firm that guides decisions like this one down the incremental path, refining existing products and discouraging the creation of new ones?

Research Roots

THREAT RIGIDITY

Researchers have shown that when faced with a situation people find threatening, people artificially limit the range of options available to them, typically to the approaches they have already been using—they become rigid in the face of the threat. However, when the situation is viewed as an opportunity, people see many more possible solution options and become much more creative with the possibilities.

Staw et al. (1981)

The new venture environment is simply friendlier to the process of opportunity creation. It is easy to see why leaders like Ross Perot left IBM to create Electronic Data Systems, and Steve Wozniak left HP to create Apple Computer, instead of developing those opportunities within their large firms. But the entrepreneurial environment shows us that structure can be used to encourage, rather than inhibit, opportunity creation.

Entrepreneurial structure: The internal market

The new venture environment works as a market. Most large firms work as hierarchies. But imagine if the opportunity creation function within a large firm could be restructured to operate more like a market. Markets already exist within some companies. 3M uses a market-like system to manage employee time; employees are given one day a week to work on whatever ideas they like. One of the many results is the Post-it note. Art Fry, a 3M employee, was working on this idea in his own time and, of course, the Post-it became one of 3M's biggest successes. Another example is Koch Industries, a large privately owned US corporation trading in oil and fertilizers. It practices "market-based management," which gives employees decision rights and performance-related pay. And in

Silicon Valley, employees at highly successful Google can use 20% of their time to work on whatever projects they want.

The core idea is that a large corporation should represent a portfolio of differentiated opportunities that have some technology or market commonality. Ideas might originate anywhere, and the objective is to create a structure to nurture them at an appropriate level so their potential can be realized with minimal risk. An internal market functions on some or all of the following principles, derived from elements of the new venture structure function:

- *Open the market to all potential innovators.* Offer time, freedom or autonomy to people who have the drive to explore new opportunities. Provide structure so that anyone with an idea can submit a proposal for funding.
- *Open the market to all potential investors.* Anyone with profit-and-loss responsibility in the firm can apply to manage a fund. Investment returns are included in the profit/loss results of the investor's business unit. Fund sizes are set annually (at the most frequent). Decision-making for investing in new projects is distributed outside the CEO office, potentially even to outsiders—for example, individuals from the venture capital industry might be permitted to invest in internal projects.
- *Encourage iterative opportunity development.* The initial funder

Research Roots

ASKING IN THE CORPORATE ENVIRONMENT

In the courtroom, lawyers abide by the rule of: "Never ask a question you don't know the answer to." Unfortunately, many businesspeople follow the same philosophy. This limits innovation and creative thinking. And it leaves many corporate managers feeling hamstrung by constraints.

If the solution to this is asking, why don't more corporate managers do this? Because they fear the unknown, what might happen if they are to go off-script? So much of a corporate manager's role is based on planning and executing on those plans, that there is no room left for improvisation.

Asking, however, can actually lead one to have more control over outcomes than just moving forward with forecasted assumptions. Here are a few steps you can take toward becoming a successful asker in a corporate setting:

- *Start small.* Start making small asks of people you have a collegial relationship with. For example, ask another manager to combine efforts with your team on a project. Or ask an external partner you work with to collaborate with you in a new way.
- *Manage expectations.* If you are going to make a bigger ask or enter into a more open-ended conversation, prepare your colleague ahead of time. Since the default communication style in the corporate environment is causal, it can catch people off guard when one communicates in a more open, co-creative way. Letting someone know ahead of time that you want to have a different type of conversation, one that is open and allows both of you to explore possibilities, increases the likelihood of your ask getting thoughtful consideration rather than just surprise.
- *Listen.* After you make the ask, listen closely to the response. Hear the words, but also hear what the person is not saying. If they answer "no," or refuse to engage, is it because they feel they do not have decision-making authority?
- *Seek out others who are open.* If you do hit an impasse with an individual who is uncomfortable co-creating with you, seek those in their organization who may be so inclined, or who might have the managerial latitude to creatively address your ask.
- *Report back.* Build a culture of asking in your team and within your organization by sharing your ask stories. Share both successes and failures. Talking about your ask journey will grow your confidence as you see the positive outcomes generated—from both your successes and failures. And it will encourage others to get out and start asking as well (Whiffen, 2015).

Research Roots

THE TALENTED ENTREPRENEUR

Many economists regard an abundant supply of talented entrepreneurs as central to the vitality of an economy. Such assertions have been influential in public policymaking in support of entrepreneurship, which policymakers often link to job creation and economic growth. However, there is relatively little evidence-based public policy, i.e. policy based on the aggregate results of research studies.

A recent study by Mayer-Haug and colleagues sought to provide such evidence by analyzing what aspects of entrepreneurial "talent" are systematically associated with different kinds of performance outcomes among SMEs (small and medium-sized enterprises). The research amalgamated data from 183 prior studies covering over 50,000 firms. It considered five proxies for entrepreneurial talent: experience and skills, education, planning capacity, the founding team, and network strength. Several key findings emerged. First, the researchers found a robust connection between an entrepreneur's network and various measures of firm performance, suggesting that aspects of good performance derive from a more diverse cast of characters than the entrepreneur alone. This suggests that promoting richer network connections between firms and their stakeholders might be considered an objective of public policy. Second, the study found that different aspects of talent were related to different kinds of firm performance, e.g. employment growth, profitability, firm survival. This suggests that policymakers need to craft specific public policies to encourage particular outcomes, rather than offering general support for entrepreneurship (Mayer-Haug et al., 2013).

of the project is not permitted to exclusively provide follow-on funding. Other funders (internal and external) must participate. This has several implications. First, external funders such as VCs, partners or customers can help validate an opportunity. Second, internal funders have to be cooperative and quick to compete with external sources of funding for the best new opportunities. Third, this approach restrains the "escalation of commitment" that initial funders can fall into—throwing good money at an opportunity that is clearly bad.

- *Eliminate minimum investment sizes.* Investments can be scalable based on the industry and the opportunity. This encourages people to fund projects that don't initially impact the bottom line and encourages people not to prematurely overfund uncertain projects; instead, add funding iteratively as the opportunity is proven.

- *Make everything negotiable (within the philosophy and values of the company).* Just like in venture capital, ownership, salary, amount of funding, nature of the business plan, milestones, and much more are all jointly agreed by funders and creators. Equity in opportunities can be bought and sold both in internal and external markets at market rates. Intellectual property owned by the firm can be secured by the new opportunity team, and vice versa.

- *Support projects that compete with the core business.* And share company resources that might complement the new venture. Better for competition to come from inside than outside.

- *Embrace failure.* Offer employees the assurance that if they explore an idea and it fails, they won't be fired or penalized. Build a culture and a structure that uses failure as a mechanism for learning, not for weeding out employees.

After bringing many of these principles inside the firm, HP established a close relationship with Silicon Valley venture firm Foundation Capital, to learn how to manage opportunities from VCs and exchange ideas about future trends.

SAFETY IN FAILURE WITHIN LARGE ORGANIZATIONS: QUESTIONS AND ANSWERS

How should a professional negotiate a margin of failure with the boss?	The employee should consider expectations and affordable loss. Setting outrageous expectations for a new project or a new product may help get resources approved but makes it difficult to deal productively with any shortfall in the results. Be realistic with the boss. Second, and particularly with highly uncertain projects, evaluate the level of affordable loss, or the level of downside that the individual and the firm can tolerate. If managed effectively, failure will never get to a point where the project generates losses that the individual or the firm can't afford. This helps to make the post-mortem of failed projects less of an emotional exercise and something people can learn from objectively.
Should failures be discussed before or after they happen?	Failure should be discussed in advance in the context of where the pitfalls may lie (so that they can be avoided or leveraged) and in terms of how much will be invested in the project. A project can still be considered successful as long as it stays within the predefined affordable limit—a key insight for being able to redefine losing as successful with a large organization. Also, every project deserves an "after-action review"—a chance to look at what the team liked and did not like about the project, what was learned from the project and how to take that learning into the organization and into the next iteration of the project.
How can a manager make it safe for his or her team to innovate?	Walk the talk. Learn from his or her own failures. Share that learning with the team. Conduct "after-action reviews" with the team for all projects. Promote people who have been able to learn from failure, and communicate those stories. This is clearly not something that can be put into a policy manual—it is an enacted part of a team or firm culture.

GORE APPLICATION QUESTIONS

- What are some potential pitfalls of the Gore model?

- How does the Gore model help us think about managing spin-offs?

- In what situations might the Gore model offer benefit?

- Which aspects of the Gore model seem most compelling to your organization?

Practically Speaking

BREATH OF FRESH AIR

Adventurers from New York to Nepal have long appreciated Gore-Tex. The material's seemingly paradoxical ability to keep the weather out while enabling perspiration to escape enables a wide range of functional and comfortable outerwear. And as the firm that delivered this innovation, W.L. Gore & Associates, has passed its 50th birthday, we celebrate by taking a closer look at how the company has stayed entrepreneurial for more than half a century.

No climate for innovation

W.L. "Bill" Gore started his career at DuPont in 1945 and joined a team finding applications for a novel polymer called

Practically Speaking *(continued)*

polytetrafluoroethylene—Teflon, to the rest of us. Bill experimented with the material as a tough, heat-resistant coating for wiring, an application he felt offered great potential given the likely rise of the computer. Convinced of its technical merits, he tried unsuccessfully to persuade DuPont to develop Teflon-coated cable. Frustrated, in 1958 he created his own firm with his wife Vieve in their basement. W.L. Gore & Associates' cable product created a market. Within 10 years, the firm employed more than 200 people, and Gore cable was used on a mission to the moon.

Fabric of life

Strong competition in the cable industry kept Bill and his son Bob focused on innovation. Continuing to work with Teflon, the pair figured out how to heat and stretch the material so it could be woven as fabric, and Gore-Tex was born. But even before that, Bill had started carefully crafting W.L. Gore & Associates' organization so it could embrace innovation in the way his previous employer had not.

The committed associate

Employees of W.L. Gore are called associates. In the non-hierarchical "lattice" structure, Gore empowered all his employees with the same level of authority. Leaders could emerge only if other associates committed to follow them, and associates had the choice of which projects to work on. The intent and outcome of the structure was to enable good new ideas to grow organically at the discretion of the team. And the teams also had the support of Gore, as he let them do just about anything that would not jeopardize the entire company.

Smaller sizes

Gore quantified optimal team size and constructed his organization accordingly. He felt that when a team at a manufacturing facility exceeded 150 people, two things happened. First, the team lost a sense of cooperation, shifting decision responsibility from "we" (the team) to "they" (some anonymous bureaucracy). Second, accomplishment per person started to decrease. Consequently, when manufacturing teams exceeded 150 people, Gore split the operation in two.

Patently successful

The approach works. Today, W.L. Gore & Associates has created innovative products in areas you probably know, such as clothing and shoes, and in many more that range from guitar strings to dental floss, space suits to sutures. Gore is one of the 200 largest private firms in the US, and consistently makes Fortune's annual list of the "100 Best Companies to Work For" in the US. Today, with more than US$2 billion in annual sales, 2,000 patents, and more than 8,000 employees worldwide, the company continues to defy the common expectation that large cannot also be entrepreneurial.

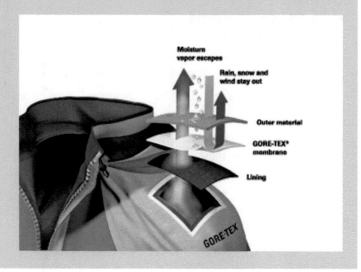

Practically Speaking

A GUIDE TO THE PROCESS

Despite the popular malignment of process, it has an intended function: to help organize, coordinate, and facilitate the actions of many individuals within a large organization. The problem is not the process, but the implementation of the process—what it is actually meant to accomplish. To provide a view into a different possible implementation of process, consider the story of insurance software provider, Guidewire. When John Seybold and his partners founded Guidewire in 2001, he knew little more about the insurance industry than an informed consumer. But as chief technology officer of the upstart company, he also knew he and the team had to learn quickly if they were going to convince mainstream insurers to scrap their aging mainframes and adopt Guidewire's Java-based solutions.

Process objective: Flexibility

The team members looked at the problem and made a decision. Above all, they would be flexible—flexible product, flexible business model, and flexible organization. They expected to gain insights every day from customers, partners, and competitors, and they wanted to be able to immediately benefit from everything they learned.

Process implementation: Sprint

Guidewire organized around small, nimble project teams. But here comes the twist: a project team's assignment lasts only a month. At the start of a month, each "sprint team" picks from the list of the most important tasks to be tackled. The team selects a leader for the month and devours the task. At the end of the month, the team wraps up the project, reflects on its progress, reprioritizes, picks a new task, and the process starts all over.

The key to keeping the whole organization moving toward success is the "master backlog" list of projects. As new ideas are generated and new requests come from customers, they are added to the backlog. No changes to priorities are made during a monthly sprint. But at the start of each new month, the organization reprioritizes the entire backlog and assigns only those tasks that top the list to the next month's sprint teams.

At the end of each month, each team has a specific deliverable—something that must be completed, tested, documented, and ready for a customer. In fact, it is the customer who reviews the deliverable and decides whether to accept it or not. Doing this forces the team to focus on creating something usable and complete, and gives the customer a strong voice within the organization.

Every day, each sprint team meets for 10 minutes in the morning at their whiteboard to discuss what it did yesterday and what it hopes to accomplish today. Individual priorities and performance are as transparent as team performance. Completely transparent. At the end of each month, the teams examine the process to discuss what worked well, what did not work, and what they want to change when they reassemble for the next month's sprint.

Process outcome: Innovation

The success of the process can be demonstrated in the numerous industry awards and client references Guidewire has garnered. But Seybold describes an unexpected benefit:

Practically Speaking *(continued)*

When we first did this, I thought seeing the huge backlog and the small projects we finished in a month would discourage the team. But exactly the reverse happened. They said wow—we're in control and look at what we did. It was a real morale booster, and it has continued to be.

John Seybold

Guidewire employs more than 1,000 people and counts more than 200 international insurers in its growing customer base—successful but still small compared with the insurance giants they sell to. Nonetheless, this process has continued to scale and work for Guidewire. By the way, if you are skeptical about this version of process within a large organization, you may be interested to know that virtually all Guidewire's large, conservative clients in the insurance industry use precisely this approach, learned from Guidewire, within their teams implementing Guidewire's software.

Principles of process

Process generally does what it is designed to do. What Guidewire demonstrates is that it is possible to offer insight into developing new products and entering new markets. More subtly, they offer ideas on selecting, promoting, and training people inside a large firm as well as insight into what might help entrepreneurs stay with the venture as it grows into a large firm. They have implications for the strategic planning process inside a large firm—particularly for acquisitions of startups and corporate venture funds. And they inform research and development partnerships and technology licensing. Though the odds are against the large firm that aspires to be entrepreneurial, there are ways to overcome the three main structural constraints and design a process that enables rather than inhibits innovation. As you think about your own organization, it is not necessary to do everything Guidewire has done. Elements of the process, such as monthly priority reviews or customer acceptance of deliverables, can be implemented in an organization without moving to small sprint teams. Also, an entire large organization does not need to have the same process. Teams, groups, cells, or divisions charged with creating new opportunities might design their own process in the same way teams within insurance firms implementing Guidewire software decided to. Regardless of what the actual implementation looks like, it is liberating to consider how you might change the rules of the organization to encourage entrepreneurial action.

GUIDEWIRE APPLICATION QUESTIONS

- How easy is it for you to terminate a dead-end project?

- Do you have a place for the customer in your organization?

- What kind of people will this kind of organization attract?

- Do you have a regular way to revise and optimize teams?

- Is your organization generating innovation at the rate you expect?

- Do your employees feel they make a visible and measurable contribution toward the success of your firm?

- Do you have the visibility you need in the innovation process in your organization?

And, while it might be no surprise that Microsoft regularly meets with VCs to shop opportunities too small for the software giant to bring to market, the trend is one that extends to companies in more traditional industries. Internal market elements drive new products at firms that include Coca-Cola and Citigroup and give energy to talent management at American Express.

Different structure, different outcome

Let's return to the new product proposal still sitting on your desk. Imagine the firm runs an internal market, and you have a block of real money to invest in real opportunities. It is separate from your operating budget. Your peers also have funds of different sizes; they, too, may invest to create opportunities. In fact, you may be competing with one of them for a piece of ownership of the proposal on your desk. This fund is dear—you had to apply for it from treasury and you carry it on your unit's profit and loss. You will benefit both financially and professionally if you can turn it into something. Instead of a large research and development budget, it is a source of innovation for your business unit. How would that change how you decide between the new product proposal and the small marketing outlay?

TAKEAWAY: A FRESH LOOK

Understanding expert entrepreneurial approaches and applying them to the large firm offers a new perspective on the questions facing executives charged with innovation and growth. Clearly, these approaches offer insight into developing new products and entering new markets. More subtly, they offer ideas on selecting, promoting, and training people inside a large firm as well as insight into what might help entrepreneurs stay with the venture as it grows into a large firm. They have implications for the strategic planning process inside a large firm—in particular for acquisitions of startups and corporate venture funds. And they inform research and development partnerships and technology licensing. Though the odds are against the large firm that aspires to be entrepreneurial, there

Research Roots

HIGH-PERFORMANCE VENTURES CREATE THE MOST SOCIAL VALUE

In The Illusions of Entrepreneurship, Scott Shane (2008) surveys research on small businesses in order to highlight that the general public and economic policymakers tend to hold many misconceptions about entrepreneurship. One interesting misconception is the idea that new ventures are a public good because they generally create jobs. The truth is that a few new ventures that grow strongly are responsible for most of the job growth. This highlights what we have talked about in this book—that learning principles used by expert entrepreneurs who have demonstrated an ability to launch high-performance ventures that create new products and markets and new large firms is not only good for you but also good for society because it is the high-performance ventures that create the most social value.

are ways to overcome the three main structural barriers to acting entrepreneurially within a large organization.

What Now?

☐ In your organization, at what number of employees does your "achievement per employee" level off (e.g. Gore)?

☐ How will you change selection and promotion of people inside a larger firm, in light of these ideas?

☐ If you were to create an "internal market" for opportunities, who would be your "buyers," who would be your "sellers," and what would a transaction look like?

☐ Identify two existing research and development partnerships and/or licensing relationships that seem to be built upon these effectual ideas (they may have snuck in). Can you identify how they came to be, and how you might initiate, run or re-design others more effactually?

☐ Think about what you are going to tell your CFO when she asks for revenue projections on a project to develop a new product.

So What?

Large organizations are built to withstand entrepreneurial efforts involving the effectual principles laid out in this book. But in order to continue to grow, they need specially designed solutions to overcome their over-reliance on research, prediction, and big bets in the pursuit of new opportunities.

Think It Through

☐ What might help entrepreneurs stay with the venture as it grows into a large firm (Bill Gates is exceptional; most founders leave or are forced out as the venture grows)?

☐ Is there an optimal size for any firm?

PART V

Applications of effectuation

In this next section, we hope you appreciate that effectuation is more than entrepreneurship. Rather it is a way of describing human decision-making and human action, which can be applied as easily to the starting of a new venture as it can to the solving of a problem in the world. And though we take on only the topics of how firms communicate their unique identity (Chapter 21), how people deal with creating technology businesses (Chapter 22), and how the entrepreneurial method is similar to the scientific method (Chapter 23), we hope you will consider these chapters your gateway out into the open ocean. And as your voyage faces uncertainties not detailed in this book, we hope you figure out how to apply some elements of effectuation to help you on your way.

Whatever you can do or dream you can, begin it. Boldness has genius, power and magic in it.

Johann Wolfgang von Goethe

CHAPTER 21

New ventures start without a brand.

But all start with something more central, potentially more useful and free.

An identity.

Brand as venture identity: Marketing you

■ ■ ■

As the prospective founder, owner, manager, and first employee of a new venture, you may well look with awe at the world's greatest brands. Names like Apple, Coca-Cola, Toyota, and Nike must give employees at these organizations an incredible advantage in the market. And here you are with nothing but an idea and a little inspiration (perhaps enhanced by the caffeine from that Coca-Cola).

The purpose of this chapter is to think about marketing a new venture. Not from the perspective of the things you don't have (a recognizable brand, a large communications budget, and a team of PR people), but from the perspective of what you do have—an identity. An identity not only

prepares you to start taking action without spending money but also helps set a foundation for what the brand will be as the venture grows, the communications message will be from the very first day, and the product or service areas the firm might or might not operate in.

We should say at the outset that no one identity is necessarily better than another. Consider the following two examples. Cypress Semiconductor, based in San Jose, California, makes programmable chips for custom computers that go into everything from automobiles to medical devices. Founder and CEO T.J. Rogers, named one of America's toughest bosses by *Fortune* in 1993, exercises with his direct reports at lunch and has a license-plate holder that reads, "Cypress: We eat nails."

EXPLAINED: THE RELATIONSHIP BETWEEN THE ENTREPRENEUR'S PERSONAL IDENTITY AND THE VENTURE IDENTITY

There are many opinions about what venture identity means. We think of venture identity as the "persona" of a firm, designed to be consistent with and facilitate the attainment of business objectives. Venture identity is not a brand. Venture identity is not a logo. It is the philosophy, values, norms, and personality of the firm. Brand and logo should reflect parts of the venture's identity, but only parts of it. When the venture starts, those elements of logo and brand don't exist at all. So at the start, personal identity and venture identity are largely the same thing. This illustrates another way an entrepreneur's means are important, and also the imprint an entrepreneur leaves on a venture she creates.

THREE THOUGHTS ON FIRM NAMES

Perhaps the most obvious connection between personal identity and venture identity is naming the firm after yourself (McKinsey & Co., for example). Beyond that, the name can still communicate much about the identity of the venture. Twitter does as good a job of illustrating light, quick communications as Costco does of setting the expectation of finding low prices.

Should the firm name be the same as the product name?

There is no right answer. The logic for making the names the same is that stakeholders have a hard enough time learning a single new name, so why spend the effort teaching two. Companies like Oracle (the name of the firm and of the firm's core database software product) illustrate the simplicity of this approach. Firms interested in creating a portfolio of products separate the two and may focus on product brands more than on the company brand, such as Proctor & Gamble.

Who is going to use your name, and is it suited to the different applications?

Think about all the people who are going to use your name. If they speak a different language, what does your name mean in their language (recall that the Chevrolet Nova did not sell well in Mexico because the name means "doesn't go" in Spanish)? Consult the dictionary. If the press is a big part of your marketing effort, will they write you up in a comparison list with your competitors? If so, choose a name at the top of the alphabet. Will you speak your firm name to a lot of people? If so, it had better be spelled phonetically. Will your name go onto consumer packaging? If so, keep it short and think about the graphic elements of the letters (lots of curves—S, O, G—versus lots of angles—L, E, A). Will you do a lot of telephone business? A seven-character name can help match it to a phone number in the US.

How can you ensure your firm name is unique?

This has gotten easier and harder at the same time: easier because you can Google the word you are hoping to use and see what comes up and check an Internet registration site (www.register.com, for instance) to see whether and how the word is being used. Harder because everyone else can do this, too, and so there has been an explosion of site registrations and new company names. If you want something unique, you are going to have to be creative, search other languages, combine pieces of existing words, or even add special characters.

"As our new company logo, I'm not quite sure it's sending out the right message."

of the venture, but it continues to be true as the venture grows. The reason is that your startup's identity could not be created by the marketing department (even if you had one) in a vacuum. Rather, it is a reflection of the systematic and often mundane internal and external actions that employees (or the sole employee) of the firm take every day. But simply taking action does not guarantee that a desirable or coherent identity will emerge. To achieve that, you must do the following:

Contrast that with the Vermont Teddy Bear Company, a folksy outfit known for people calmly sipping tea during meetings. What do the two companies have in common? Both are enormously successful. Both have a strong identity. And for both, the identity of the firm, an extension of the founder's identity, helps attract employees and partners and provides a basis for choosing which activities make sense for the business and which don't. Yet their identities could not be further apart. Clearly, there is no one right identity; the question is how to create and use your identity.

YOU ARE THE IDENTITY; THE IDENTITY IS YOU

It will be of little surprise, after reading about "means" in Chapter 10, to learn that your means are directly connected with the identity of your venture. Never is this truer than when you are the sole employee

Research Roots

IDENTIFY YOURSELF

It has long been known that non-pecuniary motivations are an important reason why some individuals take the plunge into entrepreneurship. In a recent paper, Fauchart and Gruber probe the nature of these motives, finding many ventures to be expressions of the founders' self-identities. Based on a sample of 49 founders who had created businesses in the sports equipment industry, the researchers found three basic categories of founder identities. They describe these as:

- *Missionaries.* These are founders that are advancing a cause, believe in contributing to a better world, and see their firms as instruments of that cause.

- *Communitarians.* These are founders that see themselves as supporting their communities by bringing something useful to them, often based on their knowledge of community needs.

- *Darwinians.* These are founders that view business as business, and themselves as professional, competitive players seeking to make money.

Fauchart and Gruber (2011) noted that several of the founders they interviewed were hybrids of two or three of the pure identities, which is consistent with the view that many entrepreneurs have a complex set of motives for founding a venturea.

Faithfully reflect your personality and values

Your firm's identity has to reflect your authentic personality. It must be consistent whether directed at customers, partners, employees, media—any stakeholder who has contact with the company. Of course, when you have been successful at co-creating your venture with stakeholders, this consistency emerges naturally. The goal is to succinctly understand, down to the level of individual words, the core principles of the company, principles that help stakeholders relate to the value proposition of the firm. It has to be unique, and it has to be genuine. HP, for example, has distilled it to a single word: "Invent," that goes all the way back to the founders working together in a Palo Alto garage. What will it be for you?

IDENTITY IS THE SUM OF MANY SMALL ACTIONS

Once you understand the persona of your venture, it is easy to see how your daily actions either reinforce or undermine it. A major life sciences company with an identity built around safety made the decision to buy Volvos for its company-owned cars. That may not have been the most cost-effective decision, but it certainly is the one most consistent with the company's identity. Mark and Stacey Andrus (see Chapter 13) employed their own re-use desires to make pita chips from day-old bread, and then proceeded to do their marketing by giving away their own

product (initially, they used pita chips to keep people in line for sandwiches, and once they moved into the chip business full time, they used the chips as their primary promotional item).

BE CONSISTENT

Every day presents opportunities for actions that are not consistent with the corporate identity. Whether it's making a hire, launching a product innovation, writing a press release or forming a partnership, managers need to hold the action up against the corporate identity. If it is not coherent, don't do it. One of the uses of a good corporate identity is that it helps managers figure out what the company is "not." In the 1970s, Pierre Cardin had an identity tied with luxury. But Pierre Cardin has slipped a long way from the cover of Vogue, where it once was, to the discount stores where it is today. Pierre Cardin failed one corporate identity test at a time. Looking at new opportunities, partners and customers from the perspective of the identity of your new venture can offer an efficient way to select activities that are a good fit as well as those that are not.

IMPLEMENT BEYOND THE LOGO

Identity is much more than a logo. Over the past 15 years Apple Computer, the computing pioneer, has consciously become Apple (notice "Computer" is conspicuously absent), the hip provider of trendy lifestyle technology. In the process, the company's design firm, Mark Anderson Design, worked on literally hundreds of projects to effect the shift. Some, such as letterhead, corporate signage, and product packaging, might be obvious. But other projects, like designing the annual report, press releases, and even the appearance of company offices, might not be so obvious. Corporate identity is a message that benefits from reinforcement at every opportunity.

Another example is Starbucks Coffee Company. Brief text outlining the mission statement is printed on the back of every partner's (employee's) business card. That way, all employees carry text with them that describes the corporate identity in the form of what the company does. They share

---

QUESTIONS

- Where does identity come from?
- How can I use identity as a foundation for marketing in a startup?
- Is it expensive to build identity?

it with every professional contact they meet. It is a powerful and nearly costless way to communicate with space otherwise left blank.

QUIXOTE: APPLYING IDENTITY

Personal identity is people's conception of themselves and how they relate or belong to broader social categories. Entrepreneurs often explain their actions and decisions in terms of their identities ("what kind of person I am"), rather than their goals or preferences ("what I want and like"). Sometimes the identity has to do with being an entrepreneur, however idiosyncratic that might be; in other cases, it comes from other areas of their lives—such as religious faith, political affiliations, childhood traumas, aesthetic pursuits, or even loyalties to sports teams.

Identity often plays an important role in decisions, especially important life decisions (such as starting a new career in entrepreneurship), and can be especially helpful in situations of high uncertainty.

We find powerful examples of this in great literature, such as the fable of Don Quixote. In Quixote's case, knowing what a knight would do in any circumstance makes him decisive even when the consequences are uncertain. His decision-making ability is deeply rooted in his sense of identity—in knowing who he is and what a person like him should do.

I know who I am and who I may be, if I choose.

Miguel Cervantes Saavedra
(1605–1616)

In other words, identity consists of having a strong affinity for particular ways of living and deciding, rather than for any particular consequences. Entrepreneurs, in general, appear to realize the value of creating and sustaining strong identities, which can guide them when it is not otherwise clear what they should do. Identities may be fictive or real, freely chosen or socioculturally constructed, good or evil. Often, entrepreneurial identities develop incrementally in the course of building a venture—think of how the identities of Bill Gates and Steve Jobs both changed and became more pronounced during the course of their entrepreneurial careers.

Terry Heckler: Creator of enduring brands

Terry Heckler, founder of Heckler Associates in Seattle, Washington, has helped create dozens of successful brands from scratch—ranging from Redhook Beer and Jansport Backpacks to Panera Bread and Starbucks, one of his earliest adventures in brand building.

Heckler's adventures, chronicled on his company's website, give us a glimpse of how his firm constitutes brand from identity—often starting with the founder.

Contrary to popular wisdom, Starbucks was not founded by

on to embody strong corporate identities as the fledgling ventures grew into global brands but also helped rebrand existing companies and create brand extensions as they expanded their horizons.

Take the case of the St. Louis Bread Company, Panera, which hired Heckler Associates to redefine the brand, articulate its mission and values and identify core attributes. Again, the Heckler vision of the quintessential moment of use can be observed in the logo and all design aspects associated with the name and the stores. The website describes the core of the identity as follows: Food as it should be.

Howard Schultz, who came in much later to become the driving force behind the growth of the company. The original Starbucks, a tiny shop in Seattle's Pike Place market that sold imported fine roasted coffee beans, was founded in 1971 by three friends: Gordon Bowker, Jerry Baldwin and Zev Siegl—a writer, a literature teacher, and a history teacher, respectively.

All three founders were fans of Moby Dick and so wanted to name their company Pequod, the name of Captain Ahab's ship in what, in their opinion, was the greatest American novel. Heckler pointed out to them that nobody would ever buy a cup of Pequod and suggested instead the name Starbos—the name of a local mining camp in the Northwest

during the 1800s. In fact, Heckler described his vision of "the quintessential moment of use" of the product—a miner's hand reaching for a green can of coffee inside the camp's tent in the beautiful cool and damp surroundings of Mount Rainier in the rainy Northwest. The three friends jumped on the name because it evoked the name Starbuck, first mate on the Pequod!

And so a great brand began its journey as a patchwork stitched together from the romantic dreams and values of its founders and roughly blessed by a young commercial artist who would go on to become a kingmaker in his own right. Heckler Associates has not only created successful brands for a number of new ventures that went

The central image of the logo was a painterly line illustration of a woman with flowing hair caressing a loaf of bread. She came to be known as "Mother Bread" and symbolized the core essence of the brand's differential. Interestingly, the process of making sourdough bread requires a small piece of the dough used to make the previous batch of bread dough. This starter piece is often called the "mother." Whenever Panera opens stores in a new region, a piece of the original starter that was created in the 1980s is lovingly carried to the new bakery to ensure that original Panera quality and character will rise again and again.
(Panera, 2010)

Jansport Backpacks's story also reveals the importance of the quintessential moment of use. The company was founded in the 1960s by Murray Pletz and his cousin Skip Yowell, who won a design competition sponsored by Alcoa for an aluminum flexible frame backpack. Since neither of them knew how to sew, Murray induced his girlfriend, Jan Lewis, by offering not only to name the company after her but also to marry her. When ski-maker K2 Corp bought the company in 1972 and tried to change its name,

all the employees resigned. They wanted to work for Jansport and not for something called K2. When hiking in the Alps, it was Jan's name they wanted to point to on their customers' backs. K2 gave in and retained Jansport.

Heckler's philosophy of the quintessential moment of use is not a mystical one—it is utterly pragmatic and focused on the user as co-creator of the brand. Observe his blog on the very definition of "brand" in the box that starts on the next page.

WHAT'S A BRAND?

If we're brand building, we had better know what we're building. Here is how some smart brand builders define a brand . . .

1. "Branding supersedes logic. Accordingly, brands are primarily aspirational and exist to build emotional attachment to a product or company."—David Aaker, Professor
2. "Products are made in a factory, but brands are created in the mind. Simply put, a brand is a promise." —Walter Landor
3. "By definition, brand is whatever the consumer thinks of when he or she hears your company's name." —David F. D'Alessandro, Brand Warfare
4. "A brand is a fundamental promise, a name for your business strategy and what you're prepared to enforce. It's not what you say, but what you are or aspire to become."—Keith Rienhard, CEO, DDB Worldwide
5. ". . . branding is the promise you keep . . . Brand is the intersection between core company (or product or service) strengths and what customers value."—Joseph Lepla, Lepla Parker Integrated Branding Quorum Books
6. Brand. (1) A name, usually a trademark of a manufacturer or product, or the product identified by its name. (2) Particular type of something, a distinctive type or kind of something.—Encarta
7. "A brand is a combination of features (what the product is), customer benefits (what needs and wants the product meets) and values (what the customer associates with the product). Brand is created when marketing adds value to a product, and in the process differentiates it from other products with similar features and benefits."—Timothy Mooney, Brand Strategies
8. "I am going to define a brand as an entity that satisfies all the following four conditions; (1) Something that has a buyer and a seller. (2) Something that has a differentiating name. (3) Something that is created rather than is naturally occurring. (4) Something that has positive and or negative opinions about it in consumers' minds for reasons other than its internal product characteristics."—Adam Morgan, Eating the Big Fish
9. "A brand is an intangible but critical component of what a company stands for. A consumer generally does not base a relationship with a product or a service, but he or she may have a relationship with a brand. In part, a brand is a set of promises. It implies trust, consistency, and a defined set of expectations."—Scott Davis, Brand Asset Management
10. ". . . A brand is a concept that provides the thread of unification within a business that yields a consistently broader brand value experience. So many businesses are a series of disconnected silos under-leveraging their brand. They think of their brands as products rather than total experiences."—John Wong, Brand Imperatives
11. "Branding is something you do to cows. Branding is what you do when there's nothing original about your product."—Roy Disney quote from WSJ article, April 3, 2004.

We could go on and on, but it gets to be the same thing over and over, "a brand is a promise." It sounds like a good sound bite. It doesn't help me much as a brand builder. A promise sets up some kind of a performance expectation. When I pick up an orange with the intention of taking a bite, there is the promise it will taste like an orange. When I pick up an orange with a Sunkist logo on it, it also promises me it will taste like an orange. Of course, the Sunkist orange is signalling it's a branded orange, but both the branded and unbranded oranges are presenting a promise. All kinds of generic unbranded entities make promises.

We think a brand can be anything someone is trying to own and make special. Ownership can be legal as well as just in people's minds. It could be a company, product, service, program, organization, group, person, sensory experience or ranch. You name it and someone has probably tried to make it a brand. We like this definition because it's simple and can deal with any branding situation. There are many different brand classifications, types and roles they can play. When brands are defined by equity qualifications or specific value variables people can quickly find themselves dealing rhetorically with what is or isn't a brand. We've been in situations where certain marketing people have told us, "It's only a brand if it has a consumer facing and revenues of a certain level."

(Heckler, 2010)

GRAPHICAL PRACTICALLY SPEAKING: DUCATI'S UNIVERSAL IDENTITY IN PICTURES

Ducati builds sleek Italian racing motorcycles—machines more often referred to as art than transportation. Though not exactly a startup, Ducati is a niche player with a startup-sized marketing budget in an industry that includes superpowers like Honda, Yamaha, and Kawasaki. Ducati has to be incredibly thoughtful and consistent in how it communicates. It has built, at a very low cost, an identity that appeals cohesively to the huge range of stakeholders it serves. The core values of Ducati, the passion for racing, Italian design, performance, and speed come through in every small thing the company does. In the photographs we present here, consider not only how Ducati communicates its identity to each individual stakeholder but also how it uses one stakeholder to co-communicate with another, effectively building a community around the identity:

Ducati for employees

Using a photo from Ducati in the 1920s, the company reinforces its racing history by updating the photo with new employees.

And the Ducati parking lot is reserved for Ducati owners—anyone driving anything else must park farther away.

Ducati for new customers

Instead of hiring models, Ducati uses its own employees and customers for its advertising.

Ducati for existing customers

Every two years Ducati puts on a paid event called "World Ducati Week." The gathering draws tens of thousands of attendees, who both participate and entertain (here the rock band Simple Minds play for free, as they are "Ducatistas"— Ducati owners.

Ducati for vintage bike owners

The company created a vintage motorcycle rally called the "Motogiro D'Italia" and a motorcycle museum to bring enthusiasts into the tribe. Both are supported by attendance fees and sponsors.

Ducati for the press

Always interested in free press placements (PR), Ducati invites journalists to events. This journalist from the *Daily Telegraph* enjoyed the "Motogiro D'Italia" so much, he turned it into a front-page piece.

Ducati for suppliers

Critical to Ducati's bike delivery, the firm invites suppliers to attend special events at MotoGP and Superbike races, connecting partners with racing, customers, and with the company.

As you appreciate the consistency and thoroughness of this set of corporate-identity-building actions, think about how much money Ducati might have spent on any one of them. Corporate identity can offer a great advantage, but it doesn't have to be expensive to build.

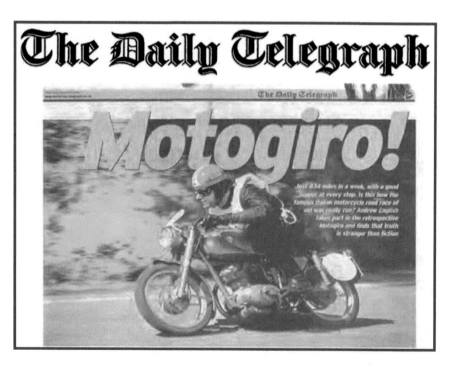

IDENTITY ACTION PLAN

Creating a plan for how to communicate your corporate identity is a straightforward process. It takes quite a bit of work, but there is no magic to it:

Step 1: Articulate your corporate identity

The goal is to reduce the elements of corporate identity to a few key words. These reflect the unique philosophy, values, norms, and personality of the firm that will inspire potential customers, employees, and partners. Articulating this identity is not something you do on your own. It is something you do with all stakeholders, inside and outside the firm:

*   Ask yourself why you started the venture.
*   Ask your cofounders why they joined you in the venture.
*   Ask your customers why they (would) buy from you.
*   Ask your partners why they work with you.

Step 2: Assess your current actions

Are the things you do every day aligned with the identity you want to create and communicate? One easy way to start a personal assessment is by using your own "to do" list, email inbox, or telephone call log. With your key identity ideas in mind, go through the list and underline actions that are consistent with the identity you defined and cross out actions that are not. This should prepare you to generate ideas around questions such as:

*   What current activities reinforce the elements of your corporate identity?
*   Is there anything you do that conflicts with your corporate identity?
*   What new activities might you initiate to communicate or reinforce your corporate identity?

Step 3: Put your corporate identity to work

Identity is a differentiator for your venture. At the start, it may be the only differentiator. You need to figure out how to use that uniqueness to help you accomplish your objectives. We have suggested some examples with corresponding questions. The list is by no means complete, but our hope is that it will serve as a starting point as you consider your own context:

*   *Obtain/retain customers.* Do your existing customers have a way to share their enthusiasm for your identity with you?
*   *Differentiate.* Is it clear to your stakeholders how your identity clearly distinguishes your offering from that of your competitors?
*   *Build partnerships.* What potential partners might be willing to help you achieve your objectives because they share your values and elements of your identity?
*   *Improve visibility.* Are there members of the press and analyst community who relate to your identity and are willing to bring their passion to disseminating your message?
*   *Add new products or markets.* In what new areas might your identity give you a competitive advantage?

TAKEAWAY: IDENTITY IS SOMETHING YOU CREATE EVERY DAY

As you move ahead, you will be able to continue to take greater and greater advantage of your corporate identity. Just keep in mind that corporate identity is something you create every day through the things you do, and it should provide you an advantage in communicating with every stakeholder who touches your venture.

■ ■ ■

So What?

A corporate identity is nothing more complex than a reflection of what you stand for on a daily basis. Shaping this identity, reinforcing it through actions and communicating it effectively are central to the value you are creating. And it gives you a competitive advantage.

What Now?

- ▪ What are the elements of value in your identity?

- ▪ Can you distil them to a single word? At most five?

- ▪ What parts of your overall opportunity does this identity enable you to ignore? (And not just the obvious choices that simply don't fit.)

- ▪ Is your identity tied to a single product? Does that seem problematic?

- ▪ What other opportunities are suggested under the umbrella of that identity?

- ▪ What is it about your venture's identity that inspires you to come to work in the morning?

- ▪ What is it about your venture's identity that inspires your customers, suppliers, and employees to work with you?

- ▪ What can you do to communicate and accentuate your identity?

- ▪ What ideas can you borrow from Ducati?

Think It Through

Irrelevance is the enemy of every startup. With so much activity and so many new ideas and new firms and new products coming out every day, the job of breaking through all that noise to make your firm relevant to your customers, your employees, and your partners is challenging.

As you use social media, public relations, and word-of-mouth to promote your current effort, begin to formulate your own theory of cutting through the noise:

- ▪ What ideas have been most successful in getting your attention?

- ▪ Were those ideas presented consistently?

- ▪ How many times do you think the entrepreneur had to tell her story?

- ▪ What medium(s) are most effective?

SO WHAT
IF YOU THOUGHT
OF IT FIRST?

PENWILL

Just because something doesn't do what you planned it to do doesn't mean it's useless.

Thomas Edison

Technology

Technology poses an interesting question to an effectual approach. Is it a means? Is it an outcome? Can technology be developed effectually? Can a causally developed technology go to market using an effectual approach? The short answer is yes. The purpose of this chapter is, now that you understand effectuation, to explore some of the different ways of applying effectuation to different problems, and at different points in the process of creating a new venture. And while this chapter is designed to help you with technology, we hope it will also encourage you to think about how effectuation applies to other specific kinds of firms. Service firms or capital-intensive businesses for example, have unique challenges that might benefit from effectual thinking. And while those are not addressed in this book, we offer

them here to provide ideas for areas where you might see if you can apply effectuation on your own. For now, we focus our attention on two areas where effectuation intersects with technology. The first considers the situation where effectuation is applied to commercializing an existing technology. And the second looks at a situation where an effectual approach is used to develop a technology.

TECHNOLOGY AS A MEANS

In 2005, the most recent year in which we could find this count taken, there were about 1.5 million patents in effect in the US. Of those, about 3,000 were deemed commercially viable by the director of public affairs for the US Patent & Trademark Office (Klein, 2005). While the pessimist may say that patenting is wildly

unsuccessful and the optimist may say that patent lawyers have a great business, the effectuator looks at these technologies which made it to patent and are still available for commercialization and sees a rich set of means—the starting points of new possibilities.

Before we continue, we note that the US Patent & Trademark Office is not the only place to find new technology means. The corners of corporate R&D labs, university research, and even amateur inventors expand the possibilities of hidden technology means further still.

Research Roots

LEAD USERS

The notion of lead users became popular in marketing in the 1990s as an antidote to the problem of rapidly changing markets and competition from new products. Despite rationally managed new product development processes and sophisticated market research, marketers knew the failure rate of new products was greater than 90%. However, based on earlier work, researchers already knew that in many fields users not only knew much more about their needs than market researchers, but in many instances actually developed most of the innovations in their industry. For example, 82% of commercialized scientific instruments were developed by users rather than producers. And the origin of many new firms was linked to the commercialization of products users had developed for themselves, often as enthusiasts. For example, mountain bikes and desktop computers were both commercialized in the 1970s by entrepreneurs who started off as mountain bike and computer enthusiasts (von Hippel, 1986).

While marketers have tried to use lead users as a needs-forecasting laboratory for what users more generally are going to need in the future, entrepreneurs recognize they can't afford the luxury of trying to predict which users provide signals of what the market more generally is going to want. More recent research draws the connection with effectuation and lead users who are willing to make a commitment (Coviello and Joseph, 2012), updating both the interaction with these users, and the product innovation process more generally (Berends et al., 2014).

Research Roots

IN PRAISE OF VENTURESOME USERS

Early stakeholders are crucially important in effectual ventures, none more so than lead users. Yet economic and management thinking largely fails to do justice to the role that lead users play in new ventures. In a wonderful book and series of articles, Amar Bhidé describes the vital role played by the venturesomeness of lead users for the development of new firms. Bhidé points out that lead users are important partners with entrepreneurs because they often shoulder some risk when they try new products and services. They may not know whether a product is going to work, let alone work well for them. Users also face uncertainty about the value of a new product, particularly if a critical mass of other users are needed to make the product (and venture) viable. Many new products also require considerable learning before users can get full value out of them, including acquiring a taste for them. And finally, lead users may risk a considerable downside if a venture fails completely, leaving them without any product support in the future. For all these reasons, lead users are co-developers of new products and services in the true sense of the word: they have "skin in the game." As Amar Bhidé (2008) reminds us, their willingness to be involved, to play a venturesome role in the genesis of new firms is a vital enabler of the entrepreneurial process.

Research Roots

EFFECTUATION IMPROVES RESEARCH AND DEVELOPMENT PROJECT PERFORMANCE

Brettel et al. (2012) transfer the principles of effectuation in corporate research and development management and show, using a survey of 400 research and development projects, that research and development managers tend to use effectuation in more uncertain projects and that using effectuation improves the performance of these projects.

The Engineer and the Entrepreneur

While we may poke fun at the pessimist and the optimist above, there is a meaningful difference in the way engineers and the way (effectual) entrepreneurs view the same technology (one clear example is presented in the story of the CD, later in this chapter). For an engineer, a technology is a solution to a problem. And the job that needs to be done is the realization of a technology that addresses the problem in a way that is sufficiently better than what is currently available. The rest, as engineering or mathematics faculty may write on the board after starting the solution to a complicated problem, is Q.E.D. (abbreviation for the Latin phrase *quod erat demonstrandum*—"that which was to be proven"). As anyone who has seen those letters written on the board knows, however, the hard work is about to begin.

TECHNOLOGY AS BOTH MEANS AND OUTCOME

	Company	Effectual Aspect of the Process	Outcome
Effectual Technology Commercialization (technology as means)	CD	Finding stakeholders willing to commit to a use for the invention	Not only the creation of the audio CD, but also its application in computer data storage
	Novozymes	Building a network of partners to turn the invention into a business	Re-organization of an engineering group to include individuals who perform the entrepreneurial role
Effectual Technology Development (technology as outcome)	GenShock	Using the means of potholes in Boston roads as the basis of a new technology	An innovation that turns bumps in the road into green energy
	Voxiva	Applying means of experience in refugee communications systems to healthcare	An inexpensive, simple, and accessible means of providing certain kinds of healthcare

Practically Speaking

THANK YOU FOR THE MUSIC

Quick trivia question: What was the first audio title pressed on to CD? Answer: ABBA 's The Visitors, 1982. Since this historic moment in culture and technology, more than 200 billion CDs have been sold, and the format has provided a foundational element for the digital music revolution, as well as a friendly way of storing large quantities of data that has greatly enhanced computer functionality. But where did the CD originate, and how can it help us think about innovation?

Practically Speaking *(continued)*

A sound invention

The answer to the first question is more modest than you might expect. James T. Russell, from Washington State in the US, is an engineer and an audiophile. As much as he loved music, his technical education reminded him that every time he listened to a vinyl record, the friction from the needle degraded the recording material and over time reduced the quality of the sound. Russell had designed and built the first electron beam welder, so when he joined Battelle Laboratory in 1965, he had already thought of combining his audio problem with his electron solution to create a recording device that would never touch the material, and could deliver top quality music after thousands of hours of listening.

No noise in the market

From a technology perspective, Russell was successful. He patented the first digital-to-optical recording and playback system in 1970. In the process of refining it, Russell earned another 25 patents for himself and Battelle. But, for the next 12 years, the invention went little further than the patent office. Battelle, which had 25 years earlier invented the dry copy process and licensed it to Xerox was unable to persuade the market to listen to the possibilities offered by its new CD.

Invention to innovation

Eli S. Jacobs, a New York venture capitalist, captivated by Russell's invention, formed a company called Digital Recording Corporation (DRC), which provided funding to Battelle to continue R&D and adapt the technology to store and play video. But it was not until Philips and Sony got involved that enough pieces came together to turn the CD into an innovation. Philips owned Polygram Records, so it had access to both music content and distribution. Sony added the credibility, which established an industry standard around Russell's CD format. And while Sony and Philips extended their fortunes by weaving CD technology into the computer storage industry, Russell, Battelle, and DRC were not able to profit from the invention until 1988, four years before the patents expired.

Unexpected entrepreneur

Two useful insights are audible in this story. The first is that even large firms can act entrepreneurially. Philips and Sony were able to do what Russell, Battelle, and DRC could not—create a market. And while scientists or creative people can invent, it is entrepreneurs who innovate by making markets for new ideas. The second insight is a more subtle entrepreneurial activity: the process of transformation. Applying something invented for one thing (CD audio) to something completely different (computer data storage). Like so many things in the world (Edison created the original phonograph using components from the telephone and the telegraph), it turned out that CDs have multiple purposes. Doing something unexpected with technology to create a market is what makes an entrepreneur.

In contrast, entrepreneurs see the job that needs to be done as that of building a bridge between a technology and its application to something valuable in the world. Indeed, as mentioned, the "entre" part of entrepreneur means "between" in French, so it's actually part of the job description. Technology may offer a foundation for one end of the bridge, but it's unclear as to where the other end of the bridge will ultimately lead.

In some ways an engineer can be likened to the predictor—the person trying to make a forecast of an uncertain future and then optimizing a single solution for that future. The engineer or/and the predictor may be correct. And when they are, the returns are grand. But statistically speaking, their chances of guessing or predicting correctly in an uncertain environment are perhaps 3,000/1.5 million or about 0.2% if we take the patent data as representative of this strategy. For an effectual entrepreneur starting with a technology, the concept of means is more flexible. As we saw in Chapter 10, the means you begin with enable you to start the effectual process. But by the time the process starts generating goals and products and firms and markets, you will use some of your means and not others. You will combine them with the means of others to create novel combinations. And so, instead of seeing a technology as a solution to a single problem, a technology is only a starting point for an effectual entrepreneur. A vehicle to initiate conversations with prospective stakeholders. Something that may or may not be used in the product, firm or market artefact which results from the process. And something that is available to be deformed, adapted, or exapted during the process (please see Chapter 11). Like effectuation in general, this approach simply increases the odds of finding a viable solution. Not only does it enable more possible solutions, it also engages the stakeholders in the process to bring enhancements or adaptations to the technology that are selected as a function of interest—interest that may reflect the interest of a broader market.

One of the greatest risks for technologists is falling in love with their technology to such an extent that they fail to even see opportunities for transforming it into actual products and markets. But when technologists genuinely strive to transform themselves into entrepreneurs, amazing new futures become possible for all of us.

> Technology is a word that describes something that doesn't work yet.
>
> Douglas Adams

Moreover, when the effectual process is done right, new technologies may emerge from existing ones.

TECHNOLOGY AS AN OUTCOME

Throughout this book, we talk about outcomes of the effectual process in terms of products and firms and markets. And while those terms cover a lot of ground, the chapters in this section of the book more precisely describe the variety we intend. In the next chapter for example, the markets that result from effectuation might not be traditional commercial markets you expect from a business school class, but markets in social change and markets in human hope. Here too, we are careful to include technology as a specific class of outcome that might result from an effectual process. That said, it is a special class of technology that results from an effectual process. It is technology that already has some of the hard work done—the work of engaging the stakeholders who are critical in turning that technology invention into a useful and valuable innovation.

In principle, the transformation of means and partnerships into a new technology happens in the same way effectuation happens generally. An entrepreneur starts with what they have. They interact with others. Stakeholders make commitments according to affordable loss. Contingencies are embraced. And ultimately, those commitments aggregate to form the pieces necessary to create a valuable outcome.

In practice, some special aspects of creating technology effectually merit further discussion.

Practically Speaking

FUEL PROOF

Google offers a tool called "Trends," which lets users graph the number of searches on a keyword over time. For the word "biofuel," searches peak on April 30, 2008, which, coincidentally, was the date an article entitled "Scientists want to stop using food to make biofuel" was in the news. And if Google Trends are any indicator of general sentiment, interest in biofuel has fallen by well more than half since spring 2008, dropping precipitously even prior to the global financial crisis. Whatever politics, preferences or conspiracy theories might be at work here, the fact remains that despite any historical correlation between biofuel production and food prices, first-generation biofuels based on corn, soy, and rapeseed have lost public appeal and will likely not expand beyond today's production levels to provide the cure to our energy woes.

End of the story? Not for Per Falholt, chief scientific officer at Novozymes. Today, biofuel is made by physically grinding corn, breaking down the starch into sugar with enzymes, converting the sugar into ethanol with microorganisms and distilling the ethanol. Per's research team of 150 scientists, in seven different locations around the world, designed the enzymes converting waste corn stalks or wood chips into clean fuel. Technically, Novozymes is successful. Novozymes is at the center of the process. From their expertise, they know that other vegetation also offers the sugars necessary to make energy, and they have been working on a second generation of enzymes capable of producing "cellulosic" biofuels based on refuse or crops such as switchgrass, grown on marginal land. But there is a cost. Corn, rich in sugar, converts easily into fuel, at around US$1.88 per gallon. Corn stalks require more effort and consequently more cost to convert, around US$2.35 per gallon. With fossil-based fuel priced at less than US$100/barrel, the economics don't work.

Must Per and his team wait patiently until the price of oil goes up for the next chapter of the story? Not necessarily. While scientists invent, entrepreneurs shape, package, and deliver an innovation that is useful and valuable. For Per and his scientific team at Novozymes, this means changing from white lab coat to white dress shirt to transform second-generation biofuel technology into a business. Their new tasks:

Re-engineer partnerships

First generation biofuel production involves a long "value chain" of partners: farmers, grain processors, processing plants, financiers, and oil companies. But second-generation biofuel can start with waste. That long chain of partners might now include organizations ranging from paper companies and municipalities that would pay to dispose of corn stalks and wood chips, to owners of marginal land where the acreage is not profitably cultivated today. Any of these partners could benefit by working with Novozymes to design a new business model around second-generation biofuel.

Reconsider the customer

If you buy corn to make fuel, you build large factories to drive down processing costs with volume production. If you help cities or companies save money disposing of waste, smaller distributed facilities located near that waste might be desirable. And while input is a cost in the first generation, it is maybe free or even a source of income in the second. Partners may also buy the finished product, as activities like paper processing have significant energy demands.

Practically Speaking *(continued)*

Re-weight involvement

Today, Novozymes is a technology supplier to only a single step in the process. The firm counts on external entrepreneurs to turn its inventions into innovations. Though this limits risk, it also limits the company's ability to shape the market. In the second generation, Novozymes may go beyond existing partnerships with grain processors and oil companies to build business models for cities or even design processing plants for industry in order to ensure its invention becomes the catalyst of a genuine innovation.

Biofuel illustrates the power entrepreneurs can have over markets. The fate of second-generation biofuels, potentially a big answer to the problem of greenhouse gas emissions, lies in the hands of the entrepreneur as much as the technologist. As with everything technical, from Internet search engines to hybrid car engines, the real innovation lies in creating the opportunity.

One of the approaches observed in expert entrepreneurs is the ability to invert a problem and imagine how even unpleasant surprises can provide the foundation for new opportunities. Problems ranging from climate change to malnutrition present transformation opportunities to make both impact and money.

Research Roots

PARTNERS OVER PATENTS: OPEN INNOVATION

The popular idea of open innovation (Chesbrough, 2006) encourages entrepreneurs to make technologies widely available so customers, partners and suppliers can co-create with the entrepreneur.

The first is specific to means. Technology lends itself to solutions to a wide variety of problems. A visionary technologist might imagine teleportation, clean energy from particle physics, or curing cancer with nanomachines. The effectual approach to developing a technology starts more modestly. Certainly, an entrepreneur begins with aspirations that might include, for example, a clean energy future. But the difference lies in the doing. Instead of starting with particle physics, the example we highlight in this chapter starts with potholes and the energy lost by a vehicle every time it hits a bump in the road. That insight is local and more amenable to practical "doing." So when you read the story of GenShock, consider how the entrepreneur's unique means of being in Boston, being at MIT, realizing the problem in a vehicle, and then working on a solution for a vehicle make the creation of the GenShock technology more manageable, and more doable with existing or modest resources.

So one element of creating technology using effectuation lies in the application of means. The pragmatic approach to starting a project with things that are reasonably readily at hand. The second is working with partners. Though the lone inventor is perhaps as romanced a notion as the mythical entrepreneur (Chapter 1), even Thomas Edison worked extensively with collaborators inside his firm and with industrial partners outside his firm to bring his innovations to light. Continuing with the GenShock example, one of the problems facing the entrepreneur is where to start. Building a technology that turns potholes into energy is something that could be useful to anyone from automobile manufacturers, to public transit operators, to commercial transport companies or to the government and military. Letting stakeholders self-select into the technology development process connects development with commercialization. It increases the likelihood that the technology which results from the process will be more than invention—it will be a useful innovation that is designed to be adopted.

One final note on developing technology effectually. It is also possible to take an effectual approach to organizing and leading a technology firm. We cover that topic in our discussions of Guidewire and W.L. Gore (Chapter 20) and refer you to those stories and ideas when you are ready to put all the pieces together.

Practically Speaking

SHOCKING VENTURE

Quick math test. If an average passenger car gets 22.5 miles per gallon, but only uses about 15% of the energy from fuel to move the vehicle and its passengers and power its accessories, how far could a perfectly efficient passenger car travel on a gallon of fuel? In case you don't happen to have a calculator handy, the answer is an even 150 miles to the gallon. Sounds pretty good. But what happens to the other 85% of the energy? Some is lost to heat. Some is lost to aerodynamic drag. And some forms the basis of entrepreneurial opportunity.

Practically Speaking
(continued)

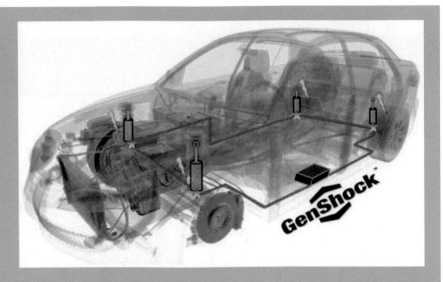

Impactful idea

As a student at MIT in Cambridge, MA, Shakeel Avadhany had plenty of opportunity to consider these facts while idling in Boston area traffic. But it was the infamous Boston potholes that launched his current venture, Levant Power. Bouncing down the street, Avadhany realized that these bumps not only cause headaches, they also cost fuel efficiency. The shock absorbers in his car were turning vibration into lost heat. His solution? Capture the energy. Build a shock absorber that generates electricity for the battery or the accessories.

Harnessing harvest

If Avadhany can achieve the midrange of the 1%–6% efficiency he hopes for, his idea could cut fuel use by more than 250,000 barrels in the US alone. Every day. More math says that if every car in the world were equipped with Levant GenShocks, it would save drivers US$15 billion per year at an oil price of US$40/bbl. Small solutions to big problems can generate enormous opportunities. And though Levant is still tiny, early results are positive. The firm has already received two rounds of investment during challenging economic times, it is working on a contract with the US military to supply its GenShock to military vehicles and it received an Innovation of the Year award from Popular Science.

Powering partners

Avadhany cannot drive down this road alone. In addition to building technology, he has also built partnerships with the US Army, testing his technology in military vehicles for performance and durability, and with Battelle National Labs to explore the possibilities of using his technology in capturing ocean energy. Together with resources, both these partners guide him to places where there is a need for his technology—effectively creating demand and product at the same time.

Open road

Should entrepreneurial ideas at the intersection of energy and automobiles intrigue you, it might be interesting to know where the remaining opportunities lie. If universally adopted, Avadhany's GenShock could take at most 6% out of the "rolling resistance" figures. That leaves 94% of the harvest open to other entrepreneurs with clever solutions. Certainly, there will be bumps, but it is the job of the entrepreneur to turn those into opportunity.

Practically Speaking

HEALTH OF NATIONS

Consider a few of the mega trends in the world today. Healthcare costs are significantly outpacing inflation or economic growth and 25% of the global population has no access to healthcare at all. At the same time, there are more cellular phones in the world than people. It is not hard to fit these facts together and imagine a business that uses technology to deliver better, less expensive, and more widely available healthcare. So clear, perhaps, that you may be wondering why you haven't done it yourself.

Entrepreneurial shape

The answer is that you are not Paul Meyer. In the weeks after the Balkans conflict ended, Meyer founded IPKO, the first and largest internet service provider in Kosovo. It provided critical communications for civilians and aid workers. And a healthy return for Meyer. Before that, Meyer was in West Africa, setting up computer systems to help reunite refugee children with their families. Deploying connectivity and computers in rugged, developing regions, knowing how information flows in these environments and understanding the people who need and use the information are assets unique to Meyer.

Vital action

But it is important to see exactly how this knowledge helps him. Ideas are cheap and plentiful. It is action that creates opportunities. With three co-founders, Meyer formed Voxiva in March 2001. The mission was to create a business that uses technology to deliver better, less expensive, and more widely available healthcare. And the action—the important part—was to distil simple elements of the healthcare delivery process into text messages. Whether collecting data on the spread of communicable disease or helping pregnant mothers through preparations for childbirth, Voxiva turns a cheap cellular handset into a readily available doctor. Anywhere and everywhere:

Peru. The first deployment in 2002, in the sparsely populated Andean foothills, showed that Voxiva could make contagious disease information, previously updated monthly on paper, instantly available, reducing costs by 40%.

Iraq. In 2003, Voxiva won an £815,000 contract to deliver a system for monitoring the spread of disease across the country as the population recovered from war.

Rwanda. In the spring of 2004, the firm focused its attentions on HIV/AIDS, deploying an information system across the country. The initiative was so successful it led to expansion in South Africa, Nigeria, Madagascar, and Uganda, and garnered support from Columbia University.

India. On February 1, 2004, Voxiva launched an initiative to monitor the spread of Japanese encephalitis in India. The initiative was so compelling that it drew Madhu Krishna from her position directing the Bill and Melinda Gates Children's Vaccine Program in India to join the start up.

United States. Emerging and war-torn economies are not the only beneficiaries of better, cheaper, and more available healthcare. Voxiva's Text4baby, the largest mobile health service in the US, provides information to more than 150,000 mothers a week and just launched in Russia.

Practically Speaking *(continued)*

Mexico. Care4life is Voxiva's mobile-enabled diabetes education and management service. Initially developed in partnership with Instituto Carlos Slim de la Salud, it is now being launched in the US.

Entrepreneurial condition

So do you have to be Paul Meyer to achieve this kind of impact? The answer is no, but there are at least two things to learn from him. Anyone could have undertaken what Voxiva set out to do 10 years ago. And the first takeaway is the importance of action. The second is less obvious, that is, how dependent action (and outcome) is on the person who takes it. Someone with experience in a big pharmaceutical company might have taken action with corporate partners. Someone more social might have enabled peer-to-peer support instead of information delivery and data capture. What would you have done?

Research Roots

SCIENTIFIC DISCOVERY AND ENTREPRENEURIAL INNOVATION

Building on the work of technology historians such as Joel Mokyr and Robert Friedel, a recent book by Matt Ridley (2015) argues that core scientific research is not strongly connected with commercial innovations or with economic growth. His book *The Evolution of Everything: How New Ideas Emerge* reviews historical scientific developments (e.g. Prince Henry's fifteenth-century investments in the science of mapmaking, nautical skills, and navigation) and current ones (the identification of the Higgs boson). Ridley compares these efforts with "garage-style" innovations from the likes of Thomas Edison. His conclusion is that despite the large investments in scientific research, the economic results of technological innovation result from efforts that are closer to the ground, closer to the customer, and are in essence more entrepreneurial than they are scientific.

TAKEAWAY: EFFECTUATION AS A TECHNOLOGY

As you begin to think about building your own venture to deliver interstellar flight or providing the next huge trend in cellular phones, consider this. Throughout this book, we work to make the case that effectuation is a general process. An engine that enables the co-creation of new artefacts in the world. You may choose to apply that engine to a new venture, a new technology, or, as we describe in the next chapter, a technology for addressing social problems in the world.

■ ■ ■

So What?

Technology can be a valuable element in the effectual process, regardless of whether effectuation is applied to the development of the technology, or to the commercialization of technology that was created using a more causal R&D approach.

What Now?

Consider each of the different paths.

- [ ] Look at a series of existing technologies, and imagine how you might use each as a "means," a starting point in the effectual process.

- [ ] Look at a series of existing problems in the world, problems that have not yet seen a compelling technology solution. Imagine how you would pursue a solution to each starting with an effectual approach.

Think It Through

Technology is only one example of a resource available to new ventures seeking a unique point of differentiation. This chapter opens up questions about any such resource, from a specialized business model, to the ownership of a unique piece of land. Are those outcomes or inputs? And depending on how you look at them, how do you manage them?

CHAPTER 23

What the scientific method did for nature, the entrepreneurial method can do for society.

Entrepreneurship as a technology for social change

■ ■ ■

Mercy Corps is an organization devoted to helping people in crisis—a worthy, though not unusual sounding, non-government organization (NGO), until you take a closer look. Mercy describes its mission as "helping turn crisis into opportunity for millions around the world." And when you notice that the staff is made up of engineers, financial analysts, project managers, public health experts, and logisticians, the news that the organization acquired a commercial bank (Mercy Corps acquired Andara Bank in Indonesia in 2008) starts to make sense. By blurring the lines that distinguish a charity from a business, Mercy Corps offers us one introduction to the idea of the social entrepreneur. Improving access to microfinance in Indonesia supports the organization's mission. Making money in the process does not detract from it. Though this example is located in tropical Indonesia, it is a small step toward a revolution that may destroy the artificial and unnecessary distinction between a for-profit venture and a charity. And when you look around, revolutionaries can be found everywhere in the financial services industry, from Muhammed Yunus, creator of the Grameen Bank, to the team behind Kiva, a person-to-person micro-loan website.

BIRTH OF THE SOCIAL BANK

When Muhammed Yunus, founder of Grameen Bank, realized he could afford to lend enough money for a whole village to rebuild its economy—the princely sum of US$27—he did just that. Only later, as he expanded his loans to multiple villages, did he bump against the cardinal rule of banking—loans without collateral ought to be deemed unbankable. The entire microfinance industry is now beginning to wake up to the notion of lending against cash flows as opposed to collateral—a point reinforced by Damian von Stauffenberg, the founder of Microrate, who emphasizes this as the key delineator between traditional lending and microfinance as well as the main differentiator between the best and the worst microfinance organizations in the industry.

Practically Speaking

THE CARING ENTREPRENEUR

The next time you pick up a prescription, take a look at the price of the product—not the portion you pay after insurance, but the actual price. Pharmaceuticals are expensive. And that translates into good business. Industry profits are in the 20% range, and with the aging population driving demand, today's global pharma sales are expected to reach US$1.3 trillion by the year 2020.

Counter intuition

An opportunity of that scale attracts entrepreneurs by the score, but none quite like Victoria Hale. She wants to make pharmaceuticals that don't make money. Yes, you read that correctly. Her firm, Institute for OneWorld Health, describes itself as a non-profit pharmaceutical company. OneWorld is her solution to the problem facing people in countries such as India who simply cannot afford many modern pharmaceutical treatments—clearly a worthwhile endeavor, one whose foundation is worth understanding.

Recycling science

Hale comes from the industry. She has a Ph.D. in pharmacology from the University of California, San Francisco (one of the top medical schools in the US), and she has worked for both the US Food and Drug Administration and Genentech. Those experiences enabled her to see "opportunity" where others saw waste. Every day, patents on profitable pharmaceuticals expire, enabling anyone to produce and distribute the compound without paying a royalty. Every day, research and development projects are cancelled because the resulting product could not find a profitable market. While useless to large pharma firms, these events could offer technology at a price OneWorld and its customers could afford.

Practically Speaking (continued)

Taking the first step

Also known as "black fever," kala-azar (formally visceral leishmaniasis) is a disease transmitted by sand flies. If left untreated, the resulting internal organ damage is nearly always fatal. Half a million new cases are estimated worldwide annually, largely in India, Bangladesh, and Nepal. Starting with an "off-patent" antibiotic, OneWorld assembled partners from the commercial, non-profit, and government sectors to develop, test, and approve paromomycin—a compound capable of curing a black fever victim for less than US$10. Paromomycin distribution started in 2007 in India, and if Hale has her way, the compound could eradicate the disease completely.

Making the opportunity

Entrepreneurs are often described as "creative," but perhaps "creators" is a more apt term. Had Hale not dragged a solution from the dustbins of pharma and built partnerships to create a new business model that gets cheap remedies to "unprofitable" markets, it is unlikely that the need would be served today. In other words, while so many aspiring entrepreneurs search for opportunities waiting to be discovered, real entrepreneurs roll up their sleeves to make opportunities that make the world we live in.

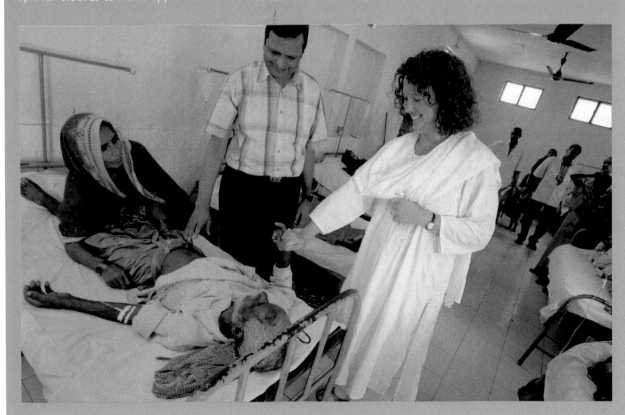

ONEWORLD APPLICATION QUESTIONS

- Are there any industries that could not offer social benefits employing a Victoria Hale approach?

- How might the for-profit pharma companies work more closely with OneWorld in a way that is productive for both?

- What would a competitor of OneWorld look like?

This chapter is devoted to understanding the basis of a revolution, independent of geography or industry. As you read, consider how entrepreneurs resolve the question of doing what they ought against doing what they can, and how the principles we have explicated in this book work in the social sector.

MARRYING SOCIAL CHANGE AND PROFIT

What holds individuals back from accomplishing what Hale and Yunus demonstrate can be done? How might we encourage more people to realize that they don't have to choose between doing something socially productive and making a profit?

Practically Speaking

THE MIGHTY ENTREPRENEUR

Rana El Chemaitelly is a mother of three; an independent businessperson who ran her own digital photography company for 12 years until the service became a commodity; an engineer with a B.E. in mechanical engineering and a Master's in engineering management; and an instructor at the American University of Beirut, Lebanon. Before you read on, close your eyes for a moment and consider how you might combine these resources to form the basis of a new venture.

Inputs in design

Now, with your own possible solution in mind, consider two observations that influenced El Chemaitelly's thinking. The first was that she found her students at the American University unprepared for their studies in engineering and unsure of what they might do with their education when they graduated. And the second was that her own seven-year old son was so captivated by video games that he was missing out on many of the social aspects of childhood.

Prototyping progress

El Chemaitelly transformed her resources and observations into an initiative called "The Little Engineer" (TLE). Launched in her home in 2009, while tyres burned and riots raged in other parts of the city, TLE was intended to teach hands-on science and technology to kids in an interactive and positive environment. After school, TLE provided robotics, energy and engineering instruction, challenges and competitions to creative little engineers.

Building up

In just three years, what was a cottage project has become a full-fledged venture. Today, TLE has programs for students from 6 to 16 years old, and it is working on an offering for 18 year olds. There are currently six TLE locations, with plans to open more in Tripoli, Bchamoun, Saida, and Jbeil this year. Some 750 children have already participated in TLE, and the firm has rolled out a mobile station—a complete center inside a truck—to bring TLE to schools that want to try it and areas where it is not possible to open a physical location.

Practically Speaking *(continued)*

Constructive stuff

Along with the growth of the business, El Chemaitelly has also received international recognition for social impact. Last year she was identified as one of the most promising entrepreneurs in the Middle East and North Africa (MENA) region by the Massachusetts Institute of Technology. She was awarded the "Coup de Coeur Femme" by Medventures for the Mediterranean and was recently declared a Laureate in the Cartier Women's Initiative Awards.

Building the future

Amid all the glamor, there are at least two things that El Chemaitelly offers us in understanding entrepreneurship. The first is how many different possibilities exist, even from a modest starting point. Compare your original idea with what she has actually done. Imagine how you might take another completely different direction from the same starting point. Good ideas and available resources are plentiful, but it is what the entrepreneur does that matters. And then consider the longer-term implications of her efforts. In her own way, El Chemaitelly is in the process of shaping engineering education. Policymakers and administrators can only dream of the changes that she is bringing to life. By proactively creating something new, tangible, and valuable, her influence will be felt by the next generation of engineers who will design the world of the future.

- *Change the tax code.* Perhaps the answer lies in making social enterprise more attractive at a regulatory level—reducing the tax burden on income from products or services provided by organizations that deliver social good. Tax codes vary across countries and even local governments, but one theme is reasonably consistent: taxation schemes clearly delineate between charity and for-profit enterprise. A graduated approach that appreciates the spectrum of different business models might serve to encourage more firms to serve the common good by making a profit.

- *Take political action.* The separation of these two realms is enforced at the political level, perhaps needlessly. While one arm of the government is focused on bringing money in through taxation, a completely different arm is focused on pushing money out to socially beneficial programs. What if these two bodies were to collaborate? What if they set up a scheme that allowed people like Hale and Yunus to take on the social needs of the community while at the same time generating a profit?

- *Teach and preach.* Educators hold sway among the educated populace. There is certainly more opportunity to open the dialog about ways to break down the artificial separation between charity and profit.

Whether accomplished through a Socratic dialog kind of an approach, or an evangelical Billy Graham style, the opportunity exists.

Entrepreneurship. But where are the revolutionaries? Will this problem be resolved by the top-down approach the first three alternatives represent? Probably not—which is why we focus on the power of the entrepreneur. As a maker of new worlds, the entrepreneur is not bound by assumptions such as "Doing something socially productive can't also make money." Why not? If there is an interest in doing both, the only question for the entrepreneur is how.

THE "ENTREPRENEURIAL METHOD"

To gain insight into whether the separation thesis that entrepreneurs must choose between doing well and doing good is valid, we go back more than 200 years to the story of Josiah Wedgwood. As founder of the famed Wedgwood pottery works, he is associated with the accumulation of great wealth. The manufacture and transportation of delicate pottery in those days was a challenging process. In addition to his Etruria pottery works, Wedgwood created a school to teach unskilled laborers the craft of fine painting. Wedgwood also undertook several major public works projects, digging the canals that connected the River Trent with the River Mersey. In neither case was his motive solely altruistic. There were not enough skilled artisans to meet the demand for Wedgwood

pottery. The roads were so uneven that much pottery was smashed before it was even delivered. Yet Wedgwood was able to deliver social good alongside profit from fine pottery. It is interesting to note that the Wedgwood fortune also funded Wedgwood's grandson Charles Darwin as he made a voyage that would generate what scientists claim to be the most significant advancement in scientific thinking of the millennium.

Wedgwood's example demonstrates that for many entrepreneurs, there is no line between what for-profit ventures do and what social ventures do. Many entrepreneurial ventures simply do both (we encourage you to go to the directory of Practically Speaking stories at the back of the book and find more than a dozen additional social entrepreneurship

stories across the different chapters). And perhaps more important, what we find is that the same underlying method is at work in both cases.

Comparing the entrepreneurial method with the scientific method

The scientific method is based on the premise that the world can be systematically studied and understood in terms that do not include divine revelation or intervention (Sagan, 2002). It also incorporates the idea that the work of navigators, inventors, and craftsmen can be a model for scholars (Bacon, 1620). At the heart of the scientific method is the belief that Nature's potential can be harnessed for the achievement of human purposes.

Research Roots

SOCIAL ENTREPRENEURSHIP IN PERSPECTIVE

Social entrepreneurship has a long and illustrious history dating back at least into the nineteenth century when some Victorian industrialists recognized the need to combine social progress with economic success. Therefore, early models for social entrepreneurship include the great American chocolatier Milton Hershey and the British Quaker firm Cadbury's (also a chocolatier), both of whom sought to combine the creation of social value with their commercial successes.

Research on social entrepreneurship highlights that what is common in all kinds of social entrepreneurship is a drive to create social value rather than just personal or shareholder wealth. Social entrepreneurs are usually creating something new, whether accidentally or deliberately, whether that's in the non-profit or for-profit sector. It also has been noted that social entrepreneurs are addressing social problems often perceived as failures of commercial market forces to meet social needs, or government failures to meet them.

One important issue highlighted by research on social entrepreneurship is challenges in mobilizing resources for new social ventures. When ventures are created on a not-for-profit basis, they are limited from attracting startup capital the way for-profit entrepreneurs do. They may also rely heavily on the value of non-pecuniary compensation by their staff. For-profit ventures may face fewer constraints in these regards. Entrepreneurs, therefore, face important decisions about whether pursuing a not-for-profit or a for-profit model is the best way to achieve the ultimate social mission of a venture (Mair and Marti, 2006).

Practically Speaking

THE BRIGHT ENTREPRENEUR

As an expat working in Laos for a German development organization during the late 1990s, Andy Schroeter observed that nearly half the population was off the electricity grid and that the cost for the kerosene needed to run lamps was one of the highest expenditures for a household. He realized that an answer could be the basis of a bright opportunity with the potential to make both money and social progress.

Building change

Schroeter did not have funding from a venture capitalist, nor did he have a novel technology solution. Laos was recovering from 20 years of war, and the government wasn't exactly set up to foster entrepreneurship. But instead of seeking charitable contributions or support from a large NGO, Schroeter formed Sunlabob in 2000 with his own means. The mission of the firm was the same as it is today—to operate as a profitable, full-service energy-provider selling hardware and providing energy services for remote areas where the public electricity grid does not yet reach.

Practically Speaking *(continued)*

Simple trade

At this point, you might be expecting a dramatic story of innovation—how Schroeter invented a robust and inexpensive fuel cell, wireless energy transmission or perhaps cold fusion for the villagers of Laos. The reality is somewhat less glamorous but a lot more practical. Schroeter takes the most suitable alternative energy products available in the global marketplace and adapts and installs them in Laos. He is a reseller, an integrator, and a (very) local distributor. These are business ideas as common as the sunlight that powers most of what he delivers.

Entrepreneurial energy

While it is easy to equate the power of the entrepreneur with the creation of a radical new product or technology, people like Schroeter show us the real job a founder of a new ventures—crafting a market opportunity by hand. Someone has to get up in the morning and find solar panels, thermosiphon heaters or wind turbines that will perform well in the rugged environment of Laos. Someone has to build an economic model so that customers in a country where annual per capita income is US$986 can realistically afford these products. Someone has to hire the people who can install and maintain the systems. And someone has to organize the company vacation to Vietnam for those same employees. Schroeter shows us that there is no magical invisible hand of the market that does this: it is the visible hand of the entrepreneur that made Sunlabob happen.

Powering growth

As Sunlabob moves ahead, the hand of the entrepreneur continues to be visible. The venture is commercially successful—having installed more than 10,000 systems in more than 450 locations around Laos—and it has been recognized for its social impact, winning an average of one international prize or award for each year it has been in operation. A few notables include the Schwab Foundation Asian Entrepreneur of the Year award at

Practically Speaking *(continued)*

the 2010 World Economic Forum, the National Energy Globe Award 2009, Tech Awards Laureate 2008, and an Ashden Award in 2007.

Real impact. Real business. Real simple.

The venture continues to apply more of the plain technologies that made it successful. Consistent with the simplicity that got Sunlabob started, it is growing with equally ordinary approaches. In addition to serving the entire country of Laos, Sunlabob expanded services using the franchising model into Uganda, Cambodia, and Tanzania and will soon be operating in Afghanistan. In 2010, it also established Sunlabob International Pte Ltd in Singapore with the intention of serving the markets in Southeast Asia and Africa and offering a better localization service to its customers.

The entrepreneurial method is analogous to the scientific method in the notion that societies can be systematically shaped and rebuilt without massive political movements or governmental regulations. It incorporates the idea that what actual entrepreneurs do can be a model for educators and policymakers. At the heart of the entrepreneurial method is the belief that human potential can be unleashed not only for the achievement of societal purposes but also for imagining and fashioning new purposes for different groups of people at different points in time and space.

As eminent scientists have observed, even the social sciences have undergone a vast change in how they explain human behavior. It is no longer necessary to argue that people are pushed and pulled by their inner and outer environments. It is okay to model human behavior in terms of initiatives, active agency, and conscious choice. When Francis Bacon proposed that human beings could go beyond observing and passively predicting the inevitable course of nature to manipulating and controlling it, the reaction was one of shock and disbelief. After centuries of technological progress, during which millions of "ordinary" scientists have been educated to contribute to that project, we should be ready to embrace the idea that we can intervene positively in the transformation of our own social purposes and environments.

Bacon's enumeration of "experimentation" as a method of purposefully intervening in nature is a common technique of the scientific method and an essential part of all education today. So too, we hope, will effectuation become an essential part of not only entrepreneurial education but also all basic education.

WHY DONATE WHEN WE CAN INVEST?

Why is it that we invest in Genzyme or Microsoft but donate to Red Cross or Transparency International? Why is it that it takes 43 cents for a good non-profit to raise a dollar when less than 5 cents gets the average banker that same dollar, and he or she lives much better than the average NGO official? Arguments fly back and forth that one subsidizes the other and that the former is less efficient and more fragmented than the other is. And, of course, there's the same tired old claim—that one is profitable and the other is not. We find it difficult to believe that investing in software is more profitable than investing in the creative fount from which such a thing as software originated in the first place. If a piece of code that moves around a bunch of electrical impulses can create wealth, it is absurd to think that the mind that creates that piece of code is less profitable—and that the societies that foster and develop such minds are even less so. We seek answers elsewhere.

NOT ALL ENTERPRISES ARE INVESTOR OWNED—EVEN IN THE US

In the US as of 1990, there were roughly 1,700 consumer cooperatives with sales amounting to US$26 billion and representing 27% of all farm production expenditures (up from 23% in 1973).

Around the same time, non-profits accounted for 64% of all hospital care, 56% of day care for children and 20% of colleges and universities. In Japan, non-profits account for almost 75% of higher education.

In France and Italy, there are thousands of employee-owned firms. And even in the US, both employee stock option plans and fully employee-owned firms are on the increase—take, for example, worker cooperatives in the plywood industry in the Northwest. (Data from Hansmann, 2000)

For millennia, human beings did not realize how to harness and use the energies locked up in steam or in the movement and structure of atoms—just as we today struggle to usefully harness the energy locked up in the sun, wind, and corn. Similarly, we simply have not yet found the mechanisms that can unleash the potential to close the virtuous circle connecting healthy societies with healthy babies and wealthy futures. Once a society has grown the baby and the ensuing adult has produced goods and services of value, we have relatively efficient and useful ways of pricing them and distributing them to those who want them and are willing and able to pay for them. With the invention of credit, we even know how to identify some of these in advance and reap the benefits within reasonable time lags. But credit markets are relatively new in human history. There is considerable creative work ahead of

us to expand them effectively to close the larger circle of human and social improvement. We do not believe this is a task better left to the revolutionary or to the policy-maker. Instead, we find tremendous scope in innovations that already exist in today's credit markets. Moreover, these innovations can be transferred and transformed through entrepreneurial initiatives. The history of micro-credit, which we touched on at the beginning of this chapter, attests to such a profitable transfer.

ENTREPRENEURS CREATE MARKETS—WHY NOT MARKETS IN HUMAN HOPE?

Throughout this book, we describe entrepreneurs as people who create firms, products, and markets. That entrepreneurs create markets is important, because not only do markets provide the basis for economic growth (and profit), but they are also a vehicle for social change. It is with this view that it is clear that people creating social change do the same things we associate with "for-profit" entrepreneurs. So everything thus far in the book is relevant to entrepreneurs regardless of whether the legal form of the venture is for-profit or not.

Consider the following questions: Why can't we buy futures contracts in Rwandan prosperity? Or options in environmental conservation in Brazil? Or equity in the emancipation of Afghan women? If we want to participate in the upside potential of biotechnology, we can buy Genzyme stock or shares in a biotech mutual fund with a couple of clicks of the mouse. But if we want to participate in the upside potential of literacy in the Congo delta, or even youth development in South Central Los Angeles, we have to research obscure charities, mail out checks, maybe fill out tax exemption forms, and then cross our fingers and hope that our money will be put to some good use. We have no way of analyzing and selecting among competing models, monitoring our investments, trading them for liquidity, or cashing in on positive results.

Why is there a belief that investments in biotech can be profitable but investments in the eradication of human misery cannot? The latter are not even categorized as investments, but as charity, to be financed through sacrifice without the expectation of a positive return. The irrepressibly cornucopian economist Julian Simon spent his life arguing that human beings are the ultimate resource. His data run deep and long and his analyses are compellingly careful and explicit. If all economic value ultimately derives from human beings, shouldn't investments in the eradication of human misery be both viable and valuable?

As the examples in this chapter show, these questions are neither unrealistic nor unreasonable.

Already there are efforts to create private equity markets in a variety of social sector projects. People are learning that there is value in human hope, and they are asking more and more questions about ways we might all benefit from the eradication of human misery. The answers to these questions will certainly require more struggle. But the struggle is worthy of all our creative efforts—especially those of us engaged in entrepreneurship and public financial markets.

EXAMPLES OF MARKETS IN HUMAN HOPE

In 2005, a massive earthquake struck the Kashmir region in the mountains of India and Pakistan. Eighty-seven thousand individuals perished in the quake and three million survivors needed to rebuild their lives. The international aid organizations rushed in with supplies and food. And were joined by entrepreneurs.

Marc Freudweiler is the founder of a Swiss derivatives trading firm named Derilab. Freudweiler saw both the humanitarian need to rebuild the Kashmir region and the economic benefit that would result. Kashmir had been a productive area before the quake. Repairing the infrastructure would enable the businesses destroyed by the quake to resume the creation of value. Freudweiler talked with people at the UNHCR (United Nations High Commissioner for Refugees), and the Kashmir Relief Note was born.

NEW FIRM FORM: B-CORP

Until recently, firms registering in the US had to choose to be a "for profit" C-corporation, or a "non-profit" 501(c)(3) organization. Today, however, "for profit" C-corporations can designate themselves as B-Corporations. By registering at www.bcorp.org with a mission that might involve how the organization treats its employees, where the organization sources its ingredients or what the organization promises its community, the firm can become a special form of the C-corporation. Should this movement gain traction, it may even become a third choice for official registration with the US government.

The Note represented a completely novel idea—that the public might invest in humanitarian relief and receive a return on its money. The specific outcome was a financial instrument that directs part of the investment into refugee relief and part of the investment into businesses that are likely to increase in value as the region rebuilds. Investors could direct funds to the crisis and could generate a return. Doing what we ought does not have to conflict with doing what we can.

TAKEAWAY: DOING WHAT WE OUGHT; DOING WHAT WE CAN

Hopefully, after reading this chapter, you come away with the appreciation that whether a firm is for-profit or not-for-profit is a design decision that's made by you. And that the same principles apply regardless. So, what are you going to do?

Change the world?
Make money?
Why choose?

■ ■ ■

What Now?

CLOSING THE VALUE LOOP

When you find a cause that turns you on, an injustice you want to correct, or a social problem you want to solve, think like a for-profit entrepreneur:

☐ Who are your key stakeholders?

☐ What is the value proposition for each of them?

☐ How can you create a product or service that the stakeholders would want to pay for?

☐ How can the beneficiaries of your product/service become your investors?

☐ How do you close the value loop through time so that the benefits pay for the costs, even as you make a decent living at it?

☐ In short, what is your business model?

So What?

Entrepreneurship can generate sustainable solutions to social problems while reducing the need to raise donations or wait for legislation. By closing the value loop, you can raise investments and earn returns rather than count on the generosity of individual contributions or the government taxation process.

Think It Through

☐ How can we make government more entrepreneurial so it might be more supportive of some of these efforts?

☐ Unless you are taking gifts, why not be a for-profit venture?

Conclusion

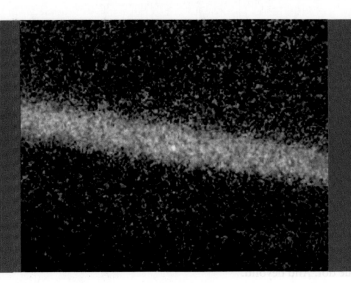

DEAR READER,

In the introduction to this book, we promised:

You will discover in this book that there is a science to entrepreneurship—a common logic we have observed in expert entrepreneurs across industries, geographic locations, and time . . . When you start a new venture—for-profit or not, individually or within an existing organization—you are not only trying to make a good living, you are engaged in expanding the horizon of valuable new economic opportunities. This book is designed to help you do that from start to finish. And in form and content, the book embodies the expert entrepreneurs' logic—bold, systematic, pragmatic, and at all times full of energy, mischief, and fun.

If you believe we have delivered on our promise, we would like to conclude with an ask of you in return. After all, this is

entrepreneurship—you have to pay with value for value delivered. So here goes:

The picture above is the only one of its kind. When the first (and only) human-made object to leave the solar system, the Voyager spacecraft, crossed into the vast space between us and the rest of the universe, it turned its camera to take a picture of earth from outside the solar system. Carl Sagan wrote about this picture in a moving way:

Look again at that dot. That's here, that's home, that's us. On it everyone you love, everyone you know, everyone you ever heard of, every human being who ever was, lived out their lives.

The aggregate of our joy and suffering, thousands of confident religions, ideologies, and economic doctrines, every hunter and forager, every hero and coward, every creator and destroyer of civilization, every king and peasant,

every young couple in love, every mother and father, hopeful child, inventor and explorer, every teacher of morals, every corrupt politician, every "superstar," every "supreme leader," every saint and sinner in the history of our species lived there—on a mote of dust suspended in a sunbeam.

. . . The Earth is the only world known so far to harbor life. There is nowhere else, at least in the near future, to which our species could migrate. Visit, yes. Settle, not yet. Like it or not, for the moment the Earth is where we make our stand.

In this book you have learned that you need not wait for the right technology or the proper resources or the massive machinery of governments or the feeble hope of the next election to rebuild your life and the world in which you seek to live. You can start today—with who you are, what you know, and who you know—and invest nothing but what you can afford to lose to begin building corridors through which your stakeholders can self-select into your valuable new venture. And together you can co-create a better world, one that neither you nor they can yet fully imagine.

So get started on your (ad)venture and make your stand on this pale blue dot. And beyond.

Bon voyage!

Directory of Practically Speaking Stories by Characteristic and Effectuation Topic

Title	Chapter	Country	Company	Green	Tech.	Social	Bus. Client	Consumer	Means	Affordable Loss	Partner	Contingency	Made vs. Found
Bags to riches	1	Cambodia	Funky Junk	■		■		■	■				■
Murkey Brew	1	USA	Starbucks					■			■		■
Everyone is doing it	2	USA	Opower	■	■		■	■	■				■
Turning a disability into a business	2	Germany	unsicht-Bar					■	■				■
Trash to cash	2	USA	Agilyx	■	■			■	■				
Turning a hobby into a business	2	USA	College Bed Lofts					■	■	■		■	■
Dragon lady	3	China	Nine Dragons					■	■			■	■
Bringing a career back from the dead	3	USA	1-800-AUTOPSY		■		■	■	■			■	■
Persist easy; swerve hard	4	India	Easy Auto		■			■	■	■	■	■	■
Fail to succeed	4	USA	MGA Entertainment					■	■			■	■
Invest in the person; not the venture	4	Global	Ashoka			■		■		■	■	■	■
Milton Hershey	4	USA	Hershey's					■	■			■	■
Product launches at Apple Computer	4	USA	Apple		■		■	■	■	■		■	
A model business	5	USA	Mannequin Madness		■			■	■	■			■
How to learn to let go	5	USA	Browning-Ferris					■	■	■	■	■	■
The making of Sears	5	USA	Sears					■					
Sustaining entrepreneurship	5	USA	eBay		■			■	■	■			■

Title	Chapter	Country	Company	Green	Tech.	Social	Bus. Client	Consumer	Means	Affordable Loss	Partner	Contingency	Made vs. Found
Boing-Boing	5	USA	Boing-Boing					■	■	■			■
The unlikely story of Freitag	6	Switzerland	Freitag	■				■					■
U-Haul: Transforming uncertainty into success	6	USA	U-Haul					■	■	■	■	■	■
Building the road ahead	7	Britain	Climate Cars	■				■	■	■	■	■	■
Building the road ahead	7	India	ForShe	■		■		■	■				■
Something from nothing	7	USA	TerraCycle	■		■	■	■	■	■		■	■
Curry in a hurry	7	Worldwide					■	■	■	■		■	■
Making a market out of a joke	7	USA	Pet Rock					■	■	■	■	■	■
The power of control	8	India	Husk Power	■	■	■	■	■	■	■	■		■
Entrepreneurial manners	9	USA	Forgetful Gentlemen		■			■	■				■
Good pill hunting	9	Ghana	mPedigree		■		■	■	■		■		■
Surprise in a glass	9	Scotland	Innis & Gunn	■				■	■		■		■
Making a clean start	9	Estonia	GoodKaarma			■		■	■	■			■
Picture perfect	10	USA	Photo Mambo						■				■
Working with what you have	10	USA	Barbara Corcran						■				■
New venture recipe	10	Denmark	Claus Meyer				■	■	■	■			■
Destination unknown	10	USA	AirBnb			■		■	■	■			■
Many happy returns	10	USA	Eco-Envelopes					■	■		■		■
Power of personality	10	USA	Estée Lauder					■	■	■	■	■	■
Up the wall	10	USA	Wacky Wall-Walkers					■	■	■			■
Charging ahead	11	Finland	Powerkiss	■				■	■	■	■		■
Chocolate magic	11	Belgium	Manon Chocolatier					■	■				■
Dust, sweat and new ventures	11	Italy	Geox					■	■	■			■
Delivering a venture	12	Kenya	Petty Errands				■		■	■	■		■

Section	Page	Country	Company
Partners' Affordable Loss	12	Romania	Bacania Veche
Opportunity in the trash	12	USA	RecycleMatch
Stacey's Pita Chips	13	USA	Stacey's Pita Chips
A mountain of partners	14	Nepal	Himalayan Health Care
A messy collaboration	14	Spain	Alucha
Hunting with the pack	14	Kenya and Uganda	Baloo Patel
A pretty collaboration	15	India	Youshine
Is a cost always a cost?	15	USA	Gardener's Eden
Twists and turns	16	USA	Contour
Creating during crisis	16	Britain	Zopa
Printed surprise	16	USA	Staples
Silly surprise	16	USA	Silly Putty
Vegetable surprise	16	USA	JR Simplot
$10 surprise	16	USA	NFTE
Railroad surprise	16	USA	Railtex
Scooter surprise	16	Japan	Honda
Ice man cometh	17	Sweden	ICEHOTEL
Investing in people	18	Columbia	Lumni
A piece of the pie	18	USA	Kenny's Great Pies
Sharing the treats among investors	18	USA	Castor & Pollux
A model for healthy change	19	India	Biocon
Disposable income	19	USA	gDiapers
The wind and the plan	19	Britain	Ecotricity
The cube without a plan	19	Hungary	Rubik's Cube
Breath of fresh air	20	USA	W. L. Gore & Company
A guide to the process	20	USA	Guidewire

Title	Chapter	Country	Company	Green	Tech.	Social	Bus. Client	Consumer	Means	Affordable Loss	Partner	Contingency	Made vs. Found
Ducati's universal identity	21	Italy	Ducati					■	■		■		■
Health of nations	22	Global	Voxiva		■	■	■	■	■		■		■
Shocking venture	22	USA	Levant	■	■	■	■		■				■
Fuel proof	22	Denmark	Novozymes		■		■						■
Thank you for the music	22	Global	Philips, Sony, Battelle	■	■		■	■			■		■
The bright entrepreneur	23	Laos	Sunlabob		■		■		■	■			■
The mighty entrepreneur	23	Lebanon	The Little Engineer		■	■			■	■			■
The caring entrepreneur	23	USA, India	One-World Health				■		■	■	■		■

Image acknowledgments

The authors and publisher would like to thank the following, for permission to reproduce their images in this book.

Start (p. ix) Tetra Images/Getty Images; New chart (p. v) © Rob Bouwman – Fotolia.com; Old map (p. 1) © Alex Staroseltsev – Fotolia.com; SUCCESS (p. 2) © Semih Akalin, www.atbreak.com; STARBUCKS PHOTO (p. 5) © kevinberne.com; Funky Junk (p. 6) © FunkyJunk Recycled; Funky Junk (p. 7) © FunkyJunk Recycled; Funky Junk (p. 8) © FunkyJunk Recycled; Light bulb (p. 11) Epoxydude/Getty Images; Loft bed (p. 13) Photo courtesy of CollegeBedLofts.com; Dinner at Unsicht-Bar (p. 14) Photo courtesy of Unsicht-Bar; Waste plastic (p. 15) © Roberto Fasoli – Fotolia.com; OPOWER (p. 16) © oPower; OPOWER (p. 16) © oPower; Empty pockets (p. 20) © Vitaliy Pakhnyushchyy – Fotolia.com; Waste paper (p. 22) © cs-photo – Fotolia.com; Coffin couch (p. 27) Photo courtesy of 1-800-Autopsy; Capsize (p. 29) © Mason Read; Failure/success signpost (p. 30) © jaddingt – Fotolia.com; Bratz (p. 32) Photo courtesy of MGA Entertainment; Bird losing fish (p. 33) © Doug Harrington Photography; HERSHEYS® chocolate bar (p. 34) Provided courtesy of HERSHEY'S®; Padmasree Harish and a rickshaw (p. 36) © Stuart Read; NEWTON (p. 38) Photo made available through Creative Commons; Ashoka image (p. 40) Photo provided courtesy of Ashoka; Graveyard cartoon (p. 42) Courtesy of Business around the Globe © 2006 Michiel Jonker; Swimming man (p. 45) Floresco Productions/Getty Images; Sears poster (p. 46) Courtesy of Sears advertizing archive; EBAY (p. 48) © eBay; Drawing from Boing-Boing book (p. 49) Courtesy of Can of Worms Enterprises; Mannequin (p. 50) © Mannequin Madness; BFI (p. 53) © TopLeftPixel; "If not now" cartoon (p. 54) © Marek – Fotolia.com; Boat Building (p. 57) © Hector Lanaeta Freeimages; Skiier (p. 58) © Ludwig Berchtold – Fotolia.com; Mouse with Helmet (p. 59) Courtesy of Boeri; Ken Lays future cartoon (p. 60) © Harley Schwadron – www.cartoonstock.com; Sinking ship (p. 63) © Corbis; Beatles (p. 63) © Corbis; Toyota (p. 63) Photo made available through Pixabay; Freitag bags (p. 65) Photo courtesy of Freitag AG; Freitag bags (p. 65) Photo courtesy of Freitag AG; Freitag bags (p. 65) Photo courtesy of Freitag AG; Freitag bags (p. 65) Photo courtesy of Freitag AG; Freitag bags (p. 65) Photo courtesy of Freitag AG; Freitag bags (p. 65) Photo courtesy of Freitag AG; U-Haul truck (p. 70) Photo courtesy of U-Haul; Bears in stream (p. 72) © Red – Fotolia.com; Climatecars (p. 74) © Climatecars; FORSHE (p. 74) Photo courtesy of Forshe; TERRACYCLE (p. 76) Photo courtesy of Terracycle; Walkman (p. 77) Photo made available through Pixabay, by fielperson; Building the world (p. 77) © Stephen Coburn – Fotolia.com; Spice (p. 79) © felix – Fotolia.com; Pet Rock image (p. 80) Courtesy of http://montaraventures. com/blog; Future signpost (p. 82) © Joe Gough – Fotolia.com; Satellite image (p. 84) Courtesy of the Office fédéral de météorologie et de climatologie MétéoSuisse; Pilots (p. 86) © Ian Andrews – Fotolia.com; FITNESS (p. 88) Photo made available through Creative Commons; Husk (p. 90) Photo courtesty of Husk Power Systems Ltd.; Old sailing ship (p. 91) © Carina Hansen – Fotolia.com; Men at sea (p. 92) © Ralph Hagan – www.cartoonstock. com; Ark cartoon (p. 95) © Off the Mark Cartoons; Goodkaarma soap (p. 96) Photo courtesy of GoodKaarma; Forgetful Gentleman (p. 98) © Forgetful Gentleman; Dougal Sharp (p. 100) Photo courtesy Innis & Gunn; Chips (p. 101) Photo made available through Wikimedia Commons; Safety glass (p. 101) Photo made available through Creative Commons; Viagra (p. 101) © istockphoto; mPedigree (p. 102) © africa924 – Shutterstock.com; Fortune teller (p. 106) Tom Le Goff/Getty Images; Learning to Sail (p. 109) Photo made available through Pixabay; Open refrigerator (p. 110) © bshphotography – Fotolia.com; ESTEE (p. 112) © Ray Fisher- Getty Images; EcoEnvelopes logo (p. 115) Image courtesy of EcoEnvelopes; Noma (p. 116) © noma; Photo Mambo (p. 120) © Photo Mambo; AirBnb (p. 121) Infographic courtesy of Anna Vital, Funders and Founders (fundersandfounders.com); Esher drawing (p. 124) © 2010 The M.C. Escher Company – Holland. All rights reserved. www.mcescher. com; Aster Buddies (p. 127) © Teri Read Photo; Manon chocolates (p. 128) Courtesy Manon Chocolates; Manon chocolates (p. 129) Courtesy Manon Chocolates; Powerkiss table (p. 130) Photo courtesy of Powerkiss; Scales (p. 131) © istockphoto; POLEGATO (p. 134) Photo courtesy of Geox; Fortune Newspapers cartoon (p. 136)

Bibliography

Ch.	Author(s)	Reference
1	Bhidé, A.	(2000) *The Origin and Evolution of New Businesses*. New York: Oxford University Press, USA.
1	Gartner, W. B.	(1988) Who is the entrepreneur? is the wrong question. *American Journal of Small Business*, 12, 11–32.
1	Gompers, Paul and Lerner, Josh	(2001) The venture capital revolution. *The Journal of Economic Perspectives*, 15(2), 145.
1	McClelland, D.C.	(1965) N achievement and entrepreneurship: a longitudinal study. *Journal of Personality and Social Psychology*, 1(4), 389.
1	Rauch, Andreas and Frese, Michael	(2007) Let's put the person back into entrepreneurship research: A meta-analysis on the relationship between business owners' personality traits, business creation, and success. *European Journal of Work and Organizational Psychology*, 16(4), 353–385.
1	SBA, 2015	Small Business Market Update, June 2015. Accessed online in March 2016 at: https://www.sba.gov/sites/default/files/Small_business_bulletin_June_2015.pdf.
1, 3	Scott, R. H.	(2009) *The Use of Credit Debt by New Firms*. The Ewing Marion Kauffman Foundation, August 2009, p. 2.
1, 5	PricewaterhouseCoopers	(2014) PricewaterhouseCoopers, National Venture Capital Association Money Tree™ Report Q4 2014/Full-year 2014. Accessed online in December 2015 at: https://www.pwcmoneytree.com/Reports/FullArchiveNational_2014-4.pdf.
2	Marmer, M. H., Bjoern, L., Dogrultan, E., and Berman, R.	(2011) *Startup genome report*. Berkeley University and Stanford University, Tech. Rep. Accessed online in December 2015 at: https://s3.amazonaws.com/startupcompass-public/StartupGenome Report1_Why_Startups_Succeed_v2.pdf.
2	Ries, Eric	(2011) *The Lean Startup: How Today's Entrepreneurs Use Continuous Innovation to Create Radically Successful Businesses*. New York: Crown Business.
2	Rogers, Everett	(2003) *Diffusion of Innovations* (5th ed.). New York: Free Press.
2	von Hippel, Eric	(1994) *The Sources of Innovation*. New York: Oxford University Press, USA.
3	Bartlett, Sara	(2002) *Seat of the Pants*. *Inc. Magazine*, October 15.
3	Bhidé, A.	(2000) *The Origin and Evolution of New Businesses*. New York: Oxford University Press, USA.
3	Dennis Jr., William J.	(1998) Wells Fargo/NFIB Series on Business Starts and Stops. Accessed online in December 2015 at: www.nfibonline.com.

Ch.	Author(s)	Reference
3	Gianforte, G. and Gibson, Marcus	(2007) *Boostrapping Your Business: Start and Grow a Successful Company with Almost No Money.* Avon, MA: Adams Media.
3	Hurst, Erik and Lusardi, Annamaria	(2004) Liquidity constraints, household wealth, and entrepreneurship. *The Journal of Political Economy*, 112(2), 319.
3	Mollick, E.	(2014) The dynamics of crowdfunding: an exploratory study. *Journal of Business Venturing*, 29(1), 1–16.
4	Aldridge Foundation	(2009) Origins of an Entrepreneur. Aldridge Foundation. Accessed online on April 20, 2010 at: www.aldrigefoundation.com.
4	Canfield, Jack and Hansen, Mark Victor	(1993) *Chicken Soup for the Soul.* Florida: Heath Communications, Inc.
4	Communication from the Commission to the Council	(1998) *Fostering Entrepreneurship in Europe: Priorities for the Future.* COM (98) 222 final.
4	Headd, Brian	(2004) Redefining business success: distinguishing between closure and failure. *Journal Small Business Economics*, 1(1), 51–61.
4	Hershey Web Site	(2010) http://www.hersheys.com/discover/milton/milton.asp (accessed May 1, 2010).
4	Jarvis, P.	(2013) 8 out of 10 statistics are . . . totally made up. TNW News. Accessed online in December 2015 at: http://thenextweb.com/entrepreneur/2015/02/07/8-10-statistics-totally-made.
4	Kessler, G.	(2014) Do nine out of 10 new businesses fail, as Rand Paul claims? *Washington Post*, January 27. Accessed online in December 2015 at: https://www.washingtonpost.com/news/fact-checker/wp/2014/01/27/do-9-out-of-10-new-businesses-fail-as-rand-paul-claims.
4	Kirchhoff, B.A.	(1997) Entrepreneurship economics. In *The Portable MBA in Entrepreneurship*, ed. W.D Bygrave. New York, NY: John Wiley & Sons, Inc.
4	Knaup, Amy E.	(2005) Survival and longevity in the business employment dynamics data. *Monthly Labor Review*. Washington: May 2005, 128(5), 50.
4	Petroski, Henry	(2006) *Success through Failure: The Paradox of Design.* Princeton, NJ: Princeton University Press.
4	Pozin, I.	(2012). How to Avoid Being a Startup Failure. Forbes, November 28, 2012. Accessed online in December 2015 at: http://www.forbes.com/sites/ilyapozin/2012/11/28/how-to-avoid-being-a-startup-failure.
4	Sandage, Scott	(2006) *Born Losers: A History of Failure in America.* Boston: Harvard University Press.
4	Shepherd, Dean	(2003) Learning from business failure: propositions of grief recovery for the self-employed. *The Academy of Management Review*, 28(2), 318.
4	Shepherd, Dean	(2009) *From Lemons to Lemonade.* Wharton School Publishing. Upper Saddle River, NJ.
4	Twain, Mark	(1897) *Pudd'nhead Wilson's New Calendar, Following the Equator.* Hartford: American Publishing Company. p. 124.
4	US Small Business Administration	(2009) Frequently Asked Questions About Small Business. Accessed online, April 23, 2010: http://www.sba.gov/ADVO/stats/sbfaq.txt.

Ch.	Author(s)	Reference
4	Wagner, E.	(2013) Five Reasons 8 Out of 10 Businesses Fail. Forbes. September 12, 2013.
4		(2008) Fortune Magazine. March.
5	Benz, M. and Frey, B.	(2008) Being independent is a great thing. Working paper, Institute for Empirical Research in Economics.
5	Fatjo, Tom and Miller, Keith	(1981) *With No Fear of Failure: Recapturing Your Dreams through Creative Enterprise*. New York: Word Books.
5	Hsu, Caroline	(2005) Entrepreneur For Social Change. *US News and World Report.* November 31.
5	PricewaterhouseCoopers	(2013) *The Startup Economy.* Accessed online in December 2015 at: https://www.pwcaccelerator.com/pwcsaccelerator/docs/pwc-google-the-startup-economy-2013.pdf.
6	Cantillon, R.	(1755) Essai sur la nature du commerce. Accessed online in December 2015 at: http://oll.libertyfund.org/titles/285.
6	Christensen, Clayton M.	(1997) *The Innovator's Dilemma.* Boston: Harvard Business School Press.
6	Drucker, Peter	(1985) *Innovation and Entrepreneurship.* London: Collins.
6	Ellsberg, D.	(1961) Risk, ambiguity, and the savage axioms. *Quarterly Journal of Economics*, 75, 643–669.
6	Kim, W. Chan and Mauborgne, Renée	(2005) *Blue Ocean Strategy.* Boston: Harvard Business School Press.
6	Knight, Frank	(1921) *Risk, Uncertainty and Profit.* Boston, New York: Houghton Mifflin Company.
6	McGrath, R. G.	(1999) Falling forward: real options reasoning and entrepreneurial failure. *Academy of Management Review*, 24(1), 13–30.
6	Miner, J. B. and Raju, N. S.	(2004) Risk propensity differences between managers and entrepreneurs and between low-and high-growth entrepreneurs: a reply in a more conservative vein. *Journal of Applied Psychology*, 89(1), 3–13.
6	Smith, Adam	(1759) *The Theory of Moral Sentiments.* Millar, London.
6	Smith, Adam	(1776) *An Inquiry into the Nature and Causes of the Wealth of Nations.* W. Strahan and T. Cadell, London.
6	Taleb, Nassim Nicholas	(2007) You Can't Predict Who Will Change The World. Accessed online in December 2015 at: www.forbes.com.
6	Tetlock, P.	(2005) *Expert Political Judgment: How Good Is It? How Can We Know?* New Jersey: Princeton University Press.
7	Carroll, Lewis	(1874) *The Hunting of the Snark.* London: Macmillan.
7	Schumpeter, Joseph	(1934) *The Theory of Economic Development.* Cambridge: Harvard University Press. (New York: Oxford University Press, 1961.) First published in German, 1912.
8	Bandura, Albert and Cervone, Daniel	(1986) Differential engagement of self-reactive influences in cognitive motivation. *Organizational Behavior and Human Decision Processes*, 38(1), 92.
8	Moore, D.A. and Healy, P. J.	(2008) The Trouble with overconfidence. *Psychological Review*, 115(2), 502–517.

Ch.	Author(s)	Reference
8	Peterson, Christopher, Maier, Steven F., and Seligman, Martin E.P.	(1995) *Learned Helplessness: A Theory for the Age of Personal Control.* Oxford: Oxford University Press. p. 305.
8	Reeves, M., Haanaes, K., and Sinha, J.	(2015) *Your Strategy Needs a Strategy: How to Choose and Execute the Right Approach.* Cambridge, MA: Harvard Business Press.
9	Blauth, M., Mauer, R., and Brettel, M.	(2014) Fostering creativity in new product development through entrepreneurial decision-making. *Creativity and Innovation Management*, 23(4), 495–509. DOI: 10.1111/caim.12094.
9	Chandler, Gaylen N., DeTienne, Dawn R., McKelvie, Alexander, and Mumford, Troy V.	(2011) Causation and effectuation processes: a validation study. *Journal of Business Venturing*, 26(3), 375–390.
9	Colvin, Geoff	(2008) *Talent is Overrated.* New York: Portfolio.
9	Dew, N., Grichnik, D., Mayer-Haug, K., Read, S., and Brinckmann, J.	(2015) Situated entrepreneurial cognition. *International Journal of Management Reviews*, 17(2), 143–164.
9	Ericsson, K. A., Charness, N., Feltovich, P. J., and Hoffman, R. R. (Eds.).	(2006) *The Cambridge Handbook of Expertise and Expert Performance.* United Kingdom: Cambridge University Press.
9	Klein, G.	(2009) *Streetlights and Shadows: Searching for the Keys to Adaptive Decision Making.* Cambridge, MA: Bradford Books.
9	Wadhwa, V., Holly, K., Aggarwal, R., and Salkever, A.	(2009) *Anatomy of an Entrepreneur: Family Background and Motivation.* Kauffman Foundation Small Research Projects Research.
9	Werhahn, D., Mauer, R., Flatten, T., and Brettel, M.	(2015) Validating effectual orientation as strategic direction in the corporate context. *European Management Journal.* DOI:10.1016/j.emj.2015.03.002.
Part III	Goodman, Nelson	(1983) *Fact Fiction and Forecast.* Cambridge, MA: Harvard University Press.
10	Corcoran, Barbara and Littlefield, Bruce	(2003) *Use What You've Got, and Other Business Lessons I Learned from My Mom.* New York: Portfolio Hardcover. p. 6.
10	Hakuta, Ken	(1989) *How to Create Your Own Fad and Make a Million Dollars.* New York: Avon Books.
10	Karinthy, F.	(1929) *Chains. Everything is different,* Budapest.
10	Milgram, Stanley	(1967) The small world problem. *Psychology Today,* (May), 61–67.
10	Ronstadt, Robert	(1988) The corridor principle. *Journal of Business Venturing,* 3(1), Winter 1988, 31–40.
10	Shane, S.	(2000) Prior knowledge and the discovery of entrepreneurial opportunities. *Organization Science,* 11(4), 448–469.
11	Agogué, Marine, Lundqvist, Mats, and Middleton, Karen Williams	(2015) Mindful deviation through combining causation and effectuation: a design theory-based study of technology entrepreneurship. *Creativity and Innovation Management,* forthcoming.

Ch.	Author(s)	Reference
11	Amabile, T. M., Barsade, S. G., Mueller, J. S., and Staw, B. M.	(2005) Affect and creativity at work. *Administrative Science Quarterly*, 50(3), 367–403.
11	Ashton, Kevin	(2015) *How To Fly A Horse: The Secret History of Creation, Invention, and Discovery*. New York: Doubleday.
11	Goldenberg, Jacob, Mazursky, David, and Solomon, Sorin	(1999) Toward identifying the inventive templates of new products: a channeled ideation approach. *Journal of Marketing Research*, 36(2), 200.
11	Gould, S. and Vrba, Elizabeth	(1982) Exaptation—a missing term in the science of form. *Paleobiology*, 8(1), 4–15.
11	Knight, Frank	(1921) *Risk, Uncertainty and Profit*. Boston, New York: Houghton Mifflin Company.
11	Schumpeter, Joseph A.	(1942) *Capitalism, Socialism and Democracy*. New York: Harper and Row.
11	Schumpeter, Joseph A.	(1911) *Theory of Economic Development: An Inquiry into Profits, Capital, Credit, Interest, and the Business Cycle*. New Brunswick: Transaction Publishers.
11	Simon, H.	(1969) *The Sciences of the Artificial*. Cambridge, MA, MIT Press.
11	Smith, Adam	(1776) *An Inquiry into the Nature and Causes of the Wealth of Nations*. W. Strahan and T. Cadell, London.
11		TripAdvisor.com, Accessed online, December 2015.
12	Shackle, G. L. S.	(1966) *The Nature of Economic Thought*. Cambridge: Cambridge University Press, p. 765.
12	Thaler, Richard	(1985) Mental accounting and consumer choice. *Marketing Science*, 4(3), 199.
12	Thaler, Richard	(1999) Mental accounting matters. *Journal of Behavioral Decision Making*, 12(3), 183.
13	Joyce, James	(1922) *Ulysses*. Paris: Sylvia Beach.
13	Wiltbank, R., Dew, N., and Read, S.	(2015) Investment and returns in successful entrepreneurial sell-outs. *Journal of Business Venturing Insights*, 3, 16–23.
13		Cite Wiki http://en.wikipedia.org/wiki/ Bootstrapping
14	Davidson, D.	(2001) S*ubjective, Intersubjective, Objective*. Oxford: Clarendon Press, pp. 43–45.
14	Fischer, Eileen and Rueber, Rebecca	(2011) Social interaction via new social media: (how) can interactions on Twitter affect effectual thinking and behavior? *Journal of Business Venturing*, 26(1), 1–18.
14	Vargo, Stephen and Lusch, Robert	(2004) Evolving to a new dominant logic for marketing. *Journal of Marketing*, 68(1), 1–17.
15	Cialdini, Robert	(2006) *Influence: The Psychology of Persuasion*. New York: Harper Paperbacks.
15	Flynn, F. J., and Lake, V. K.	(2008) If you need help, just ask: underestimating compliance with direct requests for help. *Journal of Personality and Social Psychology*, 95(1), 128.
15	Schotter, Andrew	(2003) Decision making with naïve advice. *American Economic Review*, 93(2), 196–201.
15	Smith, Adam	(1798) *Lectures on Jurisprudence*. Oxford: Oxford University Press, pp. 493–494.

Ch.	Author(s)	Reference
16	Austin, R. D., Devin, L., and Sullivan, E. E.	(2012) Accidental innovation: supporting valuable unpredictability in the creative process. *Organization Science*, 23(5), 1505–1522.
16	Harmeling, S. S. and Sarasvathy, S. D.	(2013) When contingency is a resource: Educating entrepreneurs in the Balkans, the Bronx, and beyond. *Entrepreneurship Theory and Practice*, 37(4), 713–744.
16	Silver, A. David	(1985) *Venture Capital—The Complete Guide for Investors*. New York: John Wiley.
Part IV	Knecht, G. Bruce	(2002) *The Proving Ground*. New York: Grand Central Publishing.
18	Hoffman, Auren	(2003) Going by the Board. Businessweek/Bloomberg. Accessed online in December 2015 at: http://www.bloomberg.com/news/articles/2003-08-05/going-by-the-board.
19	Bartlett, Sara	(2002) *Seat of the Pants*. *Inc. Magazine*, October 15.
19	Bhidé, A.	(2000) *The Origin and Evolution of New Businesses*. New York: Oxford University Press, USA.
19	Brinckmann, Jan, Grichnik, Dietmar, and Kapsa, Diana	(2010) Should entrepreneurs plan or just storm the castle? A meta-analysis on contextual factors impacting the business planning-performance relationship in small firms. *Journal of Business Venturing*, 25(1), 24.
19	Hall, R. E. and Woodward, S. E.	(2010) The burden of the nondiversifiable risk of entrepreneurship. *The American Economic Review*, 100(3), 1163–1194.
19	Nicolini, Davide, Mengis Jeanne, and Swan, Jacky	(2012) Understanding the role of objects in cross-disciplinary collaboration. *Organization Science*, 23(3), 612–629.
19	Osterwalder, Alexander and Pigneur, Yves	(2010) *Business Model Generation: A Handbook for Visionaries, Game Changers and Challengers*. New Jersey: John Wiley and Sons, Inc.
19	Sahlman, Bill	(1997) How to write a great business plan. *Harvard Business Review*, 75(4), 98.
20	Blekman, T.	(2011) *Corporate Effectuation: What Managers Should Learn from Entrepreneurs!* The Hague: Academic Service.
20	Blekman, T. and Konijnenburg, R.	(2012) Orkestratie van Effectuation: Het Organiseren van ondernemend gedrag. BIM Media BV. 288 pages. Ondernemend Gedrag. The Hague, The Netherlands: Academic Service.
20	Faschingbauer, M.	(2013) *Effectuation: Wie erfolgreiche Unternehmer denken, entscheiden und handeln*. Stuttgart: Schäffer-Poeschel Verlag für Wirtschaft Steuern Recht.
20	Mauer, R.	(2015) Thinking different. In: Baker, T. and Welter ,F., editors. *The Routledge Companion to Entrepreneurship*. New York: Routledge, pp. 116–130.
20	Mayer-Haug, K., Read, S., Brinckmann, J., Dew, N., and Grichnik, D.	(2013) Entrepreneurial talent and venture performance: a meta-analytic investigation of SMEs. *Research Policy*, 42(6), 1251–1273.
20	Read, S., P. Margery, and N. Dew	(2013) Innovation by design, the hybrid organization, *Kindai Management Review*, 1(1), 67–79.
20	Shane, Scott	(2008) *Illusions of Entrepreneurship*. Hartford, CT: Yale University Press.
20	Staw, B.M., Sandelands, L.E. and Dutton, J.E.	(1981) Threat rigidity effects in organizational behavior: a multilevel analysis. *Administrative Science Quarterly*, 26(4): 501–524.

Ch.	Author(s)	Reference
20	Wasserman, N.	(2015) *The Founder's Dilemmas: Anticipating and Avoiding the Pitfalls That Can Sink a Startup* (The Kauffman Foundation Series on Innovation and Entrepreneurship). New Jersey: Princeton University Press.
20	Whiffen, S.	(2015) Assets to Action. Working paper
21	Cervantes Saavedra, Miguel	(1605–1616) *El Quijote*. Madrid: Juan de la Cuesta.
21	Fauchart, E. and Gruber, M.	(2011) Darwinians, communitarians, and missionaries: the role of founder identity in entrepreneurship. *Academy of Management Journal*, 54(5), 935–957.
21	Heckler, Terry	(2010) http://www.hecklerassociates.com/blog (accessed online May 1, 2010).
21	Panera	(2010) www.panera.com (accessed online May 1, 2010).
21	Dumaine, Brian	(1993) Fortune Magazine, October 18.
22	Berends, H., Jelinek, M., Reymen, I., and Stultiëns, R.	(2014) Product innovation processes in small firms: combining entrepreneurial effectuation and managerial causation. *Journal of Product Innovation Management*, 313, 616–635.
22	Bhidé, Amar	(2008) *The Venturesome Economy: How Innovation Sustains Prosperity in a More Connected World*. Princeton, NJ: Princeton University Press, p. 429.
22	Brettel, M., Mauer, R., Engelen, A., and Küpper, D.	(2012) Corporate effectuation: entrepreneurial action and its impact on R&D project performance. *Journal of Business Venturing*, 27(2), 167–184.
22	Chesbrough, H.	(2006) *Open Innovation: The new imperative for creating and profiting from technology*. Cambridge, MA: Harvard Business Press.
22	Coviello, N. E. and Joseph, R. M.	(2012) Creating major innovations with customers: insights from small and young technology firms. *Journal of Marketing*, 76(6), 87–104.
22	Klein, Karen E.	(2005) Smart Answers, "Avoiding the Inventor's Lament," *Business Week*, November 9, 2005
22	Ridley, M.	(2015) T*he Evolution of Everything: How New Ideas Emerge*. UK: Harper
22	von Hippel, Eric	(1986) Lead users: a source of novel product concepts. *Management Science*, 32(7), 791–805.
23	Bacon, Francis	(1620) *Novum Organum*. United Kingdom.
23	Hansmann, Henry	(2000) *The Ownership of Enterprise*. Cambridge, MA: Belknap Press of Harvard University Press.
23	Mair, Johanna and Marti, Ignasi	(2006) Social entrepreneurship research: a source of explanation, prediction, and delight. *Journal of World Business*, 41(1), 36–44.
23	Sagan, Carl	(2002) *Cosmos*. New York: Random House.
23	Simon, Julian	(1998) *The Ultimate Resource 2*. Princeton, NJ: Princeton University Press.

Index